Literacy's Beginnings

Literacy's Beginnings

Supporting Young Readers and Writers

Second Edition

Lea M. McGee
Boston College

Donald J. Richgels
Northern Illinois University

Allyn and Bacon
BOSTON   LONDON   TORONTO   SYDNEY   TOKYO   SINGAPORE

Senior Editor: Virginia Lanigan
Editorial Assistant: Nihad Farooq
Senior Marketing Manager: Kathy Hunter
Editorial-Production Coordinator: Annette Joseph
Editorial-Production Service: Saxon House Productions
Composition Buyer: Linda Cox
Manufacturing Buyer: Megan Cochran
Cover Administrator: Linda Knowles
Cover Designer: Suzanne Harbison

Library of Congress Cataloging-in-Publication Data

McGee, Lea M.
    Literacy's beginnings : supporting young readers and writers / Lea
M. McGee, Donald J. Richgels.—2nd ed.
        p.   cm.
    Includes bibliographical references (p.   ) and index.
    ISBN 0-205-16732-2
    1. Reading—United States.   2. Language arts—United States.
I. Richgels, Donald J.   II. Title.
LB1050.M378 1995
372.4'0973—dc20   95-7783
                                                           CIP
Printed in the United States of America
10 9 8 7 6 5 4 3 2 1   00 99 98 97 96 95

Photo Credits: p. 3: Mary H. Richgels; pp. 39, 65, 99, 135, 171, 215, 247, 293, 335: Donald J. Richgels; p. 371: Will Faller; p. 409: Jim Pickerell.

To Richard and Kristen,
and to Mary, Ted, and Carrie

Contents

Preface

POINT OF VIEW

Literacy's Beginnings: Supporting Young Readers and Writers is intended to help preservice and inservice teachers, parents, and other caregivers of young children to be aware of and supportive of children's literacy knowledge as it grows and changes in the years from birth through early elementary school. Our purpose is to provide a guide to the long continuum of literacy growth, from the very beginning years, when children's reading and writing efforts are difficult to recognize, through the early elementary school years, when children begin to receive formal literacy instruction.

We believe that children's literacy learning is developmental, but not in the sense of proceeding in an irreversible, step-by-step progression. No child's discoveries about and experiments with literacy exactly match those of another child. Furthermore, an individual child's literacy behaviors vary in sophistication depending on the task and the situation.

Literacy learning is developmental in a very commonsensical way that makes sense to anyone who has spent time writing and reading with children. Literacy learning is developmental in the sense that what an individual child knows about writing and reading changes dramatically over time. Not only do young children's constructions of literacy differ from those of adults, but children's present constructions also differ from their own former and future constructions.

We believe that teachers have an important role to play in young children's literacy learning. The subtitle of our book emphasizes the supportive nature of that role. We hope that our descriptions of literacy events involving young children and our suggestions for classroom support will help teachers to be aware of the directions in which children's literacy knowledge can move over the period covered by this book. Such awareness can make easier one of the most difficult tasks in teaching: the close observation of many different children. From a basis of careful observation, teachers can respect what children know and support children's continued learning in ways that make sense to the children.

ORGANIZATION OF THE TEXT

We present literacy learning in two parts. The first part provides an overview and important background information about children's literacy learning. In this section we describe the nature of children's understandings about written language and how this knowledge is reflected in their reading and writing. In Chapter 1 we present an overview of learning and written language. We describe critical changes in children's concepts about written language that both propel them forward as readers and writers and define the need for the following four chapters. In Chapter 2 we examine infants, toddlers, and twos as they begin their literacy experiences. In Chapter 3 we describe preschoolers and kindergartners who become novice readers and writers. In Chapter 4 we discuss kindergartners and first graders who are experimenting readers and writers. Finally, in Chapter 5 we describe conventional readers and writers.

We designate children by four terms: *beginners, novices, experimenters,* and *conventional readers and writers.* We use these terms as a shorthand way of referring to complex concepts. These terms and a term even more essential to our topic, *literacy,* have everyday connotations that are not necessarily what we intend when we use those terms.

To us, being *literate* means being able to find meaning in written symbols. This definition includes much territory left out by everyday definitions of literacy; for example, a pretend reading of a favorite storybook qualifies as a literate act by our definition, but does not usually qualify under the everyday definition. Still, our definition does not include everything that very young children do with books and writing materials. We use the two names *beginners* and *novices* to distinguish between the general meaning making in literacy events by children we call beginners and the more focused meaning making involving printed symbols by children we call novices.

Because we wanted to begin at the beginning, we include in Chapter 2 what infants do with books and writing materials. Infants have meaningful experiences with books and writing materials, but they do not find meaning in printed symbols themselves, and they do not make written marks with the intentions of communicating particular messages. Chapter 3 explains how children we call novices, though far from being literate by everyday standards, are literate by our definition. Novices do find meaning in the print symbols on signs and in books, and they do intend messages with their writing.

Chapter 4 describes a cluster of knowledges that typify experimenters. We use the term *experimenters* to capture the added awareness and intensity of involvement with written language that these children exhibit.

Chapter 5 describes what conventional readers and writers know about written language. We use the term *conventional* only to emphasize that what these children do when they read and write appears more conventional than the reading and writing behavior of children described earlier.

Although we use the terms *beginners, novices, experimenters,* and *conventional readers and writers,* we emphasize our earlier point about development. These descriptive terms are not meant to define rigid, irreversible stages. Indeed, we do not call them stages. A child may exhibit many of the knowledges in the cluster of knowledges that we associate with one of those four terms. Furthermore, a child who usually reads or writes like a novice in some situations and with some tasks will also read or write like an experimenter. The important point is that over time, children will more often resemble conventional readers and writers. Over time, they gain a richer developmental repertoire of literacy knowledge and strategies.

The information from Part 1 provides an important foundation for Part 2: Classrooms. In this part of the text we describe classrooms, teachers, and children in action. We begin in Chapter 6 by arguing that literacy learning is best supported in child-centered classrooms. Teachers need the knowledge about children presented in Part 1 to plan and organize these classrooms. Chapter 6 also presents nine characteristics of literacy-rich classrooms. Chapter 7 focuses on preschoolers and their teachers. Chapter 8 illustrates literacy learning in kindergarten. Chapter 9 describes first graders and their teachers, and Chapter 10 presents a primary classroom beyond the first grade. In each of these chapters, we consider the expectations for achievement along with describing child-centered approaches to literacy instruction.

Chapter 11 examines the literacy needs of diverse learners, including children with developmental or learning differences, with language differences, and with cultural differences. Techniques for supporting these children are described.

Chapter 12 addresses assessment and explains the use of portfolios to guide instruction and inform parents about their children's literacy growth.

Each chapter in *Literacy's Beginnings* has four sections designed to help readers consolidate and apply what they have learned. First, we list the key terms used in the chapter. Applying the Information presents a case study on children's interactions with written language similar to the many examples given in the chapter. The reader is asked to apply the chapter's concepts to this example. Going Beyond the Text suggests ways for readers to seek out real-life experiences that will test both the chapter's ideas and the readers' understandings. We ask questions and make suggestions to guide readers' planning and reflecting on those experiences. Finally, References provides a list of all publications cited in the chapter.

THE CHILDREN AND TEACHERS IN THIS BOOK

Literacy's Beginnings is based in part on a growing body of research about emerging literacy and in part on our experiences with young children, including our own children. We incorporate many descriptions of those experiences. We wish to add here two important cautions that we will repeat throughout the text. The first is about children's ages. We usually give the age of the children in our examples in order to fully represent the facts. However, we do not intend for those ages to serve as norms against which to compare other children.

Our second caution is about backgrounds. Many, but not all, of the children in our examples have had numerous and varied home experiences with books and writing materials. Their meaningful interactions with written language are often what one would expect of children from such environments. Children with different backgrounds may exhibit different initial orientations toward written language. However, our involvement with teachers whose children come to preschool or elementary school with different backgrounds has shown us that nearly all children can benefit from the informed observation and child-centered, meaning-oriented support described in this book.

The classroom support chapters of this book are based on our own teaching experiences and on our observations of teachers. Just as we have known and observed many literate young children, so also have we known and observed many very sensitive, intelligent, and effective teachers of young children. All the samples of children's reading and writing in this book are authentic cases from our own research and the research of others cited in the text.

ACKNOWLEDGMENTS

We owe a great deal to the many children whose experiences with written language were the basis for much of this book. We thank them and their parents for cooperating so generously with us—for supporting *us* in the extended "literacy event" of writing this book. We thank the teachers who shared their classroom experiences with us: Mary Jane Everett, Candice Jones, Karen Kurr, Roberta McHardy, Nancy Miller, Terry Morel, Kathy Walker, Leigh Courtney, Karen King, Jackie Zickuhr, Carolyn Vaughn, Monette Reyes, Karla Poremba, and Diane Roloff.

We owe much to the editors and their assistants at Allyn and Bacon including Nancy Forsyth, Virginia Lanigan, Annette Joseph, and Nihad Farooq. We are also grateful to Sydney Baily-Gould at Saxon House Productions for her careful handling of the manuscript during editing and production. We thank the reviewers for their helpful comments and suggestions: Ruthann Atkinson, Edinboro University of Pennsylvania; Margaret Genisio, University of Wisconsin; Toni Stiefer, Oklahoma State University.

We acknowledge the contributions of our many students. We learned from our discussions with them about literacy's beginnings and from the examples they shared of their interactions with young readers and writers.

PART 1

Learners

We begin this book by examining children—what they know about written language and how they acquire this knowledge. In Chapter 1 we describe written language and explore ways in which children learn about literacy. This chapter sets the foundation for the four following chapters, which look at children's literacy learning from infancy through the primary grades in elementary school. Chapter 2 describes literacy beginners, young children from birth until approximately three years of age. As literacy beginners, young children construct their first written symbols and learn to understand stories and other texts that are read aloud to them. Chapter 3 focuses on novice readers and writers, preschoolers and kindergartners who pretend to read and write in their play and who gain a wide range of concepts about written language. Although their reading and writing are not conventional, they form the foundations required for later, more accomplished reading and writing. Chapter 4 discusses experimenting readers and writers, children who are just beginning to break into print. Experimenters explore the written language system and make many important discoveries that lead them to more conventional reading and writing. They begin to spell and can read familiar, predictable stories with the support of repeated readings. The final chapter in Part 1, Chapter 5, describes conventional readers and writers. Children who read and write in ways that we consider "really" reading and writing, but who are yet far from being mature, accomplished readers and writers. These chapters provide teachers with information about the range and variety of knowledge that young learners bring to classroom experiences.

CHAPTER 1

Understanding
Literacy Learning

Throughout this book, you will encounter numerous and varied instances of children's reading and writing. The picture we paint of literacy development during early childhood will be composed of hundreds of real-life examples. You might want to preview some of these examples in the figures and vignettes to be found in every chapter. Among these are descriptions of toddlers reading by responding to pictures in favorite storybooks and writing by scribbling, kindergartners exploring connections between sounds and letters in their own writing and in books and poems that their class reads together, and second graders responding to fiction and non-fiction trade books and composing stories and reports. This chapter establishes the foundation for these descriptions. How is it that even very young children can be considered literate? How and why do they begin to make sense of others' written language and to use written language for their own purposes? How and why do their understandings of written language differ from adults' and from other children's?

In the first section of Chapter 1, we explore how children learn, and in particular, how they learn written language. We describe schemas, or concepts, and the importance of these mental constructs to learning. We apply Piaget's and Vygotsky's principles of learning to explain the connection between language and concept acquisition, especially the acquisition of special concepts about written language.

In the second section of Chapter 1, we examine concepts about written language in more detail. We begin with a description of two children, Ted and Carrie, as they use reading and writing in their play with their father. We pose the question, "What concepts do Ted and Carrie have about written language as reflected in their reading and writing?" We describe Ted's and Carrie's concepts about written language meanings—messages that are communicated through written language. We explain their concepts about written language forms—what they know about how written language looks and is organized, including knowledge about letters, words, and texts. We discuss their understandings about how meanings are linked to written language forms and show that Ted has an awareness of the conventional link between form and meaning (using relations between sounds and letters to communicate meanings). Finally, we describe their concepts about the functions of written language and show that Ted and Carrie use reading and writing for a variety of purposes.

In the last part of the chapter we focus on how children's concepts about written language change as they gradually acquire more conventional concepts about reading and writing. Acquiring concepts about written language is a developmental process. Young children begin with many unconventional concepts about written language, but these concepts form an important foundation for later conventional reading and spelling. Finally, we introduce five assumptions about children's literacy learning that provide a foundation for the view of literacy acquisition as it is presented in the rest of this book.

Key Concepts

concepts	features	personal experiences
schemas	related concepts	*tabula rasa*

zone of proximal development	metalinguistic awareness	phonetic cue reading
scaffolding	concept of word	phoneme
meanings	meaning-form links	cipher reading
forms	sound–letter relationships	orthographic reading
letter features	functions	beginners
mock letters	selective cue reading	novices
linearity	logographic reading	experimenters
left-to-right organization	alphabetic reading	conventional readers and writers

LEARNING LANGUAGE

Reading and writing are language and thinking processes, and understanding how children acquire these processes provides important insights for teaching. Piaget (1955) and Vygotsky (1962) examined how children acquire language and other knowledge. Both were interested in the relationship of language learning and thinking. We use their theories first to explain learning in general and then to explore how learning and language acquisition are related.

Schemas and Learning

An important idea from both Piaget's and Vygotsky's theories is that learning occurs as children acquire new **concepts,** or **schemas.** A concept or schema is a mental structure in which we store all the information we know about people, places, objects, or activities.

Schemas

Consider the concept "pineapple": take a moment to write down everything called to mind by the mention of the word *pineapple.* The word probably brings to most people's minds several **features** of pineapples (that they are fruity, sweet, juicy, hard to eat, spiky, fresh, or canned) and several **related concepts** (Hawaii, fruit salad, fruit cocktail, sharp knife, piña colada, bananas, mangoes, garbage—lots to throw away with fresh pineapples).

The word *pineapple* also may bring to mind actual experiences with pineapples (such as the time you bought a rotten one or the time you did not use the knife you usually use for coring a pineapple—what a disaster!).

The reason that people recall knowledge about features, related concepts, and **personal experiences** associated with the word *pineapple* is that concepts or schemas are organized. That is, as we have personal experiences with pineapples (seeing them at the grocery, eating them, preparing them, and so on), we make mental associations among the word *pineapples,* the concept that word stands for,

and the sights, sounds, tastes, smells, and sensations that contributed to our forming that concept. We see that pineapples have spikes at the top, so we automatically make a mental association between the concept "pineapple" and the quality
"spiky." We taste that pineapples are sweet, so we automatically make another mental association, this time between the concept "pineapple" and the taste "sweet."
Thus, concepts are organized through associations.

We have schemas for many things, including objects, such as "trophy" or "din-
ing room table," people, such as "president of the United States" or "fashion model,"
places, such as "college" or "home," and activities or events, such as "going to the
dentist" or "looking for a job." Thinking and learning depend on these many
schemas or concepts. Thinking involves calling to mind information from schemas
and using that information to make inferences, predict, draw conclusions, or generalize. For example, suppose we see someone at the grocery store pulling on the
green spiky top of a pineapple. We might make an inference that this person is testing the "ripeness" of pineapples.

Similarly, learning involves adding to or changing schemas. Suppose we see,
for the first time, someone save the green, spiky-leafed top of a pineapple, root it,
and grow it as a house-plant. We might modify our pineapple schema to include
the new feature "decorative," and it may become newly connected to such concepts
as "houseplant" and "asexual reproduction" (growing a new plant from a leaf, root,
or stem of an old plant, rather than from a seed).

Infants and Schemas

Children begin life with few concepts—or even none. Children's minds may be
thought of as vacant structures, or empty schemas. There are only empty slots where
features can go. This is the **tabula rasa,** or blank slate, notion of the young child's
mind. One of Piaget's greatest insights was a suggestion of how children acquire
the knowledge to begin filling those slots with features and making connections
among schemas. He suggested that the infant's mind is actually far from a blank
slate. It is true that young children have no (or very little) knowledge of content or
the things (such as pineapples) that will eventually occupy their minds. However,
children do have considerable inborn knowledge of processes. They seem to know
how to go about acquiring content knowledge, or knowledge of things.

Piaget's idea was that young humans learn through action. They are born with
special schemas for how to act and how to respond to their world. These action
schemas bring children in contact with reality (things) in ways that produce knowledge of the world. More action produces more knowledge. As children acquire
knowledge and continue to act, changes result in the things they are in contact with
(for example, milk gets spilled) and changes result in previous knowledge (for example, the schema for milk changed to include the idea that milk does not behave
like a cracker—it doesn't keep a shape). The action schemas themselves change as
active, problem-solving children evolve more effective strategies for making their
way in the world.

Two very important conclusions can be drawn from Piaget's theory of how children learn. One is that children create their own knowledge by forming and re-

forming concepts in their minds. The second conclusion is that children's state of knowledge—or view of the world—can be very different from one time to the next, and especially different from an adult's.

The point we wish to emphasize is that, because children construct their own knowledge, this knowledge does not come fully developed and is often quite different from that of an adult. Thus, there are differences between how an adult understands reading and writing and how a child understands reading and writing. It is important for us to remember that such differences are just as real, just as natural (that is, they derive from the way in which children are set up to learn), and just as understandable as differences between an adult's and a child's understandings of what a pineapple is.

The Relation between Language and Learning

Piaget's and Vygotsky's views differ on the role that language plays in the acquisition of schemas. We have already discussed the importance of action to Piaget's idea of learning. Children's actions may physically change objects in the world. A child may pull or stretch a lump of modeling clay, changing its shape. But then that same action may change the child's concept of modeling clay, adding the feature "stretchy," and it may allow the child to see a connection between modeling clay and bread dough (NOVA, 1985).

But can children change their schema for modeling clay to include the notion that it is stretchy without their hearing or using the word *"stretchy"*? Can they pretend that modeling clay is bread dough without hearing someone else say, or being able themselves to say, that both are "stretchy"? Another way to put these questions is to ask: How important is it for the child to have the word *stretchy* available as a label for what is experienced in such a situation? Piaget and Vygotsky would answer this question differently. Vygotsky placed more importance on the child's having language along with action in order to learn. He stressed the importance of having someone with the child who could supply that language. According to Vygotsky, a mother who says to her child, "Look at that stretchy clay!" plays a vital role in her child's learning about clay. Vygotsky placed a strong emphasis on the social component of cognitive and language development.

Social Basis for Learning

Vygotsky argued that all learning first takes place in a social context. In order to build a new concept, children interact with others who provide feedback for their hypotheses or who help them accomplish a task they could not do on their own. Children's or adults' language is an important part of the social context of learning. Suppose that a child's concept of the letter *W* does not include its conventional orientation (upright). This child may write $\bigwedge$ and call it *W*. Another child who observes this writing may say, "That's not a *W*, that's an *M*." This feedback provides the child with a label for the new concept, *M,* and prompts the child to reconsider the concept of *W* by adding an orientation (upright).

Vygotsky believed that children need to be able to talk about a new problem or a new concept in order to understand it and use it. Adults supply language that fits children's needs at a particular stage or in response to a particular problem. Language can be part of a routinized situation. It can label the situation or parts of the situation, or it can help pose a problem or structure a problem-solving task. As the child gradually internalizes the language that was first supplied by an adult, the language and a routine task that helps in solving the problem become the child's own.

An example of a child's internalizing the language of a routine is how the child learns to use the words *all gone*. The parents of a child might repeatedly hide a favorite toy and then say, "All gone!" Then they reveal the toy and say, "Here it is!" This becomes a game for the child. Eventually, the child may play the game without the adult, using the same language, "All gone" and "Here it is."

We can draw two important conclusions from the "all gone" example. First, it suggests that language and cognition really emerge at about the same time. Perhaps using the word *gone* helps children to solve the cognitive problem of object permanence, or perhaps *gone* suddenly acquires a fascination for children who have just solved that problem, making it a word they are very likely to use (Gopnick & Meltzoff, 1986; Meltzoff, 1985).

Second, it suggests that learning is a matter of internalizing the language and actions of others. A young child's ability to play the game of "all gone" alone means that he or she has internalized the actions and language of his or her mother or father. For Vygotsky all learning involves a movement from doing activities in a social situation with the support of a more knowledgeable other to internalizing the language and actions of the more knowledgeable other and being able to use this knowledge alone.

Zone of Proximal Development

Vygotsky spoke of a **"zone of proximal development",** which is an opportune area for growth, but one in which children are dependent on help from others. An adult, or perhaps an older child, must give young children advice if they are to succeed within this zone and if eventually, by internalizing that advice, they are to perform independently.

When children are working in their zone of proximal development, they complete some parts of a task, and adults or older children perform the parts of the task that the younger children cannot yet do alone. In this way, young children can accomplish tasks that are too difficult for them to complete on their own. Adults' or older children's talk is an important part of helping young children—it scaffolds the task. **Scaffolding** talk gives advice, directs children's attention, alerts them to the sequence of activities, and provides information for completing the task successfully. Gradually, children internalize this talk and use it to direct their own attention, plan, and control their activities.

Figure 1.1 presents a letter that five-year-old Kristen and her mother wrote together. After Kristen's second day in kindergarten she announced, "I'm not going to school tomorrow. I don't like being last in line." Apparently, Kristen rode a different bus from any of the other children in her classroom and the teacher called her last to line up for the buses. When Kristen's mother reminded her of all the things she liked to do in school, Kristen replied, "Okay, I'll go [to school], but you tell Mrs. Peters [the teacher] I don't want to be last all the time." Kristen's mother said, "We'll write her a note. You write it and I'll help." Kristen agreed and wrote Mrs. Peter's name as her mother spelled it. Then Kristen said the message she wanted to write ("I always don't want to be the last person in the line"). Her mother said, "The first word is *I*. You can spell that. What letter do you hear?" Kristen wrote the letter *i*, but when her mother began saying the word *always* slowly for Kristen to spell, she refused to spell any more words. So Kristen's mother wrote *always* and then spelled the word *don't* for Kristen to write. She suggested that she write one word and Kristen write one word. As shown in Figure 1.1, the final letter is a combination of Kristen's writing, with invented spellings (*t* for *to*, b for *be*, *Lst* for *last*, and *pwsn* for *person*) as she listened to her mother say each sound in a word, and her mother's writing. Kristen could not have accomplished the task of writing this letter without her mother's scaffolding.

A year and a half later, Kristen ran into the kitchen where her mother was preparing dinner and handed her the note shown in Figure 1.2. This note reads, "I hate when you brought me to Penny's house" (Penny is Kristen's baby-sitter). Kris-

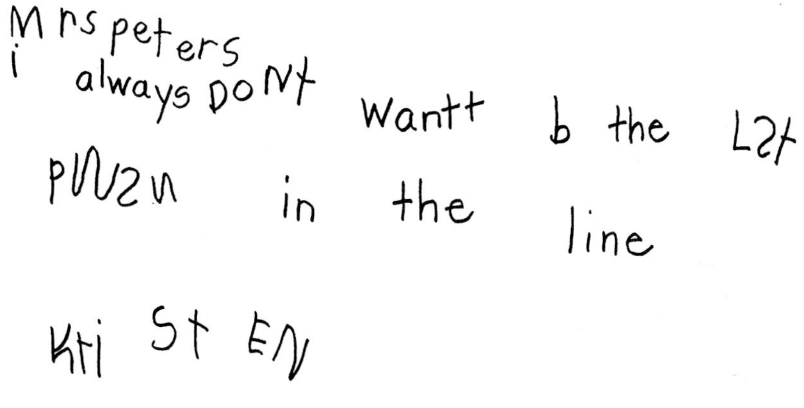

Figure 1.1 *Kristen's Letter to Her Teacher*

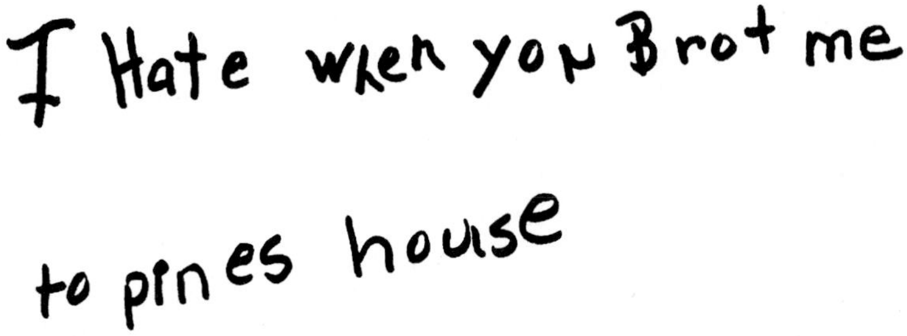

Figure 1.2 *Kristen's Letter to Her Mother*

ten had written the note in her room by herself after her mother was late picking her up. This note illustrates the results of scaffolding and working within the zone of proximal development. In kindergarten, Kristen needed her mother's scaffolding to write a letter of protest to her teacher. She needed her mother's support to hear sounds in words, to keep track of what she had written, and to sustain the effort of writing. At the end of first grade, she could write a letter of protest on her own, inventing spellings and reading to keep track of her message as she wrote.

LEARNING WRITTEN LANGUAGE

Children learn about written language in much the same way in which they learn anything else, including spoken language. They acquire and modify schemas or concepts for various aspects of written language knowledge. They use inborn abilities, and they depend on interactions with others. There are both Piagetian and Vygotskian perspectives on learning written language.

A Piagetian Approach

Children's written language learning can be explored from a Piagetian perspective. This view of literacy development emphasizes stages of development. From this view we would expect that reading and writing behavior at some stages would be very different from conventional reading and writing because it reflects concepts of reading and writing *as the child has constructed them*.

Children's concepts of reading and writing are shaped more by what they accomplished in preceding developmental stages than by their simply imitating adults' behavior or following adults' directions. At an early stage, many children write words such as K l m v s t. This word writing reveals that their concept of words might be stated something like this: "Words are a string of letters with spaces between." Of course, words are not strings of randomly selected letters; yet, many preschoolers and kindergartners operate with this concept (Ferreiro & Teberosky, 1982). They may write a string of letters and bring it to their teacher and ask, "What did I write?" They do so because they have a concept of a written word that is very different from an adult's concept. It does not matter that children see adults using letters related to sounds in a particular order. They may actually resent an adult's insistence that they have not spelled a word at all. Adults need not be alarmed about such unconventional concepts. Children eventually develop new, more conventional concepts as they gain experience reading and writing.

Children's understandings about written language parallel their understandings in other areas (Ferreiro, 1985), and the means by which they reach those understandings are the same. For example, at one stage children discover a principle of syllabication as a solution to the puzzle of how to make their written words correspond to their talk. They write one letter for each syllable in their spoken message. This idea suits their writing needs well at this stage. This principle is very similar to the principle of one-to-one correspondence in counting. It is learned through problem-solving action; then it is challenged by additional data that the child receives from the environment. Children soon begin to encounter many words that do not follow the principle of one letter per syllable. In the face of this difficulty, they act to reach new levels of understanding and eventually discover the alphabetic principle on which the English writing system is based. They may at first be happy with an early solution to the written language puzzle, but before long experience forces them to reconstruct old concepts to account for new discoveries (again, whether it is a concept for the written word or one for "pineapple").

A Vygotskian Approach

Children's written language learning can also be explored from a Vygotskian perspective. This view of literacy learning emphasizes social interaction and places less emphasis on predetermined stages of behavior than does a Piagetian view. It focuses instead on the social aspect of young children's literacy behaviors, especially on their intending to communicate with others (Harste, Burke, & Woodward, 1983; 1984) and on their using routines to learn about written language (Snow, 1983).

A very young child's drawing and writing do not always look meaningful. When adults cannot understand what a child intended, they often assume that nothing was intended. However, it is just as important with written language as with spoken language for adults to show children that they know that the children intend to convey meanings. One of the best ways of insuring that this is done is for the child and adult to have routine ways of interacting during literacy events.

We illustrate the importance of expecting children's writing and reading to be meaningful in the following example.

Figure 1.3 looks like a meaningless conglomeration of random letters, pictures, and scribbles. We know better, however, because one of the authors was present when Cody wrote it. It is actually a very meaningful piece; its composition was not at all haphazard.

Figure 1.3 *Cody's Drawing and Writing*

Four-year-old Cody was staying for a few hours with one of her mother's friends. After they had spent time looking at books together, the friend asked Cody if she wanted to write her own book. Cody said she could write her name. She said, "My name is C-O-D-Y" as she wrote the letters CODY (see Figure 1.4). Next, Cody wanted to write an *S*, but said to her friend, "I can't write *S*. Will you write *S* for me?" The friend wrote the large *S* shown in the upper right in Figure 1.3 and then urged Cody to draw a picture for her book. Cody said she would draw herself and proceeded to draw her face, hair, mouth, nose, and eyes (see the face in the upper left in Figure 1.3). When she had finished her drawing, Cody wrote three wavy lines and identified them: "I wrote a bedtime story" (see Figure 1.5). Next, Cody said, "I need a blanket." She scribbled all over the top of her bedtime story (that is, over her wavy lines—making them look like Figure 1.6) and announced, "There is my blanket." Finally, she asked her friend, "How do you spell your name?" Her friend said, "L-E-A." First Cody said "A" and then "E" as she wrote those letters (seen in the bottom right of Figure 1.3). Then she asked, "Now how do you write *L*?" and wrote the backwards *L* in her friend's name shown in Figure 1.3.

It is probably clear by now that the haphazard-looking drawing in Figure 1.3 is a bedtime story. Because the three wavy lines were so quickly covered up, Cody's friend could not ask her to read the bedtime story, and so we may only guess what

Figure 1.4 *Cody's Signature*

Figure 1.5 *Cody's Bedtime Story*

Figure 1.6 *Cody's Picture of a Blanket*

it is about. However, this written record of it survives, complete with Cody's name, her friend's name, and a picture of Cody under a blanket.

It is fascinating to note Cody's sophisticated knowledge about written language. She writes names with real letters. Her story is composed of wavy lines that simulate the lines of print on a book's page. This shows that she knows that a story involves a lot more writing than a name does. She strives for unity—the very opposite of haphazardness. She even connected her self-portrait with her bedtime story by putting it under a blanket. It is important to note that all of this would have gone undetected and unsupported if her adult friend had not treated Cody as a writer, communicating the message to Cody that, like the authors of the books they had read together, Cody could write a book. This example provides evidence of the power of the zone of proximal development and the scaffolding of a more knowledgeable other. Cody's friend invited Cody to read and write and let Cody take the lead in defining reading and writing. In this interaction, Cody revealed her current concepts about written language and extended her concepts about the formations of the letters *S* and *L*.

CHILDREN'S CONCEPTS ABOUT WRITTEN LANGUAGE

We have shown that children acquire spoken language as they acquire concepts about objects, people, places, and events. In this part of the chapter we describe in detail children's concepts about written language. We begin with a case study of Ted and Carrie as they are playing restaurant.

Ted's Delight: Two Children's Reading and Writing

Ted, who is eight years old, and his sister Carrie, who is three years old, were playing in the corner of the living room. They had set up their card table playhouse. Taped on the playhouse was the sign shown in Figure 1.7.

Figure 1.7 *"Ted's Delight" Sign*

Ted and Carrie had collected Carrie's plastic play food and doll dishes and put them behind the playhouse. When their father entered the room, he looked at the sign and said, "Oh, I think I need some lunch." The children asked him to visit their restaurant. He entered the playhouse, and Carrie presented him with a menu (Figure 1.8).

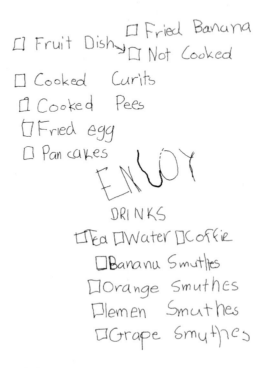

Figure 1.8 *"Ted's Delight" Menu*

Carrie asked, "May I take your order?" Her father read the menu and said, "I'll take pancakes and coffee." Carrie checked off two items on the menu and took it out to Ted, who was behind the playhouse. He pretended to fix pancakes and pour coffee. Ted brought the dishes into the playhouse to his father, who pretended to eat with much relish. When he had finished he asked, "May I have my check, please?" Carrie picked up a pad of paper and a pencil and wrote a check (Figure 1.9). Her father pretended to pay the check and left the playhouse.

Figure 1.9 *Carrie's Check*

Later that evening, the family discussed the restaurant play. Ted said he had made the sign so that the playhouse could be a restaurant. He had asked Carrie if he could use her toy food and dishes. She had wanted to play, too. Ted said that he and Carrie decided to write on the menu the names of the play food they had. In the middle of his writing the menu, Carrie insisted on helping him. "She wrote the letter that looks like a backwards *J* in the middle of the menu," Ted reported. "I had to turn it into the word *Enjoy* to make sense."

Ted's and Carrie's Concepts about Written Language

What do Ted's and Carrie's reading and writing reveal about their concepts of written language? First, the sign and menu Ted wrote suggest that he is learning that written language communicates meanings. His sign communicated a message to his father: a restaurant is open for business. Ted also knows that the messages communicated in written language should be meaningful given the written language context. Ted knew that the "backwards *J*" that Carrie wrote somehow had to be incorporated into a message that could be communicated on a menu. Random letters on menus do not communicate meaningful messages. Ted made the random letter meaningful by incorporating it into the word *Enjoy*. Carrie also showed that she knows that written language communicates messages. Even though we cannot read her check, her behavior as she gave it to her father (and her father's reactions to the written check) suggests that her writing communicates a message something like "pay some money for your food."

The sign and menu indicate that Ted is learning about written language forms—what written language looks like. These two writing samples certainly look like a sign and a menu. His menu is written in the form of a list. The content of his menu is organized as a menu is usually organized—drinks and food are grouped and listed separately. Carrie is also learning what at least a few written language forms look like. The writing on her check looks something like the letters *E* and *J*. Even though Carrie's letters are not yet conventional, they signal that she is paying attention to what letters look like. Much of what she notices about letters corresponds with what adults notice about letters. Although Carrie's *E*'s sometimes have too many horizontal lines, she has obviously noticed that horizontal lines are included on letters. And, even though Carrie's *J*'s seem to be backwards, she does include the hook expected on this letter. There is one exception. Carrie put a circle on her letter *E;* most letter *E*s do not include circles. Figure 1.10 (Carrie's name written as her preschool teacher wrote it) suggests why Carrie may have included the circle on her *E*. Carrie noticed that her preschool teacher wrote circles on her letters, so Carrie may have decided to put the same circles on her own letters.

Figure 1.10 *"Carrie" as Written by Her Preschool Teacher*

Ted's spelling errors on the menu suggest a great deal about his knowledge of how forms and meanings are related. Ted knows that certain letters (written language) are associated with certain sounds; he wrote *pees* for *peas*. He knows that the letters *ee* often take the sound of long *e*.

Both Ted's and Carrie's behaviors indicate that they understand many ways in which written language is used. Carrie knows that a waitperson writes something when a customer orders and when the customer asks for the check. She seems to be learning, just as Ted is, that writing and reading are functional. Ted and Carrie used written language to get their customer into their restaurant (they made a sign), to let their customer know what was available to eat (they made a menu), and to let their customer know how much the meal cost (they wrote a check).

Concepts about Written Language: Meanings, Forms, Meaning-Form Links, and Functions

Ted and Carrie have learned a great deal about written language, but their knowledge is not unique. As researchers have studied young children in similar literacy events, they have discovered that all children—even those who are not traditionally reading and writing—acquire concepts about four aspects of written language:

- Meanings
- Forms
- Meaning-form links
- Functions

"Ted's Delight" also provides insights into *how* children acquire concepts about written language. Ted and Carrie were learning about written language as they played, and their play reflected how they had seen written language used in real life. Their father provided an important component to their play; he entered the dramatic play as a playmate rather than as a parent who might correct Ted's spelling or Carrie's letter formations. He responded to Ted's sign and menu just as he would respond to a sign and menu at a real restaurant. He responded to Carrie's writing just as he would when presented with a bill in a real restaurant. Thus, children acquire concepts about written language as they participate in family activities using reading and writing for real purposes. Ted and Carrie had many opportunities to be involved in activities in which their parents read and wrote (e.g., going to restaurants as a family) and to practice being readers and writers with a supportive player (e.g., pretending to run a restaurant). Children learn about written language as they use it and as they interact with other written language users (Baghban, 1989; Cook-Gumperz, 1986; Scollon & Scollon, 1981; Taylor & Strickland, 1986).

Written Language Meanings

Reading and writing are meaning-making activities (Halliday, 1975). They involve communication of **meanings** between the reader and the writer. As we read, we construct meanings and explore messages that authors communicate through written language. As we write, we construct meanings that we communicate to readers through written language. Ted and Carrie demonstrated their meaning making through reading and writing. In order to communicate the message "restaurant," Ted wrote the sign "Ted's Delight."

Children display their awareness of text meanings in many ways. When asked to read a grocery list, four-year-olds reply, "green beans, bread, coffee." When dictating a letter, five-year-olds say, "I love you." When asked what a traffic sign might say, they reply, "Watch out for children walking." Young children's concepts about meaning are related to their experiences in which different kinds of texts are used. Four-year-olds know the meanings associated with grocery lists because they know the kinds of things found in a grocery store and have shopped with their parents as they read from a grocery list. Young children's concepts about meanings are tied to their awareness of the context in which written language is used and to the variety of written text forms they have observed.

Reading and writing, of course, are only a few of the ways in which we can communicate meanings. We also communicate meanings through facial expression, gesture, dance, art, conversation, and music. For young children, communicating in spoken language and play are very closely related to communicating in written language. In the following example, Mary's play with her dolls illustrates how children's talk, actions, and play communicate meanings in ways that are similar to communicating meaning in written language (Wolf, 1984).

Mary was playing with cardboard boxes and two dolls. One of the dolls was "Mommy" and the other was "baby." Mary stood one of the cardboard boxes up next to the dolls and said, as if she were "baby," "Mommy, I want to ride the elevator." Then Mary said, as if she were a narrator in a story, "And they talked and talked." As she spoke, the cardboard box began to tip over. Mary said, as if she were "Mommy," "See, it's dangerous, it's tippy, that's why you have to go with grown-ups" (Wolf, 1984, p. 846).

In this literacy event, Mary communicated meaning—a story about a mother and her little girl who were going to ride an elevator—through her actions, talk, and props. The story's meaning is communicated through the talk of "Mommy" and "baby" and through the talk of a narrator. Although Mary was involved in make-believe play, some characteristics of her spoken language make it more like a written language story than an oral conversation. For example, Mary narrated. Having a special person who communicates part of a story is found in written stories, but not in oral conversation. Another characteristic of Mary's play signals that her language is more like written than like spoken language. Mary kept the talk of the people in her play ("Mommy" and "baby") related to the meaning of the make-believe story she was developing. She did not allow the real situation of the cardboard box nearly falling over to interfere with the story's meaning. Rather, she incorporated the box's falling over as part of the meaning in the story. "Baby" in the make-believe story could not ride the elevator because the *elevator,* not the box, was tippy.

This literacy event demonstrates that young children learn to communicate written-language-like meanings in their play and spoken language. It might not seem surprising or special that children use spoken language to practice what they will need to use in written language. As expert readers, we assume that what we write, we can read aloud and say; what we say aloud, we can write. However, as Mary's play demonstrates, written language is not exactly "talk written down." Meanings in written language are communicated in special ways that differ from the ways of spoken language.

Written Language Forms

Learning written language **forms** means knowing what written language looks like. Carrie was learning what one kind of written language form—alphabet letters—looked like. Ted knew what several kinds of written language forms—menus, words, and letters—looked like.

We review next children's concepts about alphabet letters, words, sentences, texts, and left-to-right organization.

Alphabet Letters

Carrie's writing illustrates one aspect of children's alphabet learning—learning **letter features.** Features are attributes of an object; for example, the features of the letter *L* include a vertical and horizontal line. Children acquire concepts about the features of letters, as Carrie did (Lavine, 1977).

One way to find out about children's knowledge of letter features is to ask them whether letters are alike or different (Gibson, Gibson, Pick, & Osser, 1962). We might give children the letter *O* and the letter *U* and ask if they are alike or different. (The two letters differ on the feature *closed* versus *open.*) We might show children the letters ꓮ and *A,* which differ on the feature *rotated* versus *upright.* Three-year-olds know that the letters *U* and *O* are different, but they do not know that the letters ꓮ and *A* are different. They know the feature *closed* versus *open,* but they do not know the feature *rotated* versus *upright.* In contrast, seven-year-olds know that both sets of letters are different, because they know both features.

Children also demonstrate their knowledge of letter features in their writing. Figure 1.11 presents one preschooler's writing. This writing looks as if it might include letters, but a close inspection reveals none of the twenty-six Roman alphabet letters. Clay (1975) called letters such as these **mock letters.**

In Figure 1.12, a five-year-old Chinese girl has labeled her picture by writing two symbols that resemble Chinese characters, although neither is a real Chinese character. The writing in both Figures 1.11 and 1.12 demonstrates young children's unconventional concepts about letters and characters, which they will later use conventionally.

Words

Children also learn about the features of words. If we wanted to know about children's knowledge of word features, we might ask them to sort cards into two piles, one pile for "words" and one pile for "not words" (Pick, Unze, Brownell, Drozdal, & Hopmann, 1978).

On the cards we would write long and short words and nonwords (such as *keld* or *cafkiton*). Even three-year-olds are willing to perform this task, and they put all the words (and nonwords) with three or more letters in the "word" pile. Thus, their

Figure 1.11   *Mock Letters*

Figure 1.12   *A Five-Year-Old's Drawing with Mock Chinese Letters*

notion of words is that words consist of strings of at least three letters. In contrast, first graders put all the words (including single-letter words, such as *a,* in the word pile, but they reject real words that they cannot read (such as *obese*). Their concept of words is that words may have only one letter but must be readable and meaningful to the reader. It is interesting to note that children's concepts about words begin to develop before they can read or write conventionally, and their concepts change over time.

Children also demonstrate their knowledge of word features in their writing (Clay, 1975; Sulzby, 1986). Figure 1.13 presents a letter that Michael wrote. His writing indicates a beginning awareness of words as subunits of longer text. Michael wrote his letter in six different colors of magic markers. In the third line of his letter he wrote the word *Michael* in blue, followed by the words *you so* in orange. In the fourth line he wrote the word *swet* (sweet) in purple, the word *you* in orange, and the words *Dr. McGee* in black. Of importance is the fact that Michael never changed colors in the middle of words; he only changed colors at word boundaries. Michael's use of colors to separate words indicates his growing awareness of words as units of language. Later, Michael will learn to signal words with the conventional feature, a space between words.

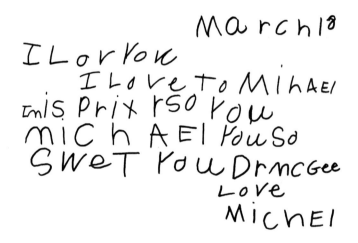

Figure 1.13 *Michael's Letter*

Sentences

Pierre's writing (Figure 1.14) indicates his awareness of sentences. His use of one line for each sentence and his emphatic periods are undoubtedly related to his kindergarten teacher's writing and to her talk about sentences and periods. However, Pierre puts periods only at the ends of sentences, and all his lines of writing marked by periods qualify as sentences. Pierre's knowledge of a sentence as a unit in written language marked by punctuation is noteworthy in a kindergartner. Even some second and third graders struggle to identify sentences in their writing; their compositions often consist of one long sentence.

Texts

There are many of kinds of texts, including poems, recipes, maps, newspapers, dictionaries, books, magazine articles, *TV Guides*, and directions. One thing young chil-

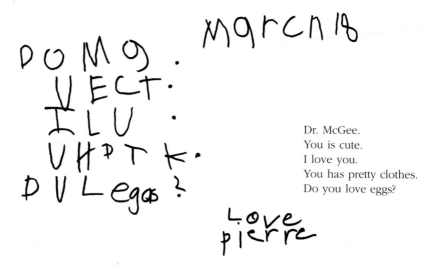

Dr. McGee.
You is cute.
I love you.
You has pretty clothes.
Do you love eggs?

Figure 1.14 *Pierre's Sentences*

dren learn about these different text forms is how they look. Figure 1.15 presents a preschooler's story. This writing looks like a story—it fills a page with horizontal lines of writing and demonstrates a concept of **linearity.**

Figure 1.16 presents a nine-year-old's letter to her principal. The form of the letter reflects Andrea's concepts about letter form, including a greeting, body, and signature. The content is also organized, with a statement of a problem and solution and with arguments for why the principal should consider the solution.

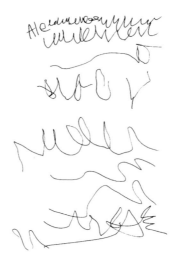

Figure 1.15 *A Preschooler's Story*

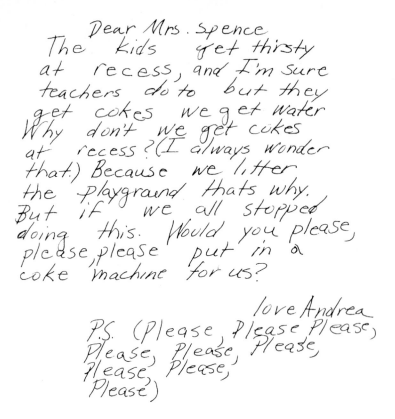

Dear Mrs. Spence
The kids get thirsty at recess, and I'm sure teachers do to but they get cokes we get water Why don't we get cokes at recess? (I always wonder that.) Because we litter the playground thats why. But if we all stopped doing this. Would you please, please, please put in a coke machine for us?

love Andrea
P.S. (Please, Please Please,) Please, Please, Please, Please, Please, Please)

Figure 1.16 A Persuasion Letter

Left-to-Right Organization

Some kindergartners know that letters and words are organized from left to right in written English. Many kindergartners point to the top left line of print when asked where to begin reading (Johns, 1980). They often write mock cursive stories (such as in Figure 1.15) by writing from left to right.

However, learning **left-to-right organization** is not a simple task. Jane's writing (Figure 1.17) demonstrates the difficulties children can experience with left-to-right organization. Prior to writing the story presented here, Jane frequently wrote mock cursive stories from left to right. But in the writing in Figure 1.17, left-to-right organization is not apparent. Jane began this story by drawing a picture of a chicken. She decided to write "Kentucky Fried Chicken." To begin her invented spelling message, she said to herself, "Tucky, /t/, /t/" and wrote a letter *T* near the outstretched leg of her chicken. Next she concentrated on the sound of *ck* in her word *tucky*. She wrote several *C*s scattered around the page. Then she said, "Fried, /f/, /f/" and wrote an *F* and an *R*. Finally, she tried to write the word *chicken* and wrote the letters *CK* (looks like *CH*) and *N* (looks like *W*) (Newman, 1983, pp. 863–864).

Figure 1.17 *"Kentucky Fried Chicken"*

From "On Becoming a Writer: Child and Teacher" by J. Newman, 1983, *Language Arts, 60,* p. 864, October 1983. Copyright © 1983 by the National Council of Teachers of English. Reprinted with permission.

Jane listened to the sounds in the words *Kentucky Fried Chicken* in order, but did not write her letters in order from left to right when she spelled the words. In this case, it is not that Jane did not know left-to-right organization (she had demonstrated that knowledge many times in her previous stories). Rather, it seems as if she abandoned left-to-right organization to concentrate on another aspect of written language, the relation between sounds and letters.

Metalinguistic Awareness of Written Language Units

We have been using words such as *letter, word, sentence,* and *story,* which make it easy to describe written language. They constitute *language about language.* Children's understanding of and ability to use language about language is a particular kind of knowledge called **metalinguistic awareness** (Yaden & Templeton, 1986). Children acquire several aspects of metalinguistic awareness. One aspect is the ability to examine a written language form apart from the meaning associated with the form (Templeton, 1980). For example, the word *dog* can be examined as a written

language form—it is composed of three letters with the graphic shape of ⌐_⌐ .

The word *dog* also has meaning—a hairy, four-legged animal. Young children have difficulty examining form apart from meaning. When asked to name a long word, they might reply "bus." They are likely to say "paper clip" when asked to name a short word. Young children use the meaning of a word to determine whether a word is long or short. Older children who have metalinguistic awareness would use the form of the written word to identify and name long and short words, such as *encyclopedia* and *I.*

The example of saying that "paper clip" is a short word illustrates another aspect of metalinguistic awareness, **concept of word.** A child who gives this answer does not realize either that the question "What is a short word?" implies that only one word should be given or that *paper clip* is two words. Concept of word has several components, including the ability to identify a single word in a spoken sentence, the ability to identify a single word from a written sentence, and the ability to answer the question, "What is a word?" (Downing & Oliver, 1973–1974).

Meaning-Form Links

We use the term **meaning-form links** to refer to the way in which meaning is connected to written forms. Ted used the conventional meaning-form link in English—he used letters associated with certain sounds (**sound–letter relationships**) so that his written words corresponded to spoken words and the concepts related to those spoken words. He wrote *pees* using *ee* (as in the word *tree*) to represent the sound of long *e*. Despite Ted's unconventional spelling, we are able to construct the expected meaning (the small, round, green vegetables) because we look for correspondences between expected meanings on a restaurant menu and the letters he chose to represent the sounds in the name of the food item peas.

The link between letters in written words and sounds in spoken words is obvious to experienced readers, but it is not always clear to beginning readers and writers. Younger children, like three-year-old Carrie, are usually unable to make the kind of meaning-form links displayed in Ted's spellings; they make other kinds of links between meanings and written forms.

Pictographic Meaning-Form Links

One way in which children link meaning with written forms is to make their written forms look like the meaning they intend, using pictures, or pictographic writing. Pictographic writing consists of signs or symbols that look like objects and actions (Gelb, 1952).

Dexter is a kindergartner who uses pictures as a link between meaning and written forms. He said that the word *deer* began with the letter *O* because "It's [the letter *O*] shaped like a deer" (Dyson, 1984, p. 23). Dexter even drew an *O* and turned it into a deer by adding a set of antlers. To children like Dexter, units of written language, such as letters, directly represent meaning by looking like the meaning. A letter *O* can convey the meaning of "deer" if a writer makes the letter look like a deer.

Meaning-Form Links through Syllables

Sometimes children explore a syllable link between spoken language and written language. For example, Heather memorized the poem "Twinkle, Twinkle Little Star." Her kindergarten teacher wrote the poem on a chart and asked Heather to read it and "point to each word." Heather performed the task by reading and pointing as follows.

Text:	Twinkle	Twinkle	Little	Star		
Heather:	Twink	le		Twink	le	

Text:	How	I	Wonder	What	You	Are
Heather:	Lit	tle	Star		How	I	Won

Heather hesitated and then pointed back at the beginning of the poem:

Text:	Twinkle	Twinkle	Little	Star
Heather:	Won	der		What	You

Text:	How	I	Wonder	What	You	Are
Heather:	Are					

Then Heather stopped, pointed to the remainder of the text, and said, "I don't know what the rest says." Heather used a strategy of linking each written word to a spoken syllable.

Sound–Letter Correspondences as Meaning-Form Links

The conventional link between meaning and forms is that letters (individually or in common patterns) stand for the important sounds in words. For example, the four important sounds in the word *bank* (the sounds of *b, æ, ŋ,* and *k*) are represented by four letters. Jane demonstrated that knowledge when she listened very carefully to sounds as she said "Tucky Fried Chicken."

The links that children explore between meaning and written forms illustrate reading and writing as symbol-using activities. Because reading and writing are symbol-using activities, they are related to children's other symbol-using activities—talking, drawing, and imaginary play.

Relations among Talking, Drawing, Writing, Reading, and Playing

Talking, drawing, writing, reading, and playing are related because they are symbol-using media (Vygotsky, 1978). A symbol is a representation of something—an object, action, experience, or idea—that exists separately from what it represents. We draw symbols for houses—we do not create real houses on paper. Similarly, we write a symbol for a house (the word *house*). In dramatic play children create symbols by transforming objects and people into different objects and people. For example, a child might say, "I'll be the doctor and you hand me the scalpel," while pointing to a plastic knife. In this play, the child uses talking to become a doctor and to transform the knife into a scalpel. The child becomes a symbol for doctor and the knife becomes a symbol for scalpel.

Children often use many symbolic systems interactively to create meaning. They may draw, write, and even act out stories during writing (Fueyo, 1989).

Written Language Functions

Ted and Carrie's restaurant play demonstrated their awareness of purposes for using written language. Ted and Carrie used written language to identify and label; they created a restaurant by making a written sign declaring that their card table play-house was a restaurant. Ted and Carrie used written language to direct behavior; their written sign directed their father's behavior by prompting him to act like a customer. Their writing also directed their own behavior by prompting them to take on the roles of waitress and chef.

Written language is used to meet a variety of needs. Neighborhood store owners want customers to buy their merchandise, so they tell people about their goods through signs and announcements in their windows and through newspaper advertisements or flyers. People want to relax after work, so they read detective novels, best-sellers, or magazines. An important part of learning to read and write involves learning more about the **functions** that written language serves.

Functions of Spoken Language

Children have a head start learning about written language's functions because they already use their spoken language to meet a variety of needs. Children, like the adults around them, use their spoken language in functional ways. Halliday (1975) identified seven functions of spoken language. These functions represent different ways in which we use language. Table 1.1 summarizes Halliday's seven functions of language using examples from children's spoken language as illustrations of each (Halliday, 1975).

Unique Functions of Written Language

Since children are acquainted with using spoken language for several purposes, it is not surprising that they learn how to use written language to accomplish a variety of goals as well. In fact, many of written language's purposes are the same as those of spoken language. Table 1.1 also presents several examples of written language that serve each of Halliday's seven functions.

Much of becoming literate—becoming a capable reader and writer—involves learning uses of language that are unique to reading and writing. There are several benefits to using written language rather than spoken language. We use written language when we want to send information over distances and over time and when we want to remember something. Written language is also useful for communicating with people we really do not know well. There are three additional unique functions of written language: to establish identity, to record information, and to increase knowledge.

Establishing identity. Young children quickly recognize written language's ability to establish identity. Ted and Carrie established that the card table was a

Table 1.1 *Halliday's Language Functions*

Language	Function	Spoken Language Examples	Written Language Examples
Instrumental	satisfies needs and wants	"I want to watch Big Bird." "I want the colors."	advertisements, bills, reminder notes, sign-up sheet
Regulatory	controls others	"Don't use purple." "Andrew, stop."	traffic signs, policy statements, directions
Interactional	creates interaction with others	"Let's go in the playroom." "Who wants the rest?"	personal lettters, notes, personals in the newspaper
Personal	expresses personal thoughts and opinions	"I like Mr. T." "I'm not tired."	editorials, diaries, autobiographies, journals
Heuristic	seeks information	"What does this say?" "What is that?"	letters of request and inquiry, application forms, registration forms
Imaginative	creates imaginary worlds	"You be Judy and I'm Peewee." "This is a big green haystack."	poetry, drama, stories
Informative	communicates information	"Dad's giving a speech tonight." "The flowers opened."	wedding announcements, obituaries, dictionaries, textbooks, reports, telephone books

Adapted from Halliday, 1975.

restaurant by making a sign that declared it to be a restaurant. Another example of children's use of written language to establish identity involves two groups of preschoolers who were arguing about the use of a large refrigerator box. One group insisted that the box should be a dollhouse. The other group wanted it to be a fire station. Two boys in the fire-station group went to a mother helper and asked her to write the words *fire station*. They copied her writing on a large sheet of paper and taped it to the box. One child pointed to the sign and said, "This is not a house. This is a fire station" (Cochran-Smith, 1984, p. 90).

    Recording information and increasing knowledge.   Researchers have argued that written language serves at least two other functions not served by oral language (Stubbs, 1980). One function is to record information. Writing allows information to become permanent and transportable. Another function of written language is to increase knowledge. Because information can be recorded and reread, facts can be accumulated. These facts can be studied and considered critically, which may lead to new discoveries and theories. This new knowledge is made possible by studying in detail the accumulation of past knowledge.

Both these functions of written language can be observed in list making. People make lists to help organize what they need to get done. Writers often brainstorm lists of ideas before they begin to write. Sometimes it is through their lists that they discover a new idea—something they want to write about. Children also make lists. It may be through their list making that they first begin to explore the recording and increasing knowledge functions of written language. Taylor (1983) described several young children who used written language in a variety of ways, including making lists as a part of club activities. The children made many lists that negotiated who were to be members and who were not, lists of furnishings they needed for the clubhouse, and lists of jobs to do for the club.

CHILDREN'S CHANGING CONCEPTS ABOUT WRITTEN LANGUAGE

We have shown how children's concepts change as they have more experiences that include reading and writing. Children have many unconventional concepts about words, alphabet letters, and meaning-form links. Yet all children's concepts become increasingly more conventional. Although the journey to becoming a mature reader and writer is long, what happens during the journey is as valid as the end point. Knowing how children's concepts about written language develop is critical for understanding children's reading and writing. Here we discuss major changes in children's concepts about word reading as just one example of their growth toward conventional literacy.

Development of Conventional Word Reading

As children's word reading ability develops, they use at least three different concepts of how to read. The first is sometimes called **selective cue reading** (Juel, 1991) and sometimes called **logographic reading** (Ehri, 1991). For example, many preschoolers, on seeing the sign at a Baskin-Robbins Ice Cream Store, know that the sign says "Baskin-Robbins." Similarly, they may know that the label on their cereal box reads "Rice Krispies." This is an important accomplishment for preschoolers—they realize that print in the environment communicates meaning.

In addition, preschoolers are willing to reread their favorite books. They may turn the pages and label characters and actions depicted in the illustrations or use the illustrations to retell the story. Sometimes the stories children tell as they reread favorite books match the text nearly verbatim (Sulzby, 1985).

Yet if "Baskin-Robbins" or "Rice Krispies" or the text of a favorite story were printed on a card, preschoolers could not read the words. How, then, can preschoolers read words from familiar environmental print signs or from their favorite storybooks? They do so by assigning meaning to logos and illustrations found in familiar print contexts. This is a visual concept of word reading; it depends on seeing print in familiar environments, such as the front of an ice cream store or pages in a favorite book.

The second concept is called **alphabetic reading** (Ehri, 1991).With this, children who know at least some alphabet letters come to realize that alphabet letters are associated with certain sounds. When they first acquire this concept, children may perform **phonetic cue reading** (Ehri, 1991); they read printed words by remembering some sound–letter associations. For example, they may be able to read the word *mom* because they recognize the letter *m* and associate it with the sound /m/.

At this early point in alphabetic reading, knowledge about letters and sounds is not complete. For example, children who can remember *mom* by using the association of the sound /m/ with the letter *m* can not read the nonsense word *mim;* they cannot yet separate each letter and associate it with a single sound, or **phoneme.** They are not yet able to sound a word phoneme by phoneme (/m/, /i/, and /m/) and then blend the phonemes into the nonsense word *mim*. They might say, "Mom" when reading the word *mim*.

Children operate according to a later version of the alphabetic reading concept when they perform **cipher reading** (Juel, 1991). At this point they process words more completely, including being able to segment words phoneme by phoneme. Cipher readers can read nonsense words such as *mim* by decoding or ciphering phoneme by phoneme. This is primarily an auditory concept of word reading. Children read words by segmenting them phoneme by phoneme; they know letters associated with phonemes, and they use the sounds associated with letters to remember words.

The third and last concept children use as they develop word reading ability is called **orthographic reading** (Frith, 1985). This process involves associating familiar spelling patterns with sound segments. For example, the word *night* includes the *ight* spelling pattern, and this pattern is always associated with the sound segment /īt/. With this concept of word reading, children associate more than single sounds with single letters. They automatically notice familiar letter patterns and associate these patterns with sound segments (Adams, 1990).

Consider a word beginning with the letter *d*. When orthographic readers—who have had much experience with English text—see the *d*, their visual perception mechanisms are primed to expect the second letter to be any vowel, including *y*, or one of only two consonants, *r* and *w*, that commonly follow *d* in English spelling. They are not expecting any of the other consonants. In fact, such expectations feed one another, so that readers come to expect high-frequency sequences of letters.

This is mostly a visual concept of word reading. However, it is far different from the visual concept of selective cue or logographic reading. With orthographic reading, children are so familiar with the sequences of letters in written words that they automatically see letters in groups, or clusters.

We have used word reading to provide just one example of children's changing concepts about written language. We describe similar changes in spelling concepts in Chapters 4 and 5. Word reading and spelling are examples of meaning-form links. Changes also occur in children's concepts of written language meanings, forms, and functions. The rest of Part 1 is about such changes.

A Developmental Approach

Moving from one concept of word reading to another is a time of transitional knowl-edge about written language, when children's understandings are about to undergo significant reorganizations, resulting in more conventional literacy behaviors. A pos-sible indicator of such transitional periods is children's "out of sync" reading of their own writing, for example, writing a story using sound–letter correspondences to spell but using storytelling (rather than reading) to read (Kamberelis & Sulzby, 1988).

This is further evidence that literacy acquisition is a fundamentally developmen-tal process. That is, literacy concepts undergo significant changes, and only the last concepts to develop are what we might call conventional. Children naturally go through different stages as they approach mature reading and writing, and the knowledge acquired within each stage is critical for making the transition to a more sophisticated stage. There is no single, preconventional form of reading and writing.

We capitalize on the developmental nature of literacy acquisition in the re-mainder of Part 1 in this book. We describe young children as they go through four stages: beginning literacy, novice reading and writing, experimenting reading and writing, and conventional reading and writing.

Beginners are very young children who have meaningful experiences with books and writing materials, experiences that lay necessary foundations for later lit-eracy development. The children we call beginners, however, do not find meaning in printed symbols themselves, and they do not make written marks with the in-tentions of communicating particular messages.

Novices are aware that printed texts communicate messages, and they write with the intention to communicate meaning, although the ways in which they read and write are unconventional. They learn to name and write some letters of the alphabet, and they make texts that have visual features appropriate to their purposes (e.g., a list that looks like a list rather than a sentence or paragraph, even though it may not con-tain readable words). They read back and assign meanings to their own writing that match their purposes for writing, and they read other texts in ways that depend on vi-sual clues from the immediate environment (e.g., a picture of an ice cream cone on a sign that says "Ice Cream"). They are logographic readers and nonspellers.

Experimenters use many more conventional tools and strategies than novices, but most people would not yet mistake them for conventional readers and writers; they are in a transitional period. They use literary language, they can name and form nearly all the letters of the alphabet, they develop an awareness of words, they be-come inventive spellers, and they read with the support of familiar, predictable text. They are at the beginning of alphabetic reading and spelling.

Conventional readers and writers read and write in ways that most people in our literate society recognize as "really" reading and writing. For example, they use a variety of reading strategies, know hundreds of sight words, read texts written in a variety of structures, are aware of audience, monitor their own performances as writ-ers and readers, and spell conventionally. They are fully alphabetic readers and spellers, and they are becoming orthographic readers and writers.

These are only short descriptions of the four identities of developing readers and writers that we will use throughout this book. Chapters 2, 3, 4, and 5 are devoted to filling out our descriptions of beginners, novices, experimenters, and conventional readers and writers. For now we want to emphasize the developmental nature of literacy acquisition implicit in our presenting these four identities. We stress that these four identities (beginners, novices, experimenters, and conventional readers and writers) are only abstractions; no single accomplishment establishes a child as a novice, an experimenter, or a conventional reader and writer. The boundaries between these identities are fuzzy; children often waver between them. We use them only to help organize and elaborate the vast amount of information we now have about how children's literacy competence changes from birth to the primary grades.

ASSUMPTIONS ABOUT LITERACY LEARNING

We close the chapter by describing five assumptions about literacy learning. These assumptions are drawn from our discussion of how children learn, concepts that children acquire about written language, and the developmental nature of children's literacy acquisition. The first three assumptions deal with *what* children learn about written language. The last two assumptions have to do with *how* children learn about written language.

Even Very Young Children Know about Written Language

At the time of the literacy event "Ted's Delight," Carrie was only three years old. She already knew a great deal about being literate. She knew when to write an order and a check in a restaurant. Her writing included many features of written language form. Within the restaurant play activity, Carrie was a reader and a writer. We will show later in this book that even infants begin learning about reading as they interact with books or other print items and with their parents or other readers.

Teachers can expect that children will begin their school literacy experiences with important and useful knowledge about reading and writing. They can examine each child's literacy knowledge and insights, with the understanding that the kinds and amounts of knowledge each child has depend on the child's interactions with reading and writing.

Young Children's Reading and Writing May Be Different from Adults' Reading and Writing, but It Is No Less Important

Young children's notions about written language are often quite different from adults' notions about written language. Carrie's letter *E* (Figure 1.9) was not a conventional letter *E*. Heather's reading was different from an adult's reading of the poem "Twinkle Twinkle Little Star." Even at school age, children's notions about certain aspects of written language are different from adults' notions. At that stage, children are developing their own ideas about written language, which will eventually come to be more like adult ideas.

Teachers do not expect children to conform to adult models of correctness. They expect that children's reading and writing efforts will not always look like what adults consider reading and writing. Teachers provide many opportunities for children to try out what they know, without making them conform to an adult model.

Reading and Writing Are Similar and Interrelated Activities

Reading and writing are highly interactive and interrelated. In real literacy events it is hard to separate reading from writing. Ted and Carrie wrote and read what they wrote. Their father read their writing. Children learn about reading by writing and learn about writing by reading. This makes sense, because both reading and writing have a common element—written language. They are both meaning-making activities. Reading and writing are related to other meaning-making activities, including talking, drawing, and playing. Children's knowledge of written language is often displayed in these activities.

Teachers recognize that children's literacy knowledge and learning is often interwoven with many activities in addition to reading and writing. In the classroom, teachers encourage children and provide opportunities for them to talk, draw, read, write, and play. Teachers also look for ways to help children apply their knowledge of written language in literacy events that include several meaning-making activities, such as occurred in Ted and Carrie's restaurant play or Mary's dramatic play.

Young Children Acquire Literacy Knowledge as They Participate in Meaningful Activities

The key to young children's literacy learning is their participation in meaningful activities in which reading and writing are used. Ted and Carrie's restaurant play activity was a highly meaningful one—it was a favorite playtime activity. Michael's writing was part of a letter-writing activity, and he sent his letter to a frequent visitor to his classroom. It was important to Kristen not always to be last in line for the bus, hence her letter to her teacher.

Teachers expect that children are best supported in their literacy learning in meaningful activities in which reading and writing are used to meet everyday needs. Thus they plan literacy events in their classrooms, knowing that children seem to learn about reading and writing as they use reading and writing.

Young Children Acquire Literacy Knowledge as They Interact with Others

Children's reading and writing efforts are supported by others who respond to their efforts in ways that make them readers and writers. Carrie's father responded to Carrie's writing just as he would respond to a written check in a real restaurant. His response supported Carrie's writing.

In the classroom, children's literacy efforts are best supported by teachers' interactions with children and by children's interactions with each other. Teachers need to know effective ways of responding to children's literacy efforts that will extend and challenge children's learning.

Chapter Summary _____

Children's learning is dependent on having experiences that lead to the formation of concepts or schemas. Concepts are mental constructions about objects, people, events or activities, and places. Learning is a matter of acquiring new concepts or adding to and changing old concepts. Language is critical for learning when it provides labels for new concepts and when language is used to scaffold children's attempts at difficult tasks.

Children develop special concepts about written language that they use in reading and writing. Their concepts about written language meanings reflect their experiences with different kinds of texts, such as stories, grocery lists, and traffic signs. They create concepts about written language forms, including learning about letter features, words, sentences, texts, and left-to-right organization. They develop understandings about meaning-form links including unconventional concepts such as using pictographic writing (where the form of the writing looks like its intended meaning) and syllabic reading (where one printed word is read as one spoken syllable). Finally, children develop concepts about the functions of written language including using reading and writing to label and record.

Children's concepts about written language change and grow with their reading and writing experiences. Children begin with unconventional concepts and gradually acquire concepts that lead to conventional reading and writing. Children's word reading and spelling abilities are examples of the developmental nature of literacy acquisition. In both, they begin with unconventional visual strategies that then give way to more conventional auditory strategies involving sound–letter relationships. Finally, children achieve mature word reading and spelling as they once again focus on visual aspects of words to facilitate reading and spelling. In the orthographic stage of word reading and spelling, children are aware of alternative spellings and use these to spell and read words.

We believe that the best help for children's literacy acquisition is based on the following assumptions. Even very young children know about written language. Their literacy achievements, though different from adults', are significant. Children's reading and writing (and speaking and listening) are interrelated. Children grow in reading and writing by participating in meaningful activities and interacting with others.

Applying the Information _____

A case study of a literacy event follows. Read this case study carefully and think about the four domains of written language knowledge. Discuss what each of the children in the case study is learning about written language (1) meanings, (2) forms, (3) meaning-form links, and (4) functions. Consider what each child shows about the five assumptions of literacy learning given at the end of this chapter.

Four children and their sitter were sitting around the kitchen table. It was a rainy afternoon and the children had become restless. The sitter earlier had decided to read a book to the children to entertain them. She read *George Shrinks* (Joyce, 1985), a story of a little boy's adventures when he shrinks to the size of a mouse. Then the sitter suggested that the children draw a picture about the story.

Kristen, a two-year-old, immediately grabbed a marker and began to draw (see Figure 1.18). Ryan, a three-year-old, selected a marker and said, "I'm going to

Figure 1.18 *Kristen's Picture*

Figure 1.20 *Danielle's Picture*

draw his brother." (George's little brother, who has not shrunk, is a prominent character in the story.) Ryan's picture is presented in Figure 1.19. Danielle, a four-year-old, complained, "I can't draw a cat." The sitter said, "Sure you can. A cat has pointed ears and whiskers." Danielle's cat is shown in Figure 1.20. The sitter commented, "Hey, that's a good cat."

Then she asked, "Is that George?" as she pointed to the other object in the picture. She continued, "Would you like to write about that?" Danielle said, "No, you write it. Write 'The cat is going to eat him.' "

Kristen joined in the conversation. She gave her drawing to the sitter and said, "I drew, um um, something." Ryan said, "Write on mine, too." The sitter asked, "What shall I write?" Ryan replied, "Um, um, his brother."

Matthew, a six-year-old, had been drawing and writing quietly while the other children talked to the sitter (see Figure 1.21). The sitter noticed his picture and writing. She asked him to read his story. Matthew read, "The cat thought George was a mouse." Then he said, "I can tell the story. George was sleeping in his bed. After he woke up he shrinked small as a mouse and he was so little than a book . . . "

Ryan interrupted, "I can tell the story, too. There's George. The cat came out to get George. The, but, um, the cat didn't eat him." Meanwhile, Danielle had noticed Matthew's picture and writing. She drew another picture of a cat (Figure 1.22). She asked the sitter, "How do you spell 'cat'?" The sitter said each letter as she wrote them. Then Danielle wrote what looks like a colon. Next she copied the word *George*. She said, "*G,* what's that next let-

Figure 1.19 *Ryan's Picture*

ter?" Matthew replied, "An *e*." Danielle said, "It doesn't look like an *e*." Matthew responded by adding a mark to his letter *e*. Danielle continued to write words by saying each letter aloud to herself. After she was finished, the sitter asked her to read her writing. Danielle replied, "It says just what Matthew's writing says."

Figure 1.21   *Matthew's Picture and Story*

Figure 1.22   *Danielle's Writing*

Going Beyond the Text

Observe a literacy event with at least two children. One way to initiate a literacy event is to prepare for some dramatic play with children. Plan a dramatic play activity that could include reading and writing. For example, plan a restaurant play activity. Bring dramatic props, such as an apron, dishes, and a tablecloth, as well as reading and writing materials, such as large sheets of paper, small pads of paper, crayons or markers, placemats with puzzles, and menus. Suggest to two or three children that they might want to play restaurant and propose that they use the paper and crayons in their play. Observe their actions and talk. Use your observations to find out what the children know about written language meanings, forms, meaning-form links, and functions.

References

ADAMS, M. (1990). *Beginning to read: Thinking and learning about print.* Cambridge: MIT Press.

BAGHBAN, M. (1989). *You can help your young child with writing.* Newark, DE: International Reading Association.

CLAY, M. M. (1975). *What did I write?* Aukland: Heinemann Educational Books.

COCHRAN-SMITH, M. (1984). *The making of a reader.* Norwood, NJ: Ablex.

COOK-GUMPERZ, J. (Ed.). (1986). *The social construction of literacy.* Cambridge: Cambridge University Press.

DOWNING, J., & OLIVER, P. (1973–1974). The child's conception of a word. *Reading Research Quarterly, 9,* 568–582.

DYSON, A. H. (1984). Emerging alphabetic literacy in school contexts toward defining the gap between school curriculum and child mind. *Written Communication, 1,* 5–55.

EHRI, L. (1991). Development of the ability to read words. In R. Barr, M. Kamil, P. Mosenthal, & P. Pearson (Eds.), *Handbook of reading research* (2nd ed., pp. 395–419). New York: Longman.

FERREIRO, E. (1985). Literacy development: A psychogenetic perspective. In D. R. Olson, N. Torrance, & A. Hildyard (Eds.), *Literacy, language, and learning* (217–228). Cambridge: Cambridge University Press.

FERREIRO, E., & TEBEROSKY, A. (1982). *Literacy before schooling.* Exeter, NH: Heinemann.

FRITH, U. (1985). Beneath the surface of developmental dyslexia. In K. Patterson, J. Marshall, & M. Cotheart (Eds.), *Surface dyslexia* (pp. 301–330). London: Erlbaum.

FUEYO, J. (1989). One child moves into meaning—his way. *Language Arts, 66,* 137–146.

GELB, I. J. (1952). *The study of writing.* Chicago: University of Chicago Press.

GIBSON, E. J., GIBSON, J. J., PICK, A. D., & OSSER, H. (1962). A developmental study of discrimination of letter-like forms. *Journal of Comparative Physiological Psychology, 55,* 897–906.

GOPNICK, A., & MELTZOFF, A. Z. (1986). Relations between semantic and cognitive development in the one-word stage: The specificity hypothesis. *Child Development, 57,* 1040–1053.

HALLIDAY, M. A. K. (1975). *Learning how to mean.* New York: Elsevier.

HARSTE, J. C., BURKE, C. L., & WOODWARD, V. A. (1983). *The young child as writer-reader, and informant* (Final NIE Report No. NIE-G-80–0121). Bloomington, IN: Language Education Departments, Indiana University.

HARSTE, J. C., WOODWARD, V. A., & BURKE, C. L. (1984). *Language stories and literacy lessons.* Portsmouth, NH: Heinemann.

JOHNS, J. L. (1980). First graders' concepts about print. *Reading Research Quarterly, 15,* 529–549.

JOYCE, W. (1985). *George shrinks.* New York: Harper and Row.

JUEL, C. (1991). Beginning reading. In R. Barr, M. Kamil, P. Mosenthal, & P. Pearson (Eds.), *Handbook of reading research* (2nd ed., pp. 759–788). New York: Longman.

KAMBERELIS, G., & SULZBY, E. (1988). Transitional knowledge in emergent literacy. In

J. Readence & R. Baldwin (Eds.), *Dialogues in literacy research* (pp. 95–106). Chicago: National Reading Conference.

LAVINE, L. O. (1977). Differentiation of letter-like forms in prereading children. *Developmental Psychology, 13,* 89–94.

MELTZOFF, A. Z. (1985). In *Baby talk* (NOVA transcript No. 1207). Boston: WGBH Transcripts.

NEWMAN, J. (1983). On becoming a writer: Child and teacher. *Language Arts, 60,* 860–870.

NOVA (1985). *Baby talk* (NOVA transcript No. 1207). Boston: WGBH Transcripts.

PIAGET, J. (1955). *The language and thought of the child*. Cleveland, OH: World.

PICK, A. D., UNZE M. G., BROWNELL, C. A., DROZDAL, J. G., JR., & HOPMANN, M. R. (1978). Young children's knowledge of word structure. *Child Development, 49,* 669–680.

SCOLLON, R., & SCOLLON, S. (1981). *Narrative, literacy, and face in inter-ethnic communication*. Norwood, NJ: Ablex.

SNOW, C. (1983). Literacy and language: Relationships during the preschool years. *Harvard Educational Review, 53,* 165–189.

STUBBS, M. (1980). *The sociolinguistics of reading and writing: Language and literacy*. London: Routledge & Kegan Paul.

SULZBY, E. (1985). Children's emergent reading of favorite storybooks: A developmental study. *Reading Research Quarterly, 20,* 458–481.

SULZBY, E. (1986). Children's elicitation and use of metalinguistic knowledge about word during literacy interactions. In D. B. Yaden, Jr., & S. Templeton (Eds.), *Metalinguistic awareness and beginning literacy* (pp. 219–233). Portsmouth, NH: Heinemann.

TAYLOR, D. (1983). *Family literacy*. Exeter, NH: Heinemann.

TAYLOR, D., & STRICKLAND, D. (1986). *Family storybook reading*. Portsmouth, NH: Heinemann.

TEMPLETON, S. (1980). Young children invent words: Developing concepts of "wordness." *The Reading Teacher, 33,* 454–459.

VYGOTSKY, L. S. (1962). *Thought and language*. Cambridge: MIT Press.

VYGOTSKY, L. S. (1978). *Mind in society. The development of higher psychological processes* (Michael Cole, Trans.). Cambridge: Harvard University Press.

WOLF, D. (1984). Research currents: Learning about language skills from narratives. *Language Arts, 61,* 844–850.

YADEN, D. B., JR., & TEMPLETON, S. (1986). Introduction: Metalinguistic awareness—an etymology. In D. B. Yaden, Jr., & S. Templeton (Eds.), *Metalinguistic awareness and beginning literacy* (pp. 3–10). Portsmouth, NH: Heinemann.

solicited comments from her mother or father by pointing to something in the picture or making comments and asking questions. She learned to answer questions. Gradually, she learned to listen to more of the story her mother or father was reading. Kristen discovered that, just like her mother and father, she also had certain roles to play in bookreading (Ninio & Bruner, 1978; Taylor & Dorsey-Gaines, 1988).

4. Pictures in Books Are Symbols

Another aspect of literacy learning involves discovering that the shapes and colors in pictures represent things—pictures are **symbols** for objects and actions. Kristen showed that she had discovered this when she found her crayons after she saw a picture of crayons in a favorite book. She was discovering not only that pictures are interesting to look at, but that they are also representations of real things. Children learn that pictures in books are not things; rather, they represent things (Snow & Ninio, 1986). Kristen learned that she was not patting real objects when she patted the pictures in her books; they were only symbols for real things that she could pat.

5. Books and Print Communicate Meaning

A crucial outcome of children's early experiences with books and other kinds of print is that they learn that books and other print materials communicate meaning—they tell a message. Kristen learned to look through catalogs so that she could talk with her mother about familiar animals or objects. She learned that her storybooks showed pictures of familiar objects and events.

Learning to "mean" (Halliday, 1975), to understand what others say and do, is involved in nearly every activity, not only in literacy activities. It is the great undertaking of life—we constantly try to understand the messages that bombard us and to send messages to others. We use many cues to help us understand others and to help others understand us. We use the situation we are in and its clues to meaning (characteristics of the location or people's clothing), as well as spoken language and its clues to meaning (words, stress, and intonation). Because our society is a literate one, another powerful set of clues to meaning is written language. Written language, too, is used along with situation (getting out a checkbook at the grocery store), with spoken language ("That will be $81.47"), and with written symbols (81.47 printed on the computer display of the cash register).

Children learn to use these cues, including the written language cues, to make meaning. We are not implying that infants look at print and try to read it like an adult does. However, when an adult reads print aloud, tells a story, or talks about pictures in a magazine, infants and toddlers try to make sense of what is going on. They attempt to understand the situation, the talk they hear, and the visual symbols they see.

"Look at All These Raindrops": Experiences with Crayons and Markers

Kristen received crayons as a Christmas present when she was fifteen months old. Her first attempts at drawing were rapid back-and-forth swipes at paper (see Figure 2.1). She would quickly make a few marks and push the paper on the floor, indicating that

Figure 2.1 *Back-and-Forth Lines*

she wanted another sheet of paper. Kristen would try to write whenever her mother or father were writing. When she was twenty-one months old, Kristen began making round-and-round lines and dots. Her mother and father began drawing to entertain her. They drew people, houses, flowers, cats, dogs, and other familiar objects.

When Kristen was two years old, she began making jagged lines and single straight lines. She often labeled her pictures "dots." At that time, Kristen often commanded that her parents draw "a little girl," "a little boy," or any other object she could think of. She also asked them to write "Kristen," "Mommy," "Daddy," and the names of all the people she knew.

At twenty-seven months of age, Kristen made concentrated efforts to control her marks. She would slowly draw a continuous line all around the edges of her paper. It seemed as if she were pushing the crayon around the paper and watching its progress. She began making circular shapes of just a single line or a few lines (see Figure 2.2). One day she drew the picture presented in Figure 2.3. Her mother asked

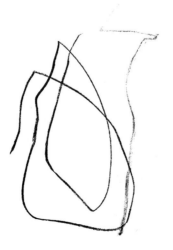

Figure 2.2 *Circular Shapes*   **Figure 2.3** *"ABCs"*

her, "What did you write?" and Kristen replied, "ABCs." This was a rare occurrence. At this time, Kristen did not often choose to use her markers or crayons to draw. Rather, she insisted that her mother or father draw or write. She also frequently refused to answer when her mother asked, "What did you draw?"

Once, when Kristen was two and a half years old, her mother began drawing a face. She stopped after drawing the shape of the head, and she asked Kristen to point to where the eyes, nose, mouth, and hair should go. Kristen pointed to where each feature belonged. Her mother coaxed her to draw some eyes. Kristen tried to put eyes on the face, but became frustrated. She announced, "I can't draw that." One morning, Kristen's mother convinced her to draw by saying, "Just do some lines and dots and circles." Kristen selected a blue marker and made several quick line strokes down her page (see Figure 2.4). After making several of these marks, she cried, "Look at the rain." She made several more marks, saying, "More rain. Look at the rain, Mommy." Then she began making dots, saying, "Look at all these raindrops."

A few days later, Kristen was encouraged to make a picture for her aunt. She made a single line down her page and said "B" (see Figure 2.5). She made another line and said "C." She continued making lines and naming letters. As she gave her picture to her aunt, she said, "Look at the ABCs."

By the time Kristen was three years old she was drawing people (see Figure 2.6). She would draw a circle, add two lines for arms, two lines for legs, and some dots for eyes. After drawing the person in Figure 2.6, Kristen said, "This is a picture of Daddy."

What Kristen Learned

As a part of these rich experiences interacting with her parents and with crayons, markers, and other writing materials, Kristen learned at least five concepts about drawing and writing.

Figure 2.4 *"Rain" and "Raindrops"*

Figure 2.5 *"ABCs" Again*

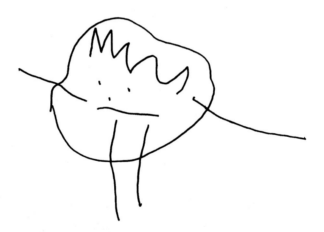

Figure 2.6 *"This is a picture of Daddy"*

1. Drawing and Writing Are Pleasurable

Children enjoy drawing and writing. Adult observers sense children's intense concentration as they hold tightly to both markers and paper and watch intently the shapes they create (Taylor & Dorsey-Gaines, 1988). Kristen often chose drawing and writing over other activities. For her, getting a new box of crayons or a set of markers was an important occasion, followed by hours of pleasurable drawing and writing.

2. Movements Are Controlled

Children learn motor "schemes" for drawing shapes and lines (Gardner, 1980). **Motor schemes** allow children to control their movements so they can make intentional shapes and lines. In order to be able to put circles and dots on a page where they intend them to go, children must learn how to control their movements. Kristen showed that she was learning to control her movements when she intently watched the progress of her crayons as she drew. As with Kristen, most children first develop motor schemes for making back-and-forth marks, round-and-round lines, dots, and jagged lines. Later, they make circlelike shapes and single lines (Gardner, 1980). Eventually, children learn to make as many as twenty basic scribbles, which become the building blocks of art and writing (Kellogg, 1969).

3. Drawing and Writing Involve Certain Routines

For toddlers and two-year-olds, drawing and writing are likely to involve others. Young children draw both to engage their parents' attention and to engage other children in play. Kristen quickly learned many routines that initiated drawing and writing as social interactions. She would say to her friends, "Let's make ABCs," or to her father, "Let's draw. You draw. Draw a little girl." When her father suggested that she draw (because he suspected she needed a new activity), Kristen replied, "No, you draw." Kristen, like other young children with willing parents, engaged in "command-a-picture" or "command-a-word" routines (Lass, 1982). In these routines, children name a word, letter, or object, and parents write or draw it.

4. Drawing and Writing Can Be Named

Children learn to label their lines and shapes. Gardner (1980) reported that he often drew things for his son. One time he drew a bird and, while drawing, talked about birds. Later, his son drew round-and-round lines, which did not resemble a bird in the least, and called his picture "bird." Gardner called this **romancing.** Many children romance both drawings and writing. They draw with no apparent intention to create something specific or meaningful, and when they finish, they label their creation, as Gardner's son did. Kristen romanced writing "the ABCs" (Figures 2.3 and 2.5). Such drawings are not really representational drawings or symbols because they do not objectively resemble the object labeled. However, romancing pictures and drawings—not planning what a written mark will be or even intending it to be meaningful, but rather labeling it or assigning meaning to it after the mark is completed—is a step in the direction of creating symbols in representational drawing. Children are led in this direction when their parents treat even their unintentional drawings as if they were intentionally representational. They ask children "tell me about your picture." This is an example of **ascribing intentionality,** when parents act as if what children do is intentional. Ascribing intentionality moves children onward toward representational drawing.

5. Drawings Are Symbols

Sometime between the ages of two and five, children begin to plan their drawings, and these drawings begin to resemble recognizable objects. When children's drawings begin to look to an objective viewer like what children label them, they are called **representational drawings.** The drawings become recognizable symbols.

Children learn that not only can they name their drawings, but their drawings can also become representations of things. Kristen demonstrated the beginning of this knowledge as she drew her "rain" picture. She drew lines and noticed that they looked like rain. Then she made dots that she called "raindrops." Kristen learned that she could not only make lines and dots, but she could also make "rain" and "raindrops." She used her lines and dots as symbols.

Children's early representational drawings or symbols depict humans. Most children's early representational drawings of people consist of a circle with two vertical lines reaching downward. These drawings are called **tadpoles** (see Kristen's drawing of her father in Figure 2.6).

Kristen's story provides one example of a young child's early literacy concepts. Yet we could ask whether all young children have experiences like Kristen's and whether they all learn the kinds of concepts that she learned. We could also ask *how* Kristen acquired so many literacy concepts at such an early age. Obviously, one of the important variables in Kristen's learning was the nature of the interactions she had with her parents as they shared books and wrote together. In the next section we discuss further how children acquire literacy concepts and describe the influence of home experiences in supporting young children's literacy learning.

HOME INFLUENCES ON LITERACY LEARNING

Literacy learning begins in the home. Children's first experiences with literacy are mediated by the ways in which parents and other caregivers use reading and writing in their lives. There are two critical components at work here for children's learning: first, children's interactions with others create contexts for learning (see Chapter 1 and the discussion of Vygotsky's zone of proximal development); and second, literacy is embedded in everyday living activities. Parents help socialize their young children into the activities that are expected in everyday living, including reading and writing. Kristen's mother and father valued literacy, and reading and writing were an important part of every day of their professional and personal lives. Therefore, they included Kristen in these activities and had every expectation that Kristen would learn to read and write and eventually participate in the same kinds of literacy activities.

One way in which parents invite very young children to participate in literacy activities is to read storybooks aloud. In fact, one of the best predictors of children's reading achievement in school is the number of hours they were read to as preschoolers (Wells, 1986). We also know that preschoolers who interacted more with their parents as they read aloud have larger vocabularies and better story understanding as five-year-olds than do children who contributed less during storybook readings (Dickinson & Tabors, 1991). Clearly, reading aloud with young children is an important vehicle through which they acquire literacy concepts.

Other literacy activities in the home may also contribute to children's literacy learning. Parents and children interact as they read environmental print—print that is found on everyday objects such as coupons or food containers. They may talk together as a parent composes a letter or list or as a child asks a parent to write (as Kristen enjoyed having her parents draw and write on her command).

Finally, some activities that do not include print, reading, or writing may contribute to children's later reading and writing achievement. Some researchers (Heath, 1984; Snow, 1991) argue that certain kinds of oral language patterns are very much related to the kinds of language used in literacy instruction and in reading and writing in school. For example, many parents ask preschool children to recount or retell daily activities in much the same way that teachers ask children to retell events from stories they read.

Next we describe home support for children's literacy learning as children and parents or other caregivers share books, participate in other literacy events, and engage in oral language interactions.

Booksharing

Sharing books with children is a frequent activity in many homes. Children and parents enjoy the close and special rapport that is established when reading and rereading favorite stories. The benefits from such activities are many. Children gain new experiences and understandings. They develop new strategies for constructing meaning from stories, and their vocabulary and language abilities grow (Whitehurst et al., 1988).

We relate the interactions between three children and their parents as they shared books together. These interactions demonstrate the strategies used by parents and other caregivers to support young children's construction of meaning. They also show how children's abilities to construct meaning expand as a result of participating in booksharing interactions.

Kristen and Her Mother Share *Billy Goats Gruff*

Figure 2.7 presents a portion of the dialogue between Kristen and her mother as they shared *Billy Goats Gruff* (Hellard, 1986). Kristen was seventeen months old at the time of this interaction. The dialogue demonstrates that Kristen already knew much about meaning construction; she labeled objects (saying "tee" as she pointed to a picture of a tree) and sought confirmation of her label (she repeated "tee" each time, looking at her mother as if for confirmation of her meaning and label). Kristen also monitored her meaning; she observed her mother's reaction to her label.

Kristen's mother used several strategies to encourage Kristen to participate actively in the booksharing interaction and to expand on what Kristen could currently do. She allowed Kristen to take charge of the reading by turning pages, even when doing so interrupted the reading. She provided feedback to Kristen's labels ("Yes, it's a tree") and helped Kristen focus on the more important narrative elements of the story. She hugged and shook Kristen and used her voice to attract Kristen's attention to a character, the troll.

It is noteworthy that none of the story text was read in this bookreading episode. Kristen's mother knew that Kristen found her talk, not her reading of the text, most meaningful. Although Kristen contributed very little language in the interaction, she was actively participating. She turned pages, used gestures and movements, gazed at her mother, and said words.

Figure 2.7 *Kristen and Her Mother Share* Billy Goats Gruff
(Hellard, 1986)

Brackets indicate portions of the dialogue that occurred simultaneously.

Kristen: (brings *Billy Goats Gruff* to her mother, sits on her mother's lap, holds book, and turns book with cover facing up)

Mother: Three billy goats gruff. (points to each goat on the cover) Look, a little one. (points to a small goat) A middle-size—

   K: (opens book and turns two pages, gazes at picture, and points to a picture of a tree) tee (looks up at her mother)

   M: Yes, it's a tree.

   K: (points to another tree) tee (looks up at mother again)

   M: Hm, um

   K: (points to another tree) tee

   M: (points to picture of troll, puts her arm around Kristen, and shakes them both) (changes voice to deeper tone) Look at the Trollllll. I'm going to eat you up.

   K: (laughs, turns page)

   M: Look. The first Billy Goat—

   K: (shakes her head, points at troll)

   M: Oh, yes, I see. (lowers voice) The Trolllll.

   K: (laughs, turns page, points to tree) tee

Elizabeth and Her Mother Share *Where's Spot?*

A portion of the interaction between Elizabeth (twenty-six months) and her mother as they shared *Where's Spot?* (Hill, 1980) is presented in Figure 2.8. In this interaction, Elizabeth followed both the story and the story text much more closely than Kristen did. In addition, Elizabeth contributed more language to the reading episode. However, her mother still contributed the majority of talk.

Elizabeth used many of the same meaning making strategies that Kristen used. She took charge of the interaction by turning the pages and making comments. She labeled objects in the pictures ("There's a doggy in there") and answered her mother's questions.

Elizabeth's mother used many strategies for expanding and supporting Elizabeth's participation in this booksharing event. First, she highlighted an important narrative element (action and character motivation) by telling Elizabeth that the mother dog was looking for her puppy. She continually used this as a context for helping Elizabeth understand why the dog was looking behind doors and under beds. She matched her reading style to Elizabeth's ability to participate in the booksharing (as did Kristen's mother) by interweaving her talk with reading the text (Altwerger, Diehl-Faxon, & Dockstader-Anderson, 1985). The story text seemed to be included as part of a conversation she was having with her daughter about the story.

She helped Elizabeth find meaning from the words of the text by using her explanations and expansions on the story as a support for meaning construction. In addition, she asked Elizabeth questions that called for labeling ("What's in the piano?") and provided feedback to her daughter's answers (correcting Elizabeth when she mistook the mother dog for the puppy).

Figure 2.8 *Elizabeth and Her Mother Share* Where's Spot? *(Hill, 1980)*

Paraphrased text is underlined. Brackets indicate portions of the dialogue that occurred simultaneously.

Mother: We are looking for Spot. Let's turn the page. He's a little tiny puppy. Can you see if you can find him <u>behind the door.</u> Is he there?

E: (turns to next page)

M: No?—What's inside the clock? Is he in there?

E: He's in there.

M: That's a snake. That's not a little dog.

E: Let me read it.

M: Okay.

E: It's a snake.

M: Turn the page. Where's Spot? Let's see if we can find the puppy. Is he—

E: (turns back to look at snake again)

M: Let's see what's behind the next page. We need to find Spot. Is he in there? (points to piano)

E: There's a doggy there (points to Mother Dog, Sally)

M: He's looking for another doggy. Spot's not there.

E: There? (points to Sally on next page)

M: Yes. That's a doggy. He's looking for another doggy, a puppy. Is there a puppy <u>in the piano?</u>

E: No.

M: What's a piano?

E: A, a

M: What is that?

E: What is that?

M: It's a bird.

E: Let's close it up. (closes flap on piano)

M: Let's see if we can find that puppy <u>under the stairs.</u> Is he in there?

E: Uh uh

M: No puppy in there. He's looking for the puppy <u>in the closet.</u> Is he in there?

E: No puppy in there. He's upstairs.

Jon-Marc and His Father Share
The Story of Ferdinand

Figure 2.9 presents part of a booksharing interaction between Jon-Marc, a three-year-old, and his father. Jon-Marc listened carefully and looked intently at each illustration as his father read *The Story of Ferdinand* (Leaf, 1936). He interrupted his father at times to ask questions and make comments. Like Elizabeth, one of the meaning-making strategies Jon-Marc used was to ask questions. He not only asked about the meaning of words, but also about reasons for story events and actions. He asked, "Why (did they have to take Ferdinand home)?" He listened carefully to his father's explanations and asked clarifying questions ("Is that why they wanted to fight in the drid?").

Another strategy Jon-Marc used to make meaning was to apply his understanding of events in the real world to make inferences about story events. Jon-Marc asked if Ferdinand would (go home) "And . . . and . . . and love her mother cow?" This question reveals that Jon-Marc used inferences to predict story events (after going

Figure 2.9 *Jon-Marc and His Father Share* The Story of Ferdinand
(Leaf, 1936)

Text is presented in all capital letters.

Illustration: Ferdinand (very large bull) jumping around after having been stung by a bee. Five men are jumping with joy in the background.

   Father: HERE WAS THE LARGEST AND FIERCEST BULL OF ALL. JUST THE ONE FOR THE BULL FIGHTS IN MADRID.

Jon-Marc: What does drid mean?

   Father: Madrid. That's the name of a city. Ma–drid, that's the name of a city, a city in Spain.

   Father: (reads several more pages of text)

Illustration: Ferdinand in a small cart going over the mountain. A bull ring is the background.

   Father: SO THEY HAD TO TAKE FERDINAND HOME.

Jon-Marc: Why?

   Father: Because he wouldn't fight. He just wouldn't fight. He didn't like to fight. He just wanted to smell the flowers. (Note, this is a paraphrase of the text that had just been read on the previous pages.)

Jon-Marc: Is that why they wanted to . . . to . . . to fight in the drid?

   Father: In Madrid? Yeah, they wanted . . . they wanted him to fight in Madrid. Madrid's the name of a city. They wanted him to fight the matador. But he didn't. He just wanted to go home and smell the flowers.

Jon-Marc: And . . . and . . . and love her mother cow?

   Father: Yeah, and . . . and love his mother.

Jon-Marc: Where's her mother cow?

   Father: Well, she's back in the book a little bit.

---

home, Ferdinand would love his mother). It also illustrates that he used his own life as a frame of reference for understanding the story. Jon-Marc probably went home to love his mother, so he inferred that Ferdinand would be going home to love his mother.

Jon-Marc's father, like Kristen's and Elizabeth's mothers, was skillful at adapting the booksharing event to Jon-Marc's abilities. He knew that Jon-Marc was able to sit and listen to long stretches of text. Jon-Marc's father expanded on information from the text and related to Jon-Marc's concerns (he explained that Madrid is a city), and he provided more adult models of language ("And love his mother"). He drew attention to information in the text as a way of helping Jon-Marc understand the story. He repeated information from the story text to answer Jon-Marc's question and, therefore, made explicit the causal relations among events in the story ("They wanted him to fight the matador. But he didn't. He just wanted to go home and smell the flowers.") All of his talk was contingent on Jon-Marc's talk; that is, it was in response to Jon-Marc's questions and comments.

Meaning Making in Booksharing

Table 2.1 presents a summary of the strategies that these three children used to construct meaning as their parents shared books with them. They used these *processes,* or strategies, to understand or construct meaning from the stories read aloud to them. These **meaning-making strategies** become part of the booksharing routines that we described earlier in the chapter. Children know that they play certain roles during booksharing, and these roles enable them to construct meaning.

As shown in Table 2.1, one meaning-making strategy that children use is to **label objects.** They learn that they can talk about things and actions in pictures by naming them (Snow & Ninio, 1986). Later, they can talk about things by describing them and comparing them to other experiences or people. A second meaning-making strategy is to **ask questions** (about word meanings, characters, actions, character motivations, and causal relationships between events). Children actively seek more information (Yaden & McGee, 1984; Yaden, Smolkin, & Conlon, 1989), sometimes as a way of monitoring their understanding of the pictures and story. Children also **connect their lives to the story** (Snow & Ninio, 1986). They draw on their "scripts" of daily

Table 2.1 *Meaning-Making Strategies and Supporting Strategies*

Children's Meaning-Making Strategies	Parents' Supporting Strategies
label objects	provide labels
ask questions	adjust reading style
connect story to life	raise cognitive level
make inferences	give feedback and extend
use parents' talk	draw attention to narrative elements
pay attention to narrative elements	follow children's lead
	up the ante

activities—their knowledge of what goes on, for example, at bedtime (McCartney & Nelson, 1981)—to make sense of descriptions of these activities. Children **make inferences** about actions, motivations, and relationships. They make explicit what is implied in the story text. They incorporate and expand on information provided by their parents. At first young children listen to their parents' talk about the story as a way of constructing meaning. Later, they use the words of the text read aloud to construct meaning. Finally, children **pay attention to salient narrative elements,** such as characters, actions, relationships between events, and character motivation. They learn to use what they know about stories to better understand and remember stories.

Table 2.1 also presents a summary of the strategies that the parents used to support and stretch their children's participation in meaning making. These **supporting strategies** encourage children to participate, provide information, and expand on their parents' contributions. It is as if parents demand that children help coconstruct the meaning of the story as they read and talk together.

As shown in Figure 2.10, parents **provide labels** for objects and characters, **adjust their reading style** to their children's ability to participate, **ask questions** that require children to label objects, and draw attention to important narrative elements. An important strategy that parents use is to **raise the cognitive level** of talk by commenting on and asking about character motivations and logical relations. These questions and comments require children to analyze characters, make predictions based on understandings of character motivations, and make inferences. Parents also provide feedback to their children as they expand on and **extend** their children's comments. Parents allow their children to take the lead in booksharing interactions. Early on, parents permit children to turn pages and identify topics of discussion. Later, parents follow their children's leads by making comments and asking questions contingent on the content of the children's talk. Finally, parents **up the ante** by encouraging children to participate in ever more cognitively demanding ways and by taking on more and more of the meaning making independently.

Obviously, children learn a great deal from these rich interactions, and their learning is related to their future success as readers in school (Dickinson & Tabors, 1991; Wells, 1986). That is, children not only learn strategies or processes for making meaning as they interact with books, they also learn concepts about the nature of stories and the language in books. They learn the special kind of language related to written stories and other text, decontextualized language (Dickinson & Smith, 1994). **Decontextualized language** is language in which all the information must be conveyed in the words or language itself. Unlike conversation, in which much meaning can be conveyed by looking at the same object or events or carefully watching facial expressions or listening to tone, decontextualized language must convey meaning linguistically in the words that are spoken or read. Young children also learn that stories have certain narrative or literary elements and qualities that are particularly important in the process of constructing meaning. We call the knowledge that children acquire of narrative elements and how they work in stories the **concept of story.**

Concept of Story

Before we describe a child's **concept of story** and how it changes, we need to describe an adult's *story schema.* We know that adults know a great deal about stories. In its simplest form, a story contains at the outset a state of equilibrium followed by a disruption of that equilibrium. Then, a character recognizes the disruption, and an action aimed at repairing the disruption ensues. The story ends with a reinstatement of the initial equilibrium (Leondar, 1977, p. 176).

Cognitive psychologists used the notion that all stories have a basic structure to create **story grammars** (Mandler & Johnson, 1977; Thorndyke, 1977). Story grammars are sets of rules intended to represent the kinds of content that people think are included in stories and how that content is organized. Table 2.2 presents a story grammar and a sample story (McGee & Tompkins, 1981, based on Stein & Glenn, 1979).

Of course, young children have not yet acquired the same concept or schema of a story that adults have. However, children's concept of story is very important

Table 2.2 *Story Grammar*

Story Components	Story Example *The Old Woman and Her Curious Cat* (by Lea M. McGee)
Main characters (animals or people)	There once was an old woman and a very curious cat
Setting (description of location)	who lived together on a tiny farm.
Action or event (introduction of problem)	One day the cat overheard his friends the blackbirds talking on the roof of the barn. He got so curious about what they were saying that he climbed to the very top of the roof. Once he got up there he realized that getting back down was not going to be easy.
Goal (formulation of a goal)	The cat decided to ask the blackbirds to fly down and tell the old woman of his predicament.
Attempt (actions that solve problem)	The blackbirds agreed to help if he promised to have the old woman set out bread crumbs for them during the winter. The cat promised, so the blackbirds few down on the shoulder of the old woman and told her where her cat was.
Resolution (outcome of actions)	The old woman quickly got a ladder and climbed up to rescue her cat. The cat kept his promise and had the old woman set out bread crumbs for the blackbirds that winter.
Reaction (character's feelings about goal attainment)	And as for the cat, he never climbed to the barn roof again.

Adapted from McGee, L. M., & Tompkins, G. E. (1981). The videotape answer to independent reading comprehension activities. *The Reading Teacher, 34,* p. 428. Reprinted with permission of the International Reading Association.

in learning to construct meaning from stories. Children give hints about what their concept of story might be in the kinds of stories they tell (Botvin & Sutton-Smith, 1977). Children gradually acquire a concept of story or story schema that is like an adult's story schema (Applebee, 1978). They come to know that stories have characters and settings, that some action triggers the character to form a goal, that the character performs actions to try to achieve the goal, and that the story ends with the character's obtaining (or not obtaining) the goal.

Importance of concept of story.   Children's concept of story, in part, influences how they understand stories, retell favorite stories, tell original stories, and ask questions about stories. For example, when toddlers or two-year-olds retell stories they may label only objects in pictures (Sulzby, 1985). The objects they label may have little or nothing to do with the story (such as the tree Kristen labeled as she shared *Billy Goats Gruff*). This situation would be expected if a child had a simple concept of story with little understanding of the elements shown in Table 2.2.

Other Literacy Activities

Children observe and participate in a variety of other activities in addition to sharing books. Children are included in shopping trips for which parents read lists, clip coupons, or write checks. They observe as parents write reminder notes or help older children with homework. The number of literacy events in the home and the willingness and ability of parents to include their children in these activities are related to the amount of knowledge that young children have about literacy. Children whose homes include more frequent literacy events (such as parents' reading magazines and books and writing letters or lists) know more about how reading and writing are used (Purcell-Gates, 1994). Two important literacy events for preschoolers are interactions with environmental print and drawing and writing (Burns & Casbergue, 1992).

Interactions with Environmental Print

Environmental print items play an important part in the beginning literacy experiences of toddlers and two-year-olds. Many children have more experience with environmental print items—toy packages, street signs, and food labels—than they have with books. Children learn to recognize meaning in environmental print by being immersed in daily activities involving items that include print (Goodman, 1980). As children eat breakfast they see a box of Rice Krispies and they hear talk about eating the Rice Krispies. They observe and listen in the grocery store as their parents look for Rice Krispies. As children acquire language, they learn to talk about "Rice Krispies" just as they learn to talk about "ball" or "baby" or "car." Just as children learn that things in pictures have names and can be labeled, they learn that things like cereal boxes and cookie packages can be named as well.

Many toddlers and two-year-olds do not notice or pay much attention to the print on their cereal boxes or cookie packages; nonetheless, the print is there. The print on the packages becomes part of what children know about those objects. Later, children will recognize just the print and stylized picture or logo without the object being there.

Interactions with Drawing and Writing

Many children, like Kristen, enjoy scribbling and drawing with markers, pens, and crayons. Parents encourage their children to engage in these activities by having writing materials and paper available. They also provide support in other ways. For example, how did Kristen learn to make her first written symbol—her "rain"? Kristen's parents probably played an important role in her transition into a symbol maker by providing her with crayons, markers, pencils, and paper. Kristen knew where these materials were, and she was encouraged to seek them when she wanted to draw. Her parents often modeled reading and writing. They wrote as part of their daily activities, and they drew pictures at Kristen's request. They provided examples of what adults produce when they write and draw.

Parents do something more subtle that helps their children become symbol makers. One of the most important things parents do is act as if their children are doing something before their children can actually do it. Kristen's parents often did this when Kristen made lines, dots, and circles. They acted as if her lines were really a representational drawing. While Kristen was drawing, she often sat with her father and mother. They would say to her, "What are you *drawing?*" It is clear that Kristen's parents expected that she would make drawings and name them. They were ascribing intentionality to her scribbles.

Oral Language Interactions

In the next section of the chapter we describe oral language interactions that are closely related to the kinds of language patterns found in books or other text.

Decontextualized Oral Language Interactions

Snow (1991) and Heath (1984; 1989) argue that certain oral language interactions are more like the language found in books and other texts than are other oral language interactions. Some language interactions require that children sustain a topic (talk for extended times about one topic without the support of another speaker), focus on **nonimmediate** events or objects (talk about things that the speaker cannot see at the time of talking), and make clear relationships between ideas and events (use logical reasoning, including making talk contingent on or connected to a previous speaker's talk). We described such talk as decontextualized language (Beals & DeTemple, 1993; Heath, 1986). These language interactions are not only connected to language found in books, but also to some language events in schools.

Some children have many opportunities to observe adults as they use decontextualized language to recount events of the day, plan for future events, give explanations, or tell stories. Similarly, some parents encourage their children to participate in such language activities and support their children's attempts by asking questions, providing prompts, and expanding on children's comments (Beals, 1993). These experiences may be quite important for children's later literacy success. Children who are experienced in using decontextualized language are likely to be more successful in school language and literacy activities (Beals & DeTemple, 1993; Heath, 1984).

Differences in Home Literacy
and Language Interactions

We can now return to the question of whether all children learn the same concepts about literacy that Kristen learned and whether her literacy experiences are like those of most young children. We have shown that there are many ways in which literacy is supported in the home long before children go to school—in the ways in which parents and other caregivers interact with children as they share books, draw and write, read environmental print, and engage children in certain oral language routines. Any of these experiences has the potential of helping children become better readers and writers later, when they enter school.

By and large we know that middle class, mainstream families are likely to engage their children in many of these language and literacy activities. But of course, families differ from one another, and the inclinations of children differ as well. Therefore, even children in the same family do not have exactly the same literacy and language experiences.

It is especially difficult to make generalizations about early literacy and language experiences across social class and ethnic lines. Some researchers have found infrequent uses of reading and writing in low-income homes (Purcell-Gates, 1994), although variations within these families also point to difficulties in generalizing across families. Some researchers have shown that the ways in which parents share books with children differ (Heath, 1984), and sometimes parents have difficulty reading with their young children (Edwards, 1989). Other researchers have documented rich and frequent literacy experiences in low-income families (Taylor & Dorsey-Gaines, 1988).

Some researchers have found differences in the ways in which parents in Mexican American and Chinese American families include their children in decontextualized language experiences (Heath, 1986; Pease-Alvarez, 1991). Heath (1989) argues that in many cultural groups children are not expected to use certain language patterns. It is safe to say that not all children come to school with experiences or concepts like Kristen's and that teachers should expect and celebrate the richness these differences bring to the language mix of the classroom. The next section of the chapter describes how teachers can enhance even very young children's literacy learning in child care and nursery school settings.

IMPLICATIONS FOR CHILD CARE
AND NURSERY SCHOOL

Soon after they are born, many children spend many of their waking hours in the care of adults at child care centers and nursery schools. We do not believe that infants, toddlers, and two-year-olds ought to have structured literacy activities. However, teachers in these situations can take advantage of what we know about how parents support literacy learning to provide appropriate opportunities for young children to explore literacy.

Literacy Materials

Teachers can provide literacy materials even for very young children. Books should be in easy-to-reach locations. We recommend that nursery schools and child care centers have at least one **book nook** set up in an out-of-the-way place in each room (Schickedanz, 1986). Some teachers of toddlers prefer to keep books in large baskets which they can bring out during booksharing time. Paper, crayons, and markers should be available on a daily basis. Toddlers and two-year-olds enjoy trying out new kinds of pencils, markers, and crayons. They also enjoy using new colors and writing on new textures.

Environmental print items can be used in a housekeeping center, or they can be brought in as part of other activities. One teacher of toddlers kept a bag of familiar environmental print items (such as a McDonald's bag, cereal boxes, and candy wrappers) to use during talk time. Talk time is a special time during the day when she invites one child at a time to sit on her lap in a rocking chair and talk with her. The environmental print items are one of the things the children might select to talk about.

Children's Literature

Teachers need to be sensitive to the kinds of books that are most appropriate for the children they work with. Infants enjoy **board books** because the pages are easier to turn and the books are more durable. Experts on children's literature also recommend **Mother Goose** and rhyme books for infants and toddlers (Huck, Hepler, & Hickman, 1987). A list of appropriate Mother Goose and rhyme books for young children is presented in Table 2.3.

Table 2.3 *Books with Mother Goose Rhymes for Infants, Toddlers, and Two-Year-Olds*

Ahlberg, J., & Ahlberg, A. (1979). *Each pair each plum*. New York: Viking.	Galdone, P. (1986). *Three little kittens*. New York: Clarion.
Cauley, L. (1982). *The three little kittens*. New York: Putnam.	Hill, E. (1982). *The nursery rhyme peek-a-book*. New York: Price/Stern/Sloan.
Chorao, K. (1977). *The baby's lap book*. New York: Dutton.	Marshall, J. (1979). *James Marshall's Mother Goose*. New York: Farrar.
de Paola, T. (1985). *Tomie de Paola's Mother Goose*. New York: Putnam.	Wright, B. F. (Illustrator). (1916). *The real Mother Goose*. New York: Rand McNally.
Galdone, P. (1985). *Cat goes fiddle-i-fee*. New York: Clarion.	

Concept books capitalize on toddlers' growing language abilities (Huck, Hepler, & Hickman, 1987). They encourage children to label pictures. Simple ABC and counting books with few objects per page are especially appropriate for naming. Older toddlers and two-year-olds can be introduced to **first storybooks** (Friedberg, 1989), many of which, such as *The Runaway Bunny* (Brown, 1942) and *The Gingerbread Boy* (Galdone, 1975), include repetition or patterns. Table 2.4 presents a list of suggested storybooks for toddlers and two-year-olds.

Responding to Children's Literacy Activities

We believe children should see teachers read and write and that they should be invited to read and write daily. Exemplary nursery school teachers read aloud to small

Table 2.4 *First Storybooks for Toddlers and Two-Year-Olds*

Brown, M. (1942). *The runaway bunny.* New York: Harper.	Hill, E. (19809). *Where's Spot?* New York: Putnam.
Brown, M. (1947). *Goodnight moon.* New York: Harper.	Hughes, S. (1985). *Bathwater's hot.* New York: Lothrop, Lee & Shepard.
Burningham, J. (1971). *Mr. Grumpy's outing.* New York: Holt.	Hutchins, P. (1971). *Rosie's walk.* New York: Macmillan.
*Carroll, R. (1932). *What Whiskers did.* New York: Walck.	*Keats, E. (1974). *Kitten for a day.* Danbury, CT: Franklin Watts.
*Carroll, R. (1970). *The Christmas kitten.* New York: Walck.	Kuskin, K. (1959). *Which horse is William?* New York: Harper and Row.
Clifton, L. (1977). *Amifika.* New York: E.P. Dutton.	*Ormerod, J. (1981). *Sunshine.* New York: Puffin.
Crews, D. (1978). *Freight train.* New York: Greenwillow.	*Oxenbury, H. (1982). *Good night, good morning.* New York: Dial.
Freeman, D. (1968). *Corduroy.* New York: Viking.	Rice, E. (1981). *Benny bakes a cake.* New York: Greenwillow.
Galdone, P. (1973). *The little red hen.* New York: Scholastic.	Slobodkina, E. (1947). *Caps for sale.* New York: Addison.
Galdone, P. (1973). *The three bears.* New York: Scholastic.	Tolstoy, A. (1968). *The great big enormous turnip.* Danbury, CT: Franklin Watts

* Wordless books

groups of children. Two-year-olds sometimes enjoy sharing books in groups of two or three children. This number of children allows teachers to sit close to the children just as parents do in one-on-one booksharing. Teachers can use the same strategies and routines in sharing books with children that parents use. Effective teachers are very willing to share favorite books again and again. They are more likely to talk about the story than to read the text. They invite children to participate by asking questions and making comments. Effective teachers use gestures and intonation to enrich the story meaning, and they tell how pictures and story actions are related to children's real-life experiences.

Chapter Summary

Very young children begin their literacy learning when they interact with their parents and other caring adults as they share books or other kinds of print items. Young children who have opportunities to draw and to talk about their drawing are also on their way to knowing about literacy. Infants, toddlers, and two-year-olds are not yet literate (as we describe *literate* in the preface of this book), but they do have many literacy behaviors and they do know something about literacy. They find reading and writing activities pleasurable, and they have bookhandling skills and participate in booksharing routines. Young children gain control over their arms, hands, and fingers as they develop motor schemes for creating shapes they have in mind. They know that the shapes they draw and the pictures they view can be named, are symbols or representations of reality, and communicate meaning.

Young children's home experiences have a powerful influence on their literacy learning. Children acquire literacy concepts through booksharing, other literacy activities (including interactions with environmental print and drawing), and in decontextualized oral language routines.

As children share books with their parents and other caregivers, they acquire meaning-making strategies. They know how to (1) label objects and characters in pictures, (2) acquire additional information through asking questions and seeking confirmation, (3) draw on their own experiences and link this information to the text, (4) make inferences about information not presented in the text or illustrations, (5) use information provided in their parents' or other caregivers' talk about the pictures and text, and (6) pay attention to particular narrative elements. As children gain experience with stories, they acquire a concept of stories, and this concept undergo changes and become more complex as the children have more experiences with stories.

Parents support children's meaning making in many ways. They (1) label objects and pictures, (2) adjust their reading style to children's abilities, (3) ask questions, (4) raise the cognitive level of the talk by analyzing, predicting, and making inferences, (4) provide feedback to children by expanding on their comments, (5) let children take the lead by responding to their comments and questions (make contingent responses), and (6) up the ante by expecting children to take on more of the responsibility for meaning making.

Parents also support children as they interact with environmental print. They respond to their children's drawings in ways that signal that these drawings are meaningful (ascribe intentionality). Finally, they invite children to participate in decontextualized oral language experiences, including giving explanations and telling stories.

Teachers can also play an important role in young children's literacy learning. They can make literacy materials available, offer literacy experiences, and respond to children's literacy attempts. Table 2.5 presents a summary of what literacy beginners know about written language meanings, forms, meaning-form links, and functions.

Table 2.5 *Summary: What Literacy Beginners Know about Written Language*

Meaning	Meaning-Form Links
know booksharing routines	make symbols
learn meaning-making strategies	**Functions**
use decontextualized language	draw and share books as pleasurable activities
develop concepts about stories	use books and drawing to gain the attention of others
use decontextualized language	
Forms	
develop motor schemes	
recognize the alphabet as a special set of written signs	

Applying the Information

Complete the following case study. Discuss Steven's literacy knowledge and behaviors. Also discuss the role Steven's baby-sitter plays in Steven's learning.

When Steven was nineteen months old, he retold *Bears in the Night* (Berenstain & Berenstain, 1971). He turned the book so that the cover faced him right-side-up. He turned past the first page (title page) quickly. Figure 2.10 presents Steven's retelling.

When Steven was twenty-five months old, he enjoyed drawing with his baby-sitter. She would encourage him to get his crayons, and he would color while she folded clothes or cleaned. He often made nonsense sounds as he colored. His sitter would talk to him as she worked. She would imitate his sounds and he would imitate hers. Sometimes Steven would sing songs he knew as he colored. Figure 2.11 presents one of Steven's pictures. He said, "This is a car."

Figure 2.11 *Steven's Drawing*

Figure 2.10 *Steven Retells* Bears in the Night
(Berenstain & Berenstain, 1971)

Story: Bears investigate a sound in the night by creeping out of bed, down a tree, and up a hill.

Steven: (points to moon) moon (points to lantern) i-eet	TEXT: IN BED Illustration: Seven bears in bed. Open window with a crescent moon. A lantern hangs on the wall.
(turns page, points to moon) moon (points to lantern) i-eet	TEXT: OUT OF BED Illustration: One bear out of bed, otherwise similar to previous page.
(turns several pages rapidly, gazes at picture for several seconds)	TEXT: UP SPOOK HILL Illustration: Bear going up hill with lantern in hand. Moon in sky. Owl at the top of hill
(turns page) shakes head, points at owl OOOOOOOOOOO	Illustration: The word "WHOOOOO," an owl, and four frightened bears jumping up.

literal meaning	analytic talk	causal relationships
inferential meaning	letter features	spectator stance
evaluative meaning	mock letters	pretend readings
storybook reading style	metalinguistic awareness	emergent readings
amount of participation	text features	contextual dependency
timing of opportunity to talk	concept of story	sign concept
	story-as-a-whole	logographic reading
level of cognitive demand	sequence	phonological awareness

WHO ARE NOVICE READERS AND WRITERS?

In this chapter, we examine the literacy learning of many preschoolers, kindergartners, and even some first graders whom we call **novice readers and writers.** Our choice of words to describe these children's reading and writing is intentional: in everyday usage, the words *novice* and *beginner* are nearly synonymous. Our decision to use the word *novice* in this chapter and the word *beginner* in Chapter 2 signifies that although we describe a change in literacy behaviors, we recognize that there are overlaps and interactions between our two concepts of beginning literacy and novicelike literacy.

Learning about written language is a gradual process. Children's literacy development is a matter of their taking small steps and making minor adjustments in their hypotheses. Children form new hypotheses in response to the discovered inadequacies of past strategies. Thus, it is not possible to identify a single criterion of novice literacy. A child may act like a literacy beginner in one literacy event and like a novice reader or writer in another event. Still, careful observers will notice that in some literacy events children begin using written language in ways that signal new insights about literacy. In this chapter, we will describe the many indications that children have constructed new understandings about literacy.

New Insights about Communicating with Written Language

Preschoolers sometimes use written language in ways that differ from those beginners use. They go beyond labeling their written marks as beginners do (in Chapter 2 Kristen called her written lines and shapes "ABCs"). *Novices intentionally create written symbols that they use to communicate a message.* Carrie's writing in the "Ted's Delight" literacy event in Chapter 1 is a good example of a novice's writing that is intended to communicate a message. Carrie wrote a check (Figure 1.9) as a part of restaurant play with her brother and father. Although her writing is not conventional, her behavior as she handed the check to her father indicated that she intended her writing to mean something like "pay for your food."

Figure 3.1 shows Thomas's writing. He gave his writing to his mother and said, "I have a message for you." His mother asked, "What does it say?" and Thomas

Figure 3.1 *Thomas's Message*

replied, "um, um, I love you." Thomas's writing is unconventional; in fact, it does not even have letters, just round-and-round scribblelike lines. However, Thomas intended his writing to be read, and he knew that his mother would find it meaningful.

Novice readers and writers also signal their new insight that written language communicates meaning when they construct meaning from the printed words and logos found on environmental print. They may recognize "Raisin Bran," "McDonald's," and "Coca-Cola" on the familiar cereal box, fast-food restaurant sign, and drink can. However, novices go beyond simple recognition of meaning in familiar items or contexts that happen to include printed symbols and words. *Novices react to the meaning communicated in printed signs and labels even when they are not located on the items they represent or in the context in which they are usually found.* They construct meaning from the symbol of the printed words and logos. They recognize the Raisin Bran and McDonald's logos even when the actual object (the box of cereal) is not present or when the familiar context (the restaurant building) is not available.

Examples of Novices

Three literacy events involving Quentin, Kristen, and Courtney are described next. These children have had many experiences sharing books with their parents and nursery school teachers.

Quentin is three and a half years old. He frequently draws with his older sister as she does her homework. Sometimes she draws pictures and writes words or letters at Quentin's request. One day, while his sister was doing her spelling homework, Quentin drew a large circle with one line radiating down from it. He pointed to this primitive *Q* and said "Quentin." Later, when his mother was checking his sister's spelling words, he gave her his paper and said, "I wrote mine."

Kristen is thirty-two months old. One day, while she was riding in the car with her mother, she said, "Pizza man." Her mother looked and finally spotted a Domino's pizza sign. This sign consists of two domino shapes in red, white, and blue and the word *Domino's*. Kristen's family frequently has a Domino's pizza delivered to their home. Kristen had never been to a Domino's pizza place because Domino's only delivers pizzas—it is not a restaurant.

Courtney is twenty-nine months old. When her mother signs birthday cards or makes lists, she gives Courtney paper and pens or crayons and suggests that Courtney write too. One day, as her mother was writing a letter to accompany a birth-day card, Courtney said, "I write 'Happy Birthday to you' " (see Figure 3.2). Court-ney's mother suggested that they send her letter too.

Figure 3.2 *"Happy Birthday to You"*

What They Are Learning

Quentin's, Kristen's, and Courtney's behaviors and talk indicate that they intend for their written symbols to communicate messages and that they recognize that mes-sages can be communicated in written symbols. What is significant about these events is that Quentin, Kristen, and Courtney constructed meaning from *written symbols that they constructed or noticed on their own.*

Kristen constructed the meaning "pizza man" from a printed sign and logo with-out the clues of an actual pizza, a delivery man, or a familiar location associated with eating pizza. Her behavior indicated a new understanding that printed sym-bols communicate messages. She knew that written marks in environmental print are significant. Quentin constructed the meaning "Quentin" by printing something like a letter *Q,* and Courtney constructed the meaning "Happy birthday to you" by writing round-and-round and jagged lines. Their behavior, too, indicated their awareness that printed symbols communicate messages. It is significant that the messages Quentin and Courtney constructed were part of a larger activity involving writing to communicate. Quentin joined his sister as she practiced her spelling words, and Courtney joined her mother as she wrote a birthday message.

Are They Reading and Writing?

This important question has been the center of controversy for the past few years. Tra-ditionalists define *reading* as the ability to identify words printed in isolation or in sim-ple stories. Similarly, they define *writing* as the ability to write identifiable words in isolation or in simple stories. After careful observation of children such as Quentin, Kris-ten, and Courtney, some educators have argued that we need a new definition of read-ing and writing (Baghban, 1984; Goodman, 1980; Harste, Woodward, & Burke, 1984).

We believe that *children are novice readers when they intend to get meaning from written symbols,* even when those symbols are highly familiar signs, labels, and logos. Kristen did not say that the Domino's pizza sign said "Domino's"; rather, she indicated that it meant "pizza man." Obviously, Kristen was not reading the words on a sign as a conventional reader would; nevertheless, she constructed meaning from the sign. Even when signs and labels appear in situational context, novice readers frequently respond to the written symbols rather than merely to the context. Three weeks after Kristen identified the pizza sign, she asked, "What does that *name say?*" about a familiar sign on a Baskin Robbins ice cream store. For months Kristen had said, "I want ice cream," as she passed the store. Because a picture of an ice cream cone is prominently displayed on the front of the store, we might conclude that Kristen was merely interpreting a picture (of an ice cream cone) or recognizing a familiar context (an ice cream store) when she said, "I want *ice cream.*" However, Kristen's later request that her mother tell her what the *name said* demonstrated her awareness of the written sign and its power to communicate.

We believe that *children are novice writers when they* **intend to communicate** *meaning with written marks.* Quentin communicated meaning when he made his printed symbol *Q.* It is important to notice that Quentin's writing was not yet conventional; he did not write his full name, *Quentin,* nor did he form the letter *Q* perfectly. Still, he intended to write something that was meaningful—a symbol for his name. Courtney communicated meaning when she made her jagged and round-and-round lines. She did not include any letters or words in her writing at all, but she intended her writing to convey the message "Happy birthday to you."

Repertoire of Knowledges

Some researchers have described developmental sequences of children's literacy acquisition (for example, Ferreiro & Teberosky, 1982; Thomas & Rinehart, 1990). Some of these ideas are presented in Chapter 1. Because we distinguish between literacy beginners and novice readers and writers, it may seem as though we favor a developmental approach to literacy learning. We believe that children's *knowledge* grows and changes as they have more and different literacy experiences. However, we also believe that the *strategies* children use to acquire literacy for themselves are similar for infants, preschoolers, and young elementary schoolchildren.

Some researchers have noted that children seem to display a **repertoire of literacy knowledges** as they engage in different kinds of literacy activities (Dyson, 1991; Sulzby, 1985). That is, when performing one kind of literacy task, children might display one level of literacy knowledge, and when performing another task, they might display another level of literacy knowledge. We have observed many children who display different kinds of literacy knowledges in different literacy events. At the time Kristen's mother noted her new awareness of printed symbols in some environmental signs, she also noted that Kristen was not responding to all environmental signs, nor was she using her written marks to communicate messages. After Courtney wrote her birthday message, she spent several months writing lines and shapes that she labeled as letters or words but that she did not intend to be messages.

We believe that children draw on a variety of understandings about literacy as they participate in literacy events. Although we use the terms *literacy beginner* and *novice reader and writer* (and later *experimenting reader and writer* and *conven-*

tional reader and writer) as useful devices for describing children's literacy behaviors and understandings, we do not intend for these words to be used as labels for young children. Rather, we believe that our descriptions of beginning literacy and novice reading and writing will provide teachers with useful guides for carefully observing what children do with reading and writing in specific literacy events.

MEANING

Novice readers and writers learn to construct meaning from an ever-increasing variety of texts, including menus, *TV Guides*, telephone books, grocery lists, coupons, and, especially, stories. Novice writers make meaning by creating an increasing variety of written symbols.

Constructing Meaning from Environmental Print

By the age of two and a-half or three, many young children find some **environmental print** symbols meaningful (Goodman & Altwerger, 1981; Hiebert, 1978). Most young children learn to recognize McDonald's, Coke, and Burger King at remarkably early ages. Other young children may point to the word *Crest* on a tube of toothpaste and say "toothpaste" or might point to the word *Cheerios* on a cereal box and say "cereal." Novice readers are not reading the words on environmental print; rather, they know the kinds of meanings usually associated with the objects and actions signalled by the environmental print item.

Children's first experiences with environmental print also occur in contexts that make the meaning of the printed symbol obvious (Laminack, 1990). A McDonald's sign is located in front of the place where children get hamburgers. The McDonald's logo is on the bag that holds the hamburgers and on the paper in which the hamburger is wrapped. This kind of print is **contextualized written language.** It appears in a context or situation that usually helps cue the meaning; it is similar to contextualized oral language. Children naturally apply their oral-language strategy of paying attention to the context as a way of constructing meaning from environmental print.

Eventually, children no longer need the actual physical context to signal meaning. When children are familiar with printed symbols such as the McDonald's logo, the context of the building or hamburger is not necessary to cue its meaning. Children find the printed symbol itself meaningful. They operate with the knowledge that written language symbols communicate meaning. Many children begin to ask "What does that say?" about environmental signs. They know that the signs they see communicate some message that might be interesting to learn about.

For example, a few months after Kristen read the Domino's Pizza sign she said, "Look, Mom, Barbie." Her mother had received an advertisement for ordering magazines. The advertisement included a page of perforated stickers on which the magazine titles were printed. One of the magazines was *The Barbie Magazine,* and the word *Barbie* was printed on the sticker in pink stylized letters just as it appears on the doll box. There was no picture of a Barbie doll on the sticker, and the sticker with *Barbie* written on it was more than halfway down a page of nearly a hundred stickers. Kristen recognized the word *Barbie* without the clues of a toy store, a doll, or even a picture of a doll.

Children expect meaning from many kinds of print items in addition to environmental print. For example, four-year-old Takesha was asked to read a handwritten grocery list. She said, "Green beans, coffee, and bread." She also offered to read a telephone book and said, "Takesha, 75983." Although Takesha did not really read the grocery list or the telephone book, she knew the meanings associated with these kinds of print and used this knowledge to read.

Constructing Meaning from Literature

In order to construct the meaning of a story being read to them, children must listen to the words of the story. Of course, most books for children include pictures that provide salient contextual cues for understanding the stories. Eventually, however, children must learn to rely only on the text and not on picture context to construct meaning from stories that they read. These strategies are particularly important for later success in reading (Dickinson & Smith, 1994; Dickinson & Snow, 1987).

Constructing Story Meanings in Groups

Most children's early experiences with constructing story meanings take place as they share stories with a parent or other adult. These sessions are highly personalized; they capitalize on children's experiences with particular stories. As children approach school age—preschool or kindergarten—their storybook experiences will be in many-to-one situations. Teachers are likely to share books with groups of children rather than with one child at a time. In group story-sharing situations, children are not as close to the pictures as they are in one-to-one story sharing situations. Thus they have to rely more on the words of the text to construct story meaning than on extensive viewing of pictures.

Effective preschool and kindergarten teachers are skilled in capturing each child's attention as they share books with small groups of children (Cochran-Smith, 1984). Still, young children must learn to pay attention not only to what the teacher is doing and saying (showing pictures, asking questions, making comments, and reading text), but also to what their classmates are doing and saying.

Mrs. Jones is a preschool teacher who is skillful in sharing books with her class of four-year-olds. Figure 3.3 presents a portion of the interaction among nine four-year-olds and Mrs. Jones as she shared *There's a Nightmare in My Closet* (Mayer, 1968).

Children's meaning-making strategies. The children's comments and questions demonstrate that they understood much of the **literal meaning** of the story. Obviously the children understood that there was a nightmare in the closet; they knew that the character needed protection. Their comments and questions demonstrate that they also made many inferences about implied meanings in the story. They made inferences about motivations for the character's actions (he shut the door "Cause he doesn't want the nightmare to come out"); about the character's

Figure 3.3 *A Portion of the Interaction as Mrs. Jones and her Pre-kindergartners Share* There's a Nightmare in My Closet *(Mayer, 1968)*

Brackets indicate portions of the dialogue that occurred simultaneously.

Mrs. J: (shows cover of book, invites children to talk about nightmares, reads title and author, and reads first page of text stating the character's belief that a nightmare once lived inside his bedroom closet)

Child 1: He got toys and a gun on his bed.

Mrs. J: Umm, I wonder why?

Child 2: So he can protect him.

Mrs. J: Protect him. Umm. (reads text about closing the door to the closet)

Child 1: Cause he's scared.

⎡ Child 3: He's a scaredy cat.
⎣ Child 1: My momma take the light off, I'm not scared.

Child 4: He might lock it.

Mrs. J: Why would he lock it?

Child 4: Cause he doesn't want the nightmare to come out.

Mrs. J: (reads text about character being afraid to even look in the closet)

Child 1: Cause the wind blow.

Mrs. J: The wind blows?

⎡ Child 3: Yeah, the curtain's out.
⎣ Child 2: It's blowing.

Mrs. J: It must have been a dark, windy night. (continues reading text, making comments, and asking questions)

Children: (continue making comments and asking questions)

Mrs. J: (reads text about character deciding to get rid of the nightmare)

Child 1: I guess he ain't cause that's not a real gun.

Mrs. J: (turns page to illustration of the nightmare coming out of the closet and walking toward the boy in the bed)

⎡ Child 1: There he is.
⎣ Child 5: Why he's awake?

Mrs. J: Well what did it say? He was going to try to get rid of his nightmare, so he stayed awake waiting for his nightmare.

---

traits ("He's a scaredy cat"); and about reasons for the character's feelings (he was afraid "cause the wind blow"). The children also made predictions about upcoming story events. Just before Mrs. Jones turned to the last page of the story, which contains an illustration of a second nightmare peeking out of the closet, one child predicted, "There's gonna be another one."

In addition to making inferences and predictions about sequence and causal relations, the children projected themselves into the story ("My momma take the light off, I'm not scared"). They also evaluated the story meaning based on their knowledge of the real world ("I guess he ain't [getting rid of the nightmare] cause that's not a real gun.")

In addition, the children paid attention to each other's comments. When one child commented about an action of the character ("Cause he's scared"), another one agreed ("He's a scaredy cat"). Similarly, when one child noted that "the wind blow," another child added, "Yeah, the curtain's out."

This short story interaction illustrates that four-year-olds in group story-sharing can construct many kinds of meanings (Martinez, 1983). They understand what the author says—the **literal meaning.** They understand what the author implies—**inferential meaning.** They make judgments about what the author says—**evaluative meaning.**

Teachers' support for meaning making.   Several researchers have examined the ways in which teachers share storybooks with young children and have found that teachers have different **storybook reading styles** that vary along three dimensions (Dickinson & Smith, 1994; Martinez & Teale, 1993; McGill-Franzen & Lanford, 1994). First, teachers' storybook reading styles differ according to the **amount of children's participation**. Some teachers expect children to do a great deal of talking during the storybook reading. They ask questions to encourage children's comments, and when children make comments, these teachers extend and clarify them. Other teachers expect children to sit quietly throughout the storybook reading, keeping still and looking at the teacher or book.

Second, teachers' storybook reading styles differ in the **timing of opportunity to talk** during storybook reading. Some teachers encourage most talk during their reading of the story. Like Mrs. Jones (in Figure 3.3) they ask children questions, make comments, and invite predictions throughout the reading of the story. Other teachers encourage talk before and after reading the story but usually read the story with little talk.

The third dimension on which teachers' storybook reading styles vary is the **level of cognitive demand** that teachers make on children's responses. Some teachers expect children to make inferences about a character's motivations or to discuss the causal relations among events. They expect children to talk about the meanings of words and to predict outcomes, or they want children to recall the important events of a story. Other teachers have children chime in as they read a repetitive refrain in a story or ask children to recall the name of a character. This latter approach is less demanding cognitively than talking about word meanings, predicting outcomes, or recalling important story events.

In general, teachers who encourage more talk from children and whose questions are cognitively demanding, requiring **analytic talk** (see Chapter 2 for a discussion of how parents support children's meaning making), provide better support for children's meaning making (McGill-Franzen & Lanford, 1994). Timing of talk about stories—whether before, during, or after storybook reading—does not seem to influence children's meaning making. However, going back at the end of the story to recall the major events and to share personal responses to the story as a whole may be particularly important (Martinez & Teale, 1993; McGee, Courtney, & Lomax, 1994).

Constructing Meaning in Writing

As we described the new literacy insights that signal a child's becoming a novice writer, we discussed children's new interest in participating in the sending of the message and not just in the activity of writing. Much of novice writers' message making is a part of playful activity. They imitate their parents' or siblings' sending messages in their dramatic play. One day, when Giti and her mother had returned from having a snack at the Big Wheel Restaurant, Giti walked around with a pencil and paper and stood in front of her mother with the pencil held over the pad just as she had seen the waitress at the restaurant do. She said, "You want?" Her mother dictated "Hot dog," and Giti wrote a jagged line. Then her mother said "French fries," and Giti wrote again. After several minutes of this game, Giti said "Ready?" just as her mother had when she was ready to leave the restaurant (Baghban, 1984, pp. 61–62). Giti's behaviors indicated her intention to write something meaningful. She wrote the food orders that her mother dictated. The "words" she wrote ("French fries" and "hot dog") reflected Giti's growing awareness of the content expected in a written food order.

Children's interest in producing written messages can also be initiated through school experiences. Two-year-old Natalie made the zigzag lines in Figure 3.4. She wrote left-to-right zigzags with her right hand and right-to-left zigzags with her left hand. After her first zigzag, she said, "I did it! That's my name. I'll spell your name." Then she made another zigzag and said, "That's your name, Daddy." For others she said, "That's Mary's," and "Don's is easy," and, "That's your name, Mommy." We asked Natalie where she learned to write. She said, "I do it at school," referring to her day care center.

Figure 3.4 *Natalie's Name Writing*

Similarly, Vang's kindergarten teacher provides many real-life experiences, such as flying kites, finding caterpillars, and visiting the zoo (Abramson, Seda, & Johnson, 1990). She believes that these experiences are particularly important for the learning of her children, whose first languages include Hmong, Spanish, Laotian, and Cambodian. Several days after visiting the zoo, Vang drew a picture of an elephant and wrote what appears in Figure 3.5a, saying "elephant." Then he drew a picture of a second, smaller elephant and discussed it with his teacher (Abramson, Seda, & Johnson, 1990, p. 69)

Vang: Teacher, look it. I made baby. Baby el-fant.

Teacher: A baby elephant. Oh, that's great. Can you write "baby elephant"?

Vang: Sure!

Vang wrote what appears in Figure 3.5b. Vang knows that writing can be used to label drawings. The meaning he constructed ("elephant" and "baby elephant") is highly dependent both on his picture and on the teacher's suggestion.

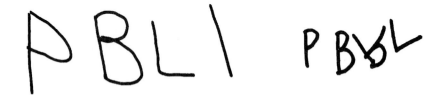

Figure 3.5a *"Elephant"*   **Figure 3.5b** *"Baby Elephant"*

From Abramson, S., Seda, I., & Johnson, C. (1990). Literacy development in a multilingual kindergarten classroom. *Childhood Education, 67,* 68–72. Reprinted by permission of the author and the Association for Childhood Education International, 11501 Georgia Ave., Ste. 315, Wheaton, MD. Copyright © 1991 by the Association.

Much of children's meaning making in writing depends on their experiences with meaningful uses of reading and writing. Giti would not have used writing to create a food order if she had not observed orders for food being written. Natalie would not have taken up name writing if she had not associated writing at school with classmates' names and then been encouraged by her parents. Vang would not have created a message in his journal if he had not had a highly meaningful trip to the zoo or observed his classmates' daily journal writing and his teacher's responses to those written messages.

WRITTEN LANGUAGE FORMS

While they are developing new insights about written language meanings, novices also demonstrate new awarenesses about written language forms. In particular, they acquire a great deal of knowledge about alphabet letters, names, and text.

Alphabet Letters

In this section, we describe what children seem to be learning as they begin to name and write alphabet letters. We start with what children must learn before they can recognize and name any specific alphabet letters.

Knowledge Prior to Learning to Name or Write Alphabet Letters

Before they learn to name any alphabet letters or to write recognizable letter forma-tions, children discover a great deal about alphabet letters and written language. One thing young children learn is that alphabet letters are a special category of visual graphics that can be named. Lass (1982) reported that her son began calling each of the letters in his alphabet books or in environmental print signs *B* or *D* when he was still a toddler. It seemed as if Jed had learned to recognize the special category we call letters. He called all the visual graphics (letters) in his category *B* or *D*.

A second thing that children learn about alphabet letters before they can name them is that alphabet letters are associated with important people, places, or ob-jects. For example, Giti noticed the letter *M* in the word *K-Mart* and called it "Mc-Donald's." She also noticed the letter *Z* on one of her blocks and said, "Look, like in zoo." (Baghban, 1984, pp. 29–30). Notice that Giti did not call the letters *M* or *Z* by their names. Rather, she associated their unique shapes with two meaningful places where she had seen those shapes.

Knowledge of Letter Names and Formations

As preschoolers, some children learn the names of many letters and acquire the abil-ity to write several recognizable alphabet letters. By the age of three, some children can name as many as ten alphabet letters (Hiebert, 1981; Lomax & McGee, 1987). By age four, some children can write some recognizable letters, especially those in their names (Hildreth, 1936). It takes some time even for these early letter learners to acquire the names of all the alphabet letters. Even precocious youngsters who become accomplished readers and writers prior to entering kindergarten take about six months to learn all the letter names (Anbar, 1982; Lass, 1982), Children may take as long as two or three years to perfect writing their names (Hildreth, 1936). In this area, as in all literacy learning, there is wide variation in the age at which children acquire certain knowledges (Morgan, 1987). Many children entering kindergarten do not recognize any alphabet letters and cannot write their names.

Other Knowledge

As children learn to name alphabet letters and to write recognizable letter forma-tions, they also acquire other kinds of knowledge about letters and written lan-guage. We suspect that it is this other knowledge that children learn while they are learning to name and write letters that may be especially important for their writ-ten language understanding. We discuss next two of these other knowledges— knowledge about letter features and metalinguistic knowledge about letters (McGee & Richgels, 1989).

Knowledge about letter features.   **Letter features** are the special lines and shapes that make up letters. For example, the letter *T* is made up of a horizontal and a vertical line; the letter *O* is made up of an enclosed, continuous curved line; and the letter *N* is made up of two vertical lines and a diagonal line. Children must learn to pay attention to letter features in order to distinguish between letters (for example, between the letters *w* and *v* or *l* and *i*). Natalie's grandmother tried to use Natalie's interests in zigzags and in name writing to call her attention to the features of *N*. After Natalie completed the writing shown in Figure 3.4, her grandmother began showing her how to make the letters of *Natalie*. Natalie was not interested, and her grandmother gave up after "NAT." But then Natalie made another, short zigzag, and her grandmother said, "You made an N!"

Children show that they pay attention to letter features in their writing. Figure 3.6 presents Carrie's writing, which consists of both mock letters and conventional letters. As we described in Chapter 1, **mock letters** are letterlike shapes with many of the same features of conventional alphabet letters. In Figure 3.6 Carrie wrote a conventional letter *O* and the mock letters resembling *T* and *E*. These mock letters have several of the conventional letter features of these letters, but also have some unconventional features (the small circles at the bottom of the letters and the extra horizontal line in the mock letter *E*).

Figure 3.6 *Carrie's Writing*

From McGee, L., & Richgels, D., (1989). "K is Kristen's": Learning the alphabet from a child's perspective. *The Reading Teacher, 43,* p. 211. Reprinted with permission of the International Reading Association.

Metalinguistic knowledge about letters.   Even when children intend to write messages and those messages include letters and mock letters, children's talk about their writing reveals that they are still discovering what they know. Figure 3.7

Figure 3.7 *Ashley's Thesis*

presents Ashley's writing. She wanted her aunt to play with her, but her aunt was busy writing her thesis. Ashley decided to write the thesis for her aunt. Ashley said as she wrote, "Aunt Linda helps people learn to read. She is a good teacher. The End." As she said "The End," she pointed to the letter that looks like a backwards *N* on the bottom left of her paper. She said, "Hey, I wrote an *N*." This literacy episode illustrates that sometimes novice writers discover letters after they write.

Ashley's comments also reveal that she is able to talk about alphabet letters as objects of interest. Her talk showed that she knew what the letter *N* looks like. Such awareness of one's own knowledge about alphabet letters is called **metalinguistic awareness.** Many children signal their attention to what letters look like and their own awareness of alphabet letters as they write together.

Children's Concepts about Alphabet Letters

Even when children know the names of several alphabet letters and use mock letters and real letters in their writing, they have unadult-like concepts of what those letters are. Many children do not think of letters as units of written language that are parts of words and related to sounds; rather, they think of letters as belonging to or symbolizing something meaningful.

Anders told his mother that the letter *a* in *Safeway* was "one of mine" (Goodman, 1980, p. 28). Santiago said about the letter *S,* "That's Santiago's." When asked, "Does it say 'Santiago'?" he replied, "No, it's Santiago's" (Ferreiro, 1986, p. 19). Dexter said, "*N* spell my grandmama." His grandmother's name was Hele*n* (Dyson, 1984, p. 262). These children's comments about letters show that they did not have the same concepts about letters that more accomplished readers have. Santiago did not think of *S* as a letter, as representing the sound of the letter *S,* or even as part of his name. Instead, he thought of the letter *S* as belonging to him.

Signatures

Just as children learn to name and write alphabet letters and acquire concepts about what alphabet letters are, they also learn to write their names and acquire concepts about what written names are.

Writing Signatures

Children's ability to write recognizable signatures develops in an identifiable pattern (Hildreth, 1936). Their ability depends on their growing motor control, awareness of letter features, and knowledge of letters as discrete units. Figure 3.8 presents Robert's name-writing attempts over a nine-month period while he was in a prekindergarten program for four-year-olds. The first example of his signature, produced in early September, was a jagged line. Like Robert's early signatures, many children's initial attempts at writing their names contain no letters at all; they are frequently a single line or shape. Such signatures may reflect that children are relatively unaware that the letters in their names are discrete units.

As children gain practice writing their names and begin to notice written language in environmental print or in their parents' writing, they start to produce a

Figure 3.8 *Robert's Signatures*

number of discrete, letterlike symbols as a part of their signatures. In the second example of Robert's signature, produced in October, there are five letter-like shapes. These shapes do not include many letter features. In contrast, in the third example of Robert's signature, produced in December, there are again five shapes, but they include many letter features. This signature has a recognizable *R* and *o*. Eventually, children include more conventional formations for all the letters in their signatures. They begin to place the letters in order and to include every letter, although at first the letters are likely to be scattered around the page or in scrambled order.

The fourth example of Robert's signature, produced in February, includes a symbol for each letter of his name; the letters are recognizable, but not conventionally formed. The letters are in order and written linearly. The fifth and sixth examples, produced in March and May, show his growing control over writing. The letters are conventionally formed, and by May, the writing indicates Robert's growing control over letter size and proportion.

Children's Concepts about Signatures

As children learn to recognize and write their names, their notions about signatures are quite different from those of adults. Ferreiro (1986) described Mariana, who claimed that she could write her name. She wrote five capital letters (*PSQIA*) as she said "Mariana" several times. When asked, "What does it say here?" about the letters *PS,* she replied, "Two Mariana." When asked, "What does it say here?" about the letters *QIA,* she replied, "Three Mariana" (Ferreiro, 1986, p. 37). Her answers reflect that Mariana believed each letter she wrote would say her name.

Mariana's comments about her name illustrate that children do not conceive of signatures as words composed of letters that represent sounds. Their ideas about signatures are interwoven with their concepts of alphabet letters.

Texts

Novice readers and writers learn a great deal about different kinds of writing, and they use this knowledge to create a variety of texts. Specifically, they increase their knowledge about story texts.

Text Features

Novice writers produce many different text forms. Carrie wrote a restaurant check (Chapter 1, Figure 1.9); Ashley wrote a thesis (Figure 3.7); and Courtney wrote a birthday message (Figure 3.2). Later in this chapter we will describe Johanna's birthday list (Figure 3.14) and Jeremy's "Book of Poems." Much of these texts was included in their talk as they wrote and in the contexts in which the texts were produced. When we look only at Courtney's writing, it does not appear to be a text. It is only apparent that it is a text when we pay attention to her talk, to her actions (she put her writing in an envelope), and to the context (she and her mother were writing birthday cards). It is interesting to note that function plays an important role in novices' creation of texts. Courtney created a birthday message as she participated in the functional activity of sending birthday greetings.

Sometimes the forms found in children's writing signal their growing awareness of the different features of texts. Figure 3.9 presents two pieces of Christopher's writing. Although Christopher composed both his pieces using a combination of mock

Figure 3.9 *A Story and a Grocery List*

letters and conventional alphabet letters, the two compositions look quite different. One composition was written in the home center when Christopher decided to go grocery shopping with two friends. Christopher said, "I need candy, milk, bread, and cereal." The other composition was written at the writing center. Christopher later read this story to the teacher: "My dad went fishing but he didn't catch any fish. I caught a big fish."

It is easy to distinguish Christopher's grocery list from his story both by the meaning he assigned to his writing and by how each piece of writing looks. The story includes two main characters (Dad and Christopher) and contrasting event descriptions of those characters (Dad couldn't catch any fish; Christopher caught a big fish), whereas the grocery list includes four food items (candy, milk, bread, and cereal). The story is composed of three horizontal lines of text with an illustration; the list is composed of a vertical line of text. These features of Christopher's writing indicate his growing awareness of **text features.**

Knowledge about Text Organizations: Concept of Story

Christopher's story and grocery list demonstrate that he had the growing awareness of the kinds of content found in different texts and how that content should be organized that is particular to novice readers and writers. We have called this kind of knowledge about stories **concept of story,** or story schema (see Chapter 2).

Novice readers' and writers' concepts about stories grow as they gain experience with more complex stories. One of the most important ways in which novices' concepts of stories change is that they begin to understand **story-as-a-whole.** Novices learn two important organizational structures that can be used to link events together in stories: **sequence** and **causal relationships.** Novices learn that events in stories occur in sequence and that some events in stories cause other events to occur. They discover that the event of a character falling down while skating is related to the event of scraping a knee—falling down caused the characters's knee to become scraped.

When children grasp sequence and causal relations and center their stories on a main character, their concept of story is similar to an adult's story schema (see the story grammar presented in Chapter 2, Table 2.2). As children use their understandings of sequence and causal relations to link story events together, they are able to perceive of stories-as-wholes. They seem to be able to recreate a story world in their imagination in which they can consider events "before" and events "after." They consider stories from the perspective of "there and then" (Genishi & Dyson, 1984). Younger children who label objects or actions in each individual picture seem unable to move away from the concrete single event captured in each illustration. They consider stories from the perspective of "here and now." Applebee (1978) called children's ability to step back and view story events as part of a larger whole their assuming the **spectator stance.** They begin to take on the role of a spectator in a story world they create as they share stories with their parents or other adults.

As children gain experience with stories, they begin exploring the imaginary world created by the interaction of a story's reading, other children's responses, and their teacher's talk (Rosenblatt, 1978). Children learn the particular ways language is used in stories (literary language), the kinds of characters found in stories, and the characteristics of specific kinds of characters (Crago & Crago, 1983; Meek, 1982). Children's awareness of literary language and their ability to enter a story's world is frequently observed in their imaginary play. Three-year-old Nat demonstrated this ability when he called his cereal "porridge" and said, "We are the three bears. My chair's broken" (Voss, 1988, p. 275). Another three-year-old invited her mother to enter her story world soon after they had shared *Three Little Kittens* (Galdone, 1986). Kristen was "cooking" on her play stove. As she slipped on her hot-pad mitten, she said, "Oh, Mother dear, Mother dear. My mitten, my mitten here. Hey, Mommy, you be the mother."

The Importance of Concept of Story

Children's concept of story influences many aspects of their literacy behaviors. Children draw on their concept of story as they listen to stories read aloud and construct the stories' meanings. They know to focus on the main characters and their characteristics, including motivations and problems. They know that the events in a story will be related to one another in a specific order. Their questions during storybook reading reveal their attention to these elements (see Figure 3.3).

Children also draw on their concept of story as they compose stories. Christopher included main characters and contrasting events in his fishing story (Figure 3.9). As children play, draw, write, and sing, they weave characters and events in and out of their familiar story settings (King & McKenzie, 1988). They create their own stories not only by making up characters and events, but also by mixing in characters and events from familiar stories.

Novices also use their concept of story when they attempt to retell stories (Hough, Nurss, & Wood, 1987). A special kind of retelling is when children look at favorite picture books—ones they have shared many times with their parents or teacher—and attempt to reread them on their own. These retellings or rereadings are called **pretend readings** (Pappas, 1993) or **emergent readings** (Sulzby, 1985).

Young children's earliest emergent readings typically consist of labeling parts of the illustrations or naming actions found in the pictures. Children at this stage do not usually attempt to relate the objects or actions in the illustrations to one another, and, therefore, they do not tell a story. Figure 3.10 presents four-year-old Ben's emergent reading of *Deep in the Forest* (Turkle, 1976). Ben's emergent reading of this wordless book consists largely of labeling pictures.

Figure 3.11 presents Johanna's emergent reading of *The Very Hungry Caterpillar* (Carle, 1969). This emergent reading retells the events of the story in a sequence

Figure 3.10 *Ben's Emergent Reading of* Deep in the Forest
(Turkle, 1976)

Bear. Bear. Bench. Oh oh. He's eating it. Broke chair. Jumping on the bed. The people. Crying. Bear. She found him. She chased that bear. Find his mother.

Figure 3.11 *Johanna's Emergent Reading of* The Very Hungry
Caterpillar *(Carle, 1969)*

Once upon a time there was a little egg on a leaf. It popped and out came a little caterpillar. One day he was hungry and he ate one apple. He was still hungry. At Sunday he had
two pears. He was still hungry. At Saturday he ate three pineapples and he was still hungry.
Then he ate four strawberries. He was still hungry so he ate a chocolate piece of cake, a
piece of pear, some sausages, and then he was fat. He made a cocoon and he pushed his
way out. And he became a beautiful butterfly. That's the story.

and includes some of the language found in the text (notice the use of past tense
and the repetition of the phrase "he was still hungry").

Children's emergent reading depends on more than just their concept of story.
Although Ben's emergent reading took a simpler form than did Johanna's, Ben had
only shared the book a few times with his mother and he was reading to a stranger.
In contrast, Johanna had shared *The Very Hungry Caterpillar* dozens of times and
was reading to her mother.

Concepts about Other
Organizational Features of Texts

During the preschool and kindergergarten years, children listen to more than just
stories. They enjoy poems, songs, and informational books. Just as they gain a growing awareness of the characteristics of storybooks and the organizational patterns in
stories, children learn how informational books are organized. From listening to informational books read aloud, children learn that these books tell about classes of
things, such as trucks or squirrels or tunnels (Pappas, 1993). Unlike stories, which
tell about a particular squirrel (the main character) and his problem, an informational book tells about squirrels in general, what they are like (a description of their
characteristics), and what they do (a discussion about their behaviors). Children's
concepts about informational texts also influence their emergent readings, retellings,
and compositions of such texts.

MEANING-FORM LINKS

Novice readers and writers find print in the environment meaningful, engage in
emergent readings, and communicate messages in their writing. They link meaning
with form in their reading and writing by using the context and talk. Eventually,
however, novices become aware that print plays an important role in communicating messages.

Contextual Dependency

Novice readers and writers rely on contextual dependency to link written forms with
meaning. **Contextual dependency** means that written forms convey meaning

through the context of their use or through children's talk about their writing. Thomas's message (Figure 3.1), Courtney's birthday card (Figure 3.2), Vang's journal entry (Figure 3.5), Ashley's thesis (Figure 3.7), Christopher's story and grocery list (Figure 3.9), and many other examples of writing found in this chapter have a common characteristic: the use of contextual dependency to link written form to meaning. If we took the children's writing out of the context in which it was written and did not know what the children said about their writing, we would not be able to determine the message that the child writer intended to communicate. We can only know the messages that novice writers convey when we know the context in which they wrote and when we listen to what they say about their writing. Clay (1975) called children's dependency on context to link meaning and form the **sign concept.** The sign concept is evident when children use the context of play to construct meaning in their writing and reading. Novice readers also rely on contextual dependency to construct meaning from environmental print. We have shown that novice readers find printed symbols in environmental print meaningful. However, if novice readers were shown words from meaningful environmental print symbols written on a card, they would not be able to bring meaning to that print. What novices notice about environmental print is not the printed words by themselves, but rather the colors, styles and shapes of letters, special logo designs, and pictures as a whole. The entire sign or label acts as a symbol or sign that means, for example, "McDonald's" or "pizza man." First, the sign or label assumes meaning because of the actual context in which it is found. Then, the entire sign or label itself becomes a context that signals meaning. Children depend on the whole context of a sign or label and not just the words on the sign or label in order to link a meaning to it. For example, Kristen was able to read *Barbie* because of its unique print and stylized lettering.

Using contextual dependency to read environmental print is called **logographic reading** (Ehri, 1991). In logographic reading children attend to the unique visual features of words, such as the stylized print, color, size, or pictures found in environmental print signs and labels; they focus on logos.

Moving beyond Contextual Dependency

Although novice readers and writers depend primarily on the context in which their writing is produced and in which written symbols are found to link meaning and form, some use more than context to link meaning and form. Many researchers have explored children's concepts about the links between meaning and print (Dyson, 1982, 1985; Ferreiro & Teberosky, 1982; Sulzby, 1985). They have found that not all children have the same concepts about the relations between meaning and form, that their concepts about the relations between meaning and form change as children gain experience using written language, and that children's knowledge of meaning-form links is very complex (Ferreiro, 1986).

We will describe three children's responses to a writing task which illustrate their knowledge of links between meaning and form in their writing. The task involves asking children to write a story and then read it (Sulzby, 1985).

Figure 3.12 presents Constance's story writing and her message ("I like you to visit me. You are nice.") Constance's writing and reading demonstrate the use of contextual dependency to link written form with meaning (Constance's writing conveys her intended message only because she tells us her message). However, Constance's writing also indicates that she has noticed something else about print. Note that Constance repeated several of her mock letters and that these letters seem to appear in recurring patterns. Constance has noticed that written English includes only a few shapes (twenty-six letters) that are used over and over in words (Clay, 1975). Although Constance's writing uses contextual dependency to convey its meaning, it also shows that she is aware that the way print looks has something to do with the messages conveyed in writing. Her understanding of how written forms communicate meanings is like logographic reading. She relies on context to convey the meaning of her story, but shows that she knows that print is important in this process.

Figure 3.13 presents John's writing and story ("I have a dog. He is big. He is my best friend.") As John read the story he swept his finger from left to right across each line of text as he said each sentence. John, too, demonstrated contextual depen-

I like you to visit me.
You are nice.

Figure 3.12 *Constance's Story*

I have a dog.
He is big.
He is my best friend.

Figure 3.13 *John's Story*

dency in making meaning from his own writing. But John has also noticed that printed text must be matched somehow to the oral message; he matched a line of text with a spoken sentence. Although not yet conventional, this matching of the text with the oral message is a precursor to a later, more-developed kind of meaning-form linking, that is, matching one spoken sound (or phoneme) with one letter (or grapheme).

Figure 3.14 presents Johanna's writing and story. She did not write an actual story, but instead wrote a list of things she wanted for her birthday.

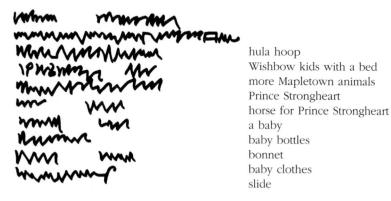

hula hoop
Wishbow kids with a bed
more Mapletown animals
Prince Strongheart
horse for Prince Strongheart
a baby
baby bottles
bonnet
baby clothes
slide

Figure 3.14 *Johanna's Birthday List*

Although her list is composed entirely of jagged lines, correlating what Johanna said with her jagged lines reveals that Johanna often matched one continuous jagged line with one spoken word. Johanna realized that the written forms she wrote should correspond with the spoken meaning she intended.

Drawing and Writing

Most novices' written texts include both drawing and writing. Dyson (1982, pp. 365–366) found that children combined drawing and writing in several ways in their texts. Sherrilynn's text (Figure 3.15) includes a cup of coffee, some houses, a wheel, a golf tee, and the letters *A, B,* and *g.* As she wrote she said, "I wrote some houses, your coffee, an *A* and a *B,* and some other stuff." Her text illustrates that some children draw and write about unrelated things as they create texts. This text also shows that even when children write conventionally (the letters *A* and *B* are conventionally formed), they do not always intend to communicate a message.

Lorena's text is presented in Figure 3.16. She said, "This is a dresser," as she pointed to her drawing and, "This is dresser, too," as she pointed to her writing. Her text shows that some children use both drawing and writing to communicate the same meaning. Lorena used her writing to label her drawing.

Figure 3.17 presents Johanna's picture and story writing. She read her story pointing to the print from left to right and then down the side and from right to left

Figure 3.15 *Sherrilynn's Text*   **Figure 3.16** *Lorena's Text*

Figure 3.17 *Johanna's Story*

across the bottom: "Miss Sharon and Mr. K have a new baby, Emily. I hope we will baby-sit Emily. I love Emily Grace." Johanna used her picture as a starting point, but went on to create a story world filled with characters, actions, and feelings. In this example, Johanna used writing to move beyond her picture into the world of story.

Given that children so often include drawings with writing and that they read pictures in the same ways in which they read print, researchers have wondered whether children differentiate between the two symbolic systems, drawing and writing. We might suspect that they do not differentiate between drawing and writing. However, the relation between drawing and writing is complex. Some researchers have noticed that the lines and shapes that children call pictures are different from the lines and shapes that they call writing (DeFord, 1980; Harste, Burke, & Woodward, 1981). This observation suggests that children notice differences between drawings and writing and that their own drawing and writing reflect these differences. Figure 3.18 presents three-year-old Ryan Patrick's drawing and writing. Careful observation of Ryan Patrick's product suggests that he differentiates between drawing and writing, even though the drawing is not representational and the writing is not conventional.

Figure 3.18 *Ryan Patrick's Drawing and Writing*

There are three important characteristics of children's use of drawing and writing. First, it is clear that children's drawings are an important part of their written communications, and teachers can use them to encourage children's writing. Second, the talk that surrounds both drawing and writing is crucial for understanding what children intend to communicate. Third, the talk provides useful information for finding out what children know about written language and how they learn to link meaning and written forms.

Phonological Awareness

Although novice readers and writers do not make the connection between sounds and letters, they do learn something important about oral language that, at a later time, will help them discover sound–letter relations. Novice readers and writers learn to pay attention to the sounds in oral language.

The sound system of language includes sounds in words, such as the /p/ at the beginning of *pin* and the middle of *happy,* but it also includes the qualities of sounds, such as pitch and stress and pause, which contribute to the melody of language. **Phonological awareness** comprises awareness of all of these things.

To begin to spell and read children must be able to hear sounds in words so that they can discover the relation between letters and sounds. To write the word *happy,* children must be able to isolate the word *happy* from a stream of oral speech, such as "happy birthday." Then they must be able to isolate sounds within the word *happy.* The ability to isolate the individual sounds in the word *happy* is just one manifestation of phonological awareness. Hearing every individual sound in a word is beyond the ability of novices. Still, some novice readers and writers show that they have some phonological awareness because they make up rhyming words.

The ability of novice readers and writers to create rhyming words emerges from their earlier experiences with nursery rhymes and other books with language play. The rhythm created in nursery rhymes highlights and segments speech sounds in a way that conversation does not (Geller, 1983). The syllables *PE ter PE ter PUMP kin EAT er* are naturally separated by the stress in the rhyme. This natural play with language sounds invites children to enjoy the music of language. Children who have listened to nursery rhymes and other books with language play soon begin to play with speech sounds themselves. While four-year-old James was playing with blocks in his preschool room, he muttered "James, Fames, Wames" to himself. James was demonstrating phonological awareness. This ability will serve him later when he begins to notice that certain letters appear at the same time that certain sounds of language are heard.

In the next section, we describe what children learn about the functions of written language. Function is the key to novice readers' and writers' literacy learning. Children's involvement in activities that use written language in functional ways provides the base for literacy growth.

WRITTEN LANGUAGE FUNCTIONS

One characteristic of young children is that they want to do whatever they see someone else doing. If Dad is sweeping the porch, his son wants a broom to sweep, too. We find these actions charming, but they are more than that. This willingness, even insistence, on joining in family activities forms a strong foundation for literacy learning. When Dad writes checks to pay bills, his son will want a pen and paper so that he can join in the activity of writing. Later, his son will want to join in the activity of writing checks to pay bills. Children not only observe adults' reading and writing, but they also participate in using written language, especially in their play. (Jacob, 1984, p. 81).

Many children from literacy-rich homes go beyond using literacy in their play. They use literacy as themes for play. One day Jeremy announced that he was going to make a book (Gundlach, McLane, Scott, & McNamee, 1985, p. 13). His father suggested that he use some index cards and write his book on the typewriter. After Jeremy had finished typing his cards, he and his father stapled the cards together to make the book. When his father asked him what was in his book, Jeremy replied, "A surprise" (p. 13). The next day, Jeremy's father invited him to listen to a radio program of children reading their poetry. After the program, Jeremy asked his mother and father to come into the living room to listen to him read his "Book of Poems." He opened the book he had made the previous day and said, "Page 1." Then he recited a poem that he knew. As he read "Page 2," he could not seem to remember any more poems, so he made up rhyming words and used singsong intonation. His mother and father applauded his reading.

Unlike Jeremy, who uses literacy as a way of playing and gaining the attention of his parents, Tom uses literacy in more functional ways. When Tom was four, he became angry because his mother would not buy him a new toy. His mother said that she would be paid in three weeks and that Tom could have a toy then. Tom asked how many days were in three weeks and went to his room. He made the calendar (a portion of which is presented in Figure 3.19) with a number for each of the twenty-one days remaining until he could get a new toy. Every day as his father read him a story at bedtime, Tom crossed off a day on his calendar, and on the twenty-first day his mother bought him his new toy.

Figure 3.19 *Tom's Calendar*

Jeremy's poetry reading and Tom's calendar making are examples of children's functional use of reading and writing. Jeremy created a poetry reading that was entertaining for him and his family (see Halliday's interactive and imaginative functions in Chapter 1), and Tom constructed messages so that he could plan for (and ensure) important future events (see instrumental and regulatory use of language from Chapter 1).

Family- and Community-Specific Written Language Functions

Children learn what to do with written language as they function as a part of a family that uses written language in particular ways. Naturally, what children know about the functions of written language reflects how written language has been used in their families. In most families, reading and writing are used as a part of daily living. Children in these families participate in these activities as well as observe them (Taylor, 1983; Taylor & Dorsey-Gaines, 1988). Many of the writing and reading examples presented in this chapter reflect the kinds of reading and writing found in many homes: writing birthday messages, reading menus and giving orders at a restaurant, writing and reading grocery lists, marking calendars to remember important events, and locating numbers in a telephone book.

How written language functions within different communities also influences what children learn about reading and writing. Written language functions in different ways in different communities (Heath, 1983; Schieffelin & Cochran-Smith, 1984). In some communities, print serves the practical functions of paying bills, providing information about guarantees, and affirming religious beliefs. In other communities, print is used for recreation and entertainment as well; people are likely to read for pleasure. Print serves even wider functions in other communities; it provides a means of critically analyzing political, economic, or social issues. Children growing up in these different communities have different concepts of the functions served by reading and writing.

Because teachers are members of communities that use reading and writing in certain ways, they hold views about why children should be taught to read and write that are influenced by their community's literacy values and beliefs. Most teachers come from professional communities where written language is viewed as an important source of mental stimulation, learning, and enjoyment (Schieffelin & Cochran-Smith, 1984). Print is viewed as authority; books and other printed materials are used to legitimize experiences and verify information gained through other means. Teachers often unknowingly create classrooms in which such beliefs about written language prevail. Because teachers have their own values and beliefs about literacy, they must be careful not to take them for granted and not to use them to judge others' beliefs and values.

A WORD OF CAUTION

We add two cautions to our discussion of novice readers and writers. First, we have noted the ages of several of the children we described as novice readers and writers. We believe that many children become novice readers and writers around the ages of two or three. However, children may display knowledge like that of novice readers and writers in one literacy event and knowledge like that of literacy beginners in other events. Many children display novice reading and writing literacy knowledge throughout their preschool years. Many kindergartners and first graders seem to operate with novice reading and writing knowledge. We caution that not all three-, four-, or five-year-olds will be novice readers or writers and that novice reading and writing often does not end at age five.

Second, much of the knowledge we have of young preschoolers' literacy derives from research involving middle-class families. The ages at which many of these youngsters display novice reading and writing may be deceptive; these children have had early and frequent experiences of the kind that would be expected to sup-

ference, 44th Yearbook (pp. 1–32). Claremont, CA: Claremont Graduate School.

GOODMAN, Y., & ALTWERGER, B. (1981). *Print awareness in preschool children: A study of the development of literacy in preschool children* (Occasional Paper No. 4). Tucson: Arizona Center for Research and Development, College of Education, University of Arizona.

GUNDLACH, R., McLANE, J. B., SCOTT, F. M., & McNAMEE, G. D. (1985). The social foundations of children's early writing development. In M. Farr (Ed.), *Advances in writing research: Vol. 1. Children's early writing development* (pp. 1–58). Norwood, NJ: Ablex.

HARSTE, J. C., BURKE, C. L., & WOODWARD, V. A. (1981). *Children, their language and world: Initial encounters with print* (Final Report NIE-G-79-0132). Bloomington, IN: Indiana University, Language Education Department.

HARSTE, J. C., WOODWARD, V. A., & BURKE, C. L. (1984). *Language stories and literacy lessons.* Portsmouth, NH: Heinemann.

HEATH, S. B. (1983). *Ways with words: Language, life, and work in communities and classrooms.* New York: Cambridge University Press.

HIEBERT, E. H. (1978). Preschool children's understanding of written language. *Child Development, 49,* 1231–1234.

HIEBERT, E. H. (1981). Developmental patterns and interrelationships of preschool children's point awareness. *Reading Research Quarterly, 16,* 236–260.

HILDRETH, G. (1936). Developmental sequences in name writing. *Child Development, 7,* 291–302.

HOUGH, R. A., NURSS, J. R., & WOOD, D. (1987). Tell me a story: Making opportunities for elaborated language in early childhood classrooms. *Young Children, 43,* 6–12.

JACOB, E. (1984). Learning literacy through play: Puerto Rican kindergarten children. *Research in the Teaching of English, 17,* 73–83.

KING, M. L., McKENZIE, M. G. (1988). Research currents: Literary discourse from a child's point of view. *Language Arts, 65,* 304–314.

LAMINACK, L. (1990). "Possibilities, Daddy, I think it says possibilities": A father's journal of the emergence of literacy. *The Reading Teacher, 43,* 536–540.

LASS, B. (1982). Portrait of my son as an early reader. *The Reading Teacher, 36,* 20–28.

LOMAX, R. G., & McGEE, L. M. (1987). Young children's concepts about print and reading: Toward a model of word reading acquisition. *Reading Research Quarterly, 22,* 219–256.

MARTINEZ, M. (1983). Exploring young children's comprehension during story time talk. *Language Arts, 60,* 202–209.

MARTINEZ, M., & TEALE, W. (1993). Teacher storybook reading style: A comparison of six teachers. *Research in the Teaching of English, 27,* 175–199.

MAYER, M. (1968). *There's a nightmare in my closet.* New York: Dial.

McGEE, L., COURTNEY, L., & LOMAX, R. (1994). Teachers' roles in first graders' grand conversations. In C. Kinzer & D. Leu (Eds.), *Forty-third Yearbook of the National Reading Conference.* Chicago: National Reading Conference.

McGEE, L., & RICHGELS, D. (1989). "K is Kristen's": Learning the alphabet from a child's perspective. *The Reading Teacher, 43,* 216–225.

McGILL-FRANZEN, A., & LANFORD, C. (1994). Exposing the edge of the preschool curriculum: Teachers' talk about text and children's literary understandings. *Language Arts, 71,* 264–273.

MEEK, M. (1982). *Learning to read.* Portsmouth, NH: Heinemann.

MORGAN, A. L. (1987). The development of written language awareness in Black preschool children. *Journal of Reading Behavior, 19,* 49–67.

PAPPAS, C. (1993). Is narrative "primary"? Some insights from kindergartners' pretend readings of stories and information books. *Journal of Reading Behavior, 25,* 97–129.

ROSENBLATT, L. M. (1978). *The reader, the text, the poem: The transactional theory of the literary work.* Carbondale: Southern Illinois University Press.

SCHIEFFELIN, B. B., & COCHRAN-SMITH, M. (1984). Learning to read culturally: Literacy before schooling. In H. Goelman, A. Oberg, & F. Smith (Eds.), *Awakening to literacy* (pp. 3–23). Exeter, NH: Heinemann.

SULZBY, E. (1985). Kindergartners as readers and writers. In M. Farr (Ed.), *Advances in writing research: Vol 1. Children's early writing development* (pp. 127–199). Norwood, NJ: Ablex.

TAYLOR, D. (1983). *Family literacy.* Exeter, NH: Heinemann.

TAYLOR, D., & DORSEY-GAINES, C. (1988). *Growing up literate: Learning from inner-city families.* Portsmouth, NH: Heinemann.

THOMAS, K., & RINEHART, S. (1990). Young children's oral language, reading, and writing. *Journal of Research in Childhood Education, 5,* 5–26.

TURKLE, B. (1976). *Deep in the forest.* New York: Dutton.

From Five to Seven Years: Experimenting Readers and Writers

Chapter 4 describes children who are making the transition between reading and writing as novices and becoming conventional readers and writers. We call these children **experimenters.** Experimenting readers and writers do not yet read and write in fully conventional ways; but they make several fundamental discoveries. They learn that to be writers and readers they must make systematic use of symbols. With their storybook retellings and their invented spellings, experimenters show that they are engaged in constructing their own symbol systems. Thus, they lay the groundwork for—and truly are in transition toward—eventually learning the symbol systems used by conventional readers and writers. No single characteristic or accomplishment qualifies a young child as an experimenter. We believe, however, that children who show several of the following sets of behaviors will benefit from their teachers' considering them experimenters. Experimenters

1. Know that they do not know how to read and write in the same way that adults read and write.

2. Are aware of the work involved in reading and writing. They often devote large amounts of energy to a literacy task, even when the task is a small, concentrated part of the whole process of reading and writing.

3. Attempt literacy tasks that are not necessarily a part of playing a game or a role. They sometimes respond to adults' or more knowledgeable peers' efforts to enlist them as writers or readers.

4. Have complete or nearly complete alphabet knowledge and are beyond concentrating on individual letters in their reading and writing efforts.

5. Have a baseline of writing ability that is not conventional writing, but does include many conventional features, such as conventional letters and words, especially their own names.

6. Spell—they work at using letters to write words, usually inventively. Their approach is systematic but not conventional.

7. Use language that is like the language in books and unlike the language of conversation; they are influenced by the print in their reading.

In this chapter we examine what experimenters know about written language meanings, forms, meaning-form links, and functions. We begin by describing the new insights about reading and writing that signal children's engaging in literacy activities in ways that we consider experimenting reading and writing: they concentrate on learning about conventional reading and writing through experimenting. Experimenters continue to develop meaning-making strategies, but their greatest achievements are in their expanding understandings about written language forms and meaning-form links. Experimenters gradually acquire concepts about spoken words, written words, and word boundaries. They experiment with a variety of text formats by using mock writing, dictating, copying, asking for spellings, and spelling. They use three rules to link meanings and forms: sounding literate, being precise, and using letter–sound relationships. They develop phonemic awareness and invent spellings. They use reading and writing for the purposes of experimenting, pleasing others, and preserving messages.

Key Concepts

experimenters

alphabetic language system

breaking into print

literary syntax

concept of spoken words

content words

function words

concept of written words

letter combinations

invented spelling

concept of word boundaries

informed refusals

dialogue markers

alliteration

sounding literate

scale of emergent readings

reading-like intonation

being precise

finger-point reading

voice-to-print match

sight words

message concept

phoneme

phonemic awareness

onset

rime

manner of articulation

identity of sound

letter name strategy

affrication

non-spelling

early invented spelling

purely phonetic spelling

alphabetic reading

phonetic cue reading

WHO ARE EXPERIMENTERS?

Learning about written language is a gradual process, and it is not possible to identify absolute milestones. There is no single, great accomplishment that divides beginners and novices from the experimenters described in this chapter. A child may act like an experimenter one day and then go back to the ways of a novice for a while. A child may experiment in storyreading, but not yet in spelling. Good observers notice a combination of changes that together suggest that a child is dealing with written language in a new, experimental manner.

Experimenters' New Awareness

One of the most important changes in children as they become experimenters takes place in their *attitude*. Over a period of time, a careful observer can notice a new attitude that might be described as being more aware, thoughtful, tentative, and testing. Experimenters are aware that certain conventions are related to reading and writing. They know that readers and writers attend to print as they read and write, and that print governs what is read and written. But young experimenters know that they cannot do what conventional readers do; they have not yet worked out the puzzle of what exactly readers and writers are doing. However, *experimenters work hard at trying to figure out the conventions that enable conventional reading and writing*. They focus on trying to produce conventional readings of texts and conventionally written texts. In doing so, they work at understanding how the written language system works.

By experimenting with a variety of hypotheses about how written language works, how someone really reads or writes, experimenters eventually (and gradually) come to discover an important insight about conventional reading and writing—that readers read words and that words are composed of letters related to the sounds in spoken words. That is, experimenters eventually discover that the English written language system is an **alphabetic language system,** that letters in written words relate to sounds in spoken words.

As we shall see, experimenters' understanding about the relationships between sounds and letters is not the conventional understanding that more accomplished readers and writers hold. Experimenters only gradually become aware of the conventions related to written words and how the letters in words relate to the sounds in spoken words. Yet it is this gradual understanding about words and sound–letter relationships that moves experimenters from emergent reading and writing to the beginnings of conventional reading and writing. Experimenters also acquire new understandings about written language meaning or functions, which are discussed later in the chapter. What is most important about experimenters, though, is what happens with forms and meaning-form links. Experimenters are **breaking into print;** their reading and writing attempts are influenced by print.

Because early experimenters are aware that they do not know how to read and write conventionally, they are especially prone to frustration and feelings of inadequacy. They are likely to say, "I can't write" or "I don't want to read." Experimenters need understanding, support, and patience.

If experimenters have adults' support, however, another aspect of their new attitude may appear, concentration, or engagement. Many young children show that they are experimenters by the intensity with which they work at reading and writing. Once they are helped to avoid the potential frustration of knowing that there is much that they do not know, they seem to dig in and work at one small part at a time (Sulzby, 1985b). They will work intensely when invited to read and write, especially if they know that they can request help and that they need not do a perfect, complete job. Children's appearance of working hard is the result of the careful analysis, the concentrated thinking, and the reasoned trying out that is the essence of experimentation and invention. If it is true that what they are doing at this stage is "inventing literacy for themselves" (Goodman, 1980), then it is no wonder that such hard work is involved.

Experimenters may need adults' encouragement even when they do not finish a task. For example, they may work at how to represent the sounds in a single word of a longer message they wish to write, or they may work at reading a favorite storybook by concentrating on a single page, its pictures and print, and their memory of what adults have read on that page.

An important distinction between experimenters and more conventional readers and writers is that *experimenters usually concentrate on only one aspect of conventional reading and writing at a time.* Experimenters may want to write a conventional list (for example, when sending a birthday wish list to a grandparent) and refuse to invent spellings. Or, experimenters may look at a storybook page and laboriously try to puzzle out how to read individual words using sound–letter knowledge and ignoring the powerful meaning-making strategies they have been using for years.

The important thing to remember is that experimenters are trying out many pieces of the literacy puzzle and are experimenting with each one. It is an exciting process for both the children and those who support them (Hilliker, 1988; Matthews, 1988). In this process, they gain important literacy knowledge that will be used later when they will be better able to put the pieces together.

Examples: Novices versus Experimenters

Which of these children are experimenters with written language?

> Thirty-three-month-old Giti is writing a letter to her grandmother. She announces, "For Grandma," and makes several lines of zigzag scribbles on a paper and under-lines them. Part of what she writes is clearly intended to be her grandmother's name, and another part her own name. These parts are primitive but recognizable capital *G*'s. She pretends to mail these letters (Baghban, 1984).

> Two-year-old Ian's favorite reading material is a magazine that he and his grand-mother often read together. The first time they did this, she just happened to be reading the magazine while rocking him. Then, many times over the next few weeks, they chose that magazine and talked about the pictures in it. Ian learned to say many new words from this talk. Now he gets the dog-eared magazine when-ever he visits his grandmother and asks her to read it to him.

> Five-year-old Ted has been sent to his room for misbehaving. He either does not remember or does not understand why he was sent there. With pencil and paper, he writes the message shown in Figure 4.1. He dashes out of his room, tosses this written query or protest on the floor before his mother, and runs back into his room.

> Three-year-old Sophie listens to her uncle read a storybook. She directs his read-ing, "Read that. . . . Read that." She always points first to the left-hand page and then

Figure 4.1 *Ted's Protest: "Mom, why are you punishing me? Ted"*

to the right-hand page. When they finish the book, Sophie begins pointing to individual words on a page and again says, "Read that. . . . Read that," this time for each word she points to. This pointing proceeds right to left, word by word, until Sophie's uncle has identified every word in a line.

Giti and Ian are novices. As with many children at that stage, their literacy behaviors are charming. Part of the charm lies in what they do *not* know. They do not know how inexpert their products are, thus they confidently act like readers and writers. There is an element of pretending in novices' literacy behavior. Children at this stage pretend they are readers and writers with the same intensity and confidence characteristic of their other pretend play. They believe that they *are* what they pretend to be (Chiseri-Strater, 1988).

However, sooner or later children approach written language not with a daring plunge, but with careful experimentation. This can be seen in Ted's and Sophie's behaviors. What Ted produced was a record not just of his query or protest, but also of his analysis of English words and their component sounds. Ted knew that he did not know the adult way to spell. He often consulted an authority. However, when he was left to his own devices, he knew that he could get his words on paper if he thought about letter names and sounds in words. Ted sometimes worked intensely, especially when a message was as important to him as this one was. Ted's query appears unfinished; he wrote nothing for the word *me*. It is unlikely that he knowingly wrote an incomplete message; perhaps the effort required for this writing task distracted him so much that he did not realize he had omitted a word.

Sophie knew left-to-right directionality for pages. More important, although she did not know left-to-right directionality for word reading, her careful pointing to words showed that she was able to identify word boundaries. She was exploring the power of written words, the combinations of letters bordered by spaces, to evoke particular spoken words from the reader.

EXPERIMENTING WITH MEANING

It is no accident that the list of experimenters' new behaviors at the beginning of this chapter lacks explicit statements about constructing meaning. The meaning making of experimenters is only slightly more complex than that of novices. Novices and experimenters share a basic orientation toward written language that is one of novices' greatest achievements. Both write in order to communicate a message, and both engage in interactive storybook reading using sophisticated strategies for constructing meaning. Experimenters continue to use the meaning-making strategies they devised as novices (Yaden, 1988).

For example, experimenters are likely to have a fully developed concept of story or story schema (see Chapter 2). They use their concept of story both to make sense of stories that are read aloud to them and as they compose their own stories. Later in this chapter we will describe experimenters' new attention to the literary properties of stories and informational texts. They have learned that written stories and informational books have certain language forms and word orders not found in spoken language. Experimenters are likely to use literary word order, or **literary**

syntax, when composing and recalling stories, for example, "Away we went to grandmother's house."

The most striking new achievements of experimenters are related to their greater control over form and meaning-form links. However, in the face of their students' striking achievements with form and meaning-form links, teachers should not lose sight of the important fact that children do not experiment with form in a vacuum. Solving problems of form is not an exercise for its own sake. The meaning making learned as novices is the basis of all that experimenters do.

EXPERIMENTING WITH FORMS

Experimenters are beyond exploring alphabet letter forms. They already have considerable knowledge about letters; they can name most letters, write most letters with conventional formations, and recite the alphabet. Experimenters also have metalinguistic awareness of letters; they can talk and think about the names and properties of letters ("Your *M* is upside down. I know how to make a *W* and a *M*."). Experimenters expand their awareness of two forms of written language: words and texts.

Words

One of the hallmarks of experimenters is their movement beyond letters to focus on words. They gradually develop a concept of what a word is and why that unit of written language is so important. Experimenters develop concepts about words in spoken and written language, and they learn to distinguish boundaries between written words.

Concepts about Spoken Words

Children begin to acquire a **concept of spoken words** as they come to understand that spoken language can be segmented into individual words. Young children communicate through spoken language without being able to identify individual words. But in order to read and write, they must be able to identify or segment words. Experimenters only gradually come to recognize spoken words as units of language. For example, when children are asked if *house* and *swim* are words, they say yes, because "people live in houses and people can swim." Children recognize that **content words,** such as *house* and *swim,* which represent objects and actions, are words because of their connection with meaningful objects and activities (Roberts, 1992). In contrast, children reject **function words,** such as *and* or *the,* as words, because "they are not something" (Roberts, 1992, p. 132). Thus, it is not surprising that most young children fail a variety of experimental tests of spoken word perception, such as tapping a separate poker chip for each word they hear in a spoken sentence (Downing & Oliver, 1973–1974; Huttenlocker, 1964).

Fortunately for experimenters, learning about written language does not depend on a fully developed concept about spoken words. They do not need to be able to segment a spoken sentence correctly and completely into its individual words. What experimeters do know is that spoken language can be segmented. As we will see later in the chapter, the segments of spoken language that experimenters perceive are not yet conventional. Sometimes experimenters perceive syllables or phrases as words.

Concepts about Written Words

Experimenters also do not need a fully developed **concept of written words** (knowledge that words are composed of combinations of letters; that words have boundaries, spaces; and that words have particular letters related to the sounds in spoken words) in order to move forward in learning to read and write. They demonstrate their understandings about written words by inventing words for others to read, asking about words, and attempting to spell words. As they invent, ask, and spell words, experimenters show that they are developing parts of the concept of word. We will see that they may work at recognizing combinations of letters and word boundaries, yet not understand that letters in words have a particular relationship to sounds in spoken words. Or, children may spell words using sound–letter relationships, but fail to use combinations of letters (they may spell with only one letter) or word boundaries.

Inventing and asking about words. One way in which children show their interest in words is to invent words when they write. Figure 4.2 shows one of Carrie's drawings. It includes not only many letterlike forms, but also some real letters. Some of the real letters are included in groups or composites of letters, such as the composite "CAE" from her name and the composites "Hi" and "iH," two versions of the word *hi* that her brother taught her. Carrie was beginning to use **letter com-**

Figure 4.2 *Carrie's Letter Combinations*

bination as signs, instead of using letters themselves as signs. Carrie was focusing on what expert readers and writers call *words.*

Another example of experimenters' attention to letter combinations as words is presented in Figure 4.3. This figure shows some writing that Kathy produced one day as she sat by herself in her room. When her mother asked her to read her writing, she replied, "It's just words." Notice that Kathy's writing is much like a novice's—we could not know the meaning Kathy intended to communicate unless we listened to Kathy read her writing (and in this case Kathy did not seem to intend to communicate a message). There are three things of importance to notice about Kathy's writing. First, she is experimenting with letter combinations to produce writing that she calls words. Second, she is experimenting with using spaces between letter combinations to signal boundaries between her words (we will discuss more about children's concepts of word boundaries later in this chapter). Finally, Kathy seems to be paying attention to only one aspect of written language, words and how they look, and ignoring other aspects of written language, such as meaning.

Children signal their interest in words by asking questions about words as well. One day, Carrie's father was silently reading a typewritten letter. Carrie climbed into his lap, pointed to a word in the letter that began with the letter *C,* and asked what it was. When told that the word was *concern,* she replied, "Oh. It has a *C* like my name." Carrie had noted that the word *concern* was something like her name. Both were composites of letters and both began with a *C.* Carrie then asked, "What's that word?" about several other words in the letter.

Children also indicate their interest in words by asking others to spell words for them and by making up combinations of letters and asking others to read their

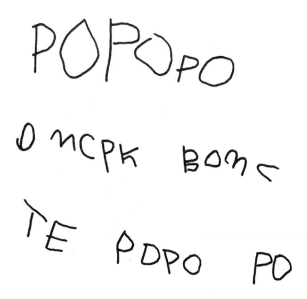

Figure 4.3 *Kathy's Words*

spellings. Figure 4.4 presents an interaction that Kathy had with her mother over spelling words. Kathy said, "Spell *baby bird,*" and her mother wrote it. Then Kathy wrote *FOO FOO* (she copied the word from the title of one of her books) and asked, "What does this spell?" Her mother read it, "foo foo," and Kathy asked, "How do you spell *dodo?*" and wrote the letters as her mother spelled them. Then she said, "Spell *fingers,*" and wrote the word as her mother spelled it. Then her mother said, "I'll write *hands,*" and Kathy said, "I'll write *hair,*" as she wrote YH2OT.

Kathy was interested in having her mother spell particular words, having her mother read words she found in her books, and experimenting with spellings of her own.

Figure 4.4 *Kathy's and Her Mother's Words*

Spelling words.   One indication of Kathy's and Carrie's attention to written words was their use of the word *word* and their use of word boundaries. Children also signal their attention to words by attempting to write words in which some of the letters in the word capture some of the sounds in spoken words (we call this **invented spelling** and devote considerable attention to this topic later in the chapter). What is important about many invented spellings is that readers can read words by attending to their spellings and that the writer must have attended to words (or some segmented portion of spoken language) in order to spell.

Bissex's (1980) description of her son Paul's learning to write provides an example. At first, like many children, Paul enjoyed simply forming letters of the alphabet. Later, he used letters to write messages, but they were messages in which the letters themselves seemed to be the only unit of form. Still later, he used the letters in combinations to make what we would call words. However, Paul's spelling and his idea of which combinations of letters counted as single words differed from those of a conventional writer.

Children sometimes dictate literary texts other than stories. Jeffrey dictated a poem to his mother as he ran back and forth across his patio.

The Running Poem
Bubble gun boppers,
Candy heart sneakers,
Sparky love.
Buster slimers,
Booger man,
Barbecue pit.
Blue ribbons win.
The end.

While the content of Jeffrey's poem relates to what he was doing (running) and seeing (his sneakers, the barbecue pit, and the family dog, Sparky), it also shows Jeffrey's understandings of the conventions of poetry forms. His poem consisted of phrases rather than sentences, and he used **alliteration**—five lines of his poem started with words beginning with the sound /b/. It is interesting that Jeffrey ended his poem with "The end," which is the formulaic ending for a story rather than a poem. Still, his poem demonstrates Jeffrey's experimentation with the specific language forms associated with poetry.

Copying and asking for spellings.   Experimenters also compose by copying. Figure 4.14 presents a story that Joel copied from his book *Bears in the Night* (Berenstain & Berenstain, 1971). His story provides several indications of a young child's experimenting. First, he wrote the words in the story in a column instead of in a line, indicating his attention to words. Second, he labored a long time producing his story. He copied each word letter by letter, and writing the entire story took

Figure 4.14 *Joel's Copied Story*

forty minutes (we show only part of his writing, which covered several pages). This demonstrates experimenters' willingness to concentrate on literacy tasks and devote considerable energy to their constructions. Joel's story illustrates his experimentation with how words from stories are made.

Writing stories by spelling.   As shown in Figure 4.15, children may compose by spelling. Ashley drew a picture and then asked her mother to help her spell. Her mother insisted, "If you write it, I'll be able to read it." Ashley said very slowly, "Nora," and wrote the letter *N;* then she said "flies," and wrote the letter *F;* and last she said "kites," and wrote the letter *k.* She wrote ASH and said, "That is my nickname, and here is my real name," (she wrote ASHLEY). Ashley's story was very primitive—she introduced a character and told one thing the character does. However, she listened to the spoken words she wanted to write and captured the initial sound of each word in her spelling. Notice that her arrangement of letters was not linear, written in left-to-right order; rather, it seems that Ashley let go of her more sophisticated knowledge about story meanings and the linearity concept in the effort of listening to sounds as she was spelling. This is a good example of experimenters' inability to control all aspects of written language as they experiment with a small part of the written language puzzle.

Figure 4.15 *"Nora Flies Kites"*

It is important to keep in mind that experimenters use some of the same conventions as more conventional readers and writers. We tend to think of children at this stage as not yet being very knowledgeable about written language. Even when we are accepting and supportive, what usually catches our attention in children's experimental products are their mistakes. However, there is much that is correct in their products, even by conventional standards.

EXPERIMENTING WITH MEANING-FORM LINKS

To become literate, children must learn that writing demands special kinds of language and special care with language. Written language uses more complex sentence structures than does spoken language. It also uses more specialized vocabulary and many conventional or formulaic expressions, such as "Once upon a time" and "Dear _____ ." In addition, written language is permanent. Unlike spoken language, it can be examined and reexamined; it can be read by people at different times and in locations different from that of the author. Carrie understood this when she wrote to her Uncle Jade who lived in a distant state (Figure 4.6). Other ways in which meaning and form are linked have to do with the fact that English orthography (spelling) is alphabetic; that is, letters represent sounds in words. Some of the earlier examples of Paul's and Ashley's writings illustrate their working out the spoken sound–written symbol relation.

Rule One: Sound Literate

One method that children use to link meaning and form might be stated: "Use special words and special combinations of words when you write or read. Everyday conversational talk will not do." Acquiring this special talk is related to experimentation with text forms, such as stories and poems. Examples of special talk include children's use of "Once upon at time" and their use of past tense in stories they tell or write.

Sounding Literate in Reading

Experimenters use **sounding literate** when they pretend to read favorite storybooks. Recall from Chapter 3 that early emergent reading consists of labeling parts of the illustrations or actions of the characters or telling a story that matches the illustrations. The stories that novices tell in their emergent readings usually do not closely match the words in the text. In conrast, experimenters' emergent readings of favorite storybooks not only closely resemble the words in the text, but also are influenced by print. At first, of course, experimenters do not watch print while they read. However, experimenters' emergent readings include much of the language of the text and, therefore, sound literate. Eventually, experimenters' emergent rereading are exact, word-for-word readings of the text, and these readings are carefully matched to the page on the text.

Figure 4.16 presents a developmental **scale of emergent readings** of favorite storybooks (Sulzby, 1985a). A major step is the transition from story retellings that are like oral language to retellings that are like written language. The intonation of written-language-like retellings is different from the intonation of conversational speech. By slowing their rate of speech and using stress expressively, children sound as if they are reading. Even though the wording may not be verbatim, a writ-

Figure 4.16 *Emergent Reading Scale*

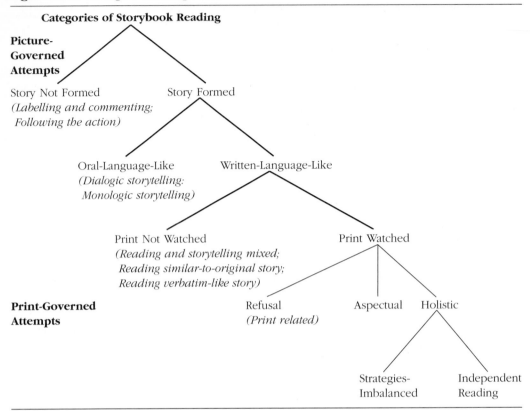

Note: This figure includes independent reading attempts only: the child is making the reading attempts without dependence upon turn-taking reading or interrogation by the adult.

From Sulzby, E. (1985). Children's emergent reading of favorite storybooks: A developmental study. *Reading Research Quarterly, 20,* p. 464. Reprinted with permission of the International Reading Association.

ten-language-like retelling may use some unusual expressions from the text; it often includes the more formal, more complex sentence structure that the child has come to expect from books (Sulzby, 1985a).

An example of an experimenter's emergent reading is provided by Carrie. Four-year-old Carrie had often listened to her parents and older brother read *The Three Bears* (1952). It was one of her favorite books. When Carrie read the entire story of Goldilocks and the three bears to her father, she included elements unique to her book's version. Table 4.1 presents a portion of Carrie's emergent reading of *The Three Bears,* in which she included descriptions of Papa Bear's repairing the roof, Mama Bear's watering flowers, and Baby Bear's doing tricks on the lawn. Although her book had illustrations of the three bears doing just those things, an important quality in Carrie's reading of the story is that she did not merely give a present-tense description of those pictures. The one time when she did just describe a picture

("The bird's just watching!"), she shifted out of a story-reading mode into a conversational mode. As she talked about a part of the illustration that she found charming, she used varied and faster intonation, in contrast to the steady, even voice and past tense of her reading.

Table 4.1 *Carrie's Emergent Reading*

Text	Reading
. . .	. . .
(From second and third pages. The illustration shows Mama Bear and Baby Bear in the foreground. She is watering tulips. He and a rabbit are doing handstands while a little bird watches. In the background Papa Bear is on the ladder repairing the roof of their house.)	(In an even voice, at a steady pace, until the end, when her voice rises)
Papa Bear pounded nails in the roof. Mama Bear watered the flowers. Baby Bear did tricks on the lawn.	"And Papa nailed the roof. Mama—Mama watered the flowers. And Baby Bear did tricks on the lawn."
	(Short pause. Laughter. Then in higher pitch, with rising and falling intonation, and faster pace)
	"The bird's just watching!"
. . .	. . .
(From twenty-first page)	(In a very high-pitched voice)
"'Someone has broken my tiny chair all to pieces!"	"'And she's broken it all to pieces!'"
. . .	. . .

Carrie's reading used language that was peculiar to the text of her very familiar book. She recreated the book's odd description of Papa Bear's behavior. Both the book and Carrie described him not as repairing the roof or fixing the roof, but as pounding nails in the roof!

Throughout Carrie's emergent reading of *The Three Bears,* she clearly indicated who was talking, at first with dialogue markers, such as "Papa said" and "Mama said," and later by using a loud, deep voice for Papa Bear, a high voice for Mama Bear, and a very high voice for Baby Bear.

In other ways as well Carrie's emergent reading was parallel to, but not a perfect replication of, the text. She frequently used the book's verb tenses in her recreation of the characters' speech. For example, in the second excerpt shown in Table 4.1, she did not have Baby Bear say—as a four-year-old might—that someone "broke" his chair; rather, she repeated the book's *has broken* in her "she's *broken.*"

Her reading also included the book's attempt at a happy ending, with the three bears calling to Goldilocks as she ran away, "Come back! We want to be friends!"

Sounding Literate in Writing

Children who are acquiring rule one, "Sound literate," also use special written-language-like talk when they dictate stories (Sulzby, 1985b). They know that dictating a story is different from telling a story. They are aware that they are authors. They do not speak in order to communicate with or to entertain their scribe. Instead, they communicate with unknown, nonpresent future readers. Children also use the rule "Sound literate" in their writing.

Figure 4.17 shows a story written by a first grader named Justin. Immediately after writing, he read it to his teacher: "A little boy. He's little. And he went across the street to do some . . . and somebody picked him up and somebody took . . . and he went with him." Later, he volunteered to read his story to his classmates: "There was a little boy. He went across the street. He went to the grocery store and somebody picked him up."

Figure 4.17 *Justin's Story*

What is interesting in this example is the manner in which Justin shifted his language, from informally reading his story to his teacher and more formally reading to his classmates. Unlike when he was reading to his teacher, when he read to the audience of his classmates Justin used a formulaic story opening, "There was," and he used **reading-like intonation.** Justin realized that written stories, when read, need special literary language forms and intonations.

Rule Two: Be Precise

A second way in which children link meaning and form might be stated: "Be precise about which words you (or your scribe) write and about which words you read back from your writing (or from someone else's). Only the words that the author formulated while writing may be read when the author or someone else reads what was written." In other words, reading is different from telling.

Being Precise in Reading

Being precise in reading begins as children's emergent readings capture the story text nearly verbatim. They have not only learned the language of the text (as when they sound literate), but they can match the text language to the exact page of the storybook. Thus, being precise leads to another kind of matching, finger-point reading. **Finger-point reading** is when children say a word from the story while pointing to a word in the printed text (Ehri & Sweet, 1991; Morris, 1993); it is also called **voice-to-print match**. At first, finger-point reading may not be completely accurate. Children may match a spoken syllable with a written word, for example. Eventually (as their concepts of spoken and written words and their perceptions of word boundaries mature), children begin to match each spoken word with a written word as they pretend read. Children who are accurate finger-point readers are not yet conventionally reading, but they are watching the print and coordinating what they say with the printed text.

Sometimes children's preoccupation with precision is so great that they will not attempt to read parts of a story that they have not memorized. Later, when they are able to identify words rather than rely on memorization, some children are similarly preoccupied—they become "glued to print" (Chall, 1983, p. 18). Sometimes, unlike mature readers (Goodman, 1967), children are so concerned with correct word identification that they neglect to attend to the meaning of text.

Rule two takes an experimenter beyond the emergent reading behaviors that followed from rule one. It is not enough to use any literate-sounding talk when reading a story. This kind of precision is part of the later stages of the emergent reading scale. Children's performances at this stage should not be dismissed as "just memorization." Their effort to retrieve the actual story shows a new sophistication about how written language works.

An example of a child's reading being governed by preoccupation with precision is Daniel's reenactment of *My Cat Likes to Hide in Boxes* (Sutton, 1974). He quickly recited the parts that he knew verbatim, but hesitated and used verbal fillers when he was having trouble retrieving the actual words of the story (Sulzby, 1985b, p. 470):

> [Quickly]   And the cat in Norway—got stuck in the doorway.
> [Slowly]   And, um, uh, the cat, oh, and the cat in /Spain-liked-to/ drive an airplane.
> [Quickly again]   But my cat likes to hide in boxes.

He also asked the researcher to read what he had not memorized: "And read this page—cause I forget that" (Sulzby, 1985b, p. 470).

We have already emphasized that young experimenters can be aware that they do not know all there is to know about writing and reading. When they are also preoccupied with precision, the result can be refusal even to attempt to read ("print-related refusals") or reading only what they are sure of ("aspectual reading"). An aspectual reader recited "Grandma," "the," "and," "the a," "and" (Sulzby, 1985a, pp. 471–472) for page after page because those were the only words she was sure of. She could identify them wherever she saw them. Words that a child can identify on sight, without using any sounding out or context strategies, are called **sight words.**

The final step on the emergent reading scale heralds a still higher level of knowledge and marks the beginning of conventional reading and writing.

Being Precise in Writing

Being precise in writing means that children are aware that written language is permanent and stable, that writing does not communicate just any message, but communicates a precise message that can be reread again and again in exactly the same way. This notion is called the **message concept** (Clay, 1975). Justin's writing (Figure 4.17) is that of a writer who does not have the message concept—who is not being precise in his writing. His reading to his teacher differed from his reading to his classmates.

Children who are able to use dictation to write stories are aware that the scribe must record their words precisely (Sulzby, 1985b). They pause to allow the scribe to catch up. They use "voice continuant intonation," in which the voice does not fall before a pause, thus letting the listener—in this case, the scribe—know that there is more to come, that the pause should not be taken to be a conversational pause, which would signal that the listener could take a turn at talking.

Children may demonstrate precision in writing by the way they attempt to reread their own writing. Figure 4.18 presents a Father's Day card that four-year-old Brooke composed. On the front of her card she drew a bird and some flowers. On the inside she wrote nine letters: *R, A, Y, g, P, G, O, G,* and *I.* Afterward she read her writing to her mother, pointing to the first five letters one at a time: "I/ love/ you/ dad/ dy." Then she paused for a few moments and pointed at the remaining four letters one at a time, reading, "ver/ y/ much/ too." Brooke is being precise by carefully matching each letter of her writing with a segment of her spoken message (in this case, a syllable).

Figure 4.18 *Brooke's Father's Day Card*

Rule Three: Use Sound–Letter Relationships

Experimenters also link meaning with written form through the use of sound–letter relationships in their spellings and emergent readings. We have provided some examples of children who invent spellings—children who look for systematic relationships between sounds and letters. For example, Ted spelled *why* with a *y* and *punishing* as PNShAn (Figure 4.1); Ashley spelled *Nora* with an *N* (Figure 4.15), and Paul spelled *buzzer* as BZR. It may appear that experimenters are using the relationships between sounds and letters just as more conventional readers and writers do, but this is not always the case.

Using Sound–Letter Relationships in Writing

In order to spell, writers need a system: they need a rather precise, analytic understanding of the relationship between spoken and written language; they need the ability to examine words one sound unit at a time; and they need an awareness of some kind of relationship between spoken sounds and letters. What this means is that young writers must first be able to segment their spoken message into its component parts—words. Then spellers must further segment words into smaller parts—eventually, into phonemes. A **phoneme** is a unit of sound (e.g., /t/, /ă/, /n/, /ĭ/, /θ/, and /ŋ/) that can contrast with another unit of sound when such units are combined to make words (e.g., *tan* vs. *tin*, *tin* vs. *thin*, *thin* vs. *thing*). In conventional spelling, phonemes are associated with single letters—such as *t, a, n,*—or with letter combinations—such as *th* or *ng*. Hence teachers call /t/ the "T sound" or /θ/ the "T-H sound."

Early inventive spellers do not usually pronounce single phonemes one at a time; this is a later-developing ability. Instead, they may pronounce a multisyllable word one syllable at a time. Even in these cases, however, their spelling efforts begin with paying attention to part of that syllable, often the first part, that is, the first phoneme. Then spellers must decide which letter to use to represent that phoneme. This is a long and complicated process that involves a great deal of conscious attention.

Phonemic awareness.   The process of attending to phonemes is part of the phonological awareness we described in Chapter 3. Phonological awareness includes attention to all aspects of the sounds of a language. One of those aspects is phonemes. Paying attention to phonemes, **phonemic awareness,** is most developed when a person can segment a word into each and every one of its phonemes, for example, segmenting the word *tan* into /t/, /ă/ and /n/. This most developed kind of phonemic awareness only gradually emerges.

Kristen's first spellings provide a case in point. She announced that she could spell and looked around the room for things to spell. She said, "I can spell phone," and repeated the word to herself, saying it slowly, stretching out the initial /f/ sound, "Ph-ph-ph-phone, phone. I know—it's spelled V." Then she looked around again and said, "I can spell window, too." Again she slowly repeated the word, stretching out the initial /w/ sound, "W-w-w-window. Window is Y."

Kristen's spellings are not conventional, but they have the characteristics of true spelling; they are systematic, and they demonstrate phonemic awareness. Using only one letter to spell each word is consistent with not pronouncing each phoneme of a word one at a time. She pronounced a whole word and paid attention to the first phoneme in that word. She was not doing the complete phoneme-by-phoneme analysis that demonstrates the most developed form of phonemic awareness, but her attention to each word was at the level of the phoneme.

When adults notice that children are beginning to attend to phonemes, they can guide children toward the fully developed, complete phonemic awareness that involves pronouncing each phoneme of a word one at a time. For many months after Kristen's first instance of spelling (with *phone* and *window*), she argued that she could not spell. She would spell only when her mother segmented spoken words for her and then invited Kristen to suggest a letter. Her mother said "Batman—/b/," and Kristen wrote *B.* Then her mother said "/t/," and Kristen wrote *T.* Kristen's mother was not yet offering a complete analysis, she was merely helping Kristen to do a little more than she could do on her own. She was helping Kristen to notice more than the beginning phoneme, but she was avoiding for a while the most difficult phonemes to match with letters, the short vowels (e.g., /ă/ in *Bat*).

Another way to help children notice more than one phoneme in a word is to help them segment syllables into two parts: (1) the first phoneme if it is a consonant (this is called the **onset**, e.g., /b/ in *Bat*), and (2) the rest of the syllable (this is called the **rime**, e.g., /ăt/ in *Bat*). Practice with onsets and rimes helps children to develop phonemic awareness (Treiman, 1991). For the second letter of Kristen's spelling of *Batman,* if Kristen's mother had used the rime, she would have said "/ăt/" rather than just "/t/" and left it for Kristen to decide how much of the rime to spell. Practice with onsets and rimes builds on what children do with rhyming words when their phonological awareness is emerging as novices (recall the "James/Wames" example from Chapter 3). For many children such as Kristen, the ability to segment spoken words into component parts is the crucial element to their becoming spellers.

Sound–letter relationships.

Once children can segment smaller-than-a-word sound units, they must also have a way to relate letters to the sounds they segment. While attending to the phonemes at the beginnings of *phone* and *window,* Kristen used two clues for choosing an appropriate letter for spelling: manner of articulation and identity of sound. **Manner of articulation** is the placement of the mouth, tongue, and teeth when speaking. Kristen noticed that her upper teeth were biting down on her lower lip both when she started to say the word *phone* and when she started to say the name of the letter *V.* Kristen also may have used manner of articulation to spell *window.* In order to say the sounds at the beginning of the word *window* and at the beginning of the name of the letter *Y,* a speaker's lips are rounded into a distinctive O shape.

Manner of articulation provides a way to spell not only consonant sounds (as in Kristen's spellings of *phone* and *window*), but also some of the most difficult sounds to spell, the short vowel sounds. Say the short *e* sound and then the letter name *E.* Now say the short *e* sound and the name of the letter *A.* While the manner of articulation for the short *e* and the letter name *A* are not exactly the same, they are closer than the manner of articulation of the short *e* and the letter name *E.* Therefore, children sometimes use the letter *a* to spell the sound of short *e.*

With *window* and *Y,* there is another possible explanation of Kristen's spelling. She may have used **identity of sound.** Both *window* and the name of the letter *Y* start with /w/ (the letter name *Y* is made up of two phonemes /w/ and /ī/). Spellers can use the phonemes in the letter names and associate them with the phonemes in the spoken words they wish to spell. Ashley did this when she linked the phoneme /k/ in the letter name *K* with the phoneme /k/ in the word *kite* (Figure 4.15). We might also expect a young speller to associate the phoneme /ch/ in the letter name *H* with the phoneme /ch/ in the word *chain,* as in the invented spelling HAN.

It is interesting that Kristen ignored the identity of sounds at the beginning of the word phone and at the end of the name of the letter F (both are /f/) when choosing a spelling for phone. This is just one example of how even beginning invented spelling is systematic, but not always in the same way in which conventional English spelling is systematic.

Ted's spelling of the word *why* with a *Y* shows another way of linking letters and sounds—using the name of the letter to represent a sound segment in a word that sounds like the letter's name. This is called the **letter name strategy.** Spelling the word *eyes* with IZ and the word *knee* with NE are two additional examples of using the letter name strategy (Wilde, 1992, p, 39).

Sometimes children link letters with sounds by hearing sounds in spoken words that are ignored in standard spellings (and, therefore, that many adults forget are even there). Both standard spelling and invented spelling are abstract—they both ignore some sounds in words. But the standard system and invented spelling do not ignore the same things. Standard spelling ignores the affrication in *tr* and *dr* blends. **Affrication** is the burst of air that occurs in the pronunciation of these blends. That sound is not represented in conventional spellings of words that begin with the *tr* and *dr* blends. Yet that same burst of air *is* spelled with a *j* or a *ch* in other contexts, such as in *juice* and *chain*. Read (1971) found that inventive spellers repeatedly chose to represent that burst of air in the *dr* and *tr* blends. Children spelled the affrication in *try* with a *ch* (CHRIE) and in dragon with a *j* (JRAGIN). On the other hand, invented spelling ignores nasals before consonants (NUBRS for *numbers,* AD for *and,* PLAT for *plant,* and GOWEG for *going*), while standard spelling represents them.

Spelling Development

Read's (1971) work has influenced both classroom practice (e.g., Chomsky, 1971; Lancaster, Nelson, & Morris, 1982; Paul, 1976; Sowers, 1988) and research (Burns & Richgels, 1989; Vukelich & Edwards, 1988). One finding from this research is that inventive spellers progress through stages that culminate with conventional spelling (Gentry, 1982; Morris, 1981). This finding is reassuring to skeptical parents and teachers, and it is also not surprising. We have just described what inventive spellers know as a system; their spellings are not haphazard. The fact that their spelling system is not the conventional one adults use is not as important as the fact that it *is* a system. Inventive spellers know what spelling is supposed to accomplish. They must only progress to knowing how to accomplish it in the conventional systematic way rather than in their invented systematic way.

Table 4.2 describes three stages in that progression. These stages are intended to clarify the direction of change in children's spelling development. Children often show spelling behaviors from more than one stage in a single piece of writing. What is important is that over time their spellings resemble later stages more than earlier stages.

Table 4.2 *Stages of Invented Spelling*

Non-Spelling

Some alphabet knowledge

No sound-letter knowledge

Random stringing together of letters of the alphabet

No concept of word

Example: YHZOT for *hair*

Early Invented Spelling

Nearly complete alphabet knowledge

Use of manner of articulation

Knowledge that sounds can be associated with letters

Letter name strategy

Frequent omission of vowels (especially non–long vowel sounds for which a letter name strategy does not work)

Encoding of only some parts of a word

Emergence of concept of word (some segmentation of word strings at word boundaries)

Examples: K for *kite,* BD for *bird,* SWM for *swim*

Purely Phonetic Spelling

Based strictly on sound-letter correspondences

Encoding of all parts of a word

Letter name strategy for long vowels

Use of manner of articulation for short vowels

Omission of unheard vowels and nasals before consonants

Segmentation of letter strings at most word boundaries

Examples: KRI for *cry,* BRD for *bird,* BREJ for *bridge,* PLAT for *plant*

Stages are based on Gentry (1982) and Morris (1981). Examples of early invented spelling and purely phonetic spelling are from research conducted by the authors.

Table 4.2 is based on similar schemes described by Gentry (1982) and Morris (1981), who derived their stages from Read's (1975) and Henderson and Beers's (1980) work. The three stages are labeled non-spelling (because it is random, not systematic), early invented spelling, and purely phonetic spelling.

The first stage, **non-spelling,** is what novices do. They write mock cursive or letter strings to stand for messages (contextually dependent writing). This activity reflects novices' fixation with letters. This stage is primarily characterized by a lack of awareness of sound–letter correspondences. Non-spellers choose letters randomly. Because they seem to believe in some power of the letters themselves to communicate, non-spellers can also be characterized as lacking a concept of word. Individual letters in their writing are not even representative of beginning sounds in the words of their intended message.

The second and third stages, **early invented spelling,** and **purely phonetic spelling** represent the kinds of spellings that we expect from experimenters. In these two stages experimenters use letters to make words based on analyses of sound units in words and knowledge of sound–letter correspondences. They progress from only partial (initial or initial and final sounds) to nearly complete encoding of word sounds, and from representing only consonant sounds to representing consonants and vowels. At the end of this experimenting time, they may begin to incorporate some English spelling conventions for frequently occurring word parts (such as -*ed*). However, the primary characteristic of experimenters is spelling without regard for standard conventions. Instead, they systematically use sound–letter correspondences.

Children's growth in spelling does not stop at the end of the purely phonetic stage of spelling development. In Chapter 5 we will describe two more stages of invented spelling that are beyond what experimenters do.

Using Sound–Letter Relationships in Reading

Children's awareness of systematic (but unconventional) relations between letters and spoken language influences their reading. Children's reading of environmental print, storybooks, and their own writing gradually reflects their awareness of written words and the relationships between letters in words and sounds in spoken language. For example, one day a young child noticed something different about an environmental print sign that she had been reading for quite some time as *Emporium, . . .* "a San Francisco department store whose stylized spelling is dominated by a very large initial *E.* On one of this child's frequent visits to the store, she looked at its name and commented in surprise, 'Mom! That doesn't say Emporium (i.e., *m-porium*). That says *E-porium!*' " (Ehri, 1991, p. 411).

Another example of the influence of children's awareness of sound–letter knowledge on their reading occurred when Jeffrey looked at a word book (an alphabet picture book that had several pictures on a page depicting objects and actions associated with a particular letter). He was looking at the *F* page when he called out to his mother, "Do you want to hear me read this page?" Jeffrey's mother knew that he could not really read, but she was willing to be an audience as he pretended to read this favorite book. Jeffrey pointed to the word *fence* and said "fence." He pointed to each of the words *fruit tree, flag, funny face,* and *four fish* and said the appropriate word or phrase. Then he paused as he scanned the picture of a farmer driving a tractor. The words accompanying this picture were *front wheels* and *fertilizer.* Finally Jeffrey said, "I'm looking for the word *tractor* because this is a tractor. But I can't find it. All of these words have *F*'s. But tractor shouldn't be *F.* Where is it, Mom? Can you find the word for 'tractor'?"

These examples demonstrate children's attention to letters and their sounds. In the case of *Emporium,* the child was applying a letter name strategy (*m-porium*); and in the case of *tractor,* Jeffrey knew that the word *tractor* did not begin with the phoneme associated with the letter *F.*

Knowing the sounds associated with initial consonants in words and having some concept about written words helps children more finely tune their ability to finger-point read and their phonemic awareness (Morris, 1993). We have already shown that experimenters know that reading means being precise. They point to words in a favorite storybook from left to right as they say the spoken words of the text. An awareness of the sounds associated with initial consonant letters helps readers better align their pointing and their reading. For example, suppose that the following sentence is the text of a storybook.

I jumped and swam in the pool today.

An experimenter who is aware of the sounds associated with the letters *j, s, p,* and *t* is better able to monitor pointing to the written words while saying the text. Suppose the child reads "I" (pointing to *I*), "jumped" (pointing to *jumped*), and "swam" (pointing to *and*). The experimenter would notice that the word he or she is pointing to, *and*, does not match with the word last said, "swam." The child might notice that the next word begins with the letter *s,* and correct the pointing. The search for a correct match between the spoken sounds in the words he or she is reading and the letters in the words in the text could be prompted by a teacher's or parent's asking, "Does that look right? (pointing to *and*) You said 'swam.'"

The ability to use some sound–letter relationships to read and remember words marks the beginning of **alphabetic reading** (Ehri, 1991). Children who are early inventive spellers can demonstrate the beginnings of alphabetic reading in their guesses about environmental print and as they monitor their emergent readings of favorite storybooks. However, not all children who can read a few words or spell a few words conventionally are alphabetic readers. For example, Michelle could write and read the words *Mom* and *Dad*. But when she was shown the letters in the word *Mom* in scrambled order and asked to read the new word she said, "I can't remember" (Barnhart, 1988, p. 304). In contrast, Jules could write *Mom* and *Dad* conventionally, and he used invented spelling to spell *bear* (BAR), *duck* (DAC), and *caterpillar* (CAURPELR). When he was shown any of the words with the letters scrambled, he made an attempt to sound out the new words. Michelle was not yet an alphabetic reader, whereas Jules was.

Eventually children can read some words by sight. *Sight words* are words that children recognize immediately without using context or sound–letter relationships. However, to learn sight words, children may use what is called **phonetic cue reading** (Ehri, 1991). Figuring out words by using some sound–letter knowledge (as Jules did when he tried to read words presented to him in scrambled order) contributes to remembering them. For example, a phonetic cue reader could figure out and later remember that JRF is the word *giraffe,* because the letters in the word are associated with the sounds in the word *giraffe* (Ehri, 1991). Similarly, children might learn to recognize the words *tub, dog,* and *fat* because the associations between the letters and sounds (most likely the beginning and ending consonants) help them remember the words. Children whose spelling teachers would judge to be at the later early invented spelling stage or purely phonetic stage can be phonetic cue readers; they are more likely to learn to read some words by sight if they know some of the sound–letter relationships in the words (Richgels, 1995).

EXPERIMENTING WITH FUNCTIONS
OF WRITTEN LANGUAGE

We have presented much information about children's experimentation with the functions of written language. Young experimenters continue what they began as novices. They continue to use written language to communicate for a variety of purposes. Carrie's letter writing demonstrates use of written language for such general purposes as communicating over distances and for such specific purposes as thanking someone ("Thanks for all the presents"), or simply being sociable ("How is the weather?"). We have seen writing to tell stories, to voice a protest, to make a game, and to keep a list.

Three Higher Functions

What remains in this section is to emphasize three points about all this experimentation with function. One is that children at this stage of literacy development often work with an additional purpose, which is simply to experiment. Young experimenters devote large amounts of energy to literacy tasks; it seems that they realize that one purpose for reading and writing is to learn to read and write. They appear to know that you learn it by doing it. Young experimenters read and write to try out their theories of what reading and writing are.

A second point is that experimenters may engage in literacy tasks with the purpose of pleasing others; adults ask them to and sometimes they comply. Experimenters may write and read because they know that showing interest in and an ability for literacy tasks usually wins recognition and applause, just as other achievements, such as walking and talking, did at earlier ages. Reading and writing serve the function of identifying children as being interested in membership in the elite community of literates. They continue to play at adult roles that include literacy behaviors just as they did when they were novices. Experimenters may continue to pretend to be waitpersons, doctors, or receptionists, but they also work intensely at "really reading" and "really writing." They do so in ways that adults can more easily accept.

The third point about experimentation with functions has to do with rule two ("Be precise") and Clay's (1975) message concept; experimenters realize that the message they speak can be written down. The most significant function-related conceptual change of the experimental stage is the discovery that written language can preserve a writer's message exactly and precisely. Children discover that they can use written language to communicate exactly what they want to say to their cousin or uncle, to keep precise records of important messages, or to tell stories exactly as they want someone else to read them.

Transition to Conventional
Reading and Writing

We began this chapter by characterizing experimenters as children who are aware that there is a system to learn, but who do not know what that system is. Throughout the chapter we have described the variety of concepts that children must grasp in order to puzzle out the system, to become what others would judge conventional

readers and writers. Children gradually come to have many behaviors and understandings that we call conventional. The understandings that experimenters have
about written language are unconventional in many ways (for example, their using
manner of articulation to link letters and sounds or their counting syllables or
phrases as words). Yet, their reading and writing also have signs of much that is
conventional (for example, their using knowledge of literary syntax to compose stories and their using sound–letter knowledge to monitor their reading.).

We hope that this chapter does not lead readers to two misconceptions. The
first has to do with ages. Ages are not the important part of any description of children as experimenters. The children in our examples have been various ages. We
have provided their ages only to accurately present the facts in some of our real-
life examples. The ages of these children do not set norms against which to compare other children. Many children come to kindergarten and even to first grade not
acting as experimenters. We have no reason to believe that they will fail to learn to
read or write, or even that they will fall behind. Of much greater value than age is
the behavior that can be observed in a literacy event; what the child knows or learns
in the event; and how adults support that behavior, knowledge, and discovery. From
this information, teachers can gain insights that will guide instruction.

The second misconception has to do with identification of children as experimenters. Identification is not important for its own sake. It does not really matter
whether Carrie or Paul or any other child is called an experimenter. What matters
is that teachers know what literacy behaviors children are willing and able to engage in. Then teachers will understand and support children in the provision of resources, in actions, and in talk. We know that some children's literacy behaviors fall
in some manner—however imprecisely—within the broad territory described as the
experimenter's. We hope that when teachers recognize such children, they will
know how to support the children's continued development as writers and readers.

Chapter Summary

Experimenters are aware that there is a
system of written language that they only
partly understand. Still, they are up to the
adventure of exploring the unknown territory. They respond to adults' encouragement with deliberate, focused episodes of
reading and writing.

The meaning making that experimenters do is similar to what they did as
novices. They continue writing in order to
present a message, and they continue
using sophisticated strategies for interacting with books.

Some of the most striking new
achievements of experimenters are related
to their greater control over form. They

make letters of the alphabet that are recognizable according to conventional standards. They acquire a concept of spoken
and written words, and they devise means
for showing word boundaries in their
writing. In addition to knowing what
physical arrangements are appropriate for
different text forms, they know what
special language is appropriate.

Typically, experimenters can conventionally spell their names and a few other
words. Many experimenters go farther and
demonstrate their exploration of the relation between spoken language and written
language by invented spelling. They carefully analyze speech sounds in almost any

word they want to write, and match those sounds with letters. Experimenters also show new knowledge of meaning-form links by using special written-language-like talk in literacy events. Often they are aware that written language is more precise than spoken language and that what readers say depends on what writers write.

As with novices, written language serves a variety of functions for experimenters. A new purpose for their reading and writing is simply to experiment. They sometimes engage in literacy events with the additional purposes of pleasing others and being exact.

A summary of what experimenters know about written language meanings, forms, meaning-form links, and functions is presented in Table 4.3.

Table 4.3 *Summary: What Experimenting Readers and Writers Know about Written Language Meanings, Forms, Meaning-Form Links, and Functions*

Meaning Making

assign meaning to text by applying knowledge of specialized literary language (such as literary syntax, alliteration, and letter-writing conventions)

Forms

know nearly all alphabet letter names and formations

have metalinguistic awareness of letters

develop concepts of spoken words

develop concepts of written words

develop concepts of word boundaries

use specialized literary knowledge to construct a wide variety of texts

use a variety of strategies to produce conventional texts (including copying, asking for spellings, dictating, and spelling)

Meaning-Form Links

sound literate when assigning meaning to storybooks and compositions

are precise when assigning meaning to storybooks and compositions

develop phonemic awareness

use manner of articulation to associate sounds and letters in spellings

use letter names to associate sounds and letters in spellings

use identity of sounds to associate sounds and letters in spellings

spell at the level of early and purely phonetic spelling

use knowledge of sound–letter relationships to monitor emergent reading

use finger-point reading (demonstrating voice-to-print matching)

can use phonetic or alphabetic cues to learn some sight words

continued

Table 4.3 *continued*

Function

read and write to experiment with written language

read and write to please others

understand that written language is precise (develop the message concept)

Applying the Information

Two literacy events follow. The first event involves four-year-old Maria and her mother, and the second concerns a story written by five-year-old Ben. Discuss what these events show about Maria's and Ben's understandings of written language meanings, forms, meaning-form links, and functions.

Maria wrote OPMN (see Figure 4.19) on a piece of paper and asked her mother, "What does this word say?" Her mother answered, "It isn't really a word. I guess it says /o-p-m-un/" sounding out the nonsense word slowly and pointing to each letter as she said the sounds. Next Maria wrote ON (one of the few words she knows how to spell conventionally). When she asked her mother to read the word her mother said, "You know what that says." Maria said "on." Maria wrote OrNMP and OrMO and then asked her mother to read these words. Her mother again slowly sounded out the words and pointed to the letters. Finally, Maria wrote NO and said, "Mom, I know how to read this word. No."

Ben complained that he had nothing to do. His mother suggested that he write a story. He had never written one before, but to his mother's surprise, he took up the challenge. He returned in a few minutes with these three lines of letters.

Figure 4.19 *Maria's Words*

WNSAPNATMTEWDKDRWOTOTNTE
BOSAD HEDKD
FEH

He read them as, "Once upon a time the woodcutter went out in the boat and he did catch fish." Ben's mother understood why Ben ended the story as he did. Ben had been unsuccessful on a recent fishing excursion.

Going Beyond the Text

Visit a kindergarten classroom. Join the children who are writing. Notice what their writing activities are. What experimenting behaviors do you observe? What text forms are the children using? How many of them are spellers? Begin your own writing activity (writing a letter, a story, a list of some kind, a reminder to yourself, or a poem). Talk about it with the children. How many of them take up your activity and attempt similar pieces? Does the character of their writing change from what it was for their own activities? Is there more or less invented spelling, more or less word writing, more or less scribbling?

Ask the teacher if children have favorite storybooks. If so, invite children to read their favorites to you. How do they interpret that invitation? If they would rather you read to them, how willing are they to supply parts of the reading? What parts do they know best? What parts do they like best?

References

BAGHBAN, M. (1984). *Our daughter learns to read and write: A case study from birth to three*. Newark, DE: International Reading Association.

BARNHART, J. (1988). The relationship between graphic forms and the child's underlying conceptualization of writing. In J. Readence & R. Baldwin (Eds.) *Dialogues in Literacy Research* (pp. 297–306). Chicago: National Reading Center.

BERENSTAIN, S., & BERENSTAIN, J. (1971). *Bears in the night*. New York: Random House.

BISSEX, G. L. (1980). *GNYS AT WRK. A child learns to write and read*. Cambridge: Harvard University Press.

BURNS, J., & RICHGELS, D. J. (1989). An investigation of abilities associated with the "invented spelling" ability of four-year-olds of above average intelligence. *Journal of Reading Behavior 21*, 1–14.

CHALL, J. S. (1983). *Stages of reading development*. New York: McGraw-Hill.

CHISERI-STRATER, E. (1988). Reading to Mr. Bear. In T. Newkirk & N. Atwell (Eds.), *Understanding writing: Ways of observing, learning, and teaching* (2nd ed., pp. 31–39). Portsmouth, NH: Heinemann.

CHOMSKY, C. (1971). Invented spelling in the open classroom, *Word, 27,* 499–518.

CLAY, M. M. (1975). *What did I write? Beginning writing behavior*. Exeter, NH: Heinemann.

DOWNING, J., & OLIVER, P. (1973–1974). The child's conception of a word. *Reading Research Quarterly, 9,* 568–582.

EDELSKY, C. (1982). Writing in a bilingual program: The relation of Ll and L2 texts. *TESOL Quarterly, 16,* 211–211.

EHRI, L. (1991). Development of the ability to read words. In R. Barr, M. Kamil, P. Mosenthal, & P. Pearson (Eds.), *Handbook of reading research* (2nd ed., pp. 395–419). New York: Longman.

EHRI, L., & SWEET, J. (1991). Finger point reading of memorized text: What enables beginners to process the print? *Reading Research Quarterly, 26,* 442–462.

GENTRY, J. R. (1982). An analysis of developmental spelling in GNYS AT WRK. *The Reading Teacher, 36,* 192–200.

GOODMAN, K. (1967). Reading: A psycholinguistic guessing game. *Journal of the Reading Specialist, 4,* 126–135.

GOODMAN, Y. M. (1980). The roots of literacy. In M. P. Douglas (Ed.), *Claremont Reading Conference, 44th Yearbook* (pp. 1–32). Claremont, CA: Claremont Reading Conference.

HARSTE, J. C., BURKE, C. L., & WOODWARD, V. A. (1983). *Young child as writer-reader, and informant* (Final Report Project NIE-G-80–0121). Bloomington, IN: Language Education Departments, Indiana University.

HENDERSON, E. H., & BEERS, J. W. (Eds.).(1980). *Developmental and cognitive aspects of learning to spell*. Newark, DE: International Reading Association.

HILLIKER, J. (1988). Labeling to beginning narrative: Four kindergarten children learn to write. In T. Newkirk & N. Atwell (Eds.), *Understanding writing: Ways of observing, learning, and teaching* (2nd ed., pp. 14–22). Portsmouth, NH: Heinemann.

HUTTENLOCHER, J. (1964). Children's language: Word-phrase relationship. *Science, 143,* 264–265.

LANCASTER, W., NELSON, L., & MORRIS, D. (1982). Invented spellings in Room 112: A writing program for low-reading second graders. *The Reading Teacher, 35,* 906–911.

MATTHEWS, K. (1988). A child composes. in T. Newkirk & N. Atwell (Eds.), *Understanding writing: Ways of observing, learning, and teaching* (2nd ed., pp. 9–13). Portsmouth, NH: Heinemann.

MORRIS, D. (1981). Concept of word: A developmental phenomenon in the beginning reading and writing processes. *Language Arts,* 58, 659–668.

MORRIS, D. (1993). The relationship between children's concept of word in text and phoneme awareness in learning to read: A longitudinal study. *Research in the Teaching of English, 27,* 133–154.

PAUL, R. (1976). Invented spelling in kindergarten. *Young Children,* 31, 195–200.

READ, C. (1971). Pre-school children's knowledge of English phonology. *Harvard Educational Review, 41,* 1–34.

READ, C. (1975). *Children's categorizations of speech sounds in English.* Urbana, IL: National Council of Teachers of English.

RICHGELS, D. (1995). Invented spelling ability and printed word learning in kindergarten. *Reading Research Quarterly, 30,* 96–109.

ROBERTS, B. (1992). The evolution of the young child's concept of word as a unit of spoken and written language. *Reading Research Quarterly, 27,* 124–139.

SOWERS, S. (1988). Six questions teachers ask about invented spelling. In T. Newkirk & N. Atwell (Eds.), *Understanding writing: Ways of observing, learning, and teaching* (2nd ed., pp. 130–141). Portsmouth, NH: Heinemann.

SULZBY, E. (1985a). Children's emergent reading of favorite storybooks: A developmental study. *Reading Research Quarterly, 20,* 458–481.

SULZBY, E. (1985b). Kindergartners as writers and readers. In M. Farr (Ed.), *Advances in writing research: Vol 1. Children's early writing development* (pp. 127–199). Norwood, NJ: Ablex.

SUTTON, E. (1974). *My cat likes to hide in boxes.* New York: Parents Magazine.

TEMPLE, C., NATHAN, R., BURRIS, N., & TEMPLE, F. (1988). The beginnings of writing (2nd ed.). Boston: Allyn and Bacon.

THE THREE BEARS. (1952). Racine, WI: Western.

TREIMAN, R. (1991). The role of intrasyllabic units in learning to read. In L. Rieben & C. A. Perfetti (Eds.), *Learning to read: Basic research and its implications* (pp. 149–160). Hillsdale, NJ: Erlbaum.

VUKELICH, C., & EDWARDS, N. (1988). The role of context and as-written orthography in kindergartners' word recognition. In J. E. Readence & R. S. Baldwin (Eds.), *Dialogues in literacy research* (Thirty-seventh yearbook of the National Reading Conference) (pp. 85–93). Chicago: National Reading Conference.

WILDE, S. (1992). *You kan red this! Spelling and punctuation for whole language classrooms, K–6.* Portsmouth, NH: Heineman.

YADEN, D. (1988). Understanding stories through repeated read-alouds. *The Reading Teacher, 41,* 556–560.

as "It's red and it's a dirt bike." Drawing a picture or talking with a friend helps children write stories that have better narrative form.

Young authors' stories often barely qualify as stories (Calkins, 1986). Beginning writers seem to avoid the story form altogether. That is, they do not use in their writing all the story structure knowledge that they exhibit during storytelling. Many first written "stories" are not stories; rather, they are "all I know about something" pieces. They are more like inventories of information—and misinformation. Figure 5.5 shows an **all-about story** written by a first grader.

Figure 5.5 *All-About Book*

A typical all-about piece lacks story form, a precise sequence of events, and a real end. It may be a book composed of several pages, each with a picture and a caption that tells about some part of the subject the child has chosen. The captions may contain pronouns that refer to earlier mentions of the subject. Except for such pronoun usage, however, most pages could stand on their own; they have no direct link with what went before or what comes after.

Story Writing

Eventually conventional writers become skilled at doing all that is entailed in writing complex stories, that is, stories that reflect a very developed concept of story and sophisticated literary knowledge. Writers in the primary grades only begin this long process of learning to compose coherent, engaging, and insightful stories. Still, we can lay out what we might expect to find in the very advanced stories that conventional writers in these grades might compose.

Literary elements in stories.   We would expect well-written stories to include many of the literary elements already discussed, such as point of view and theme. And although we would never presume that young children would be able to write stories containing all the literary elements we expect in well-written stories (few adults can craft stories using all the elements we will describe), we can expect them to write stories that have some of these elements. After all, young readers explore many of these elements in their story discussions (see Figures 5.2 and 5.3), and children dictate stories that include some of these elements (see Ted's dictated story in Figure 5.4). We will first describe literary elements found in high-quality stories. Then we will present two stories composed by young writers and discuss the literary elements found in these stories.

All stories have seven major literary elements: setting, character, plot, point of view, style, mood, and theme (Lukens, 1990). These elements are summarized in Table 5.1. The **setting** introduces the location, time period, and weather in which

Table 5.1 *Literary Elements of Narratives*

Element	Components	Purpose
setting	time place weather	reveals mood reveals character introduces conflict
character	thoughts actions appearance words (dialogue)	reveals motives, traits must be believable and consistent
plot	problem conflict climax resolution	must be logical and consistent introduces tension propels story forward
point of view	first person third omniscient third limited omniscient objective	positions reader in story world
style	imagery figurative language word choice	reveals author's voice
mood		sets emotional tone
theme		provides consistency for story at the abstract level

the story takes place, and reveals mood and character. For example, characters who are put in harsh settings (such as a desert or a lonely island) are often revealed as resourceful, hardworking, and independent. The setting is sometimes used as an antagonist to introduce conflict to the story. For example, a character may have to travel through a snowstorm (an antagonistic setting) in order to get to school.

There are two kinds of **characters** in stories: main characters and supporting characters. The main characters are at the center of the action of the story, and supporting characters serve as helpers to the main characters. Characters are not always people (they can be animals or objects that are animated), but main characters must have human traits—we must come to know them as people. Characters are revealed through their thoughts, actions, words, and appearance. We must be able to see a character in action and hear what a character says and thinks.

A critical component of stories is the plot. The **plot** includes **episodes,** each with a problem and obstacles. The last episode in a story includes the climax and resolution of the story. The main character does not usually solve the problem simply or easily, but encounters difficulties or obstacles along the way that create **conflict**. A critical moment comes when the problem is solved (the **climax**) and the story is resolved (often happily in literature for children). Conflict is an important part of stories, because it produces tension (we do not know how the story will end, although we hope all will go well) and propels the story forward.

Point of view is the perspective from which the story is told. Sometimes the story is told by a narrator who allows the reader to know the thoughts of all the characters. At other times the narrator is a character, and we know only his or her thoughts. At other times the narrator is an objective observer; in this case the narrator tells only what an observer might see or hear and never reveals the thoughts of any characters. Point of view is particularly important, because it positions the reader inside or outside the story. When point of view allows readers inside the story, they know all the characters' thoughts and feelings.

Style is the way the author uses language, including use of imagery (descriptions that appeal to the senses, such as sight, sound, or touch), word choice, and figurative language (such as the use of simile or metaphor). Each author uses language in unique ways to describe setting and character and to uncover the plot.

Mood is the emotional tone of a story (humorous, somber, lighthearted, mysterious, frightening). **Theme** is the abstract statement about life or humanity revealed by the story as a whole. Through theme, stories achieve a consistency at an abstract level.

Literary elements in children's story writing.   What elements might we expect in primary schoolchildren's compositions? Figure 5.6 presents Ted's two-page rocket story. The setting is revealed in the story's illustrations: Ted's house before the rocket launch and out in space where the rocket crosses a planet's path. The story includes main characters ("they,"implied as the people on the rocket) and supporting characters (people seeing the rocket being launched). We know that the main characters, the people on the rocket, possess foresight, because they have a "special shield all around it in case there is an attack on the rocket."

There is one implied and one explicit conflict in Ted's story. The rocket might be attacked (conflict with other people), and the rocket must cross a planet's path

Figure 5.6 *Ted's Space Trip Story*

The rocket is blasting off! They are going through 100 galaxies! People are climbing a ladder to see them. It has a special shield all around it. In case there is an attack on the rocket. Because you never know. They are on TV also.

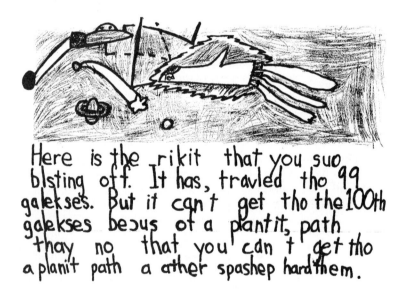

Here is the rocket that you saw blasting off. It has traveled through 99 galaxies. But it can't get through the 100th galaxy because of a planet path. They know that you can't get through a planet path. Another spaceship heard them.

(conflict with natural forces). The story is told mainly from the objective point of view (as readers, we can see into the setting and observe the actions). Only once are we allowed to know the characters' thoughts ("They know that you can't get through a planet's path"). However, the story directly addresses the readers twice ("because you never know" and "here is the rocket that you saw blasting off").

Figure 5.7 presents another story written by a primary-grade student. Although the story sometimes loses sequence, it has several characters who act in a consistent manner, as we would expect (a cat chases a chick). The author tells us about the characters by revealing their feelings (the cat is hungry, and the chick is afraid) and by showing us what they say ("Peep, peep" and "Meow"). The story has a problem (the cat is trying to eat the chick) and actions to solve the problem (the mother bites the cat, and the chick hides).

From these two stories, we can conclude that children do use many literary elements of narratives in their stories, but not necessarily all elements, nor are the elements always well developed. We understand that primary schoolchildren's stories may lack plot complexity and descriptive detail. We might expect young conventional writers' stories would gradually acquire overall story consistency, believability, and detail, but much of this development occurs after the primary grades.

Figure 5.7   *"Peep Peep" Story*

Yo tengo un pollito. El pollito hace—¡pio, pio!—. El pollito se va a jugar y viene. Tiene hambre. El pollito hace—¡pio, pio!—. El gato lo persigue. La madre lo pica y el gato hace—¡miau!— . . . Por eso la gallina y mi pollito dice la gallina y el pollito estaba escondido. Tenía miedo que el gato lo agarrará.

(I have a chick. The chick says, "Peep, peep." The chick goes out to play and comes [back]. He's hungry. The chick says, "Peep, peep." The cat chases him. The mother bites him and the cat goes, "Meow." . . . Therefore the hen and my chick say the hen and the chick was hidden. He was afraid the cat will catch him.)

Edelsky, C. (1986). *Writing in a Bilingual Program,* p. 91. Reprinted with permission from Ablex Publishing Corporation.

Expository Text

Not all texts are stories. Some texts inform or explain, rather than relate a story; these are called **expositions.** Much nonfiction takes this form. We expect conventional writers eventually to compose informative, engaging, and accurate expositions. Of course, readers and writers in the primary grades only begin the process of learning to compose highly structured informational texts and to read and remember ideas from informational books. We will first describe the forms of well-structured expository texts and then present what we know about young children's expository writing next.

Expository Text Structure

There are three important components in highly organized informational material: consistency, ordered relationships, and hierarchical relationships (Newkirk, 1987). For a text to have **consistency,** all its ideas must be related to one another. The all-about story about butterflies presented in Figure 5.5 is consistent: all of the ideas in the text are related to butterflies and feelings about butterflies. However, this text does not have ordered relationships.

Ordered relationships are ideas that are related in some order. For example, two ideas might be related because one idea is an example of or illustrates another idea. Causes and effects, problems and solutions, comparisons, main ideas and supporting details, or sequences are all ideas that are ordered—they are related to one another in specific ways. A third grader wrote the following composition about doing chores in order to receive an allowance. In this composition each sentence is not only consistent with the topic, but it is also related to the preceding sentence through sequence or cause–effect relationships.

> My mother wants me to set the table because that is my job. First, I get out the silverware and then the glasses and last the butter. When I set the table all week, I get my allowance.

The last component of expository text structures is **hierarchical relationships**. Most expository texts are complex and can be broken into one or more main topics, which, in turn, can be broken down into subtopics, forming a hierarchy. The relationships among the main topics and between the subtopics and the main topic in expositions are also ordered or related. An example of an expository text with hierarchical relationships, ordered relationships, and consistency is presented in Figure 5.8. In this composition the two main ideas (causes of forest fires and solutions to forest fires) are related by being a problem and its solutions. Each of the main topics has subtopics related to the main idea through the ordered relationships of cause–effect (for example, forest fires are caused by campfires and cigarettes, and forest fires can be prevented by staffing lookout stations, using bulldozers, and building fire lanes). The information within each of these subtopics is both ordered and consistent.

Figure 5.8 *Forest Fires: An Exposition*

Every year thousands of acres of forests are destroyed by fires. This problem is often caused by careless campers who do not put their fires completely out. Hikers and other visitors drop smoldering cigarettes in the forest underbrush. Left unattended campfires and smoldering cigarettes can cause small fires. But in dry forests, a small fire can quickly burn thousands of trees.

One solution to the forest fire problem is to man lookout stations and use helicopters to spot fires. Fires that are discovered immediately can be put out before they get too big to handle.

A second solutuion to the problem is to have experts and bulldozers on duty ready to fight fires. Bulldozers are capable of moving tons of dirt to smother fires quickly. Expert forest firefighters know the qucikest methods of controlling fires so that they do not grow out of control.

A third solution is to build fire lanes in the forests. Fire lanes are long breaks in the forest where there are no trees. These breaks prevent the fire from spreading out of control.

Adapted from McGee, L., & Richgels, D. (1985). Teaching expository text structure to elementary students. *The Reading Teacher, 38,* p. 745. Reprinted with permission of the International Reading Association.

Children's Expository Writing

Even in third grade, children's expository writing shows relatively little of the organizational structures found in well-organized expository text. Unlike their story writing, third graders' expository writing is especially undeveloped (Langer, 1986). We can nonetheless see the beginnings of expository text organization, and we will describe next four kinds of expository texts that young children may write (Newkirk, 1987).

Labels.   At first, children's expository texts consist of **labels**, that is, one-word identifications of a picture, or statements that begin with "This is a _____." Writers extend this idea by labeling their drawings and by making lists enumerating what they know ("This is a picture of the North Star and the space shuttle, and the earth, and the moon."). Figure 5.9 presents an early exposition that consists of a collection of labels for a Halloween picture. This exposition has implied consistency (all the labels are related to the topic of Halloween), but it lacks ordered or hierarchical relationships.

Figure 5.9   *Ted's Collection of Halloween Labels*

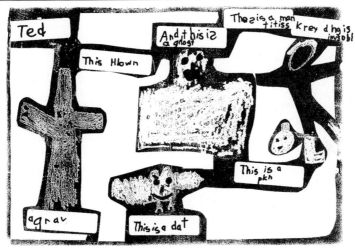

Ted. This is Halloween. And this is a ghost. This is a man. It is gray because he is invisible. A grave. This is a bat. This is a pumpkin.

Attribute lists.   Children may also organize their expository writing by writing an **attribute list** about a topic. The ideas they include in their compositions are consistent—they all relate to the topic—but they are not ordered—they are not related to one another in any specific way. Children go beyond labeling to describe information related to the topic. Figure 5.10 presents an example of an attribute list exposition describing the solar system. All the ideas in the composition are related to the topic, the solar system, but they are not related to each other, with the exception

Figure 5.10 *Ted's Attribute List*

This is a picture of space. We live on Earth. It is the only planet with 3 colors. The hottest planet we know is the sun. The second hottest one is very close to the sun. Pluto is tiny.

of two. The idea "the hottest planet we know is the sun" is related to the idea "the second hottest one is very close to the sun" by the relationship of comparison.

> ***Initial ordered paragraphs.***   Eventually young writers compose **initial ordered paragraphs,** in which the ideas are not only related to a topic (are consistent), but they are also related to one another (have ordered relationships). Initial ordered paragraphs contain at least three statements that are related to a single topic and that are logically connected or related to each other (Newkirk, 1987). Writing initial ordered paragraphs means that writers have begun learning various ways to connect ideas logically, such as through sequence, cause and effect, or compare-and-contrast relationships.

An elementary-school student wrote the paragraph shown in Figure 5.11. This student is beginning to understand how to use cause-and-effect logic to organize ideas in writing, but this paragraph barely qualifies as an initial ordered paragraph. The first idea, "the dinosaurs died," is causally related to the subsequent idea, "because of a comet that landed on the earth." But this line of reasoning does not reach a conclusion until farther into the paragraph: "The comet blocked the sun," "there was a lot of radiation," "and that killed the dinosaurs." These ideas are not only consistent, but also causally related.

> ***Ordered paragraphs.***   The most organized expository text structure consists of **ordered paragraphs**, where ideas are not only consistent and related, but also hierarchical (the main topic is broken down into subtopics). Few primary-school-age students achieve this organization in their expository writing (Newkirk, 1987), perhaps because one of the last steps in learning exposition is knowing that, to pre-

Figure 5.11 An Initial Ordered Paragraph

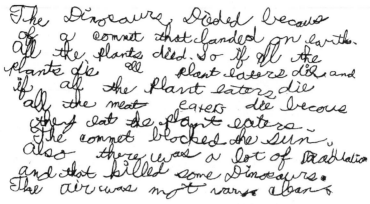

The dinosaurs died because of a comet that landed on earth. All the plants died. So if all the plants die, all plant eaters die, and if all the plant eaters die, all the meat eaters die because they eat the plant eaters. The comet blocked the sun. Also there was a lot of radiation and that killed some dinosaurs. The air was not very clean.

sent a topic well, one must find the best way to organize its content. Choosing the best organization depends on having a repertoire of expository text structures available, such as compare–contrast and cause and effect. This knowledge is also part of learning a subject thoroughly. A complete understanding of crocodiles requires knowing how crocodiles are both different from and similar to alligators. A report about crocodiles and alligators could be well organized using a compare–contrast text structure. Similarly, a complete understanding of the age of glaciers requires knowing what effects the glaciers had on plant and animal life and on the topography of the continents. A report about glaciers could be well organized using a cause-and-effect text structure. Bruner (1960) called this "the mastery of the structure of the subject matter" (p. 18). Most accomplished readers and writers are only beginning to acquire this sophisticated knowledge.

Story and Expository Writing Together: Hybrid Story-Reports

One way in which children learn to use the new form of exposition is to rely on another, more familiar form—narrative. Some young children's expository reports have a strong narrative thread. It is not, as some (e.g., Moffett, 1968) have argued, that children must make do with the narrative form because they are ignorant of any other; rather, children are using what they know best in order to take their early steps toward a new form. In some cases, we can see a strong interplay between listing and storying.

We call the use of narrative and exposition together **hybrid story-reports**. Hybrid story-reports are not just stories. They serve a different purpose from story writing; they are written primarily to convey or to preserve information. We will use another exposition by Ted to examine further the interplay between two forms, exposition and narrative.

When Ted was in second grade, he saw Halley's comet. He might have documented his experience simply by writing a collection of factual observations, but the event was too dramatic; it called for storytelling as a means of preserving important information. Ted supplemented his story-report with a drawing. Figure 5.12 shows his drawing and Figure 5.13 shows his report. Ted blended two kinds of expository form: description ("It looked like a big fuzzy blob with a big fuzzy tail," "It was a very bright object, and I couldn't see the tail") and comparison/contrast ("I had seen many pictures of the comet, but this one looked different," "When I got to look through the telescope, the comet did not look at all like it did in the binoculars," "when it last came, it was higher in the sky and brighter"). He also used such narrative elements as time sequence and dialogue. Finally, he used dramatic inventions. He wrote, "I thought we were going to have another baby," Yet Ted (who had been awakened in the night once before, for his sister's birth) knew that his mother was not expecting a baby, and he did not really expect such a development overnight!

Expository Writing as a Form That Is Unique to Written Language

We have seen that from very early ages, children are able to use what they learn about narrative form to tell, and then to write, stories. In other words, narrative

Figure 5.12 *Ted's Drawing of Viewing Halley's Comet*

regularity is that the *f* sound (/f/) is spelled only four ways in English: *f, ff ph,* and *gh.* It is true that there is no apparent reason for spelling /f/ at the end of *laugh* and *half* differently. Still, there is some regularity in how the letters for the *f* sound are used: /f/ is never spelled with *gh* or with *ff* at the *beginning* of an English word; and *ph* is used only with a special class of words, such as those that are built from *phon-* (meaning "sound") and *-graph* (meaning "write") with the exception of the word *elephant.* So, knowing the spelling regularity of the *f* sound suggests that the spellings of /f/ in *telephone,* or even *phone,* and *phonics* and *geography* and *paragraph* are to be expected; but that spellings such as *phunny* or *ghunny* or even *ffunny* are not to be expected.

Children's errors reveal their growing awareness that certain spellings can only occur in certain words and in certain parts of words. A child's writing *laff* (for *laugh*) is consistent with our observations about the usual context of *ff* (at the end of words), and so it is less wrong than writing *ghish* for *fish. Laff* is not as great a violation of our expectations as is *ghish. Laff* is wrong in a way that shows that a child is learning about English spelling conventions. Expectations about where alternative spellings of the same sound occur are automatic with mature readers and spellers. Still, acquiring such expectations is a big job and an important one for children. It is a significant part of their becoming conventional writers and readers.

As they acquire these expectations, the children we are calling conventional writers still make mistakes, but their mistakes are more and more conventional looking. Ted's space trip story (Figure 5.6) provides an example. He wrote *Thay* for *They.* Although this is incorrect, it shows that Ted understood that *ay* is an alternative to the letter name spelling for the long *a* sound (he used that letter name spelling in the same story in *cas* for *case* and *spashep* for *spaceship*). Furthermore, Ted's spelling shows that he knew that the end of a single-syllable word is a likely place for using the *ay* alternative; after all, *ay* is correct for the long *a* sound in *way, day, say, pay, stay,* and many other English words.

Ted's spelling of *Thay* is a transitional spelling—it shows awareness of an alternative way to spell the long *a* sound. Figure 5.14 presents a journal entry with several transitional spellings. In this entry, the student spelled *weigh* as *way,* showing the same understanding of an alternative spelling of the long *a* sound that Ted displayed in his space story. The spellings of *Doctor's* as *Doturs* and *office* as *offis* also are transitional (they include a vowel in every syllable and the *ff* alternative spelling of the sound /f/).

FUNCTIONS

Nowhere are both the continuities and the changes involved in children's becoming conventional readers and writers more evident than in their learning more about the functions of written language. Children continue to read and write for their own purposes, but they also learn another set of purposes for reading and writing—school-related purposes. In schools, reading and writing often entail considering the purposes the teacher has set, the special purposes the textbook authors have for writing, and the unique criteria by which classmates will judge one's writing.

In classrooms, students do not always read and write because they need to enter imaginary worlds, to gain information about their own expanding real world, to dis-

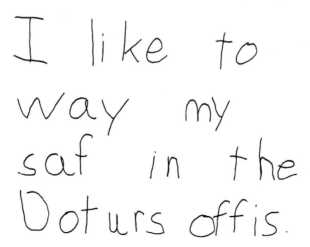

I like to
way my
saf in the
Doturs offis.

Figure 5.14 *Doctor's Office*

cover for themselves how written language works, or to create a permanent record of their ideas and wants. They also read in basal readers, and they complete writing assignments in handwriting books and in reading-skills workbooks. They have a new purpose for reading and writing: completing assignments and satisfying their teachers.

Successful elementary schoolteachers make sure that the assignments they give are congruent with children's own urges to write and read. They support children's ideas of the purposes of reading and writing. Children's reading and writing must continue to serve their own purposes, even when teachers make use of them for instruction.

However, conventional readers and writers have a keener awareness of audience than experimenters do. They have a more constant and pervasive realization that literacy involves creating meaning with someone else in mind, whether it is the author whose book they are reading, the intended reader of their writing, or the listener to whom they are reading. They understand that such meaning making is the single most important element of reading and writing.

All these factors can contribute to the creative hum of a classroom in which children still proceed from their own purposes, but in which teachers create more specifically reading-directed and writing-directed institutions than they do in preschools. These institutions can include explicit lessons, the writing workshop, the conference, the reading workshop, the author's chair, assignments, rules and expectations, and assessment (all of which we describe later).

THE TRADITIONAL END POINTS: READING AND WORD IDENTIFICATION, VOCABULARY, AND COMPREHENSION

We have not used traditional terms to describe what children learn about reading during the early elementary grades. Reading educators traditionally describe the *what* of reading learning in terms of **word identification** skills, **vocabulary** knowledge and **comprehension** ability. Those terms emphasize the view that, in order to become readers, children must do three things. They must learn to identify new words they encounter in print by sounding them out using phonics knowledge, by recognizing known word parts, and by using the context in which the words occur. They must know the meanings of, and know related words for, many of the words that they encounter in their reading. They must be able to understand what they read (for example, by knowing how the complex sentences that they are likely to encounter are constructed and by knowing how main ideas in a passage are supported by details). We agree with this description of what able readers must do. The following discussion is intended to show that the terms we have used cover the same ground and that they were used for sound reasons.

Although the descriptions *word identification, vocabulary,* and *comprehension* sound very unlike what was used in this chapter, there are similarities. The phenomena defined by the traditional perspective are not entirely different from the writing and reading processes described from our psycho-sociolinguistic perspective. The difference is in emphasis. The traditional terms emphasize an end point. Our terms emphasize development. By using the same categories and terms in this chapter that were used in the first four chapters of this book (*meaning making, forms, meaning-form links,* and *functions),* we have tried to call attention to the *origins* of conventional reading and writing, not just what they are. Our terms assume a long period of development in which children truly are readers and writers even though "the person on the street" would not think so. This is a period in which children derive important literacy knowledge that is the basis for their eventual conventional reading and writing, especially when we acknowledge their accomplishments along the way.

By the end of the period described in this chapter, children are conventional readers and writers, and the traditional terms of description work quite well. We can demonstrate this by casting two of the descriptions given in this chapter in traditional terms. The recasting for the sake of demonstration involves what we have called meaning making; we could have called the end point of development of meaning making "comprehension." We have said that conventional readers are able to construct many kinds of meanings, such as literal and evaluative meanings, from what they read; this is reading comprehension.

We have also said, however, that conventional writers are able to write for an intended audience. They can comprehend for an audience as they write by rereading their writing. This is a kind of writing comprehension that is absent in traditional uses of the term *comprehension.* We believe that this comprehension ability is not an automatic product of teacher-directed comprehension lessons in most reading programs. Children are able to construct literal and evaluative meanings from what they read because they did so when they were read to and because they were encouraged to do so when they engaged in pretend reading long before they neared the end points described in this chapter. Similarly, children do not write for an intended audience merely because a teacher reminds them to do so; this behavior follows from earlier episodes in which they were treated as authors, as if they intended to communicate, even as they merely scribbled or wrote mock letters.

Our end point and the traditional reading behaviors are both comprehension. Before that end point, however, there were important literacy-related knowledges and behaviors for which we found it necessary and helpful to use our more de-scriptive term, *meaning making*.

We could have also used the traditional term *phonics* as a label for the end-point of one of children's developing knowledges about meaning-form links. In-stead, we continued to describe the invented spelling behaviors that first appeared during the experimental period described in Chapter 4, hoping to emphasize that children experiment with sound-letter correspondences long before they are con-ventional readers or writers. They use phonics in writing as well as in reading; in fact, they use phonics in writing even *before* they use it in reading.

This is neither a matter of semantics, nor an effort to confuse our readers who come to this book with a traditional perspective. By maintaining the categories and terms we have used throughout this book, we show the importance of respecting children's early developing knowledges and allowing children to use them in their own ways for their own purposes. Invented spelling provides just one example. Let-ting children experiment early with invented spelling and talking with them about their spellings may eliminate the need for many isolated phonics lessons later, in the primary grades. If so, the same end point is achieved: children are able to use phonics knowledge efficiently for the word-identification and spelling purposes that make sense to conventional readers and writers.

Chapter Summary

Conventional readers and writers achieve a new independence in their reading and writing, but they are never alone. They are aware of the author who wrote what they read and of the audience that will read what they write. Thus, they show a keen awareness that written language is a communication process.

Conventional readers and writers are able to maintain several processes and to juggle several communication strategies in extended episodes of writing or reading. They are aware of how well or how poorly the juggling act is going; they have fix-up strategies for when it goes poorly.

Conventional readers' meaning mak-ing extends to being able to make inter-pretations and understand abstract literary elements, including point of view, sym-bol, and theme. They know the fine points of form at the word level in Eng-lish; they have a conventional concept of word. They acquire sophisticated aware-ness of story form that comprises knowl-edge about setting, characters, plot, point of view, style, mood, and theme.

These children also gain a greater knowledge of text structure than they had as experimenters, especially knowledge of expository text structure. They learn to apply their already well-developed knowledge of story structure to both un-derstanding and producing stories, and to both telling and writing stories.

Conventional readers and writers have many new performance strategies. They build on their previous understandings of what spelling is all about by adding multi-ple strategies for representing words in print, some using their earlier knowledge of sound–letter correspondences, and some using visual, contextual, and seman-tic information in new ways.

Conventional readers and writers have new, school-related purposes for reading and writing. Written language can make them participating members of a literate classroom community and can facilitate a more intense or intimate interaction between authors and audiences than was possible before they reached this stage of reading and writing.

Table 5.3 summarizes what conventional readers and writers know about written language meanings, forms, meaning-form links, and functions.

Table 5.3 *Summary: What Conventional Readers and Writers Know about Written Language Meanings, Forms, Meaning-Form Links, and Functions*

Meaning Making

- use metacognitive strategies to focus on meaning while reading, including monitoring that reading makes sense

- use strategies for generating ideas during composing, including knowing the expectations of audience

- interpret literature and move toward interpretations at the abstract level, including point of view, theme, and symbol

- use knowledge of abstract literary elements and style to compose stories and other literary texts

Forms

- have fully developed concept of word

- understand morphemes

- develop an ever-increasing stock of sight words

- know conventional spellings of an ever-increasing stock of words

- use knowledge of literary elements in narratives to compose stories that include settings, characters, and some plot elements and that signal growing control over point of view, mood, and style

- develop knowledge of how exposition is organized, using consistency, ordered relationships, and hierarchical relationships to produce gradually more-organized expository text compositions

Meaning-Form Links

- develop conventional spelling ability, including learning alternative spelling patterns, phonograms, and morphemes

- use orthographic concepts to spell and to decode words in reading (decoding by analogy)

Function

- read and write to meet a variety of personal needs

- read and write to join the classroom literate community

Applying the Information _____

In the following literacy event a first grader writes a story and shares it with his classmates. Discuss what this event shows about understandings of written language meanings, forms, meaning-form links, and functions.

Figure 5.15 displays Zachary's "whale story." He wrote this as a first draft on six sheets of paper. Later he read his story aloud to his classmates as part of an author's circle (a gathering of students who listen to others read their compositions, give compliments, and ask questions): "Made and illustrated by Zachary. To my mom and dad. Once upon a time there were two whales. They liked to play. One day when the whales were playing, a hammerhead came along. They fought for a time. Finally it was finished and the whales won. And they lived happily ever after."

After Zachary read his composition, his classmates asked him several questions, including "What kind of whales are they?" "Where do they live—what ocean?" and "How did they win the fight?" After listening to his classmates' questions, Zachary announced, "I am going to change my story by saying they lived in the Atlantic Ocean and they won the fight because they were bigger than the hammerhead and used their tails to defeat him."

Going Beyond the Text _____

Visit a third grade classroom. Observe the class during a time devoted to reading or writing. Try to identify two children whose behaviors suggest conventional reading or writing. Interview them. How aware are they of their own literacy knowledge and processes? Ask them what they do when they begin a new writing piece. How do they know when a piece is going well? What do they do to make a piece better? Ask how they choose a book to read for enjoyment. What is leisure reading like when it is going well? What makes them see what the author imagined when he or she wrote the book? How do they begin a reading assignment for social studies or science class? What do they do to be sure that they are learning from it what their teacher expects? Ask them if they would be willing to show you something they have written lately. Ask if they would read part of a book or tell about part of a book they are reading.

Do your interview subjects talk easily about reading and writing? Are they aware of what they know about literacy? Are they aware of audience in both reading and writing?

References _____

ADAMS, M. (1990). *Beginning to read: Thinking and learning about print.* Cambridge: MIT Press.

BISSEX, G. L. (1980). *GNYS AT WRK: A child learns to write and read.* Cambridge: Harvard University Press.

BLUME, J. (1974). *The pain and the great one.* New York: Bradbury.

BROWN, A. (1980). Metacognitive development and reading. In R. J. Spiro, B. C. Bruce, & W. F. Brewer (Eds.), *Theoretical issues in reading comprehension* (pp. 453–481). Hillsdale, NJ: Erlbaum.

BRUNER, J. (1960). *The process of education.* Cambridge: Harvard University Press.

Figure 5.15 *Zachary's "Whale Story"*

CALKINS, L. M. (1986). *The art of teaching writing*. Portsmouth, NH: Heinemann.

CHALL, J. S. (1983) *Stages of reading development*. New York: McGraw-Hill.

EDELSKY, C. (1986). *Writing in a bilingual program: Habia una vez*. Norwood, NJ: Ablex.

EHRI, L. (1991). Development of the ability to read words. In R. Barr, M. Kamil, P. Mosenthal, & P. Pearson. (Eds.), *Handbook of reading research*. (2nd ed., pp. 395–419). New York: Longman.

EHRI, L., & ROBBINS, C. (1992). Beginners need some decoding skills to read words by analogy. *Reading Research Quarterly, 27*, 12–26.

FREPPON, P. (1991). Children's concepts of the nature and purpose of reading in different instructional settings. *Journal of Reading Behavior, 23*, 139–163.

GENTRY, J. (1982). An analysis of developmental spelling in GNYS AT WRK. *The Reading Teacher, 36*, 192–200.

HEATH, S. B. (1983). *Ways with words: Language, life, and work in communities and classrooms*. New York: Cambridge University Press.

HUTCHINS, P. (1968). *Rosie's walk*. New York: Scholastic.

LANGER, J. A. (1986). *Children reading and writing: Structures and strategies*. Norwood, NJ: Ablex.

LEHR, S. (1988). The child's developing sense of theme as a response to literature. *Reading Research Quarterly 23*, 337–357.

LUKENS, R. (1990). *A critical handbook of children's literature* (4th ed.). Glenview, IL: Scott, Foresman/Little, Brown.

LYONS, C. (1991). Helping a learning-disabled child enter the literate world. In D. DeFord, C. Lyons, & G. Pinnell (Eds.), *Bridges to literacy: Learning from reading recovery* (pp. 205–216). Portsmouth, NH: Heinemann.

MANY, J. (1991). The effects of stance and age level on children's literary responses. *Journal of Reading Behavior, 23*, 61–85.

MARTIN, B. (1967). *Brown bear, brown bear, what do you see?* New York: Holt, Rinehart and Winston.

MCGEE, L. (1992). An exploration of meaning construction in first graders' grand conversations. In C. Kinzer & D. Leu (Eds.), *Literacy research, theory, and practice: Views from many perspectives* (pp. 177–186). Chicago: National Reading Conference.

McGEE, L., LOMAX, R., & HEAD, M. (1988). Young children's written language knowledge: What environmental and functional print reading reveals. *Journal of Reading Behavior, 20*, 99–118.

MCGEE, L., & RICHGELS, D. (1985). Teaching expository text structure to elementary students. *The Reading Teacher, 38*, p. 739–748.

MOFFETT, J. (1968). *Teaching the universe of discourse*. Boston: Houghton Mifflin.

MORRIS, D. (1981). Concept of word: A developmental phenomena in the beginning reading and writing process. *Language Arts, 58*, 659–668.

NEWKIRK, T. (1987). The non-narrative writing of young children. *Research in the Teaching of English, 21*, 121–144.

PARIS, S., WASIK, B., & TURNER, J. (1991). The development of strategic readers. In R. Barr, M. Kamil, P. Mosenthal, & P. Pearson (Eds.), *Handbook of reading research* (2nd ed., pp. 609–640). New York: Longman.

ROSENBLATT, L. (1978). *The reader, the text, the poem: The transactional theory of the literary work*. Carbondale: Southern Illinois University Press.

SULZBY, E. (1992). Research directions: Transitions from emergent to conventional writing. *Language Arts, 69*, 290–297.

TOMPKINS, G., & MCGEE, L. (1993). *Teaching reading with literature: Case studies to action plans*. New York: Macmillan/Merrill.

WARD, C. (1988). *Cookie's Week*. New York: Putnam.

WILDE, S. (1992). *You kan red this: Spelling and punctuation for whole language classrooms, K–6*. Portsmouth, NH: Heinemann.

YORINKS, A. (1986). *Hey, Al*. New York: Farrar, Straus and Giroux.

PART 2

Classrooms

In Part 2 we shift our focus to teachers and their role in supporting children's literacy learning. We begin in Chapter 6 by describing nine characteristics of a literacy-rich classroom. In Chapter 7 we demonstrate how these characteristics apply in preschool settings and we describe instructional activities that are particularly well-suited to young learners. Chapter 8 introduces a kindergarten classroom in action and explores the kinds of activities that best fit the expectations for kindergarten achievement and the needs of five- and six-year-olds. Chapter 9 presents three first-grade classrooms and describes instruction that both supports young readers and writers and meets the expectations of first-grade literacy accomplishments. Chapter 10 describes a classroom that supports the literacy learning of children in the primary grades beyond first grade. Chapter 11 examines issues related to diverse learners' literacy learning. Chapter 12 introduces techniques for assessing literacy learning and discusses using assessment to guide instructional decision making. The purpose of this part of the text is to demonstrate ways in which thoughtful teachers nudge children to more complex understandings of written language while honoring children's own explorations of reading and writing.

Literacy-Rich Classrooms

The purpose of Chapter 6 is to provide information about how teachers can support children's literacy learning in early childhood classrooms. We begin by describing child-centered instruction and developmentally appropriate practices recommended by early childhood professional organizations. Then we draw from research to identify nine characteristics of a literacy-rich classroom, and we present classroom applications for each of these nine characteristics. We introduce the kinds of children's literature and reference materials that are found in literacy-rich classrooms. We describe how to arrange a classroom library center, writing center, and special literacy-enriched centers for functional reading and writing in dramatic play and learning. We relate three classroom routines that are especially effective in engaging children in reading and writing: reading aloud and telling stories to children, daily independent reading and writing, and sharing. We make recommendations for developing literature theme units and discipline-focused themes that integrate the curriculum across the language arts, support high levels of thinking about topics across a variety of disciplines, and are culturally sensitive. We present three kinds of effective instruction that support children's learning: informal demonstrations, interactive discussions, and using modeling and think alouds. We explain how to use interest and choice as a means of grouping children for activities and instruction. Finally, we highlight the importance of assessing children's literacy knowledge for making instructional decisions.

Key Concepts

child centered

developmentally appropriate practice

developmentally appropriate literacy practice

literacy-rich classrooms

center-based classrooms

curriculum

curriculum integration

integrated language arts

integration across disciplines

culturally relevant topics

direct teaching

homogeneous grouping

heterogeneous grouping

cooperative groups

assessment

picture books

chapter books

big books

genre

traditional literature

fable

folktale

myth

legend

fantasy

realistic fiction

historical fiction

biography

autobiography

informational books

poetry

wordless picture books

pattern books

participation books

language play books

alphabet books

reference materials

visual dictionaries

dramatic-play-with-print centers

literacy-infused center

response-to-literature activities

SSR (sustained silent reading)

dramatic story reenactments	literature logs	demonstrations
grand conversations	discipline-focused themes	IRE question-asking routine
improvised pattern stories	literature theme units	interactive discussions
story extensions	multicultural literature	modeling
response journals	culturally authentic literature	think alouds

PROFESSIONAL RECOMMENDATIONS: APPROPRIATE PRACTICE IN EARLY CHILDHOOD CLASSROOMS

Early childhood professional organizations have taken an active role in defining the kinds of classroom environments, learning activities, and instruction that best support young children's learning. Early childhood professionals argue that the early childhood years, from birth through eight years of age, are crucial for all aspects of children's development: physical, emotional, social, cognitive, and aesthetic. Quality early-childhood education provides opportunities for children to grow in all these areas. Literacy learning is only one part of children's growth and development that must be considered within the larger developmental picture. Therefore, literacy development is supported within exemplary early childhood programs that focus on all aspects of children's development.

Recommendations for Exemplary Early Childhood Programs

The Association for Childhood Education International (ACEI) has recommended that early childhood programs be **child centered** (Moyer, Egertson, & Isenberg, 1987), and the National Association for the Education of Young Children (NAEYC) has argued for **developmentally appropriate practice** (Bredekamp, 1987). Teachers in child-centered classrooms use children's interests and needs as a guide for making decisions about instruction. Teachers who are child centered observe children as they participate in learning activities and listen carefully as children talk. For example, a first grader might bring in several caterpillars that she found in her yard. As other children show interest in the caterpillars, a child-centered teacher might decide to capitalize on this interest and read from several books about insects during storytime. If the children sustain interest, the teacher may plan a unit on insects and their life cycles. The teacher may observe the children as they draw or write about insects they have collected or as they reread insect poems. Based on these observations, the teacher might decide to teach some children a short lesson about spelling words with the *ed* suffix and other children how to use familiar word patterns, for example, in the word *bug,* to decode and spell similar words (such as *dug, mug, rug,* and *tug*).

Developmentally appropriate practice is similar to a child-centered early child-hood program. Teachers who use developmentally appropriate practice recognize that children's growth and development can naturally be described in predictable sequences (remember the changes in literacy knowledge discussed in Chapters 2 through 5), but that children also have individual patterns of growth and home ex-periences that have an impact on what they know and how they learn. Develop-mentally appropriate practice acknowledges that not all children learn in the same way or need the same experiences at the same time.

We wish to stress that developmentally appropriate classrooms do support and encourage children's literacy learning. This is true whether the classroom is for three-year-olds or for eight-year-olds. Unfortunately, developmentally appropriate practice has sometimes wrongly been interpreted as meaning that "reading and writ-ing are 'academic skills' that do not belong in a child-centered early childhood pro-gram" (McGill-Franzen, 1992, p. 57). In addition, many literacy activities that occur in early childhood classrooms are not appropriate for young children's develop-mental levels or learning styles.

However, it is clear that many young children have numerous experiences with reading and writing long before they come to school and that these experiences are important for their later success as readers and writers (see, for example, Chapter 2). Therefore, experiences with reading and writing *are* appropriate for young children (McGill-Franzen, 1992). We describe literacy instruction in a preschool in Chapter 7 and in kindergarten in Chapter 8. This instruction can be called developmentally ap-propriate literacy practice.

Developmentally Appropriate Literacy Practice

In **developmentally appropriate literacy practice** children's development, in-terests, and literacy knowledge guide decisions about instruction and expectations for their participation in literacy activities. Teachers recognize that children's inter-actions in reading and writing activities may be unconventional. For example, teach-ers are aware that a novice writer could not be expected to use invented spelling to write a message, but that the child might choose to write for functional purposes if invited to write a grocery list as part of play in a home center.

Developmentally appropriate literacy practice extends beyond the preschool and kindergarten into the elementary school. Table 6.1 describes appropriate and inappropriate practices for literacy instruction in the primary grades. Suggested ap-propriate practices include having children work in small groups on a variety of ac-tivities related to a central theme. For example, children might be learning about their town. They might visit the class library center and read books or listen to a tape-recorded story about a local hero. At the writing center, they might write let-ters to the mayor. In a math center, they might sort cans into groups of vegetables, soups, and fruits for distribution to an "adopted" family. At a cooking center, they might use a recipe to make no-bake cookies for an adopted family. These and other center-related activities provide children with opportunities to grow in all areas of development, including cognitive, physical, emotional, social, and aesthetic. They also support children's literacy learning.

Table 6.1 *Appropriate and Inappropriate Language and Literacy Practices*

APPROPRIATE

The goals of the language and literacy program are for children to expand their ability to communicate orally and through reading and writing, and to enjoy these activities. Technical skills or subskills are taught as needed to accomplish the larger goals, not as the goal itself. Teachers provide generous amounts of time and a variety of interesting activities for children to develop language, writing, spelling, and reading ability, such as: looking through, reading, or being read high quality children's literature and nonfiction for pleasure and information; drawing, dictating, and writing about their activities or fantasies; planning and implementing projects that involve research at suitable levels of difficulty; creating teacher-made or child-written lists of steps to follow to accomplish a project; discussing what was read; preparing a weekly class newspaper; interviewing various people to obtain information for projects; making books of various kinds (riddle books, *what if* books, books about pets); listening to recordings or viewing high quality films of children's books; being read at least one high quality book or part of a book each day by adults or older children; using the school library and the library area of the classroom regularly. Some children read aloud daily to the teacher, another child, or a small group of children, while others do so weekly. Subskills such as learning letters, phonics, and word recognition are taught as needed to individual children and small groups through enjoyable games and activities. Teachers use the teacher's edition of the basal reader series as a guide to plan projects and hands-on activities relevant to what is read and to structure learning

situations. Teachers accept children's invented spelling with minimal reliance on teacher-prescribed spelling lists. Teachers also teach literacy as the need arises when working on science, social studies, and other content areas.

INAPPROPRIATE

The goal of the reading program is for each child to pass the standardized tests given throughout the year at or near grade level. Reading is taught as the acquisition of skills and subskills. Teachers teach reading only as as discrete subject. When teaching other subjects, they do not feel they are teaching reading. A sign of excellent teaching is considered to be silence in the classroom and so conversation is allowed infrequently during select times. Language, writing, and spelling instruction are focused on workbooks. Writing is taught as grammar and penmanship. The focus of the reading program is the basal reader, used only in reading groups, and accompanying workbooks and worksheets. The teacher's role is to prepare and implement the reading lesson in the teacher's guidebook for each group each day and to see that other children have enough seatwork to keep them busy throughout the reading group time. Phonics instruction stresses learning rules rather than developing understanding of systematic relationships between letters and sounds. Children are required to complete worksheets or to complete the basal reader although they are capable of reading at a higher level. Everyone knows which children are in the slowest reading group. Children's writing efforts are rejected if correct spelling and standard English are not used.

CHARACTERISTICS OF
LITERACY-RICH CLASSROOMS

Literacy-rich classrooms provide child-centered, developmentally appropriate support for children's literacy learning. All children, whether they have many or few home literacy experiences, whether they speak English or another language at home, and whether or not they have special learning needs, thrive in such classrooms.

Learners

As a result of being in literacy-rich classrooms, children are reflective, motivated readers and writers who use literacy to learn more about themselves and the world in which they live. This use of literacy begins before the elementary years. For example, four-year-olds who listen to their teacher read about the differences between tortoises and turtles to help identify the animal that one of them brought to school are reflective, motivated readers who use reading to find out more about their world.

Being reflective means that children are thinkers; they construct meaning for themselves and can use the thinking of others to modify their meaning. Reflective readers construct personal understandings from informational books, poems, and stories. Their initial understandings are usually tentative and unfocused. Sharing such undeveloped understandings requires great risk taking. However, reflective readers and writers use their first tentative understandings to build more fully developed and complex knowledge. They often modify their understandings given additional information from books or from talking with their friends or teachers. Similarly, reflective writers compose personally meaningful stories and poems, but also take into account the needs and interests of their audience. Constructing and sharing personal meanings with others both honors the voice of children and creates a "rich broth of meaning" (Oldfather, 1993, p. 676). This concept of literacy emphasizes the social nature of learning and the importance of revising (which we describe further in Chapter 10).

Being motivated means that children are self-directed and self-motivated (Oldfather, 1993). Many children, especially in the primary grades, are expected to participate in reading and writing activities because the teacher tells them to, but motived learners also participate in many activities because they choose to.

The Classroom

The goal of all literacy instruction is not merely to produce children who are capable readers and writers (although that is certainly an admirable goal), but it is also to encourage and support children as they use reading and writing to achieve their own worthwhile personal and social goals. To achieve this aim, teachers must make careful decisions about materials, physical layout of the classroom, classroom routines, curriculum, instruction, grouping, and assessment. Drawing on research, we next describe the kinds of decisions that create the environments most supportive of literacy learning.

Materials

It makes sense that children who have access to quality literature will be highly motived readers and discerning writers. A good book inspires wonder, curiosity, deep thinking, emotional involvement, and aesthetic pleasure as well as provides models of memorable language. Research confirms that the amount of experience children have with literature correlates with their language development (Chomsky, 1972), reading achievement (Feitelson, Kita, & Goldstein, 1986), and quality of writing (Dressell, 1990). Children who are exposed to quality literature are more likely to learn to love literature and to include reading quality books as an important part of their lives (Hickman, 1979). They are more willing to sustain their involvement with a book through writing, doing projects, and participating in discussions (Eeds & Wells, 1989). Research has also shown that children whose classrooms have a large number of books in a high-quality library center choose to read more often (Morrow & Weinstein, 1982, 1986) and have higher reading achievement (Morrow, 1992). Therefore, the first characteristic of a literacy-rich classroom is: *the classroom includes an abundance and variety of high-quality literacy materials.*

Physical Layout

The physical layout of classrooms has an important impact on children's learning. The most effective classrooms for facilitating preschoolers' language and social development are center based (Field, 1980). **Center-based classrooms** have several small spaces stocked with a variety of manipulative materials. Centers encourage children's play, and all early childhood educators agree that play is the primary avenue through which young preschoolers and kindergartners learn.

Centers that encourage dramatic play are especially supportive of literacy learning when they are enriched with literacy materials. For example, children who use dramatic and literacy props in their play in a post office or a veterinarian's office center use reading and writing in functional and more complex ways (Morrow & Rand, 1991; Neuman & Roskos, 1992). As children interact with literacy in their play, they learn more about the features of print, meaning, and the functional uses of reading and writing (Vukelich, 1993).

The arrangement of space in the classroom library and writing center also affects children's reading and writing. Children spend more time reading in classrooms with well-designed library centers (Morrow, 1992; Morrow & Weinstein, 1982, 1986). They generate and test hypotheses about written language and develop self-monitoring strategies in classrooms with well-designed writing centers (Rowe, 1994). The second characteristic of a literacy-rich classroom is therefore: *teachers arrange spaces to accommodate functional uses of reading and writing, especially in library and writing centers.*

Classroom Routines

There is ample evidence that daily reading and writing experiences are crucial for children's literacy development. Children whose teachers read aloud or tell stories to them on a daily basis are highly motivated readers with extensive vocabularies and effective comprehension strategies (Dickinson & Smith, 1994; Feitelson, Kita, & Goldstein, 1986; Morrow & Weinstein, 1982, 1986). Similarly, the more time children spend reading independently, the better their vocabularies, understanding of spelling principles, and comprehension (Adams, 1990; Anderson, Hiebert, Scott, & Wilkinson, 1985).

Sharing experiences about reading and writing is also a critical component of supporting literacy development. Children who talk together about a book, write responses to literature, and share writing with classmates construct interpretations of literature, use higher levels of thinking, and write better quality compositions (Barone, 1990; Eeds & Wells, 1989; Five, 1986; Kelly, 1990). Therefore, the third characteristic of a literacy-rich classroom is: *teachers establish daily routines that include teacher read alouds and storytelling, independent reading and writing, and sharing.*

Curriculum

Curriculum is what children learn related to the disciplines of language arts and literature, social studies, science, mathematics, art, music, health, and physical education. Recent research and theory regarding the literacy curriculum suggest that children learn better when the curriculum is integrated across the language arts, and across disciplines and when it is culturally sensitive.

Integration across the language arts.   We have long suspected that **curriculum integration**—teaching broad topics that cover areas in more than one discipline—improves teaching and learning (Dewey, 1933; Vars, 1991). One way of integrating the curriculum is to capitalize on the "interrelationships of the language processes—reading, writing, speaking, and listening" (Routman, 1991, p. 272). **Integrated language arts** activities are those in which children talk, listen, read, and write. For example, writing a poem often includes talking to others about possible topics for writing, listening to others as they talk about topics or read their poems, and reading one's own composition. Therefore, a fourth characteristic of literacy-rich classrooms is: *learning is embedded within an integrated language context, which includes listening, talking, reading, and writing.*

Integration across disciplines.   Recent recommendations for curriculum development strongly support curriculum integration across disciplines (Hughes, 1991). **Integration across disciplines** means that children learn concepts and ideas related to a topic that cuts across more than one discipline, for example, incorporating earth science, geography, and math. This kind of instruction allows children to see connections among facts and theories, provides a focus for selecting instructional activities, provides for coherence of activities, allows children to study topics in depth, and promotes positive attitudes (Lipson, Valencia, Wixson, & Peters, 1993). Therefore, the fifth characteristic of a literacy-rich classroom is: *learning is focused on discipline inquiry, which allows children to integrate knowledge across a variety of disciplines.*

Cultural sensitivity.   All children belong to cultural groups that shape their attitudes, beliefs, and ways of making meaning with written language in some way (Heath, 1983). When children perceive of a writing task or a text as having content that reaffirms their cultural identities, they are more likely to become engaged in the task and to construct personal meaning (Ferdman, 1990). **Culturally relevant topics**, topics that children perceive as culturally affirming, are an important avenue to learning and literacy development (Au, 1993). Therefore, the sixth characteristic of a literacy-rich classroom is: *teachers select materials and plan instructional activities that are culturally sensitive.*

Instruction

Talk is an important component in children's literacy learning (Genishi, McCarrier, & Nussbaum, 1988; Linfors, 1988). As children talk together about their compositions, they help each other read, construct ideas, spell, use correct grammar, and clarify information (Kamii & Randazzo, 1985; Rowe, 1994). When children talk with their teachers while they are reading and writing, they learn to use reading strategies (DeFord, Pinnell, Lyons, & Place, 1990). Teachers' talk helps children compose, revise, and edit (Calkins, 1986; Graves, 1983).

Children learn more from teachers who provide explicit, direct instruction (Evans & Carr, 1985; Tharp, 1982). **Direct teaching** consists of: (a) identifying a target literacy strategy, such as using context to figure out the meaning of an unknown word, (b) identifying when children might use the behavior, for instance, when they come across a word they do not know, (c) demonstrating and explaining the steps in using the strategy through modeling and thinking aloud, (d) providing feedback as children practice the strategy, and (e) encouraging children to use the strategy in their reading. Therefore, the seventh characteristic of literacy-rich classrooms is: *learning occurs in a variety of contexts, ranging from informal activities with quality talk to more formal, direct teaching.*

Grouping

Children learn in whole-class groups, small groups, with partners, and on their own, and experts recommend that teachers use all four grouping patterns (Hiebert & Colt, 1989). Whole-class group activities foster a sense of community; small groups provide more natural one-on-one language interactions; and independent activities allow children to pursue personal interests (Berghoff & Egawa, 1991). However, the way in which children are selected for groups is an important factor in their literacy learning. In elementary schools, there is a long history of using reading ability as a criterion for selecting children for reading group membership (Barr & Dreeben, 1991). Traditionally, children grouped for reading had similar, or **homogeneous**, reading abilities. Unfortunately, research has shown that children in low-ability groups receive a different kind of reading instruction from that given children in high-ability groups (Allington, 1983).

In contrast, children whose abilities are different, or **heterogeneous,** can earn higher grades, demonstrate higher levels of critical thinking, and make better decisions when they learn in **cooperative groups** (Slavin, 1986). In these groups, children teach each other content information, guide each other in learning new strategies, or complete joint projects. Groups are also formed in which children choose books or activities based on personal interest. Therefore, the eighth characteristic of a literacy-rich classroom is: *children learn in a variety of grouping patterns, including in whole-class gatherings, small groups, individually, with partners, and when a variety of criteria are used for forming groups.*

Assessment

Assessment is a critical part of teaching. It consists of carefully observing children as they engage in reading and writing and using the information gained from observation to inform instruction. Research confirms that children's literacy learning is enhanced when teachers draw from informed observation to provide feedback on children's reading and writing (DeFord, Pinnell, Lyons, & Place, 1990) and to plan instruction (McCormick, 1994). Therefore, the ninth characteristic of a literacy-rich classroom is: *teachers assess children's literacy learning and use information from assessment to guide instructional decisions.*

The nine characteristics of literacy-rich classrooms are summarized in Figure 6.1. The remainder of this chapter describes applications of seven of these characteristics. Ways of grouping children, including using cooperative, interest, heterogeneous, and ability groups, are illustrated in Chapters 7 through 10, with particular emphasis in Chapter 10. Assessment is described in detail in Chapter 12.

SELECTING QUALITY LITERACY MATERIALS

One of the first decisions that a teacher faces is the selection of literacy materials. Using the materials left in a classroom from the previous teacher usually is not sufficient to support a classroom rich in literacy. Teachers are responsible for using their local resources to locate and evaluate materials for their literacy programs. Teachers should gather (a) a large classroom literature collection, (b) a collection of reference materials, (c) children's magazines, and (d) a variety of writing materials.

Classroom Literature Collection

Teachers in literacy-rich classrooms know a great deal about children's literature. They are aware of literary elements, are familiar with many authors and illustrators, and keep up with recent publications (Huck, Hepler, & Hickman, 1987; Norton, 1991). They select books on topics of interest to children and that represent a range of difficulty levels (Lynch-Brown & Tomlinson, 1993).

Teachers choose books in picture-book and chapter-book format (collections for preschoolers may contain only picture books, but as children get older they enjoy chapter books as well). Teachers may also include quality big books in their classrooms. **Picture books,** such as *Where the Wild Things Are* (Sendak, 1963), *Miss Rumphius* (Cooney, 1982), and *The Wall* (Bunting, 1990), present stories or information through both the words of the text and the illustrations. **Chapter books,**

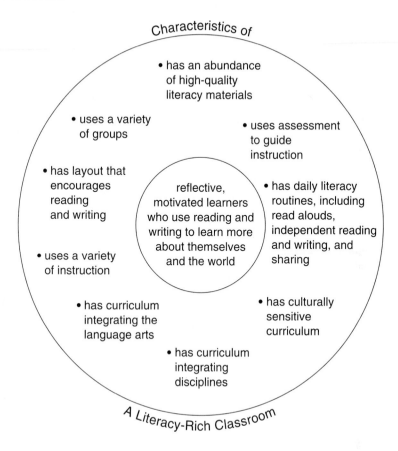

Characteristics of

A Literacy-Rich Classroom

- has an abundance of high-quality literacy materials
- uses a variety of groups
- uses assessment to guide instruction
- has layout that encourages reading and writing

reflective, motivated learners who use reading and writing to learn more about themselves and the world

- has daily literacy routines, including read alouds, independent reading and writing, and sharing
- uses a variety of instruction
- has curriculum integrating the language arts
- has culturally sensitive curriculum
- has curriculum integrating disciplines

Figure 6.1 *Nine Characteristics of Literacy-Rich Classrooms*

such as *Sarah, Plain and Tall* (MacLachlan, 1985), *Ramona Quimby, Age 8* (Cleary, 1981), and *Dominic* (Steig, 1972), present stories or information primarily through text (although some chapter books, especially informational books, may have illustrations). **Big books,** such as *The Snowy Day* (Keats, 1962), *Rosie's Walk* (Hutchins, 1968), and *On Market Street* (Lobel, 1981), are reproductions of favorite stories printed in larger-than-normal size. Other big books, for example, *The Enormous Watermelon* (Parkes & Smith, 1986), were written specifically for big-book format.

The process of locating a sufficient number of quality books can be daunting. Experts recommend that the number of books in a high-quality classroom collection should be eight to ten times the number of children (Fractor, Woodruff, Martinez, & Teale, 1993). Teachers can borrow books from local and school libraries, use bonus points from books clubs to obtain free books (Trumpet Book Club, P.O. Box 604, Holmes, PA 19043; Scholastic Book Clubs, Jefferson City, P.O. Box 3745, MO 65102), and collect inexpensive books from book clubs and bookstores that offer educational discounts. Resourceful teachers may write grant proposals to their school systems or professional organizations or work with principals to obtain funds for stocking a classroom library.

Genres of Literature

Literature is generally classified into several broad categories, or **genres**; including traditional literature, fantasy, realistic fiction, historical fiction, biography and auto-biography, informational books, and poetry. The classroom literature collection in literacy-rich classrooms includes many books from each of these genres.

Traditional literature. **Traditional literature** has its roots in the oral storytelling tradition of long ago, which still exists today. Familiar stories such as *Goldilocks and the Three Bears* (Cauley, 1981), *The Three Billy Goats Gruff* (Galdone, 1973), and *Little Red Riding Hood* (Hyman, 1983) are traditional tales once told by storytellers or family members that have been captured anew by modern illustrators. Traditional stories are found in every culture in the world, and the classroom library collection in a literacy-rich classroom should include many of these multicultural stories. Tales such as *The Brocaded Slipper and Other Vietnamese Tales* (Vuong, 1982) from Vietnam, *Beat the Story Drum, Pum-Pum* (Bryan, 1980) from Africa, and *Elfwyn's Saga* (Wisniewski, 1990) from Iceland allow children to find out about a wide variety of cultures and literary traditions.

One kind of traditional literature, **fable,** usually has animal characters and an explicitly stated moral. Most children enjoy the familiar fables of *The Hare and the Tortoise* (Castle, 1985) and *The Town Mouse and the Country Mouse* (Cauley, 1984). Fables can be found in the folk literature of many different countries. For example, *Doctor Coyote: A Native American's Aesop's Fables* (Bierhorst, 1987) includes Native American fables, and *Once a Mouse* (Brown, 1961) is an Indian fable.

Another kind of traditional literature is the **folktale**. Folktales are usually short, have flat characters (all good, evil, or tricky), and have a happy ending, with good triumphing over evil. Some folktales include animal characters, for instance, *The Three Little Pigs* (Galdone, 1970) and *Why Mosquitoes Buzz in People's Ears* (Aardema, 1975), and some include motifs such as magic or transformations, for example, *Frog Prince* (Grimm & Grimm, 1989) and *Yeh-Shen: A Cinderella Story from China* (Louie, 1982). Sometimes folktales contain a trickster, such as Anansi the spider (*Anansi the Spider: A Tale from the Ashanti,* McDermott, 1972) or Brer Rabbit (*The Tales of Uncle Remus: The Adventures of Brer Rabbit,* Lester, 1987).

A third kind of traditional literature comprises **myths** and **legends**. Myths were created to explain natural occurrences, such as the seasons, constellations, or the creation of life. They include heroes or heroines who have superhuman and magical abilities. Legends are similar to myths, but are thought to be based on true stories that grew to exaggerated proportions. Legends contain heroes or heroines who have fantastic powers. Examples of myths and legends include *The Story of Jumping Mouse* (Steptoe, 1984), *The Fire Children: A West African Creation Tale* (Maddern, 1993), and *Saint George and the Dragon* (Hodges, 1984).

Fantasy. A **Fantasy** is a story about something that could not really happen. Fantasies may contain fantastic characters, such as animals or toys who talk and

Language play books are beneficial in helping children focus on language as something that can be talked about (Geller, 1985). As children practice saying rhyming words, they learn to consider sounds of spoken language apart from the meanings associated with that spoken language. As they discover the humor in mis-interpreted word meanings, they learn to manipulate language. Table 6.5 provides a reference list of books with language play.

Table 6.4 *Participation Books*

Ahlberg, J., & Ahlberg, A. (1981). *Peek-a-boo.* New York: Viking.	Hellen, N. (1988). *The Bus Stop.* New York: Orchard.
Ahlberg, J., & Ahlberg, A. (1986). *The jolly postman or other people's letters.* Boston: Little Brown.	Hill, E. (1980). *Where's Spot?* New York: Putnam.
Carle, E. (1981). *The honeybee and the robber.* New York: Philomel.	Hill, E. (1981). *Opposites peek-a-book.* Los Angeles: Price/Stern/Sloan.
Carle, E. (1984). *The very busy spider.* New York: Putnam.	Hill, E. (1982). *Who does what?* Los Angeles: Price/Stern/Sloan.
Crowther, R. (1977). *The most amazing hide and seek alphabet.* New York: Viking.	Pienkowski, J. (1980). *Dinnertime.* Los Angeles: Price/Stern/Sloan.
Crowther, R. (1981). *The most amazing hide and seek counting book.* New York: Viking.	Pienkowski, J. (1981). *Robot.* New York: Delacorte.
Gerstein, M. (1984). *Roll over.* New York: Crown.	Pienkowski, J. (1983). *Gossip.* London: Gallery Five.
Hawkins, C., & Hawkins, J. (1991). *Old Macdonald had a farm.* Los Angeles: Price/Stern/Sloan.	Tafuri, N. (1983). *Early morning in the barn.* New York: Greenwillow.
	Tarrant, G. (1982). *Butterflies.* Los Angeles: Intervisual Communications.
	Ziefert, H., & Smith, M. (1986). *In a scary old house.* New York: Puffin.

Table 6.5 *Language Play Books*

Ahlberg, J., & Ahlberg, A. (1978). *Each peach pear plum.* New York: Scholastic.	Seuss, Dr. (Theodore Geisel) (1957). *The cat in the hat.* New York: Random House.
Carlstrom, N. W. (1987). *Wild wild sunflower child Anna.* New York: Macmillan.	Seuss, Dr. (Theodore Geisel) (1963). *Hop on pop.* New York: Random House.
Koch, M. (1991). *Hoot howl hiss.* New York: Greenwillow.	Silverstien, S. (1964). *A giraffe and a half.* New York: Harper and Row.
Komaiko, L. (1987). *Annie Bananie.* New York: Harper and Row.	Sonneborn, R. A. (1974). *Someone is eating the sun.* New York: Random House.
Lenski, L. (1987). *Sing a song of people.* Boston: Little, Brown.	Watson, C. (1971). *Father Fox's penny-rhymes.* New York: Scholastic.
Mahy, M. (1987). *17 Kings and 42 elephants.* New York: Dial.	Wells, R. (1973). *Noisy Nora.* New York: Dial.
Noll, S. (1987). *Jiggle wiggle prance.* New York: Greenwillow.	Wildsmith, B. (1986). *Goat's trail.* New York: Knopf.
Perkins, A. (1969). *Hand, hand, fingers, thumb.* New York: Random House.	Wood, A. (1987). *Heckedy Peg.* New York: Harcourt Brace Jovanovich.

Alphabet books.   **Alphabet books** use the sequence of the alphabet to organize information or a story. They appeal to both very young and older children.
In some alphabet books, a single picture represents the sound associated with an
alphabet letter. In *Eating the Alphabet* (Ehlert, 1989), one or two fruits or vegetables
are pictured and named for each letter of the alphabet. Other alphabet books tell
stories, such as the story of growing, picking, and selling apples in *Applebet* (Watson, 1982). Still other alphabet books present information about a single topic. For
example, Jerry Pallotta has written several alphabet books about a variety of topics,
including insects, frogs, and reptiles (e.g., *The Yucky Reptile Alphabet Book,* 1986).
Still other alphabet books are puzzles for readers to solve. Chris Van Allsburg's *The
Z was Zapped* (1987) invites readers to guess what happens to letters by closely examining the illustrations (such as "the *B* was badly bitten," unpaged). Table 6.6 lists
alphabet books that appeal to many ages.

Table 6.6 *Alphabet Books*

Anno, M. (1976). *Anno's alphabet.* New York: Crowell.

Baskin, L. (1972). *Hosie's alphabet.* New York: Viking Press.

Bruna, D. (1967). *B is for bear.* New York: Macmillan.

Burningham, J. (1964). *John Burning-ham's ABC.* London: Johnathan Cape.

Ehlert, L. (1989). *Eating the alphabet.* New York: Harcourt Brace Jovanovich.

Eichenberg, F. (1952). *Ape in cape.* San Diego, CA: Harcourt Brace Jovanovich.

Hoban, T. (1987). *26 letters and 99 cents.* New York: Greenwillow.

Ipcar, D. (1964). *I love an anteater with an A.* New York: Knopf.

Isadora, R. (1983). *City seen from A to Z.* New York: Greenwillow Books.

Kellogg, S. (1987). *Aster Aardvark's alpha-bet adventures.* New York: Morrow.

Lionni, L. (1985). *Letters to talk about.* New York: Pantheon.

Lobel, A. (1981). *On Market Street.* New York: Greenwillow.

McMillan, B. (1986). *Counting wildflowers.* New York: Lothrop.

Seuss, Dr. (Theodore Geisel). (1963). *Dr. Seuss's ABC.* New York: Random House.

Tudor, T. (1954). *A is for Annabelle.* New York: Walck.

Wildsmith, B. (1963). *Brian Wildsmith's ABC.* Danbury, CT: Franklin Watts.

Audiovisual Materials

Audiovisual materials are an important part of the classroom literacy program.
Teachers can borrow copies of audiotapes, films, filmstrips, and videotapes of children's literature from local or school libraries. In addition, children enjoy learning
more about favorite authors and illustrators through videotaped and audiotaped interviews. School librarians are especially helpful in locating these materials. Teachers may contact the following publishing companies for more information:
Houghton Mifflin, 2 Park Street, Boston, MA 02108; Pied Piper, PO Box 320, Ver-
dugo City, CA 91046; Weston Woods, Weston, CT 06883.

Reference Materials

Teachers carefully consider the kinds of reference materials that will best support
their literacy programs. **Reference materials** include dictionaries, thesauri, atlases,

and encyclopedias and are intended to provide information about word meanings, concepts, geography, and other familiar topics. Today many reference materials are published with detailed photographs and drawings so that even very young children enjoy looking at the illustrations in these materials. Publishers have also made available reference materials at a variety of difficulty levels. For example, very young children find picture dictionaries and encyclopedias intriguing. Two examples appropriate for young children are *My First Dictionary* (Roof, 1993) and *My First Encyclopedia* (1993). Older children enjoy locating and reading information in *The Random House Children's Encyclopedia* (1992), a single-volume text loaded with diagrams, photographs, and drawings about common topics of study in the primary grades. A specialized dictionary that appeals to primary school-age children is *The Dictionary of Nature* (Burnie, 1994).

Word books are also useful for a variety of projects. Children can use *My First Word Book* (Wilkes, 1991) to locate spellings or to practice reading familiar words. A version in Spanish (*My First Spanish Word Book*, Wilkes, 1993) is a must for classrooms with Spanish speakers and an important addition to the reference library of any classroom with a focus on multicultural issues. Primary school-children can expand their study of words using a thesaurus, such as *Roget's Children's Thesaurus* (1994).

A new kind of dictionary, the visual dictionary, seems especially attractive to young children. **Visual dictionaries** rely on illustrations to define words. *The Macmillan Visual Dictionary* (actually intended for adults) defines words by presenting labeled drawings. For example, it includes a drawing of a bird in which more than twenty body parts, such as *pin feather,* are labeled. Other visual dictionaries are written for elementary schoolchildren and focus on single topics. Such dictionaries include *The Visual Dictionary of the Universe, The Visual Dictionary of the Earth,* and *The Visual Dictionary of the Human Body* (all published by Dorling Kindersley, 1993).

Many publishers produce highly useful informational books that children may use as references to locate information about topics of study. Noteworthy are the *Eyewitness Books* (published by Knopf) and *Eyewitness Science Books* (published by Dorling Kindersley). These books present detailed photographs, drawings, diagrams, and information about a variety of life science topics, including amphibians, birds, castles, explorers, insects, mammals, plants, and the weather. Subjects addressed in the physical sciences include matter, light, energy, and the human body. Although the text of these books is often too difficult for many primary schoolchildren to read independently, the illustrations are informative and can heighten children's curiosity about scientific concepts.

Children's Magazines

Children's magazines are an important functional print item included in literacy-rich classrooms. They provide stimulating information on a variety of topics in both social studies and science, and they prompt children to experiment with new ideas in art or writing. Many teachers have found that having two or three copies of a magazine encourages children to read together or collaborate on a research project. A list of magazines appropriate for young children is provided in Table 6.7.

Table 6.7 *Children's Magazines*

Chickadee 255 Great Arrow Avenue Buffalo, NY 14207	*Stone Soup: The Magazine by Children* P.O. Box 83 Santa Cruz, CA 95063
Highlights for Children 2300 West Fifth Avenue P.O. Box 269 Columbus, OH 43272	*Super Science Red* 2931 East McCarty Street P.O. Box 3710 Jefferson City, MO 65102
Ladybug: The Magazine for Young Children Box 592 Mt. Morris, IL 61054	*Your Back Yard* 1412 16th Street NW Washington, DC 20036
Ranger Rick's Nature Magazine 1412 16th Street NW Washington, DC 20036	*Zillions* Box 3750 Jefferson City, MO 65102
Spider: The Magazine for Children Box 592 Mt. Morris, IL 61054	*Zoobooks* P.O. Box 85384 San Diego, CA 92186

Writing Materials

Teachers select a variety of writing tools and materials to support their literacy program:

- Writing tools, including colored, medium, and soft lead pencils; pens with a variety of ink colors; and markers, crayons, and chalk in a variety of colors and widths

- Lined and unlined paper in assorted colors, textures, sizes, and shapes

- Other writing materials, such as index cards, printed forms, postcards, magic slates, erasable marker boards, chalkboards, and clipboards

- Bookmaking and greeting-card making materials, such as wallpaper, contact paper, wrapping paper, used greeting cards, staplers, scissors, hole punchers, envelopes, stickers, yarn, and glue

- A typewriter, one or more computers with word processing programs, and a printer.

In addition to these materials, creative teachers will find many unusual writing materials that appeal to children, such as smelly markers, alphabet stamps, and letter-shaped cookie cutters. Children occasionally enjoy using unusual writing surfaces, such as magic slates, pebbleboard, and scratch-off paper. Office or art supply stores sell many kinds of exciting writing materials that creative teachers can adapt for classroom use.

ARRANGING SPACES FOR LITERACY USES

Teachers arrange classrooms so that there are spaces for whole-class and small-group gatherings and so that invitations for reading and writing abound. Many early childhood classrooms, especially those for preschoolers, are center based, and the centers are arranged to encourage the functional use of reading and writing. All literacy-rich classrooms include a library and a writing center, and teachers arrange these spaces so that materials are organized and easily accessible.

Dramatic-Play-with-Print and Literacy-Infused Centers

Play is an important avenue for literacy learning. Teachers can encourage literacy use in children's dramatic play by stocking centers with literacy materials (Neuman & Roskos, 1992). They can plan **dramatic-play-with-print** centers around themes and activities that are familiar to children and that have the potential for pretend reading and writing. For example, children are familiar with having their hair cut. From their experience visiting hair salons or barbershops, children are likely to have seen customers reading magazines in the waiting area and stylists writing bills and appointments. Therefore, teachers can easily capitalize on children's knowledge by setting up a hair salon–barbershop dramatic-play center enriched with literacy materials such as magazines, pads of paper, small cards, and a large appointment book. To arrange dramatic play centers enriched with print, teachers

- Select play themes that are familiar to children and have literacy potential.

- Separate the center from the classroom with movable furniture, such as bookcases, screens, or tables.

- Label the center with a sign posted prominently at children's eye level.

- Select dramatic-play props related to play themes, for example, empty food boxes, a toy cash register, plastic bags for a grocery story or plastic food, trays, and wrapping paper for a fast-food restaurant.

- Select literacy props related to play themes, for example, coupons and pads of paper for the grocery store and an appointment book, appointment cards, patient's chart, and prescription slips for the doctor's office.

- Arrange the materials within the space to suggest a realistic setting related to the play theme (Newman & Roskos, 1990).

Teachers sometimes play with children in dramatic-play centers and model new and more complex ways in which reading and writing can be used (Morrow & Rand, 1991). For example, a teacher in a hair-salon play center may comment, "I'll write you a card so that you can remember your next appointment," as she writes a child's name and date on a small card.

Teachers can enrich other areas of the classroom with literacy materials by planning **literacy-infused centers**. For example, first graders studying the ocean might have a science center that displays plastic sea animals and includes a salt water fish tank with several kinds of fish. By infusing literacy materials into these centers, teachers can increase children's engagement with the topic and stimulate more meaningful reading and writing. For example, teachers could create a literacy-infused sea creature center by displaying books, paper, markers, and a poster labeled "Today I observed" in the center. These materials would encourage children to draw and write about creatures they observed both in the fish tank and in the informational books.

Library Center

All classrooms have a library center, which houses a large part of the classroom literature collection. To provide a pleasant space for reading, listening to stories on audiotape, and talking about books, teachers

- Place the center label in a prominent location.

- Use bookshelves, hanging mobiles, or screens to partition the space from the remainder of the classroom.

- Provide space for four to six children.

- Arrange pillows, small rugs, or other comfortable seating.

- Organize the books (using last name of author or genre).

- Display several books with their covers facing outward.

- Display props for telling stories, such as three stuffed bears, a doll, and the book for retelling "Goldilocks and the Three Bears."

- Arrange a display of books and objects on a special topic, such as an author, genre, or content topic (Fractor, Woodruff, Martinez, & Teale, 1993; Morrow & Weinstein, 1986).

In addition to spaces for reading books, the classroom library may also have a space for listening to stories on audiotape (or a listening center may be established in a nearby location). A listening center includes several audiotapes of stories that are either commercially available or made by parents or other volunteers. Each tape is accompanied by at least one copy of the story. Tapes and books can be kept in plastic bags and stored in plastic bins or hung on special display racks. Figure 6.2 shows a classroom library and listening center.

Writing Center

The writing center serves a variety of purposes. For preschoolers it is an important place for groups of children and their teacher to gather, talk, write, and learn. For older primary schoolchildren the center is used for small groups of children to meet to revise or edit their writing (see the explanation of writing processes presented in Chapters 9 and 10). It may also become a publishing center.

To create a writing center, teachers arrange a large table and several chairs of comfortable height for children. The table is large enough to accommodate several children and to include displays of greeting cards, messages, signs, and special

Figure 6.2 *Classroom Library and Listening Center*

words that encourage children to write. Shelves or a rolling cart for storing writing materials are nearby. Writing materials are labeled and easily accessible on the shelves. The materials are changed frequently so that children can explore a variety of writing implements and surfaces.

LITERACY ROUTINES

Teachers in literacy-rich classrooms read aloud or tell stories daily and set aside time for children to read and write independently. Children have frequent opportunities to share their writing and engage in activities that extend their responses to literature (Hoffman, Roser, & Battle, 1993). **Response-to-literature activities** include retelling, drama, writing, talking, and other creative activities.

Teachers: Reading and Telling Stories

Teachers share literature with children by reading stories, telling stories, or showing films and filmstrips about quality literature. When reading aloud or telling stories to children, teachers should be seated slightly above the children's eye level. The children are seated so that everyone has a clear view of the teacher and the book.

Teachers plan carefully before sharing literature with children. They keep in mind the age and interests of the children as they select books to read aloud. Books selected for reading have illustrations that are large enough for a group of children to see (Glazer, 1981). Teachers preview books carefully to become familiar with story texts and illustrations and to develop purposes for sharing (we will describe more what these purposes might be in later chapters).

Frequently, teachers tell stories using special props (Cliatt & Shaw, 1988; Ross, 1980). Among the many kinds of literature props that teachers can use to tell a story are objects, clothesline props, flannel board props, puppets, and masks. *Object props* are objects that represent certain characters and actions. Object props for the story *Where the Wild Things Are* (Sendak, 1963) might include a teddy bear (to represent Max sent to bed with no supper), an oar (to represent his travels to the land where the Wild Things Are), a crown (to represent Max's becoming King of the Wild Things), a drum and horn (to use in the wild rumpus), and a plate and spoon (to represent the smell that brought Max back to his room where he found his dinner).

Clothesline props include pictures drawn to represent important events in the story. These pictures are clothespinned to a clothesline stretched across the classroom as a story is read or told (see Figure 6.3). Clothesline prop pictures that could be used to tell the story *Where the Wild Things Are* might include an illustration of Max yelling at his mother; Max sailing in the boat to the land of the Wild Things; the Wild Things rolling their eyes, gnashing their teeth, and showing their claws; Max becoming King; Max and the Wild Things creating a rumpus; Max sailing back home; and Max finding his dinner at home. Many teachers create clothesline prop illustrations by making simple drawings.

Puppets make perfect props for storytelling. Finger puppets can be made by drawing characters on paper and carefully cutting them out to include special tabs for fastening around the finger. Stick puppets can be made by coloring characters on stiff

Figure 6.3 *Clothesline Props*

paper, cutting them out, and attaching them to soda straws. Figure 6.4 presents a finger puppet and stick puppet that could be used in retelling *Where the Wild Things Are*.

Flannel board props can be made from Velcro, felt, yarn, lace, or other sewing notions. Figure 6.5 shows flannel board props that can be used in telling *Where the Wild Things Are*. Figure 6.6 presents a mask that could also be used in telling this story.

Children: Independent Reading and Writing

Teachers provide children with plenty of time to browse through and read books of their choice and to write on self-selected topics. Some classrooms and entire

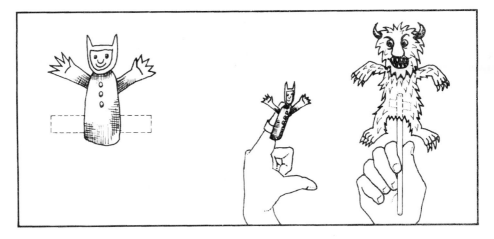

Figure 6.4 *Finger and Stick Puppets*

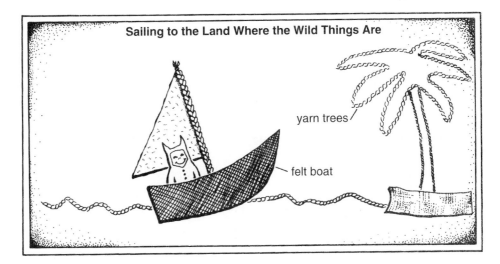

Figure 6.5 *Flannel Board Props*

curls of
paper

paper rolled
into cone

paper
plate

Figure 6.6 *Mask of a "Wild Thing"*

schools promote daily reading by using **SSR (sustained silent reading).** During
this time everyone in the classroom (even the teacher) or school (including the principal and other school personnel) reads silently for a specified period of time (usually ten to twenty minutes). However, with so many schools adopting a
literature-based reading program, time for self-selected reading is usually a part of
reading instruction (we discuss more about shared reading and reading workshops—both of which include daily reading of self-selected texts—in later chapters).

   One way to establish a daily writing activity is to have children write in a journal (Hipple, 1985; Kintisch, 1986). Each child in the classroom is given his or her
own journal. Journals may simply be small books made by stapling paper together,
or they may be more elaborate books that children or adults have bound. A special
time each day is set aside to write in journals. Children are allowed to write (copy
or draw) anything they wish. Preschool, kindergarten, and even first grade teachers
usually invite a few children each day to dictate to them. Dictations can be stimu-
lated simply by asking, "Tell me what you have written" (Hipple, 1985, p. 256).

   Another variation of journal writing that can be used in the preschool and
kindergarten is the home-school journal (Elliott, Nowosad, & Samuels, 1981). These
journals are prepared around such topics as food or toys. Two pages in the journal
are devoted to each topic: one page for home and one page for school. Children
can dictate to their teacher or write about "Food at School." They are given opportunities at school to read their dictations. Then they take their journals home to dictate to a parent or write about "Food at Home."

Children: Sharing Response-to-Literature Activities

Response-to-literature activities encourage children's emotional and intellectual involvement with literature. These activities can serve many purposes, including helping children explore the language of stories, the themes of literature, the media of
illustrations, and the connections between literature experiences and life experiences. Response activities can support children's imaginative, creative, social, moral,
intellectual, and language development (Glazer, 1981). Examples of activities include
laughing, writing, drawing, retelling, commenting, questioning, rereading, modeling
in clay, pantomiming, dramatizing, dancing, singing, cooking, and painting (Hick-

man, 1981). Teachers in literacy-rich classrooms plan a variety of these activities from which children can choose and provide time for children to engage in them.

Through sharing response-to-literature activities, children's understandings of literature are expanded and enriched.

Retelling

Children often share their responses to literature by retelling favorite stories. They are eager to retell *The Mitten* (Tresselt, 1964) after they watch their teacher tell the story using a large oven mitt and cutout pictures of a mouse, frog, rabbit, owl, fox, wolf, boar, bear, and cricket. Similarly, children enjoy using a large green sock (with button eyes sewn on and a hole cut for the caterpillar's mouth) and cut-out pictures of foods to retell Eric Carle's *The Very Hungry Caterpillar* (1970).

Children have many creative ideas for constructing their own story-retelling props. First graders used a green pipe cleaner for the hungry caterpillar and punched holes in construction paper food cutouts to retell *The Very Hungry Caterpillar*. As they retold the story, they slipped each food cutout onto the green pipe cleaner caterpillar. Third graders worked together to decide the number and content of pictures needed to retell *Nine-in-One. Grr! Grr!* (Xiong, 1989) on a story clothesline. They retold the story collaboratively—each illustrator hung his or her picture on the clothesline and retold that portion of the story.

Drama

Drama as a response to literature usually involves four steps (Heinig & Stillwell, 1981; Stewig, 1983). The first step is teacher preparation. The teacher selects literature that has plenty of action and conflict, characters who are active and have striking personalities, and a lot of dialogue. Portions of the story that are appropriate for movement, pantomime, or enactments with dialogue are identified. These selections should be easily dramatized in a short time period. Then, questions to use in discussing the story and in planning the enactment with the children are prepared. Second, the teacher reads the story aloud and uses the questions to help the children plan the enactment. Children are assigned to portray the necessary characters. Third, the teacher directs the enactment either by taking the role of narrator and acting as a side coach or by playing the role of one of the characters. Fourth, the teacher helps children evaluate their drama activity. Children can identify movements or dialogue that were particularly effective. Following evaluation, the teacher selects other children to portray the characters; the second enactment is followed by another evaluation.

Dramatic story reenactments are a special kind of drama in which children informally recreate familiar stories through play (Martinez, 1993). These enactments are spontaneous, child initiated, and child directed (as opposed to planned and guided by the teacher). They occur in classrooms where teachers read favorite stories more than once and plan a variety of other response-to-literature activities, such as painting, drawing, retelling, writing, and guided drama.

Talking

Talking about books is a natural way for children to share their responses to literature. **Grand conversations** are special kinds of talk about books that occur after reading. They are child centered and designed to explore topics that children find interesting as well as to help children reach deeper levels of understanding about literature (Eeds & Wells, 1989; McGee, 1992).

Teachers begin grand conversations by asking an open-ended question, such as "Does anyone have something to say about the story?" Then teachers facilitate children's talk by inviting children to respond and asking them to clarify or expand on their responses. Teachers can encourage interaction among the children by asking them to respond to each other (see examples of grand conversations in Chapter 5, Figures 5.2 and 5.3).

Sometimes grand conversations seem to wander, and teachers wonder if too much time is spent talking about "the part I liked best." One way of increasing the depth of talk is to stop after a few moments and ask the group to brainstorm ideas they have already talked about or new ideas they would like to talk more about (Short, 1993). Teachers can add their own ideas to the list.

Writing

Having children draw or write in response to literature is another way to help them share their thoughts about what they read. Writing (or telling) **improvised pattern stories** is an excellent response activity that connects reading and writing. These are sometimes called **story extensions.** Improvised pattern stories are stories composed by children using the repetitive pattern found in pattern books as a guide. For example, *A Dark Dark Tale* (Brown, 1981) tells the story of entering a scary house, going slowly up the stairs, and looking inside a shadowy cupboard only to find a mouse. It includes the repetitive pattern, "In the dark, dark _____ , there was a dark, dark _____ ." A group of four-year-olds retold the story using their school as the setting:

> Once there was a dark, dark school.
> In the dark, dark school there was a dark, dark hall.
> Down the dark, dark hall was a dark, dark classroom.
> In the dark, dark classroom there was a dark, dark cubbie.
> In the dark, dark cubbie there was a SPIDER!

Children can dictate their improvised stories for charts or big books. To make a big book, teachers write each line of text on large paper for children to illustrate. Children design a front and back cover (on sturdy cardboard) and make a title page. The teacher can use yarn, metal rings, or commercial spiraling to bind the book.

Another sharing activity that uses writing is to have children draw or write their responses to literature in special notebooks or small books called **response journals** or **literature logs.** Primary school-age children's written responses often consist of retellings, evaluations, and related personal experiences (Dekker, 1991). Figure 6.7 presents an entry from a first grader's response journal. Vivian responded to *Hey, Al* (Yorinks, 1986) by describing how Al felt when the bird came into his bathroom.

Figure 6.7 *Vivian's Response to* Hey, Al *(Yorinks, 1986)*

INTEGRATION ACROSS THE LANGUAGE ARTS

Reading and writing are not learned in isolation; they are learned as a part of activities that involve talking, listening, reading, and writing.

Talking and Listening

Children talk and listen for a variety of reasons, including to seek and communicate information, to make and keep friends, and to enter into imaginary play (see Halliday's functions of language in Chapter 1). Talking and listening involve informing and being informed, negotiating, hypothesizing, reflecting, and interpreting (Tompkins & McGee, 1993). Effective talkers and listeners are responsive to the thoughts and ideas of others and are able to use those thoughts and ideas to modify and extend their own ideas. Literacy-rich classrooms, therefore, are not quiet places. Teachers encourage children to talk and listen as a critical path for learning. Children do not listen exclusively to the teacher, but rather are expected to listen to one another. The teacher values and honors the voices of children.

We have already described several activities that involve children in talking and listening: reading aloud, retelling stories, drama, and grand conversations. In later chapters we will describe other talking and listening activities. As a part of these activities, teachers can extend children's talking and listening competencies by having children describe the roles played by good talkers and listeners in different activities and reflect on how effectively they talked and listened.

Literature Theme Units

Teachers can integrate activities across the language arts by using literature themes as a focus for curriculum development. **Literature theme units** are units of instruction focused on learning about authors or illustrators, genres, themes, or a single book. For example, a second grade teacher may read William Steig's *Sylvester and the Magic Pebble* (1969) aloud to a class and discover that the children are highly motivated by this story. They are eager to divide into small groups and have grand conversations. Each group brainstorms a list of topics that they would like to continue discussing. The teacher notices that several children draw pictures related to the story and that some children want to dramatize the story—they have gathered small rocks from the playground to use in their dramatization.

Now the teacher must decide whether to launch a literature theme unit. The teacher could focus the theme on William Steig as an author and illustrator. In this case, the children would read many of the other stories written by Steig, learn about his life, and possibly write him letters. Or the teacher could focus the theme on modern literary tales. *Sylvester and the Magic Pebble* is a modern literary tale, a story written by a known author but with many of the motifs found in folktales. In this case children would read other modern literary tales and discover their common motifs.

As a part of literature theme units, children engage in activities that include talking, listening, reading, and writing. For example, in a kindergarten literature theme unit comparing versions of "The Gingerbread Boy" story (Tompkins & McGee, 1993), the teacher could read five versions of the story aloud to the class, including

- Arno, E. (1985). *The gingerbread man*. New York: Scholastic (this book is also available in big book format).

- Brown, M. (1972). *The bun: A tale from Russia*. New York: Harcourt Brace Jovanovich.

- Cauley, L. (1988). *The pancake boy*. New York: Putnam.

- Galdone, P. (1975). *The gingerbread boy*. New York: Seabury.

- Sawyer, R. (1953). *Journey Cake, Ho!* New York: Viking.

Figure 6.8 presents a web of talking, listening, reading, and writing activities that could be included in this literature theme unit.

DISCIPLINE-FOCUSED INQUIRY

Teachers in literary-rich classrooms engage children in learning about the world. Through these learning experiences children read and write for meaningful purposes, and instruction in reading and writing is embedded within these activities.

Discipline-Focused Themes

One way in which teachers organize an integrated curriculum is to use discipline-focused themes to plan instruction. **Discipline-focused themes** are units of instruction organized around a broad theme that includes learning concepts across

Figure 6.8 *Integrated Language Arts Activities for*
"The Gingerbread Boy" Literature Theme

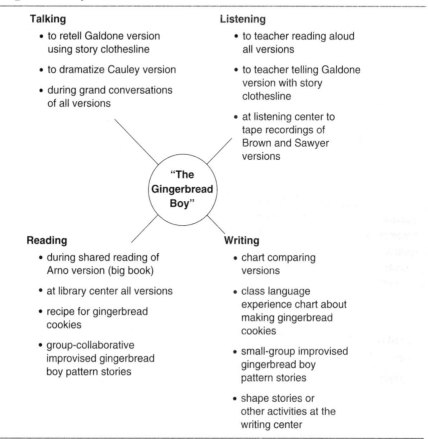

more than one discipline, active inquiry activities, and activities incorporating all the language arts.

For example, a teacher may use the theme of "growing" as a focus for learning experiences for a group of first graders. This theme explores physical changes that occur as a part of growth in plants, animals, and humans; measurement; and the literary theme "growing up." As a part of the activities included in the theme, the teacher may read aloud folktales in which plants grow to enormous sizes (such as *The Enormous Turnip,* retold by Kathy Parkinson, 1986), stories that contrast children at different ages (such as *Stevie,* by John Steptoe, 1969), poems about childhood activities at different ages (*I Want to Be,* by Thylias Moss, 1993), and informational books about growing up (such as *Pueblo Boy: Growing Up in Two Worlds,* by Marcia Keegan, 1991). The teacher may guide the children in dramatizing the stories, and children may create storytelling props to use in retelling the folktales.

The teacher may also read informational books about the growth of plants and animals (such as *How a Seed Grows,* by Helen Jordan, 1992, and several books from the *See How They Grow* series published by Dorling Kindersley (1992), including *See How They Grow: Butterfly, See How They Grow: Frog,* and *See How They Grow: Mouse*). Before the teacher reads these books, the children may dictate ideas, which the teacher may write on a "What We Know about Plants" chart (see Chapter 11 for a discussion of the KWL activity). After reading, children may have a grand conversation about the books and then dictate ideas for a second chart titled "What We Learned about Plants."

As a part of the theme children may grow bean plants, hatch butterflies, and observe a tadpole's growth. They may learn to measure plant growth and their height and weight. They may learn to make charts of plant growth and comparison charts of their own height and weight. Children may keep a science log in which they draw and write their observations of the tadpole's growth.

The teacher includes opportunities for informally learning about reading and writing that are related to the theme and plans lessons about specific strategies for reading and writing. The teacher may plan several lessons to demonstrate how to use invented spelling to write responses to stories or informational books and may talk about the formation of letters (and demonstrate good handwriting) as he or she writes on charts. The teacher may gather small groups of children to read and reread familiar stories, such as *The Enormous Watermelon* (Parkes & Smith, 1986).

Planning Discipline-Focused Themes

Planning instruction around discipline-focused themes is a complex process that requires that teachers be thoroughly familiar with the concepts taught across a wide variety of disciplines as well as the ways in which those concepts can be meaningfully integrated. Teachers who plan discipline-focused themes

- Identify a broad theme that integrates one or more disciplines. They may consult local or state curriculum guides in social studies, science, math, health, and the arts to identify themes and concepts that they are expected to teach at each grade level. Teachers should avoid loosely integrated themes and instead focus on topics that are clearly related.

- Locate resources for providing information about the theme. Two major types of resources are needed: textual and nontextual (Hartman & Hartman, 1993). Textual resources include stories (fantasy, realistic fiction, historical fiction, and folk literature), informational books (including reference books and biographies), poetry, and magazines. Nontextual resources include experts, music, art, audiovisual materials, and primary source materials (for example, a copy of a page from a diary of a Civil War soldier or newspaper articles about immigrants written in the 1920s, 1950s, and 1990s).

- Identify inquiry activities. These activities involve children in observing real phenomena (such as conducting experiments, observing class pets, collecting and classifying artifacts, or interviewing classmates or others).

- Plan activities that involve children's learning in large and small groups (such as reading aloud, retelling, dramatizing, writing in response journals, talking in grand conversations, and writing collaborative stories or poems) and independent explorations (reading and retelling stories in the library center, using the writing center, playing in dramatic-play centers correlated with the unit, or working on art projects).

- Plan literacy instruction based on the observed needs of students and the concepts outlined in the local or state language arts curriculum.

- Plan projects in which children can represent their new understandings and concepts (for example, children can collaborate in small groups and publish books entitled "How Plants Grow," or they can make a videotape of their dramatization of *The Enormous Turnip*).

CULTURAL SENSITIVITY

The curriculum in literacy-rich classrooms reflects sensitivity for children's cultures in both its content (what is taught and what children are expected to read and write) and its instruction (how concepts are taught). In most classrooms one or more students have recently arrived in the United States and speak a language other than English at home. Many classrooms include children from a variety of cultural and language backgrounds. Regardless of the mixture of children in a particular classroom, all children need exposure to literature that presents nonstereotyped information about a wide variety of cultural groups.

Culture refers to the behaviors, values, attitudes, ideals, and beliefs shared and learned by a particular group of people. As a cultural group, people live and act in particular ways together. Learning about a culture, in part, means learning about those ways of living and acting together. Many social studies curricula focus on the architecture, family life, education, dances, songs, and art of particular cultural groups. But a culturally sensitive curriculum goes far beyond learning songs or cooking new foods in the classroom.

First, a culturally sensitive curriculum eliminates the artificial dichotomies created when studying "other" cultures; it includes examples from many cultures as a part of all learning experiences. That is, the content that children study and the material they read naturally presents many different cultures. Teachers are careful to include many examples of multicultural literature in all their literature theme units and discipline-focused themes. **Multicultural literature** consists of

- fiction with characters who are from cultural groups that have been underrepresented in children's books: African-Americans, Asian-Americans, Hispanic-Americans, Native Americans, and Americans from religious minorities;

- fiction that takes us to other nations and introduces readers to the cultures of people residing outside of the United States; and

- information books, including biographies, that focus on African-Americans, Asian-Americans, Hispanic-Americans, Native Americans, Americans from religious minorities, and people living outside the United States. (Zarillo, 1994, pp. 2–3)

The best in multicultural literature presents culturally authentic information (Bishop, 1992). **Culturally authentic literature** portrays people and the values, customs, and beliefs of a cultural group in ways recognized by members of that group as valid and authentic. Most culturally authentic literature is written or illustrated by members of the cultural group. Table 6.8 lists culturally authentic multicultural books that could be used in teaching the theme "Families".

Table 6.8 *Culturally Authentic Books about Families*

Choi, S. (1993). *Hal Moni and the picnic*. Boston: Houghton Mifflin.	Johnson, A. (1990). *Do like Kyla*. New York: Orchard.
Crews, D. (1991). *Big Mama's*. New York: Greenwillow	Kuklin, S. (1992). *How my family lives in America*. New York: Bradbury.
Dorros, A. (1991). *Abuela*. New York: Dutton.	Mathis, S. (1975). *The hundred penny box*. New York: Viking.
Garza, C. (1990). *Family pictures*. San Francisco: Children's Book Press.	Say, A. (1982). *The bicycle man*. Boston: Houghton Mifflin.
Giovanni, N. (1985). *Spin a soft black song*. New York: Harper and Collins.	Say, A. (1993). *Grandfather's journey*. Boston: Houghton Mifflin.
Greene, B. (1974). *Philip Hall likes me. I reckon maybe*. New York: Dial.	Soto, G. (1993). *Too many tamales*. New York: Putnam.
Greenfield, E. (1975). *Me and Nessie*. New York: Crowell.	Steptoe, J. (1969). *Stevie*. New York: Harper and Row.
Howard, E. (1991). *Aunt Flossie's hats (and crab cakes later)*. Boston: Houghton Mifflin.	Wright, C. (1994). *Jumping the broom*. New York: Holiday House.
Johnson, A. (1989). *Tell me a story, Mama*. New York: Orchard.	

An important part of a culturally sensitive curriculum is consideration of the language of instruction. Children learn best in their home language. However, many teachers are unable to provide instruction in children's home languages. They may not be qualified speakers of the language, or there may be children with several different home languages in one classroom. Teachers should always be sensitive to children's natural tendency to use home language to communicate complex ideas. Chapter 11 provides more information about teaching children whose home language is not English.

INSTRUCTION

Learning in literacy-rich classrooms takes place in a variety of settings. Children learn informally as they talk with each other and their teacher while engaged in literacy tasks together. In such settings teachers provide models or demonstrations of how to participate in reading and writing events. Teachers also facilitate learning through interactive discussions. Finally, teachers prepare thoughtful instruction that focuses on helping children learn specific information or strategies.

Demonstrations

Demonstrations provide learners with an opportunity to see what is done during reading and writing (Smith, 1988). Teachers demonstrate when they read aloud and respond to storybooks or write with children in the writing center. During demonstrations, teachers act as readers and writers (not as teachers of reading and writing). When they talk about their reading and writing, it is for the purpose of sharing with children something interesting they have done, rather than to teach children a new understanding or strategy.

In the following example, a preschool teacher provides a demonstration of using exclamation points (Rowe, 1994). As the teacher sits in the writing center with a small group of children, she writes a get-well card to another teacher. The card reads, "Dear Carol, We hope you get well SOON ! ! !" As she finishes writing, the teacher spells the word *soon* out loud and then tells why she put so many exclamation points on her card, "S-O-O-N, exclamation point, exclamation point, exclamation point. Because I want her to get well *soon*." A few moments later two of the children talk about exclamation points as they write in the center. Kira says, "And this is (pause) extamotion [sic] point. How come?" Hana suggests, "Put three cause it's big letters," and the teacher replies, "Because I want her to get well really, really, really soon. I want to really emphasize that." Later, Christina and Hana include exclamation points in their writing (Christina writes the letters *COI* written repeatedly inside one row of a rainbow with exclamation points written repeatedly inside another row, and Hana writes her name and fills the bottom of the page with upside down exclamation points) (Rowe, 1994, pp. 168–169).

In this example, the teacher did not intend to teach about exclamation points, and, certainly, knowing how to write and use exclamation points is not something teachers would expect preschoolers to learn. However, in the act of writing and talking about her writing, the teacher provided a demonstration of exclamation points about which some children were curious and which they were willing to use in their own writing.

In another example of a demonstration, two preschoolers talk about the formation of letters. Laurel announces to Terry, "Look at my *L*." But Terry argues, "It's a *V*, you silly." While Laurel insists she has written an *L*, Terry replies, "*That* is a *V*" (Lamme & Childers, 1983, p. 47). In this case, Terry's response to Laurel's demonstration of letter writing offers Laurel a learning opportunity. It is easy to imagine that Laurel discovered that the letter *L* has to be written just right in order not to be mistaken for the letter *V*.

Interactive Discussions

Intuitively teachers believe that asking the right kinds of questions at the right moment is a powerful instructional tool for helping children acquire new knowledge and engaging them in high-level thinking. Research reveals that much of the talk that goes on in classrooms occurs in three-part **IRE question-asking routines** (Cazden, 1988; Mehan, 1979).

1. The teacher *initiates* the routine by asking a question (usually about information that the teacher knows and expects that all children should learn).

2. The student *responds* to the question.

3. The teacher *evaluates* the response by repeating the student's answer (confirming its correctness), giving praise, or signaling an incorrect answer.

This routine helps children recite factual information and provides teachers with information regarding the children's understanding of concepts they have been taught.

Teachers in literacy-rich classrooms, however, are more interested in facilitating interactions in which children construct their own meaning rather than memorize information provided by the teacher. **Interactive discussions** call for less teacher talk and more talk from children, especially talk in which children talk to each other (Cazden, 1988). Grand conversations are one example of interactive discussions in which teachers facilitate children's meaning making (see the examples in Chapter 5, Figures 5.2 and 5.3).

Teachers also help students think more deeply about their responses when they ask students to extend, clarify, or justify their responses. Teachers prompt extended and clarified responses when they ask, "What makes you think that?" or "What do you mean by . . . ?" As teachers ask students to clarify and extend their answers, they use the children's language as a part of their prompts (Cazden, 1988). For example, a teacher asks about *Rosie's Walk* (Hutchins, 1968), "Does Rosie know the fox is back there?" and the student responds, "No. He's trying to trap her." The teacher uses the child's language as a part of an extending and clarifying prompt: "What do you mean *he's trying to trap her?* Does she know it's a *trap?*"

Modeling and Thinking Aloud

In the primary grades, teachers plan instruction. Planned instruction may be in part a response to an observed need and in part in response to dictates of the language arts and reading curricula. Effective instruction informs children of the need for the task or strategy being taught, when the task or strategy might be used, and how to complete the task or use the strategy. Many teachers use a combination of modeling and thinking aloud to teach strategies. **Modeling** involves demonstrating how to perform a strategy or accomplish a reading or writing activity. **Think alouds** are when teachers tell children what they are thinking as they carry out a reading or writing task or use a strategy.

For example, a second grade teacher decides to use modeling and think alouds to teach children how to write several kinds of responses to literature. He decides to model telling about a personal experience related to the story, telling what he would have done if he were in the story, and describing parts of the story that were confusing. He plans to teach these strategies during three short lessons, or *minilessons,* after reading aloud to the children. The teacher begins the mini-lesson on writing a personal response by reading a story aloud to the children, then explaining that sometimes when he writes in his journal, he thinks of something that happened to him, some personal experience that the story reminded him of. He models this by describing a personal experience that he remembered when he was reading the story. Then he says, "I'm going to write about that personal experience today in my journal." On an overhead projector, the teacher models writing a personal response. As he writes, he reads aloud, and then rereads his response again "to make sure it makes sense." Finally, he reminds the children that as they write in their response journals, they might want to remember a personal experience and write about that. Later, the teacher may invite children to share their personal responses.

As part of direct instruction, often teachers capitalize on strategies that they observe their children using. For example, a teacher may observe that children in the dramatic-play center are writing grocery lists by copying words from food coupons in the center. The teacher may ask these children to talk about their strategy in a whole-class gathering and invite other children to use this strategy in their play.

Chapter Summary

Early childhood professional organizations stress the importance of all aspects of children's development, including their cognitive, emotional, physical, social, and aesthetic abilities. These organizations recommend that children's literacy learning be embedded within child-centered early childhood programs with developmentally appropriate practices. Exemplary early childhood programs are found in literacy-rich classrooms where children are reflective, motivated readers and writers who use literacy to learn about their world.

To create literacy-rich classrooms, teachers select quality classroom literature collections that include traditional literature, fantasy, realistic fiction, historical fiction, biography, informational books, poetry, wordless picture books, pattern books, participation books, language play books, and alphabet books. They select reference materials, audiovisual materials, children's magazines, and writing materials.

Teachers infuse reading and writing materials throughout the room to encourage functional use of literacy. They may arrange dramatic-play centers with literacy themes or enrich learning centers with reading and writing materials. They set up a classroom library center partitioned from the room, with space for four to six children, and displays to motivate reading. They also arrange a writing center large enough for several children.

Teachers establish three daily routines using reading and writing. Teachers read or tell stories, poems, or informational books daily; they set aside time for children to read and write on topics of their choice; and they plan activities in which children share their writing and responses to literature. Responses to literature may include retelling, writing, talking, or dramatizing.

The curriculum is organized around literature theme units and discipline-focused themes that include talking, listening, reading, and writing activities. In literature theme units children learn about authors and illustrators, genres, or books with similar themes. In discipline-focused themes children learn about topics related to several disciplines. All theme units include multicultural literature.

Teachers provide instruction in a variety of settings as they demonstrate reading and writing, guide interactive discussions, and provide direct teaching through modeling and think alouds. They form a variety of groups, including whole-class gatherings, small groups, and partners, and they set aside time for children to work alone. Groups usually incorporate children with a variety of different ability levels who are encouraged to work cooperatively. Teachers assess children's literacy learning and use information from their assessments, in part, to guide decisions about instruction.

Applying the Information

A description of Mrs. E's kindergarten classroom and literacy activities follows. Use the nine characteristics of a literacy-rich classroom to think about the literacy environment in Mrs. E's classroom. Discuss how Mrs. E's classroom illustrates each of the nine characteristics. We believe that Mrs. E is very supportive of literacy learning, but she is always looking for ways to improve her literacy program. What suggestions might you make about room arrangement and instruction?

Mrs. E has twenty-two kindergartners in a relatively small room. Nearly all of the children who attend this school receive free lunch (their families fall below the poverty limit established by the federal government). A map of the classroom is presented in Figure 6.9. This map illustrates that Mrs. E's room is equipped with twenty-eight desks and one table. The entire room is carpeted.

Each morning Mrs. E reads at least one selection of children's literature to the entire class. The children gather around her on the rug in the large-group area. Next, Mrs. E has experience time. During this time she might demonstrate a science experiment, have a guest speaker, or read nonfiction. Each of these daily experiences is related to a topic of study. For example, one unit of study focused on insects. A man who keeps bees visited the classroom and brought his equipment to the class. The children kept ants in an ant farm. Mrs. E read many books that had insects as characters as well as informational books about insects.

After experience time, the children usually dictate and read accounts of what they learned that day or dictate retellings of favorite stories or charts. Sometimes Mrs. E prepares her own accounts of the previous day's experience for the children to read with her. She also frequently writes short stories or poems using the content of the children's study unit and a pattern from a pattern book she had earlier shared with the children. One day she wrote

Caterpillar, caterpillar what do you see?
I see a beetle looking at me.

using the pattern from *Brown Bear, Brown Bear* (Martin, 1983) as a part of the insect unit.

Next, Mrs. E holds a five to ten minute lesson or discussion designed to motivate the children to write. During the insect unit children were encouraged to write poems, stories, and pattern stories about insects. One of the lessons Mrs. E taught was to show the children a poster she had made about the letters *b* and *c*. On the poster were several pictures of objects with names beginning with these letters (*boat, bat, beaver, cat, candy, cookie*). Mrs. E reminded the children that as they listened to words they wanted to write, they might hear some sounds like those in the words *boat* or *cat*. They could use the letters *b* and *c*.

After the lesson, the children write at their desks. Mrs. E circulates around the room asking questions, making comments, and answering children's questions. As the children finish their writing, they read their writing to each other, select books from the library center, or read child-authored poems, stories, and books that are kept on the authors' tables.

Last, Mrs. E holds author's chair. (A special chair is placed in the group area on the rug for a child to sit in as he or she reads his or her writing.) Many children have opportunities to read their writing. The children know that they may choose to "talk about their writing" or

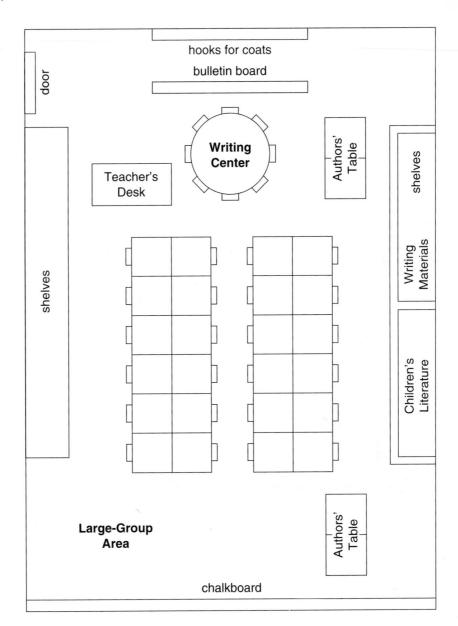

Figure 6.9 *Mrs. E's Classroom*

"read what they wrote." They feel very comfortable as the other children make comments and offer praise. Mrs. E always comments on some aspect of the content of the writing, "I didn't know there were ants called carpenters. We will need to read more about them. Will you help me find out about them?"

Going Beyond the Text

Visit a preschool or elementary school classroom and observe literacy instruction and activities. Look carefully at the literacy materials that are available in the room. Note how often children interact with these literacy materials. Observe the children and their teacher as they interact during literacy instruction and as the children work on literacy projects. Use the nine characteristics of literacy-rich classrooms as a guide for discussing your observations.

References

AARDEMA, V. (1975). *Why mosquitoes buzz in people's ears*. New York: Dial.

ABRAHAMSON, R. F. (1981). An update on wordless picture books with an annotated bibliography. *The Reading Teacher, 34,* 417–421.

ABRAHAMSON, R. F., & STEWART, R. (1982). Movable books—a new Golden age. *Language Arts, 59,* 342–347.

ADAMS, M. (1990). *Beginning to read: Thinking and learning about print*. Cambridge: MIT Press.

ALLINGTON, R. (1983). The reading instruction provided readers of differing ability. *Elementary School Journal, 83,* 255–265.

ANDERSON, R. C., HIEBERT, E. H., SCOTT, J. A., & WILKINSON, I. A. G. (1985). *Becoming a nation of readers: The report of the commission on reading*. Washington, D. C.: The National Institute of Education.

AU, K. (1993). *Literacy instruction in multicultural settings*. New York: Harcourt Brace Jovanovich.

BARONE, D. (1990). The written response of young children: Beyond comprehension. *The New Advocate, 3,* 49–56.

BARR, R., & DREEBEN, R. (1991). Grouping Students for reading instruction. In R. Barr, M. Kamil, P. Mosenthal & P. Pearson (Eds.), *Handbook of reading research, vol. 2* (p. 885–910). White Plains, NY: Longman.

BAYLEY, N. (1977). *One old Oxford ox*. New York: Atheneum.

BERGHOFF, B., & EGAWA, K. (1991). No more "rocks": Grouping to give students control of their learning. *The Reading Teacher, 44,* 536–541.

BIERHORST, J. (trans.) (1987). *Doctor Coyote: A native American Aesop's fables*. New York: Macmillan.

BISHOP, R. (1992). Multicultural literature for children: Making informed choices. In V. Harris (Ed.), *Teaching multicultural literature in grades K–8.* (pp. 37–53). Norwood, MA: Christopher-Gordon.

BLUME, J. (1974). *The pain and the great one*. New York: Bradbury.

BREDEKAMP, S. (Ed.). (1987). *Developmentally appropriate practice* (extended ed.). Washington, D.C.: National Association for the Education of Young Children.

BRIDGE, C. (1986). Predictable books for beginning readers and writers. In M. R. Sampson (Ed.), *The pursuit of literacy: Early reading and writing* (pp. 81–96). Dubuque, IA: Kendall/Hunt.

BROWN, M. (1961). *Once a mouse*. New York: Aladdin.

BROWN, R. (1981). *A dark dark tale*. New York: Dial.

BRYAN, A. (1980). *Beat the story-drum, pum-pum*. New York: Antheneum.

BUNTING, E. (1990). *The wall*. New York: Clarion.

BUNTING, E. (1991). *Fly away home*. New York: Clarion.

BURNIE, D. (1994). *Dictionary of nature*. London: Dorling Kindersley.

CALKINS, L. M. (1986). *The art of teaching writing*. Portsmouth, NH: Heinemann.

CARLE, E. (1970). *The very hungry caterpillar*. New York: Viking.

CASTLE, C. (1985). *The hare and the tortoise*. New York: Dial.

CAULEY, L. (1981). *Goldilocks and the three bears*. New York: Putnam.

CAULEY, L. (1984). *The town mouse and the country mouse*. New York: Putnam.

CAZDEN, C. (1988). *Classroom discourse*. Portsmouth, NH: Heinemann.

CHOMSKY, C. (1972). Stages in language development and reading exposure. *Harvard Educational Review, 42,* 1–33.

CLEARY, B. (1968). *Ramona the pest.* New York: Morrow.

CLEARY, B. (1977). *Ramona and her mother.* New York: Morrow.

CLEARY, B. (1981). *Ramona Quimby, age 8.* New York: Morrow.

CLIATT, M., & SHAW, J. (1988). The storytime exchange: Ways to enhance it. *Childhood Education, 64,* 293–298.

COLE, J. (1986). *The magic school bus at the waterworks.* New York: Scholastic.

COLE, J. (1987). *The magic school bus inside the earth.* New York: Scholastic.

COLE, J. (1989). *The magic school bus inside the human body.* New York: Scholastic.

COLE, J. (1990). *The magic school bus lost in the solar system.* New York: Scholastic.

COONEY, B. (1982). *Miss Rumphius.* New York: Viking.

DEFORD, D., PINNELL, G., LYONS, C., & PLACE, Q. (1990). *Report of the follow-up study, Columbus Reading Recovery program 1988–1989* (Report Vol. 11). Columbus: The Ohio State University.

de PAOLA, T. (1978). *Pancakes for breakfast.* New York: Harcourt Brace Jovanovich.

de PAOLA, T. (1989). *The art lesson.* New York: Putnam.

DEKKER, M. (1991). Books, reading, and response: A teacher-researcher tells a story. *The New Advocate, 4,* 37–46.

de REGNIERS, B., MOORE, E., WHITE, M., & CARR, J. (Compilers). (1988). *Sing a song of popcorn: Every child's book of poems.* New York: Scholastic.

DEWEY, J. (1933). *How we think* (rev. ed.). Boston: Heath.

DICKINSON, D., & SMITH, M. (1994). Long-term effects of preschool teachers' book readings on low-income children's vocabulary and story comprehension. *Reading Research Quarterly, 29,* 104–122.

DRESSEL, J. (1990). The effects of listening to and discussing different qualities of children's literature on the narrative writing of fifth graders. *Research in the Teaching of English, 24,* 397–414.

EEDS, M., & WELLS, D. (1989). Grand conversations: An exploration of meaning construction in literature study groups. *Research in the Teaching of English, 23,* 4–29.

EHLERT, L. (1989). *Eating the alphabet.* New York: Harcourt Brace Jovanovich.

ELLIOTT, S., NOWOSAD, J., & SAMUELS, P. (1981). "Me at School," "Me at Home": Using journals with preschoolers. *Language Arts, 58,* 688–691.

EVANS, M. A., & CARR, T. H. (1985). Cognitive abilities, conditions of learning, and the early development of reading skill. *Reading Research Quarterly, 20,* 327–350.

FEITELSON, D., KITA, B., & GOLDSTEIN, Z. (1986). The effects of listening to series stories on first graders' comprehension and use of language. *Research in the Teaching of English, 20,* 336–356.

FERDMAN, B. (1990). Literacy and cultural identity. *Harvard Educational Review, 60,* 181–204.

FIELD, T. (1980). Preschool play: Effects of teacher/child ratios and organization of classroom space. *Child Study Journal, 10,* 191–205.

FIVE, C. (1986). Fifth graders respond to a changed reading program. *Harvard Educational Review, 56,* 395–405.

FRACTOR, J., WOODRUFF, M., MARTINEZ, M., & TEALE, W. (1993). Let's not miss opportunities to promote voluntary reading: Classroom libraries in elementary school. *The Reading Teacher, 46,* 476–484.

GALDONE, P. (1970). *The three little pigs.* New York: Seabury.

GALDONE, P. (1973). *The three billy goats gruff.* New York: Seabury.

GALDONE, P. (1975). *The gingerbread boy.* New York: Clarion.

GELLER, L. (1985). *Word play and language learning for children.* Urbana, IL: National Council of Teachers of English.

GENISHI, C., MCCARRIER, A., & NUSSBAUM, N. R. (1988). Research currents: Classroom interaction as teaching and learning. *Language Arts, 65,* 182–191.

GLAZER, J. I. (1981). *Literature for young children.* Columbus, OH: Merrill.

GOLENBOCK, P. (1990). *Teammates.* San Diego: Harcourt Brace Jovanovich.

GRAVES, D. H. (1983). Teacher intervention in children's writing: A response to Myra Barrs. *Language Arts, 10,* 841–846.

GRIMM, J., & GRIMM, W. (1989). *Frog Prince.* New York: North-South.

HARTMAN, D., & HARTMAN, J. (1993). Reading across texts: Expanding the role of the reader. *The Reading Teacher, 47,* 202–211.

HEATH, S. B. (1983). *Ways with words: Language, life, and work in communities and classrooms*. New York: Cambridge University Press.

HEINIG, R. B., & STILLWELL, L. (1981). *Creative drama for the classroom teacher* (2nd ed.). Englewood Cliffs, NJ: Prentice-Hall.

HICKMAN, J. (1979). *Response to literature in a school environment. Doctoral dissertation*, The Ohio State University, Columbus, OH.

HICKMAN, J. (1981). A new perspective on response to literature: Research in an elementary school setting. *Research in the Teaching of English, 15*, 343–354.

HIEBERT, E., & COLT, J. (1989). Patterns of literature-based reading instruction. *The Reading Teacher, 43*, 14–20.

HILL, E. (1980). *Where's Spot?* New York: Putnam.

HIPPLE, M. L. (1985). Journal writing in kindergarten. *Language Arts, 62*, 255–261.

HODGES, M. (1984). *Saint George and the dragon*. Boston: Little, Brown.

HOFFMAN, J., ROSER, N., & BATTLE, J. (1993). Reading aloud in classrooms: From the modal toward a "model." *The Reading Teacher, 46*, 496–503.

HOWARD, K. (1971). *Little bunny follows his nose*. Racine, WI: Western.

HOWE, D., & HOWE, J. (1979). *Bunnicula: A rabbit tale of mystery*. New York: Atheneum.

HUCK, C. S., HEPLER, S., & HICKMAN, J. (1987). *Children's literature in the elementary school* (4th ed.). New York: Holt, Rinehart and Winston.

HUGHES, M. (1991). *Curriculum integration in the primary grades: A framework for excellence*. Alexandria, VA: Association of Supervision and Curriculum Development.

HUTCHINS, P. (1968). *Rosie's walk*. New York: Macmillan.

HYMAN, T. (1983). *Little red riding hood*. New York: Holiday House.

JORDAN, H. (1992). *How a seed grows*. New York: HarperCollins.

JUKES, M. (1984). *Like Jake and me*. New York: Knopf.

KAMII, C., & RANDAZZO, M. (1985). Social interaction and invented spelling. *Language Arts, 62*, 124–133.

KEATS, E. (1962). *The snowy day*. New York: Puffin.

KEEGAN, M. (1991). *Pueblo boy: Growing up in two worlds*. New York: Dutton.

KELLY, P. (1990). Guiding young students' response to literature. *The Reading Teacher, 44*, 464–470.

KINTISCH, L. S. (1986). Journal writing: Stages of development. *The Reading Teacher, 40*, 168–172.

KITCHEN, B. (1992). *Somewhere today*. Cambridge, MA: Candlewick Press.

LAMME, L. L., & CHILDERS, N. M. (1983). The composing processes of three young children. *Research in the Teaching of English, 17*, 33–50.

LASKY, K. (1983). *Sugaring time*. New York: Macmillan.

LESTER, J. (1987). *The Tales of Uncle Remus: The adventures of Brer Rabbit*. New York: Dial.

LINFORS, J. W. (1988). From "talking together" to "being together in talk." *Language Arts, 65*, 135–141.

LIPSON, M., VALENCIA, S., WIXSON, K., & PETERS, C. (1993). Integration and thematic teaching: Integration to improve teaching and learning. *Language Arts, 70*, 252–263.

LOBEL, A. (1981). *On market street*. New York: Greenwillow.

LOUIE, A. (1982). *Yeh-Shen: A Cinderella story from China*. New York: Philomel.

LYNCH-BROWN, C., & TOMLINSON, C. (1993). *The essentials of children's literature*. Boston: Allyn and Bacon.

MACLACHLAN, P. (1985). *Sarah, plain and tall*. New York: Harper and Row.

The Macmillan visual dictionary. (1992). New York: Macmillan.

MADDERN, E. (1993). *The fire children: A West African creation tale*. New York: Dial.

MARTIN, B., Jr. (1983). *Brown bear, brown bear, what do you see?* New York: Holt, Rinehart and Winston.

MARTINEZ, M. (1993). Motivating dramatic story reenactments. *The Reading Teacher, 46*, 682–688.

MCCORMICK, S. (1994). A nonreader becomes a reader: A case study of literacy acquisition by a severely disabled reader. *Reading Research Quarterly, 29*, 156–176.

MCDERMOTT, G. (1972). *Anansi the spider: A tale from the Ashanti*. New York: Henry Holt.

MCGEE, L. (1992). Meaning construction in first graders' grand conversations. In C. Kinzer & D. Leu (Eds.), *Literacy research, theory, and practice: Views from many perspectives* (pp. 177–187). Chicago: The National Reading Conference.

McGEE, L. M., & CHARLESWORTH, R. (1984). Movable books: More than novelties. *The Reading Teacher, 37,* 853–859.

MCGILL-FRANZEN, A. (1992). Early literacy: What does "developmentally appropriate" mean? *The Reading Teacher, 46,* 56–58.

MEHAN, H. (1979). *Learning lessons.* Cambridge: Harvard University Press.

MORROW, L. (1992). The impact of a literature-based program on literacy achievement, use of literature, and attitudes of children from minority backgrounds. *Reading Research Quarterly, 27,* 250–275.

MORROW, L., & RAND, M. (1991). Promoting literacy during play by designing early childhood classroom environments. *The Reading Teacher, 44,* 396–402.

MORROW, L. M., & WEINSTEIN, C. S. (1982). Increasing children's use of literature through program and physical design changes. *The Elementary School Journal, 83,* 131–137.

MORROW, L. M., & WEINSTEIN, C. S. (1986). Encouraging voluntary reading: The impact of a literature program on children's use of library centers. *Reading Research Quarterly, 21,* 330–346.

MOSS, T. (1993). *I want to be.* New York: Dial.

MOYER, J., EGERTSON, H., & ISENBERG, J. (1987). The child centered kindergarten. *Childhood Education, 63,* 235–245.

My first encyclopedia. (1993). London: Dorling Kindersley.

NEUMAN, S., & ROSKOS, K. (1990). Play, print and purpose: Enriching play environments for literacy development. *The Reading Teacher, 44,* 214–221.

NEUMAN, S., & ROSKOS, K. (1992). Literacy objects as cultural tools: Effects on children's literacy behaviors in play. *Reading Research Quarterly, 27,* 202–225.

NORTON, D. (1991). *Through the eyes of a child: An introduction to children's literature* (3rd ed.). New York: Merrill/Macmillan.

OLDFATHER, P. (1993). What students say about motivating experiences in a whole language classroom. *The Reading Teacher, 46,* 672–681.

ORMEROD, J. (1981). *Sunshine.* New York: Lothrop.

PALLOTTA, J. (1986). *The yucky reptile alphabet book.* Watertown, MA: Ivory Tower.

PARISH, P. (1963). *Amelia Bedelia.* New York: Harper and Row.

PARKES, B., & SMITH, J. (1986). *The enormous watermelon.* Crystal Lake, IL: Rigby.

PARKINSON, K. (1986). *The enormous turnip.* Niles, IL: Albert Whitman.

PEET, B. (1989). *Bill Peet: An autobiography.* Boston: Houghton Mifflin.

PEINKOWSKI, J. (1980). *Dinnertime.* New York: Price/Stern/Sloan.

POLACCO, P. (1990). *Babushka's doll.* New York: Simon and Schuster.

PRELUTSKY, J. (1983). *The Random House book of poetry for children.* New York: Random House.

RADENCICH, M., & BOHNING, G. (1988). Popup, pull down, push in, slide out. *Childhood Education, 64,* 157–160.

The Random House children's encyclopedia (rev. ed.). (1992). New York: Random House.

RHODES, L. K. (1981). I can read! Predictable books as resources for reading and writing. *The Reading Teacher, 34,* 511–518.

RINGGOLD, F. (1991). *Tar beach.* New York: Crown.

Roget's children's thesaurus (rev. ed.). (1994). New York: HarperCollins.

ROOF, B. (1993). *My first dictionary.* London: Dorling Kindersley.

ROSS, R. R. (1980). *Storyteller.* (2nd ed.). Columbus, OH: Merrill.

ROUTMAN, R. (1991). *Invitations: Changing as teachers and learners K-12.* Portsmouth, NH: Heinemann.

ROWE, D. (1994). *Preschoolers as authors: Literacy learning in the social world.* Cresskill, NJ: Hampton Press.

SAY, A. (1990). *El Chino.* Boston: Houghton Mifflin

SENDAK, M. (1962). *Chicken soup with rice.* New York: Harper and Row.

SENDAK, M. (1963). *Where the wild things are.* New York: Harper and Row.

SEUSS, DR. (THEODORE GEISEL) (1963). *Hop on Pop.* New York: Random House.

SHORT, K. (1993). *Literature circles: Talking with young children about books.* Presentation at the International Reading Association, San Antonio, TX.

SIMON, S. (1989). *Storms.* New York: Mulberry.

SLAVIN, R. (1986). *Using student team learning* (3rd ed.). Baltimore: Johns Hopkins University, Center for Research on Elementary and Middle Schools.

SMITH, F. (1988). *Understanding reading* (4th ed.). Hillsdale, NJ: Erlbaum.

STEIG, W. (1969). *Sylvester and the magic pebble.* New York: Farrar, Straus and Giroux.

STEIG, W. (1972). *Dominic*. New York: Farrar, Straus and Giroux.

STEPTOE, J. (1969). *Stevie*. New York: Harper and Row.

STEPTOE, J. (1984). *The story of jumping mouse*. New York: Mulberry.

STEWIG, J. W. (1983). *Informal drama in the elementary language arts program*. New York: Teachers College Press.

THARP, R. (1982). The effective instruction of comprehension: Results and description of Kamehameha Early Education Program. *Reading Research Quarterly, 17,* 503–527.

TOMPKINS, G. E., & MCGEE, L. M. (1989). Teaching repetition as a story structure. In D. M. Glynn (Ed.), *Children's comprehension of text* (pp. 59–78). Newark, DE: International Reading Association.

TOMPKINS, G., & MCGEE, L. (1993). *Teaching reading with literature: Case studies to action plans*. New York: Merrill/Macmillan.

TRESSELT, A. (1964). *The mitten*. New York: Lothrop.

TUNNELL, M. O. (1993). *The joke's on George*. New York: Tambourine.

TURKLE, B. (1976). Deep in the forest. New York: Dutton.

TURNER, A. (1985). *Dakota dugout*. New York: Aladdin.

VAN ALLSBURG, C. (1987). *The Z was zapped*. Boston: Houghton Mifflin.

VARS, G. (1991). Integrated curriculum in historical perspective. *Educational Leadership, 49,* 14–15.

VUKELICH, C. (1993). Play: A context for exploring the functions, features, and meaning of writing with peers. *Language Arts, 70,* 386–392.

VUONG, L. (1982). *The brocaded slipper and other Vietnamese tales*. New York: Addison-Wesley.

WATSON, C. (1982). *Applebet*. New York: Farrar, Straus and Giroux.

WILKES, A. (1991). *My first word book*. London: Dorling Kindersley.

WILKES, A. (1993). *My first Spanish word book*. London: Dorling Kindersley.

WISNIEWSKI, D. (1990). *Elfwyn's saga*. New York: Lothrop, Lee and Shepherd.

XIONG, B. (1989). *Nine-in-one. Grr! Grr!*. San Francisco: Children's Book Press.

YORINKS, A. (1986). *Hey, Al*. New York: Farrar, Straus and Giroux.

ZARRILLO, J. (1994). *Multicultural literature, multicultural teaching: Units for the elementary grades*. New York: Harcourt Brace Jovanovich.

CHAPTER 7

Supporting Literacy Learning in Preschools

In this chapter we describe how teachers provide support for children's language and literacy learning in preschools. We begin the chapter with a description of one child's reading and writing in Ms. Reyes's preschool classroom. This case study demonstrates both what we can expect some preschoolers to do as they read and write and the kind of support that adults can provide for preschoolers' reading and writing. Next we examine the expectations for language and literacy learning in the contexts of preschools—we discuss what we would expect a preschool setting to be like as well as the kinds of learnings that we could expect to occur in preschools. We describe the physical layout and materials that are found in one exemplary preschool.

In the remainder of the chapter we present four methods of supporting preschoolers' language and literacy development. First, preschool teachers infuse print into the classroom so that young children interact with print throughout the day. We show how this is done in Mrs. Miller's preschool classroom, a classroom in which all the children are considered at-risk learners (see Chapter 11 for a description of at risk). Second, preschool teachers organize group reading experiences and response-to-literature activities. We describe Miss Leslie's booksharing activities. Third, preschool teachers devise a variety of writing opportunities. They plan group writing experiences and opportunities for children to explore writing at the writing center and in other activities. Finally, teachers arrange for playful activities in which children tell stories, act out stories, and pretend to use reading and writing in special dramatic-play centers.

Key Concepts _____

"I can read" bags	sampling, predicting, confirming cycle	sign-in procedure
environmental print puzzles	Directed Listening-Thinking Activity (DLTA)	pattern writing
letter game		list making
graph	literary prop boxes	written language talk
booksharing	concept-about-story activities	dramatic-play-with-print centers
clothesline props		
booksharing techniques	big books	story telling and playing

READING AND WRITING IN MS. REYES'S PRESCHOOL CLASSROOM

Ms. Reyes teaches in a university laboratory preschool. She welcomes many visitors into her classroom. One important way of helping preschoolers become better language users is to provide them frequent and sustained interactions with adults. Good preschool teachers know that supporting language and literacy learning in their classrooms is a matter of providing children opportunities to read and write, numerous demonstrations of reading and writing, and an attentive and appreciative audience as they engage in reading and writing in their own ways.

Caitie Reads and Writes

In the following case study, Caitie reads and writes as we would expect a novice to do (see Chapter 3), and Mr. Richgels, a frequent visitor in the classroom, provides a sensitive audience for her reading and writing—an important role for preschool teachers.

Writing

During one of Mr. Richgels's visits to Ms. Reyes's classroom, he thanked four-year-old Caitie for reading a book to him during his previous visit and asked her if she would like to write a story this time. Caitie begins by reminding him that she does not know how to read.

Caitie:	I don't know how to read.
Mr. Richgels:	Well, you know how to do your own kind of reading, though—
Caitie:	Yeah.
Mr. Richgels:	—because you did that with me the last time I was here.
Caitie:	Yeah. . . .
Mr. Richgels:	Even if it's your own way that's okay . . . I know that you don't write the same way that grownups do but that's okay. You just write it the way—
Caitie:	I know what story I should write.
Mr. Richgels:	What should you write?
Caitie:	Robin Hood—that's the way—and I should write the end part.
Mr. Richgels:	Okay. That would be great.
Caitie:	But I don't have to write that up way, down way.

Mr. Richgels succeeds in assuring Caitie that she can write, and with this assurance Caitie remembers a well-known story that she can use as a prompt for her writing. One of Caitie's favorite books is a read-along book and tape, Walt Disney Productions' *The Story of Robin Hood* (Disney Productions, 1973). Her parents reported that Caitie had listened to the audiotape and followed along in the twenty-four-page picture book many times at home. Caitie begins writing her Robin Hood story by taking up a crayon and drawing the main characters, Maid Marian and Robin Hood, the two large figures with raised arms at the center and left of center in Figure 7.1. She explains as she writes, "That's Maid Marian. . . . I'm going to draw Robin Hood much taller than Maid Marian. . . . Tail, arms."

Like all the characters in Caitie's Disney book, Robin Hood and Maid Marian are animal cartoon characters. They have tails because they are foxes, and Caitie is

Figure 7.1 *Caitie's Robin Hood Story*

attentive to this detail as she writes/draws. She is attentive to many of the details in the book's illustrations. For example, at the beginning of the story, Prince John is riding through the forest in a carriage pulled by elephants, with rhinoceroses carrying his treasure chest, as Robin Hood and Little John watch from a tree. After drawing Robin Hood and Maid Marian, Caitie draws the shapes in the bottom right corner of Figure 7.1 and explains, "Those are the guys—those are the elephants. I don't draw elephants very good. . . . And rhino guys."

As she draws the figure with a big head and small arms to the right of Robin Hood, Caitie explains, "Little John's a bear." Then Caitie draws the spiral-like shape and the figure next to it at the top of Figure 7.1 and explains, "Here's Skippy's coin. The Sheriff of Nottingham took it. . . . Now I have to draw Robin Hood . . . his bow and arrow." Caitie draws the figures directly above her original large drawings of Maid Marian and Robin Hood in Figure 7.1. Mr. Richgels asks, "That's his bow and arrow?"

Caitie's talk changes from describing her drawing to speaking in character. She says in a deep voice, imitating Robin Hood, "Here, Skippy—take my bow and arrow, and here's my hat. It's a little big, Skippy, but you'll grow into it."

Again, Caitie is faithful to the version of the story of Robin Hood in her favorite book. In that version, Skippy, a little rabbit friend of Robin Hood's, is the victim of the sheriff's men. They take his birthday-present penny; Robin compensates by giving Skippy his bow and arrow and hat. Robin's words on page seven are exactly as Caitie told them, except that she added the second *Skippy,* after "It's a little big."

The last page of the Disney book shows Robin Hood and Maid Marian waving from the back window of a carriage, to which is attached a "Just Married" sign, as they leave their wedding. Keeping to her stated plan to "write the end part," Caitie now draws a picture of this carriage. It is the round object with many circles attached between Maid Marian and Robin Hood in Figure 7.1. Caitie says, "There their thing is. One wheel, two wheel, three wheel, four wheel, five wheel."

Then Caitie writes the letterlike forms at the bottom of Figure 7.1. She begins under the large figure of Robin Hood and continues to the left edge of her page. She is finished with her story, but not with her writing.

So far Caitie has used crayon, but now she picks up a pencil and announces a new project. She says, "I'm going to write my name." She writes the recognizable letters above Skippy's coin, now writing from left to right. She wrote the *C* while she was saying, "I'm going to write my name." Now she says other letter names from *Caitie* as if spelling her name, "A-I-T-I-T." But she is not finished with this different kind of writing. She says, "Now I'm going to draw my phone number." She writes her phone number with the recognizable numerals to the left of her drawing of Little John, naming each as she writes it. The last four numbers are 3100; she says, "Three, one, zero, zero. One zero, two zero."

Whether because she realizes she has left out a digit or for some other reason, Caitie decides to write her phone number again, this time beneath her drawing of Little John. She says, "I need to draw a little better." Now she writes all seven digits of her phone number, the first three left to right and the last four under them, right to left, again naming each as she writes it.

Reading

When Mr. Richgels asks Caitie to read her story, she points to the first of the mock letters at the bottom of her page. But before reading she sings a song about Robin Hood. While she sings, she takes her finger off the page and looks away from her writing, signaling that she is not intending her singing as a reading. Then she begins reading, pointing again to her first mock letter.

Remember that Caitie's drawing/writing contained several elements from the Disney book version of the story of Robin Hood, including elements from the beginning (Prince John in his coach), middle (Skippy's birthday party), and end (Robin Hood and Maid Marian's wedding coach). Her reading of her writing is even more complete. It includes all the key events and much written-language-like telling of the Disney version. In the following excerpt, when Caitie's words are the same as the Disney text, they are underlined.

> (Caitie has been reading about an archery tournament sponsored by Prince John and attended by Robin Hood and Little John in disguise. Using a low voice and the exact words of the Disney text, she quoted Prince John's declaring Robin Hood the loser. Then she steps out of her storyreading voice and speaks in an aside to Mr. Richgels.)

> Caitie: They're gonna cut Robin Hood's head off!

> Mr. Richgels: Oh no!

> Caitie: (back to her storyreading voice) And Marian cried. And then. Uh— cried—John's ready—

(Caitie makes a series of false starts and hesitations. She gets off track when, confusing Prince John and Little John, she again quotes Prince John's declaration that Robin Hood is the loser. But then she gets back on track with Little John's next line.)

>   Caitie: Kuh, uh, uh "<u>Let my friend go or else!</u>"—
>
> Mr. Richgels: Uh hmm.
>
>   Caitie: —said Little John. <u>Once Robin was free, a big fight began. Swords clashed</u>—
>
> Mr. Richgels: Yeah
>
>   Caitie: —<u>and arrows flew</u>.

As Caitie reads her writing of the Robin Hood story, she moves her finger along the line of mock letters from right to left, as she wrote them, being careful not to reach the left-most form until she is at the end of her story.

Caitie as a Novice Writer and Reader

This case study contains many examples of behaviors characteristic of a novice. Given an invitation to write and read, Caitie, who declares herself a nonreader, reveals remarkable, though nonalphabetic, reading and writing strategies. She understands much about meaning making, forms, meaning-form links, and functions of written language.

Caitie's primary strategy for meaning making was to combine three symbol systems, drawing, talking, and writing (Dyson, 1985). She began writing by picking up a crayon and drawing, but that was almost immediately accompanied by her talk—talk that ranged from description ("That's Maid Marian"), to self-evaluation ("I don't draw elephants very good"), to text creation ("Here, Skippy—take my bow and arrow"). The text she created by talking during her drawing resembled and was often reproduced in her reading of her own writing. Both originated in the text of the Disney book with which she was so familiar.

Caitie's talk played another role for her novice meaning making—a role we sometimes associate only with much more sophisticated writers. It served a planning function. This function was evident when she said, "I should write the end part," "I'm going to draw Robin Hood much taller than Maid Marian," "Now I have to draw Robin Hood," "I'm going to write my name," and "Now I'm going to draw my phone number."

Although Caitie's primary writing strategy was to draw, and she used the words *draw* and *write* interchangeably (as the examples just quoted demonstrate), she did use two other writing strategies. First, she made mock letters to create a text to accompany her pictures. She demonstrated her appreciation of the power of that text by pointing exclusively to it when reading her story. Second, she wrote her name and telephone number with conventional or nearly conventional—certainly recognizable—letters and numerals. She demonstrated her perception of these as unique texts by writing them as distinct, separate adjuncts to an already completed story, by naming the letters and numerals as she wrote them, and by using pencil rather than crayon to write them.

The Teacher's Role

It is important to note the teacher's role in this case study. Although it may appear small—it shows as only a few short turns in the quoted dialogue of the case study—it is important. Mr. Richgels's invitations to Caitie were invitations to write and read on her own terms, "in your own way." Caitie's writing and reading exemplify what even preschoolers can do when teachers help them reduce the risk of failure. Mr. Richgels was willing to accept anything that Caitie called writing as writing (for her, writing was drawing, writing mock letters, and writing her name and phone number). He allowed Caitie to define what was reading (for her, it was telling a story and pointing to print). This is a critical teacher role—allowing children to negotiate the terms of their participation. This role encourages children to take a risk and to try reading and writing in a way that lets them feel safe. They know that the person taking this role will really appreciate their reading and writing!

This case study also illustrates the benefits of good home–school communication. Mr. Richgels and Ms. Reyes were able to learn more about Caitie's listening and reading routine with her book and tape version of the *Story of Robin Hood* by sharing her at-school Robin Hood composition with her parents. Caitie's teachers were able to extend the initial composing and rereading episode to a bookreading episode by asking Caitie's mother to help her remember to bring her book to school the next day. Caitie brought the book to school and read it with much of the same language she used in her reading of her own writing. She told the complete story, included written-language-like wording, and often matched the words of the text. This not only taught her teachers more about how Caitie reads and how her bookreading is connected to her composing and rereading, it also gave Caitie a very positive experience as a reader at school.

THE PRESCHOOL CONTEXT

Every classroom is a context for the interaction of two powerful currents: what children bring to the classroom, and what teachers, parents, school administrators, school boards, and taxpayers expect of schools. A significant part of any teacher's effective support of language and literacy learning is to plan for this inevitable interaction. In one way, the children's contribution remains the same: no matter at what grade level, from preschool through the primary grades, children present teachers with all or nearly all of the array of literacy knowledges described in Chapters 3 through 5. That is, although the relative proportions represented by each group vary depending on their home and previous school experiences, it is likely that some children in any classroom will be novices, some experimenters, and some conventional readers and writers. The expectations for what children ought to learn, however, change significantly from preschool, to kindergarten, to first grade, and beyond. Society, teachers, school systems, and parents have quite definite and unique expectations about the outcomes of literacy instruction for each level.

In each of the classroom chapters that follow (chapters 8, 9, and 10), we will describe how these expectations change in a section entitled What's New Here? In this chapter, we present the expectations of the preschool context.

Ironically, there is often little or no expectation for children's literacy learning in preschools. Early childhood educators have long been concerned with the development of the whole child, including academic, social, and emotional development (see Chapter 6). We share this concern. We also believe, however, that there is an active role for teachers at all grade levels, and that part of preschool teachers' planning in the whole-child context should be to provide literacy-learning opportunities appropriate to children's social and emotional states and congruent with their developing literacy knowledge. We will show that it is possible to meet the needs of the whole child—to avoid tipping out of balance in an academic direction—while supporting literacy acquisition. In the preschool, we suggest that this approach includes offering frequent, genuine opportunities to participate in literacy events and involves an appreciation for what children know so that, as Caitie did, they can read and write on their own terms.

This teacher role is demanding, for even at the preschool level, children's knowledge and their terms for engagement are quite varied. It is, however, a necessary role. Without frequent opportunities to engage in literacy events in preschool, children whose homes offer few such opportunities are at a disadvantage in kindergarten and the primary grades. They will be less successful at learning to read and write in those grades than their peers whose homes offer many literacy opportunities.

This point is worth repeating. It is crucial that children with few experiences with written language in their homes have especially rich preschool experiences. Preschool teachers must provide demonstrations of reading and writing (which we show later in this chapter in Mrs. Miller's and Miss Leslie's classrooms). They must also engage children in reading and writing activities and become especially attentive and sensitive audiences to children's efforts. In the following sections we describe a preschool setting that surrounds children with print and encourages their reading and writing.

THE PRESCHOOL SETTING: SPACE AND MATERIALS

One of the teacher's roles in preschool is to arrange spaces and select materials that will engage children's active exploration of their environment through construction and play. This environment naturally encourages language and literacy development when children talk and play together and when reading and writing materials are an important part of these activities.

Figure 7.2 presents our design of a well-appointed and well-arranged preschool classroom with many traditional centers. The block center has bin and shelf storage spaces for large cardboard blocks, large wooden blocks, smaller wooden blocks, and durable model cars and trucks. It includes a workbench for play with pegs and hammer and wrench. On the bulletin board are posters of city skylines and their distinctive buildings (e.g., the Chicago lakefront with the skyscrapers of The Loop in the background), other distinctive buildings (e.g., Frank Lloyd Wright's Falling Water, a cantilever-constructed house over a waterfall, and the Eiffel Tower), and vehicles (e.g., ocean liners on a travel-agency poster and truck and car posters from

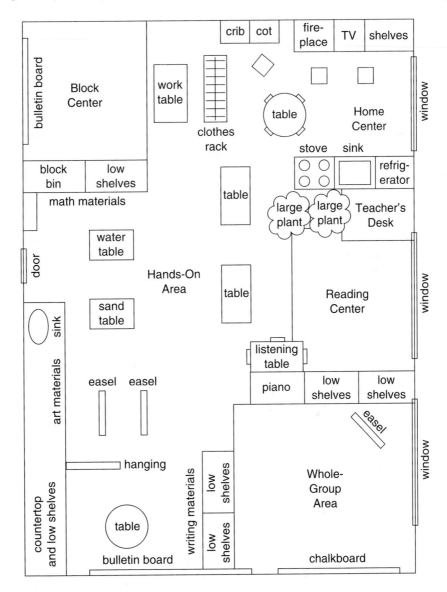

Figure 7.2 *A Preschool Classroom*

a car dealership). These posters contain the print that is part of the poster (e.g., "Chicago," "Cruise the Caribbean") as well as taped-on labels (e.g., "skyscraper," "ship"). On the workbench are hardware-store advertising flyers and a do-it-your-self carpentry book. There are two large, empty pasteboard boxes. There is a large area for playing with blocks.

The home center includes a cardboard fireplace with chairs around it, a cardboard television (such as furniture stores use in their entertainment-center displays), shelves, a kitchen set with a small table and four chairs, a small cot, a doll crib, and a doll high chair. The bookcase is stocked with magazines, including *TV Guide,* newspapers, a phone book, a few adult books, and a few children's picture books. The kitchen is stocked with plastic food, empty food containers (e.g., cereal boxes, a plastic ketchup bottle, a cottage cheese container), and several illustrated cookbooks, including *My First Cookbook* (Wilkes, 1989). Over the crib is a *Sesame Street* poster picturing Bert and Ernie and displaying their names.

Between the home and block centers is a clothing rack to serve dramatic play in the home and block centers. In both play centers, there are several small, spiral-bound, vertical-flip notebooks, small clipboards with paper, and pencils. In the home center, a waiter or waitress may use these props during restaurant play to take an order or a mommy or a daddy may use them to take a telephone message or to make a grocery list; in the block center, astronauts may use these items for a countdown checklist.

In the hands-on area are a sand table, a water table, and the art center. There are a sink and storage for supplies, including water toys and plastic aprons, and storage for and places to use children's individual collections of environmental print items, math manipulatives (e.g., Unifix cubes), musical instruments, puzzles, Legos™, clay, and science manipulatives (e.g., magnets). There is display space for content centers. All items and storage places are labeled. There is a travel poster of a beach near the sand table and one of Niagara Falls near the water table. The musical instruments are stored near the piano and an easel; sometimes the easel displays the lyrics to a song the children are learning, written on a large piece of posterboard. There are small easels for painting near the art supplies, tables for using many of the manipulatives, and a large, open area for group singing activities and for other large-group activities, such as story performances.

The reading and writing centers are on the opposite side of the room from the play centers. These contain writing materials, books (including pattern books, movable books, alphabet books, and big books), and space to use them, as described in Chapter 6. A large, round table at the edge of the writing center is the location for children's signing in at the beginning of their day and for checking out and checking in books from the classroom library.

OPPORTUNITIES TO INTERACT WITH PRINT

The space and materials just described lay the foundation for providing many opportunities for children to interact with print. When such opportunities abound, children will choose experiences that naturally support their literacy development as well as their growing emotionally, socially, and in other areas of learning, such as science, social studies, and math. In this section we describe children as they interact in a classroom rich with print. A guiding principle of infusing the classroom with print is that the print must remain functional. The focus of the reading and writing in the case study that follows is on children's reading and writing print, not learning to read specific words or learning isolated print skills.

Opportunities to Interact with Print
in Mrs. Miller's Classroom

Mrs. Miller teaches in a program for at-risk four-year-olds. She arranges her classroom so that print is included in every center, and she provides large blocks of time for children to play in the centers. First we describe the children as they play in Mrs. Miller's centers, and then we describe how Mrs. Miller interacts with the children as they play.

Children at Play

Mrs. Miller's classroom has many centers, including book, McDonald's, writing, games, art, science and math discovery, and home centers. By midmorning, children are working and playing at nearly every center. Two children are on the rug in the book center. They are looking at several books together, commenting about the pictures and talking about the stories. Then they take paper bags labeled with their names and "I can read" from a storage shelf for manipulatives. They look at the coupons, paper bags, and fronts cut from food boxes that they have taken from their **"I can read" bags.** One child gets a doll from the home center, puts it in her lap, and points to each of the items. She reads to her doll by saying a word or two for each item.

Four children are at a McDonald's center. The center is made from a puppet theater to which Mrs. Miller has attached a sign and menu. Inside the theater are empty containers for hamburgers and French fries. Two children are behind the counter in the center. Both have on hats worn by employees at McDonald's. One child is writing on an order pad, and the other is pretending to put a McDLT™ in a container. Two children are standing in front of the counter. One is dressed in a hat and heels from the home center. She is "Mama." She asks "Baby" what he wants to eat and then orders. The child taking orders announces, "That will be ten dollars." "Mama" looks in her purse for money and pays her bill.

Two children are at the writing center. A number of menus and placemats from local restaurants are displayed at the center. Also displayed are several menus composed by children. Some menus have pictures cut from magazines; some have children's mock letters or mock cursive writing; some have words children have copied from menus or newspapers; and others were written and drawn by parent volunteers. One of the menus on display was composed by Mrs. Miller. It is titled "Miller's Meals" and consists of a drawing of people eating, cutout pictures of food from the food section of the newspaper, and words. One of the children at the center is drawing and writing a menu. She announces, "I'm going to have ice cream," and draws a picture of a double dip cone. The other child comments, "I like ice cream, too. Maybe I'd better write *ice cream*. People might want ice cream on their cake."

Two children are in the games center. They play for several minutes with Legos™ and other small manipulative toys in the center. Then they remove two **environmental print puzzles** from the game shelf. The puzzles consist of boxes of brownie and cake mixes. Inside each box are pieces cut from the fronts of identical boxes. The children spread the cut-up puzzle pieces on the table. They put the puzzles together by looking at the pieces and then placing them on top of the boxes where they match. They talk together as they complete the puzzles, "I like chocolate. I could eat a whole box of these."

Two other children come to the games center and sit on the floor to play the **letter game.** A large *L* is painted on the front of a pasteboard box and a *K* on another. Attached to one of the boxes is a plastic bag containing several *L*'s and *K*'s that have been cut from construction paper and laminated. The two children play the *letter game* by sorting the letters and placing them inside the large pasteboard boxes. As they sort the letters, they say, "I'll be the *L* and you be the *K*. I know whose letter *K* is—Kelita's."

Tammy and Jonathan are painting at easels in the art center. Two index cards are clothespinned to the top of each easel; one card is on top of the other. Tammy's and Jonathan's names are on the top index cards on their easels. When they finish painting, they will unclip their name cards and take them to the bulletin board in the whole-group area where a small poster reads "I painted today." They will clip their name cards to the poster. When their name cards are removed from the easels, the two bottom cards will tell who can paint next.

One child is in the science and math discovery center. Included in this center is a **graph** divided into two segments, "No TV Last Night" and "TV Last Night." The first title is accompanied by a picture of a TV with a big *X* over it. The second title is accompanied by a picture of a TV. Under each title some squares of paper have been pasted. Many squares have children's names written on them. Most of the squares are pasted under the "TV Last Night" title. Jermain writes his name on a square of paper and pastes it under the "TV Last Night" title. Displayed on the bulletin board in the center is a graph that the children completed the day before. Under this chart are two sentences: "Two children saw no TV Monday night. Ten children saw TV Monday night."

Three children are in the home center. Two children decide to cook a meal for their babies using empty food containers and plastic food in the center. One child says, "I think I'll cook some chicken. Let me look up a good recipe." She opens a cookbook on one of the shelves in the center and begins looking through the pages. Another child is sitting in a rocking chair looking at magazines. Nearby, Mrs. Miller steps into a telephone booth made from a large box. She looks up a number in the telephone book (class telephone book with each child's name and telephone number). She says, "Ring. Ring. Is Melody home?" The child in the rocking chair says, "I'll get that," and answers a toy phone in the center. She says, "Melody is not here. Can I take a message?" She writes on a tablet near the phone and then says, "I'll give her the message. Bye-bye."

What Is Learned: Mrs. Miller's Instruction

These examples from Mrs. Miller's classroom clearly show that her students can make meanings with and understand the functions of many kinds of print. They are able to do so because she situates the print so as to maintain its original purpose and accepts her children's reading and writing even when it is unconventional. We saw her students making meanings consistent with the original functions of print when they read coupons to their dolls, used McDonald's wrappers and newspaper food advertising in restaurant play, and consulted a cookbook in their kitchen play.

Most of Mrs. Miller's children's reading and writing is not conventional. Two of the orders written as part of the McDonald's play are presented in Figure 7.3. The children said as they wrote, "Two McDLT's and a Coke" and "Three cheeseburgers and a chocolate shake." The telephone message for Melody that was taken in the home center is presented in Figure 7.4. These examples of children's reading and writing demonstrate that novice readers and writers intend to communicate meaning even when their efforts are unconventional. Mrs. Miller accepts these efforts and treats them as meaningful reading and writing.

Mrs. Miller's children benefited in still other ways from the many opportunities that she provided for interacting with print. She planned specific activities and ways of interacting with children so that they would expand their knowledge about written language forms and meaning-form links.

Effective teachers realize that children need support in moving from merely attending to the meaning of familiar print to attending to written language forms and how forms link with meanings. Case studies of the literacy learning of preschoolers have shown that children begin to learn the names of letters in meaningful environmental print words and in familiar persons' names (Baghban, 1984; Lass, 1982). This finding suggests that the familiar words in environmental print and the names of children in the classroom may be the most powerful resources for helping children learn about letters and other written language forms.

Mrs. Miller uses the writing of words from environmental print as an opportunity to focus on written language form. As part of their unit on foods, Mrs. Miller's class reads many menus and placemats. These are put in the writing center to stimulate children's writing. Mrs. Miller uses group time to compose environmental and functional print, such as the menu "Miller's Meals." As Mrs. Miller writes, she names letters and points out features of written language, such as specific letters, long or short words, or words that are repeated. She invites children to find letters they know.

Mrs. Miller frequently sits in the writing center so that she can call attention to written language features in the children's writing. In one activity, Mrs. Miller encouraged some children to dictate a "Trash Can Book." The children pasted envi-

Figure 7.3 *McDonald's Orders*   ***Figure 7.4*** *Telephone Message*

ronmental print items into books made from paper cut in the shape of trash cans. Serita made three pages in her book. She dictated, "I saved Rice Krispies from the trash. I saved Cabbage Patch from the trash. I saved potato chips from the trash." Mrs. Miller drew attention to the words *Rice Krispies, Cabbage Patch,* and *potato chips* written on the environmental print and in the words that she wrote in the book. She asked Serita to talk about how the words were alike and different in the two contexts. She invited Serita to find all the letters that were the same and name the letters she knew. Seeing familiar and meaningful words in more than one context helps children begin to move beyond context-dependent reading and writing (Hiebert, 1986). As children focus on form within the meaningful context of the environment, they begin to make connections between written forms (letters and words) and spoken forms (sounds and meaning).

Group Reading Opportunities

Our examples of children's reading and writing in Mrs. Miller's classroom included individual children's reading of environmental print. Later sections of this chapter provide other examples of children's reading by themselves. In this section, however, we discuss opportunities for children's literacy learning that are centered on group reading activities.

We begin by describing how Miss Leslie reads books aloud to her three- and four-year-olds and encourages them to participate in response-to-literature activities. A guiding principle of sharing books with children in preschool is that effective booksharing encourages interactions between the reader and his or her listeners, including listeners' individual responses to what is read. This case study illustrates the importance of going beyond merely reading aloud to children.

Booksharing in Miss Leslie's Classroom

Miss Leslie teaches in a private preschool with an emphasis on academic learning. She is careful to meet those expectations while maintaining a child-centered approach. One way in which she balances these two needs is through an activity that she calls **booksharing.** Booksharing is a highly interactive read-aloud activity in which children are expected to answer questions, make comments, and predict outcomes. Miss Leslie plans questions that help children use analytic talk and call for high levels of cognition. She also plans response-to-literature activities to extend the booksharing experience.

Miss Leslie and six three-year-olds are gathered for storytime on the rug in their classroom. The children are sitting in a square area bordered by tape on the rug. As she announces storytime, Miss Leslie points to a sign entitled "Storytime" that has a picture of a mother reading to two children. On the sign are clothespinned cards with the names of the children who are to come to storytime: Cory, Echo, Leah, Paul, Laura, and Evan. Miss Leslie points to the name on the chart as she calls each child and reminds the child to come to the rug for storytime. As the children approach the rug, she begins to sing one of the children's favorite songs, "Twinkle Twinkle Little Star."

After she and the children are settled on the rug, Miss Leslie holds up the book *The Little Rabbit Who Wanted Red Wings* (Bailey, 1987). She reads the title, pointing to each word. She reminds the children that she has read this book to them before. The book is about a little rabbit who is not happy with himself and wishes he had what other animals have. The children ask questions and make comments during the booksharing. Miss Leslie reads the text, talks about the illustrations, and asks questions. Figure 7.5 presents a segment of their booksharing.

Figure 7.5 *Miss Leslie and Three-Year-Olds Share* The Little Rabbit Who Wanted Red Wings *(Bailey, 1987)*

Text is presented in all capital letters. Brackets indicate portions of the dialogue that occurred simultaneously.

The illustration depicts a porcupine who is wearing glasses standing under a tree. Little Rabbit is sitting in a large hole in the tree looking at the porcupine.

Miss L: Now who does Little Rabbit see? (points to porcupine)

[Child 1: um um its . . .
[Child 2: Mr. Beaver.
[Child 3: Mr. Porcupine.

[Miss L: It does look a little like a beaver. This is Mr. Porcupine.
[Child 2: (reaches up and touches the picture of the porcupine) Ouch.

Miss L: Ooh, I wouldn't want to touch that.

[Child 1: Me either.
[Child 4: Oh, oh.

Miss L: His bristles would stick me. They would stick like a needle.

[Child 3: Not me.
[Child 2: He sticks you? If you touch him like this? (puts her finger on the picture of the porcupine and pulls it off as if she were stuck)

Miss L: Yes, he might. Those bristles are special. Now I wonder what Little Rabbit likes about Mr. Porcupine?

[Child 5: Glasses. (porcupine has on glasses)
[Child 1: Needles.
[Child 2: I wouldn't want to touch Porcupine.

Miss L: I wouldn't want to touch him either. But what about Little Rabbit? What do you think *he* thinks about those bristles? What do you think Little Rabbit likes?

[Child 3: um, um.
[Child 4: Glasses.
[Child 1: Needles.

Miss L: Do you think *He* wants those bristles? or maybe those glasses? (Laughs, and smiles at Child 1)

(Continued)

Figure 7.5 *(Continued)*

Child 1: Yeah.

Miss L: What would *you* like to have like Mr. Porcupine?

Child 2: I want glasses.

Child 5: Bristles.

Child 1: I want needles.

Miss L: Let's see. (looks at book) WHEN MR. PORCUPINE PASSED BY, THE LITTLE RAB-
BIT WOULD SAY TO HIS MOMMY (looks at children as if inviting them to join
in), "MOMMY, I WISH I HAD (looks back at print) A BACK FULL OF BRISTLES
LIKE MR. PORCUPINE'S."

Child 1: Mommy, I want those needles.

Child 5: I wish I had those bristles.

Child 4: I want some bristles.

Child 2: Mommy, . . .

Then Miss Leslie takes a paper bag from beneath her chair. She tells the children that it contains pictures of each of the animals Little Rabbit met in the story.
She asks the children to guess what they are. As the children guess, she pulls out
a construction-paper picture of the animal and asks, "What did Little Rabbit like
about this animal?" She clothespins each animal picture to a clothesline hung a few
feet off the floor behind her chair. She tells the children they might want to use the
clothesline props to retell the story to a friend during center time. She also suggests that they might want to draw pictures and write about the animals or Little
Rabbit in the writing center. She shows the children paper cut in the shape of a rabbit's head and tells them that the rabbit-shaped paper will be in the writing center
for them to use during center time. All the children are then free to select center
activities.

Some children go to the block center. One goes to the home center to join three
four-year-olds who have been playing there during storytime. The other three children sit down with the animal props on the clothesline. They take the construction-
paper animals and clip each one on the line. As they do this, they talk about the
story.

Miss Leslie goes to the writing center and announces that she is going to write.
Echo and Cory join her, along with three of the four-year-olds who were not participants in storytime. She says, "I think I'll draw a picture about Little Rabbit. I want
to draw his red wings." The children comment on what they might draw, "I'm going
to do Mrs. Puddleduck" and "I like trucks." As the children draw and talk, Miss Leslie
comments that she is going to write. "I think I'll write that Little Rabbit didn't like
the red wings." Cory says, "I'm gonna write, too. I'll write about her feet." Echo says,
"I don't want to write." Miss Leslie and the children continue to talk about their pictures and writing. Then Miss Leslie invites the children to read their stories and talk
about their pictures.

What Is Learned: Miss Leslie's
Roles in Booksharing

This example from Miss Leslie's preschool classroom shows that her children were active participants in the construction of the meaning of the story *The Little Rabbit Who Wanted Red Wings*. One of Miss Leslie's goals for booksharing is to enhance children's meaning-making strategies, and she uses several techniques for creating such meaning-making opportunities. The first is her skillful interaction with children during reading aloud.

Encouraging booksharing interactions. Miss Leslie uses a variety of **booksharing techniques** to help her children understand the story and to encourage their interactions. She encourages children to identify characters (she asks, "Now who does Little Rabbit see?" while pointing to the porcupine in the illustration) and to make predictions ("Now I wonder what Little Rabbit likes about Mr. Porcupine?"). She also encourages children to participate by accepting and extending their comments and questions (when Leah touched the picture of the porcupine and said "Ouch," Miss Leslie commented, "Ooh, I wouldn't want to touch that. His bristles would stick me. They would stick like a needle."). She uses questions that are intended to help children identify with story characters ("What would you like to have like Mr. Porcupine?"). She provides information that will help children understand words used in the story. (Miss Leslie commented that the porcupine's bristles "would stick like a *needle*" to clarify the meaning of the word *bristles* used in the story text.) She also recognizes all of the children's responses—even when they deviate from the story text. Miss Leslie acknowledged the prediction that Little Rabbit wanted Mr. Porcupine's glasses even though that was not a part of the story.

Miss Leslie uses gestures to help children understand the story. She points to characters and objects in the illustrations as she talks about them or reads text related to them. She uses her voice to help children understand the story. She looks at the children frequently and uses facial expressions to heighten interest in the story. Table 7.1 summarizes these booksharing techniques, which are an extension of techniques presented in Chapter 2. Teachers can fine-tune their booksharing techniques by tape-recording and analyzing a booksharing event with their children. They can use the suggestions presented in this chapter and in Table 7.1 as a guide for self-reflection about booksharing.

An important technique used in booksharing is encouraging children to predict events and outcomes. As children listen to the story text and examine illustrations, they learn to monitor their predicting efforts by evaluating or confirming their predictions. Tompkins and Webeler (1983) suggest following a three-step cycle of sampling, predicting, and confirming as an effective booksharing technique. Teachers can encourage children to participate in this **sampling, predicting, confirming cycle** by talking about the illustrations and text (sampling), asking, "What do you think will happen now?" (predicting), and then asking, "Did we make a good guess?" (confirming). This cycle is analogous to the **Directed Listening-Thinking Activity (DLTA)** (modeled after the Directed Reading-Thinking Activity; Stauffer, 1980).

Table 7.1 *Guidelines for Booksharing*

The Teacher:

   Interweaves text reading with asking questions and making comments.

   Asks children questions about characters and objects in pictures.

   Asks children to predict.

   Asks questions that help children identify with characters and actions in the story
      ("What would YOU do . . . ").

   Makes comments about characters and actions in pictures and story.

   Explains text words and concepts.

   Makes comments about relations between the story and real life.

   Predicts actions and outcomes.

   Makes statements about personal reactions to the story.

   Uses gestures.

   Points to objects and characters in pictures.

   Varies voice to indicate character dialogue.

   Answers children's questions.

   Acknowledges children's comments by commenting or further questioning.

   Extends children's questions and comments by providing additional information.

Effective teachers adapt their booksharing techniques to meet the needs of their children. Some young novice readers and writers have had few booksharing experiences. For these children, teachers spend more time telling the story and talking about the illustrations than reading the story text. Other novices have had extensive booksharing experiences; therefore, their teachers spend more time reading and commenting on the story's text. Although all teachers want to take time to comment on and discuss the language of stories, they do not need to simplify text language as they read books to children. Fox (1985) found that even three-year-olds tolerate uncertainty about the meaning of unfamiliar words in stories they particularly enjoy. As they learn the meanings of words through repeated booksharing opportunities, children begin to use the language of stories as they retell the stories, tell original stories, and later, write stories (Fox, 1985; McConaghy, 1985).

Adjusting to the needs of children.   Another reason that her three-year-old listeners were such able meaning makers is that Miss Leslie knows that the best group reading opportunities for preschoolers are often activities for well-chosen small groups rather than large groups. She has found that the six children she calls together comment more about stories when they are in smaller groups. She included two children in this group whose oral language was more mature than that of the other children. Miss Leslie believes that children learn much from interacting with other children whose abilities are slightly more mature than their own.

In addition to planning activities that she believes fit the needs of children, Miss Leslie also allows the children in her preschool class freedom of choice. She knows that children have individual preferences for and responses to books and activities. She knows which books her children enjoy, and she reads them frequently. When she discovers that she has selected a book that is uninteresting to the children (they wiggle right off the rug), she does not insist that they sit still and listen. Rather, she substitutes an old favorite and tries another book the following day. Children are allowed free choice of center activities. Note that this freedom means that a small-group reading activity can lead quite naturally to individual writing activities. Miss Leslie entices children to join in activities that they may be reluctant to select on their own. She encourages some children to write by going to the writing center herself and offering an open invitation to the children to join her there. She welcomes children who were not in the story-sharing group to the writing center.

Planning response-to-literature activities. Miss Leslie plans response-to-literature activities that extend children's opportunities for meaning making. For example, she encouraged children to use her clothesline props to retell the story during center time, and she provided special rabbit-shaped paper in the writing center to encourage children to write their own stories. Another response-to-literature activity involves special literature props in boxes to stimulate children's dramatic response to literature through play. These **literary prop boxes** include props designed to encourage children's becoming characters from favorite stories. In the *Little Rabbit Who Wanted Red Wings* literary prop box, Miss Leslie gathered several pairs of rabbit ears (made from headbands and construction paper), acorns, glasses, several pairs of rubber boots, a mirror, a pair of red wings (made from construction paper attached to an old vest), several head scarves, a toothbrush, a bowl and spoon, and two fur vests. She placed an extra copy of the book in the prop box along with the other props. Children are encouraged to use the props to act out the story or create their own stories.

Miss Leslie is concerned that her booksharing experiences enrich children's concept about stories. She knows that novice readers and writers may not have a complex concept of story. Some children may still view each illustration in a story as a separate and interesting picture; they do not connect each illustration's action to the story-as-a-whole. Effective teachers can help children strengthen their concepts of stories by sharing stories so that children focus on the story-as-a-whole. They help children move beyond understanding what is pictured in all the illustrations to understanding how the events in all the illustrations are linked.

Miss Leslie asks questions and makes comments that help children identify settings, characters, and characters' motivations. She helps children predict events and think about causes and effects during booksharing. She also plans special **concept-about-story activities** (Hoskisson & Tompkins, 1987; McGee & Tompkins, 1981). These activities are designed to help children learn five important concepts about stories, such as that all characters in stories have problems and do many things to try to solve their problems. (These concepts are presented in Table 7.2.) Activities to help children learn about story problems include having them retell stories using props or having them predict different ways in which a character might solve a problem. Table 7.2 also lists Miss Leslie's concept-about-story activities, including dramatizing, retelling, drawing, and painting.

Reading and making big books.   Miss Leslie knows that novice readers and writers begin to notice particular letters (e.g., the first letter of names) and details or style of illustrations (Kiefer, 1988). They learn concepts of print, for example, that it has lines of text and is read from left to right, top to bottom, and front to back. They refine their concepts of words, letters, and story texts. Miss Leslie knows that one of

Table 7.2 *Activities for Developing Concepts about Stories*

Story Concept	Example Activities
1. Characters are the animals and people in the story.	a. Have children draw, paint, or make characters in clay. b. Make a three-page book by having children draw and dictate what character looks like, does, and says. c. Make a book of "Story Characters I Know." Have children draw and dictate characters' names.
2. Stories take place in different places, times, and types of weather, called settings (Lukens, 1986).	a. Have children identify different places characters go in the story. b. Have children identify changes in weather in the story. c. Have children decide whether settings are real or make-believe. d. Make a list of "Story Places I Have Visited."
3. Characters in stories have problems; they do many things to try to solve their problems.	a. Compose a "Problem Book" by listing the problems of story characters and children's characters. b. Act out the story using story props. c. Have children suggest other methods of solving the character's problem. d. Use a story line to retell the story. e. Use a flannel board to tell the story. f. Play a guessing game where teacher describes a problem and children guess the name of the character.
4. Some events in stories happen over and over and some words in stories are said again and again (Tompkins & McGee, 1989).	a. Use story line to retell the story, emphasizing repeating words. b. Act out story, emphasizing repeating events and words. c. Make a list of repeated events. d. Make a big book of the story. e. Compose a story using the structure but adding new content (Tompkins & McGee, 1989).

Table 7.2 *(Continued)*

Story Concepts	Example Activities
5. Stories have a beginning that tells about characters, a middle that tells what characters do to solve problems, and an ending that tells the problem's solution (Hoskisson & Tompkins, 1987)	a. Make a four-page booklet with one page each for title, beginning, middle, and end; children should draw pictures and dictate story.
	b. Make a "The End" book. Children can dictate endings to favorite stories.
	c. Use three shoe boxes to make a story train as shown here. Make pictures of the event in the beginning, middle, and end of the story. Have children put pictures in the train and tell about the story.

Adapted from McGee, L. M., & Tompkins, G. E. (1981). The videotape answer to independent reading comprehension activities. *The Reading Teacher, 34,* 430–431. Reprinted with permission of the International Reading Association.

the easiest ways to demonstrate many of these concepts is to read from big books (Holdaway, 1979).

Big books are enlarged copies—approximately twenty inches by thirty inches—of literature selections. Many publishing companies now sell big book versions of some of their popular books. Both the illustrations and the print are large. As they read aloud to children, teachers can naturally draw attention to the print and demonstrate concepts about print as they underline text (Combs, 1987; Heald-Taylor, 1987). Because a group of children can easily see the printed text, they can talk about letters and words. As they hear the text and see the text, children also notice the link between the text and what teachers read.

Teachers who make their own big books want to select stories that children frequently request. The story should be short with only a few lines of text per page. Examples of books appropriate for teacher-made big books are *Brown Bear, Brown Bear* (Martin, 1983) and *It Didn't Frighten Me* (Goss & Harste, 1981). These are favorites of young children, they have few words to a page, and illustrations are easily made to accompany the text. Pattern books make excellent big books. (See Chapter 6, Table 6.3 for a list of pattern books.)

To make a big book, the teacher copies the text so that each page in the big book matches each page in the original book. Paint, chalk, markers, crayons, or any other media can be used to illustrate the book. It is not important that the illustrations in the big book be exact duplicates of those in the original story. Creative teachers produce illustrations that their young children enjoy as much as the original illustrations. To bind books, teachers can use large rings or spiral binding. Once big books are made, they should be included in booksharing activities frequently.

Writing Opportunities

We have described many writing opportunities in Ms. Reyes's, Mrs. Miller's, and Miss Leslie's classrooms. In this section we review those opportunities and describe what novice readers and writers can learn from them. A guiding principle of using writing to support literacy learning in the preschool classroom is to use it in a variety of ways. Thus, teachers plan for a variety of kinds of writing and allow children choices about their writing, such as what to write about or even whether to write at all.

Some writing activities are more controlled by the teacher and others are controlled by the child. In group activities, the teacher writes for children as he or she records what several children say as a part of an activity. In these activities, teachers have more control over writing. Children have a chance to contribute to the composition, but the topic and purpose of the writing activity are usually decided by the teacher. Some activities involve the teacher's recording what a single child says, such as when the teacher records a message about a picture that the child has drawn. Children in these activities have more control over writing, especially when they decide the topic and purpose of their drawing and writing.

Some activities involve children's writing. When children visit the writing center to write a note to a classmate, they initiate the writing and they choose the topic. Other activities originate in children's play. As children play house, they may decide to write a phone message. Children have most control over writing when they write for purposes of their own and on topics of their choice. It is important for children to have writing experiences over which they are more in control so that they can try out their written language knowledge.

Writing in Mrs. Miller's and Miss Leslie's Classrooms

The children in Miss Leslie's and Mrs. Miller's classrooms write as a part of many classroom activities, including writing to take orders at a McDonald's center and writing telephone messages. They write graphs in the math center and make menus as part of a food unit. They also write in the writing center, composing "Trash Can Books" and stories about "Little Bunny." We describe four preschool writing opportunities: the writing center, sign-in procedure, pattern writing, and list writing.

The preschool writing center.   Miss Leslie and Mrs. Miller created many literacy opportunities in their writing centers. They correlated many of their group activities with extending activities in the writing centers. For example, Miss Leslie put special-shaped paper in the writing center that correlated with a story she had read aloud, and Mrs. Miller wrote a menu in a group meeting and then encouraged children to write their own menus later in the writing center. Teachers plan many activities for writing centers.

Making greeting cards is always a favorite writing activity; holidays present numerous opportunities for children to write cards (Beardsley & Mareck-Zeman, 1987). Literature is another important stimulus for writing; teachers can record children's retellings of stories. Children enjoy writing on paper cut into shapes suggested by characters or themes of literature. Another favorite writing activity is for children to compose their own print items, such as menus, grocery lists, catalogs, and *TV Guides*.

Mrs. Miller knows the importance of interacting with children during writing center activities. She introduces new writing center activities during group time and follows a routine as she interacts with the children in the center. In December, Mrs. Miller plans several activities related to writing letters to Santa. First, she plans a whole-group activity in which she writes a letter to Santa using suggestions from the children. She places stationery cut from green construction paper and envelopes in the writing center. She also displays words such as *Santa, Dear,* and *Love.* Then she places a "Santa Letter" sign-up sheet in the writing center; this is a piece of paper with "I will write to Santa today" written at the top and space for four children to sign at the bottom. The children know to sign up as they enter the classroom in the morning if they want to have Mrs. Miller record their letters to Santa. We believe that preschoolers should not be required to go to the writing center to complete a particular project. Rather, they should be invited, encouraged, and enticed to go to writing centers and other writing activities.

Teachers who know what motivates and interests young children in their classrooms can create opportunities that will entice many seemingly reluctant readers and writers to participate in activities that lead to reading and writing. Such children may visit a writing center to use the typewriter or letter stamps or to engage in fingerpainting or pudding-writing activities. They may be willing to tell an adult or teacher about a picture that they have drawn, especially if that person is genuinely interested in the drawing. However, teachers must always be able to accept "no" and wait for children to be ready. We saw writing opportunities like these in Mrs. Miller's and Miss Leslie's classrooms.

The sign-in procedure. Novice readers and writers who realize that written marks can communicate messages are ready for the **sign-in procedure.** In this procedure, each child writes his or her name each day on an attendance sign-in sheet (Harste, Burke, & Woodward, 1981). This procedure is functional; it should actually serve as the attendance record of the classroom. With young three-year-olds, the procedure may consist of having children place a card with their name on it in a box or on a chart. Later, they may place their name card and a slip of paper (the same size as the name card) on which they have written their names in the attendance box. Eventually, children will sign in by writing their signatures on an attendance sheet. Naturally, three- and four-year-olds' signatures will not be conventional when they first begin the sign-in procedure (recall Robert's early signatures presented in Figure 3.8 in Chapter 3). However, by signing in daily, children gradually refine their signatures into readable names.

Mrs. Miller uses the sign-in procedure for two reasons. First, many of the children who come to her classroom have had few writing experiences prior to beginning preschool. Many children do not have crayons and paper in their homes. Before she began the sign-in procedure, few children voluntarily visited the writing center. The sign-in procedure gave the children an opportunity to write each day. As they became comfortable with that very brief writing experience, they gained confidence and began visiting the writing center for more lengthy writing experiences. The children also observed that their writing was useful; Mrs. Miller used the sign-in list to comment on children's absences.

Pattern writing.   Mrs. Miller frequently reads pattern books to her class. (See Chapter 6, Table 6.3, for a list of pattern books.) She and her children used a pattern to create their "Trash Can Books." They used the pattern "I saved the _____ from the trash can." Patterns for writing can be integrated into any unit or theme. Mrs. Miller's children used the pattern "I hate _____ , but _____ is my favorite food," as another part of their unit on foods.

It is important to keep in mind that the purpose of using **pattern writing** is to help children become more fluent and creative, rather than to make them conform to an expected pattern (Wason-Ellam, 1988). Often the most creative contribution to a pattern-writing activity is a response that breaks the pattern.

Writing lists.   Using lists is another way to solve the problems related to group dictation with small children. **List making** is effective with young children because each child can contribute several times. Lists can be made quickly, since it only takes a few seconds to write a word in the list. Miss Leslie and Mrs. Miller regularly write lists with their children as part of booksharing and environmental print reading. Miss Leslie wrote several lists with her children related to the book *The Little Rabbit Who Wanted Red Wings.* The children dictated a list of animals included in the book, a list of animal features they would like to have, and a list of wishes. Table 7.3 presents several books and examples of lists that can be written before or after their sharing.

Sometimes young children have difficulty knowing what to say when they are asked to add to a list. Some children may show their confusion by repeating what someone else dictated. We suggest that teachers write what each child contributes even when he or she repeats someone else's responses. Repeated responses provide children with opportunities for paying attention to written language forms. As the teacher and children read and reread their list, they will discover that some words are repeated and that the repeated words look the same.

What Is Learned: Using Written Language Talk

Children learn much about written language from the kinds of comments that teachers and other children make as they write. One of the most powerful literacy learning techniques that teachers can use is to talk about written language as it is being written. This kind of talk is called **written language talk.** Effective teachers use their careful observation of children in literacy events to make decisions about what kinds of written language talk might be most useful.

Table 7.3 *Making Lists with Literature*

Literature Selection	Suggestions for Lists
Brown, M. (1947). *Goodnight moon.* Harper and Row.	**1.** Things in the green room **2.** Things in my room **3.** Before I go to bed, I
Carle, E. (1974). *The very hungry caterpillar.* New York: Philomel.	**1.** Things the caterpillar ate **2.** I was so hungry I ate
Goss, J., & Harste, J. (1981). *It didn't frighten me.* School Book Fairs.	**1.** Outside my window was **2.** I'm not afraid of **3.** Fantastic Creatures
Pienkowski, J. (1980). *Dinnertime.* Los Angeles: Price/Stern/Sloan.	**1.** Animals having dinner **2.** Things for dinner
Viorst, J. (1977). *Alexander and the terrible, horrible, no good, very bad day.* New York: Atheneum.	**1.** Alexander's bad things **2.** Our bad things **3.** Wonderful, marvelous, good things

Written language talk can help children learn about written language forms. As Mrs. Miller wrote her letter to Santa with her children, she told the children she would begin her letter by writing "Dear Santa Claus." At the end of her letter, she wrote, "Love, Mrs. Miller." She explained that letters always begin with the word *Dear* and often end with the word *Love.* From this written language talk, the children learned about the text form of a letter.

Mrs. Miller also talked about alphabet letters as she wrote her Santa letter. She made comments such as, "Look, Santa begins with the same letter as Serita, *S.*" From this written language talk about alphabet letters, the children learned letter names, features, and perhaps information about sounds associated with letters.

Written language talk can help children learn about meanings. As Mrs. Miler wrote her Santa letter, she explained that the letter would start with a sentence about her good behavior in the last year. She reminded the children that Santa would want to know that in order to bring what she wanted for Christmas. Through her talk about meaning, the children learned about the kinds of language found in letters. They also learned the kinds of information appropriate to include in a letter to Santa.

Written language talk also helps children learn about meaning-form links. As Mrs. Miller wrote, she said each word. As she read her letter, she underlined the text with her hands. The children had many opportunities to connect what they heard Mrs. Miller read with the print she was highlighting. Mrs. Miller's talk about letters provided children with information for discovering sound–letter relationships. Some of the children in her class had begun making some of these discoveries. When Mrs. Miller was writing that she wanted a new sewing machine, Serita commented, "I know what letter sewing has, an *S.*" Mrs. Miller knew that Serita only made these sound–letter comments about *S* words. Still, Serita was beginning to display some sound–letter relationship awareness. We will talk more about this knowledge in Chapters 8 and 9.

Written language talk helps children learn about function. Mrs. Miller talked about taking the letter to the post office and mailing it. She reminded the children that Santa could keep her letter to remember what she wanted for Christmas. She commented that it was a good thing that Santa would have her letter because he would be getting many, many requests for gifts. She did not want him to forget what she wanted.

Children use written language talk as they watch their teacher write and as they write. Mrs. Miller encourages children to use this kind of talk and always takes time to respond to a child who makes a written language comment. She knows that children's comments provide information about written language that all the children can use to learn about reading and writing.

Play Opportunities

Play is the most important learning activity in the preschool classroom, and we have already shown many instances of children's reading and writing in their play. We described play with print in Mrs. Miller's McDonald's center and dramatic-play responses to literature facilitated by Miss Leslie's literary prop boxes. A guiding principle of play as a literacy learning opportunity is that it must remain the child's endeavor. We have emphasized that teachers must play an active, involved role in providing literacy support in preschool classrooms. Their role in children's play, however, must also be subtle. Teachers can facilitate play; they can influence it; they can even enter children's play; but they must never intrude on it. The difference between the last two items is that entering is on the children's terms, intruding is breaking the spell that children have cast with their play. In this section, we describe two active, but nonintrusive, ways in which preschool teachers can ensure that literacy learning opportunities are part of the play in their classrooms. They are Mrs. Miller's dramatic-play-with-print centers (e.g., Neuman & Roskos, 1990) and story telling and playing (e.g., Paley, 1990).

Dramatic-Play-with-Print Centers

We have described a well-appointed preschool classroom as filled with print. This description extends to the play centers, where posters, labels, and notebooks take their places with blocks, toy trucks, dress-up clothing, and plastic food. Mrs. Miller calls such centers **dramatic-play-with-print centers.**

Teachers can make a variety of dramatic-play-with-print centers (Roskos, 1988; Schickedanz, 1986). Table 7.4 describes dramatic-play-and-print props that can be used to create three such centers. If classrooms are not large enough to permit a dramatic-play-with-print center, teachers can place the props in boxes. Children can take the boxes and set up their play in any open space in a classroom.

Mrs. Miller carefully prepares her children for these centers. On the day that she introduces a center, she uses whole-group time to orient the children to the center. They discuss what happens, for example, at McDonald's. She shows the children

Table 7.4 *Dramatic-Play-with-Print Centers*

	Dramatic Props	**Print Props**
Shopping Mall Center	1. standing racks for drying clothes 2. hangers and play clothes (hang on racks) 3. cash registers 4. hats, purses, wallets 5. play baby strollers 6. dolls	1. checkbooks and play money 2. signs, such as names of departments, sale signs 3. sales slips 4. pads to write shopping lists 5. tags to make price tags 6. paper bags with store logos 7. credit cards 8. credit application forms
Drugstore Center	1. boxes for counters 2. cash register 3. empty bottles, boxes of various sizes for medicine 4. play shopping carts	1. magazines and books 2. play money 3. checkbooks 4. prescriptions 5. paper bags for prescriptions 6. labels for prescription bottles
Beauty and Barber Shop Center	1. chairs 2. towels 3. play barber kit with scissors, combs 4. telephone 5. hair clips, curlers 6. empty bottles of cologne	1. appointment book 2. checkbooks and play money 3. magazines for waiting area 4. bills

the dramatic-play-and-print props, and they discuss how the props might be used. Mrs. Miller and two or three children role-play with the center props. Several children have opportunities to play with Mrs. Miller. Later, while the children play in the center during center time, Mrs. Miller occasionally joins in. She realizes that children will think of many ingenious ways to use props in their dramatic play and that they should have plenty of opportunities to create their own unique imaginary worlds. However, she also knows that she can help expand the children's language and increase the complexity of their play by playing along with them (Neuman & Roskos, 1993).

Some of the dramatic-play-with-print centers are introduced by guests whom Mrs. Miller invites to the classroom. One of the favorite centers is the TV weatherperson dramatic-play-with-print center. This center consists of a map on a chart stand, other maps and instruments, a cardboard TV camera, and a large poster with a weather script. Mrs. Miller invites a weatherperson from a local TV station to speak to the class about weather forecasting. The weatherperson always brings a script used in a recent broadcast, several weather maps, and computer printouts of weather information. After the visit, many children want to play in the center, so Mrs. Miller posts a schedule of on-the-air casts.

Mrs. Miller realizes that children's reading and writing in dramatic-play-with-print centers provide many opportunities for her to assess their understandings about written language. For example, Figure 7.6 presents a chart Matthew filled out as a part of his play at Mrs. Miller's doctor's office play center. As Matthew wrote on this chart he said, "Your eyes look good. Your throat is red." Then he wrote the prescription shown in Figure 7.7. He said, "Take these pills ten times."

From Matthew's reading and writing in the doctor's office dramatic-play-with-print center, Mrs. Miller knows that he is constructing appropriate meanings in his writing and reading and that he uses contextual dependency to link meaning with form. He also knows the formation of some alphabet letters, linearity, and his signature.

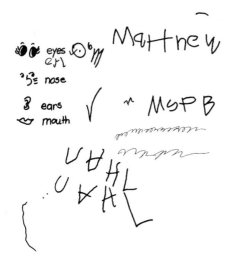

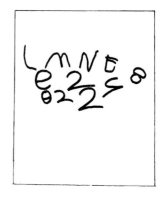

Figure 7.6 *A Doctor's Chart*   **Figure 7.7** *A Prescription*

Story Telling and Playing

In several compelling narratives about her years as a preschool teacher, Vivian Paley (1981, 1984, 1986, 1988, 1990) describes a method for combining storytelling and play. In the **story telling and playing** activity, she plays the role of scribe. She writes the stories that children dictate, and then the children perform these stories as informal drama. As children tell their stories, other children are the audience; they are free to make comments or ask questions. These interactions influence children's storytelling, and Paley accepts revisions to stories as they occur. "In storytelling, as in play, the social interactions we call interruptions usually improve the narrative" (1990, p. 23).

Paley invites children to dictate their stories as they arrive for their school day. She sits where she is accessible to all the children. As children tell their stories, Paley repeats each dictated sentence as she writes it down. She wants the storyteller to be able to correct her if she makes a mistake or to revise if a new idea comes to mind. She questions any part of the story that she is not certain she has gotten correctly. "The child knows the story will soon be acted out and the actors will need clear directions. The story must make sense to everyone: actors, audience, and narrator" (1990, p. 22). During the day she talks about the stories, always looking for and voicing connections. "Throughout the day I may refer to similarities between a child's story and other stories, books, or events, though I try to avoid doing this while the story is being dictated. I don't wish to impose undue influence on the course of the story" (1990, p. 22).

Acting out the stories at the end of the school day is equally social and open to change. Paley says, "If in the press of a busy day I am tempted to shorten the process by only reading the [dictated] stories aloud and skipping the dramatizations, the children object. They say, 'But we haven't *done* the story!' " (1990, p. 25). To play out the story, Paley reads the dictation, and the storyteller and selected classmates dramatize it. Children are free to comment on the dramatizing, and their comments often result in revision in the dramatization. "Intuitively the children perceive that stories belong in the category of play, freewheeling scripts that always benefit from spontaneous improvisations" (1990, p. 25).

What Is Learned: Letting Children Take the Lead

The literacy learning goals of a teacher in creating and becoming involved in dramatic-play-with-print centers can be described in terms of meaning making, forms, meaning-form links, and functions of written language. When children tell about a picture while pretending to read from a magazine in the waiting area of the beauty parlor and barbershop center, they show that they know written language is about making meanings. When Mrs. Miller's students examine the broadcast script, weather maps, and computer printouts of weather information that the weatherperson brings to their class, they learn about an important aspect of form, that written language comes in many formats. When Matthew says two very different and very appropriate things for his two very different-looking pieces of writing ("Your eyes look good. Your throat is red," for his doctor's chart, and "Take these pills ten times," for his prescription), he demonstrates knowledge of meaning-form links. When Melody takes a phone message, she shows an understanding of an important function of writing, that it preserves a message for later reading by someone not now present.

Paley describes the literacy-related benefits of story telling and playing in broader terms. About a three-year-old's first story, Paley writes, "She has contributed to the literature and culture of a previously unknown group of children. Now she is known, and soon she will know others through their stories, those revealed in play and those made permanent on paper. The stories are literature; the play is life" (1990, pp. 18–19).

ANOTHER LOOK: THE TEACHER'S ROLES

We have presented descriptions of preschoolers and their teachers as they are engaged in language and literacy activities. The children had multiple opportunities to learn, and the teachers used subtle instruction to support that learning. Preschool teachers *infuse the environment with print,* as Mrs. Miller did in her classroom. They *invite children to interact with print,* as Mr. Richgels did when he invited Caitie to write a story and as Vivian Paley did when she invited children to tell and dramatize their stories. They *demonstrate reading and writing by participating in literacy events,* as Mrs. Miller did when she joined in play in the home center. She pretended to phone someone, and one of the children took a message about the call. Miss Leslie sat in the writing center and said, "I'm going to write. I think I'll draw a picture of Little Rabbit. I want to draw his red wings."

Preschool teachers *model reading and writing strategies,* as Miss Leslie did when she read big books with her children and as Mrs. Miller did when she wrote a letter to Santa with her children. They *plan group activities involving reading and writing,* as Miss Leslie did during booksharing and Mrs. Miller did in composing a menu with her children. They *plan individual activities involving reading and writing,* as Miss Leslie did when she prepared storytelling props for the book she used in booksharing and as Mrs. Miller did when she organized graphing activities in the math center. Finally, *they become audiences for children's reading and writing,* as Mr. Richgels did when he listened as Caitie composed and read a story.

Chapter Summary

Preschools are engaging settings in which children gain concepts about written language while they are having experiences that allow them to grow intellectually, socially, emotionally, physically, and aesthetically. Although many parents and others do not expect children to acquire literacy skills in their preschool experiences, children can and do gain literacy knowledge when teachers invite them to read and write and accept their performances as important demonstrations of their growth. Mr. Richgels provided a rich opportunity for Caitie to read and write, and her interaction demonstrated her sophisticated understanding of written language.

Preschoolers acquire concepts about written language when their classrooms are filled with print and when teachers model how to use that print in play. Mrs. Miller's classroom included many games and dramatic-play opportunities in which children used print in entertaining and functional ways. They collected print from the environment in "I can read bags," they played with environmental print puzzles and letter games, and they acted out visiting a fast-food restaurant in their McDonald's dramatic-play-with-print center.

Young children gain understandings about written language as they participate in booksharing and response-to-literature activities. Miss Leslie demonstrated effective booksharing techniques, including using gestures and her voice to interpret stories as she read aloud and making comments. She was especially skillful in getting children to participate in booksharing by asking questions and inviting them to predict outcomes. She prepared several response-to-literature activities, such as retelling activities using storytelling props, literary prop boxes, and story concept activities. She demonstrated reading strategies and drew children's attention to print concepts by reading and making big books.

Young children acquire literacy concepts by participating in writing activities.

Children use the sign-in procedure to practice writing their signatures. They observe their teachers modeling writing as they help compose pattern writing or lists. Teachers use written language talk as they model writing and thereby provide children with many opportunities to learn more about written language meanings, forms, meaning-form links, and functions. Finally, preschoolers learn much from play, including play in dramatic-play-with-print centers and in story telling and playing activities.

Applying the Information _____

We suggest two activities for applying the information presented in this chapter. First, make a list of the nine characteristics of literacy-rich classrooms presented in Chapter 6. Then reread this chapter and locate classroom activities from Miss Leslie's and Mrs. Miller's classrooms that are examples of these characteristics. Discuss these examples with your classmates.

Second, make a list of all the literacy learning activities mentioned in this chapter, including teacher activities of infusing, inviting, demonstrating, modeling, and acting as an audience. List all the group activities described (booksharing, reading and making big books, pattern writing, writing lists, and story concept activities) and individual activities (response-to-liter-ature activities, prop boxes, sign-in procedure, card making, dramatic-play-with-print centers, print puzzles, letter games, "I can read" bags, graph making, and story telling and playing). For each of these activities, describe what children learn about written language meanings, forms, meaning-form links, or functions. For example, as children participated in booksharing with Miss Leslie, they had opportunities for meaning making by answering questions and retelling the story with storytelling props. As children wrote "Trash Can Books" with Mrs. Miller, they focused on the form of written language. They compared words in environmental print and printed forms and they named letters. Discuss your list with classmates.

Going Beyond the Text _____

Visit a preschool classroom and observe several literacy activities. Take note of the interactions among children as they participate in literacy experiences. Also note the teacher's talk with children in those experiences. Make a list of the kinds of literacy materials available in the classroom. Talk with the teacher about the kinds of literacy activities he or she plans. Compare these materials, interactions, and activities with those found in Ms. Reyes's, Miss Leslie's, and Mrs. Miller's preschool classrooms.

References _____

BAGHBAN, M. (1984). *Our daughter learns to read and write*. Newark, DE: International Reading Association.

BAILEY, C. (1987). *The little rabbit who wanted red wings*. New York: Platt and Munk.
BEARDSLEY, L. V., & MARECK-ZEMAN, M. (1987). Making connections: Facilitating literacy in

young children. *Childhood Education, 63,* 159–166.

COMBS, M. (1987). Modeling the reading process with enlarged texts. *The Reading Teacher, 40,* 422–426.

DISNEY PRODUCTIONS (1973). *Walt Disney Productions' story of Robin Hood.* Burbank, CA: Disney.

DYSON, A. H. (1985). Individual differences in emerging writing. In M. Farr (Ed.), *Advances in writing research: Vol. 1. Children's early writing development* (pp. 59–125). Norwood, NJ: Ablex.

FOX, C. (1985). The book that talks. *Language Arts, 62,* 374–384.

GOSS, J. L., & HARSTE, J. C. (1981). *It didn't frighten me.* School Book Fairs.

HARSTE, J. C., BURKE, C. L., & WOODWARD, V. A. (1981). *Children, their language and world: Initial encounters with print* (Final Report NIE-G-79-0132). Bloomington: Indiana University, Language Education Department.

HEALD-TAYLOR, G. (1987). How to use predictable books for K–2 language arts instruction. *The Reading Teacher, 40,* 656–661.

HIEBERT, E. H. (1986). Using environmental print in beginning reading instruction. In M. R. Sampson (Ed.), *The pursuit of literacy: Early reading and writing* (pp. 73–80). Dubuque, IA: Kendall/Hunt.

HOLDAWAY, D. (1979). *Foundations of literacy.* Sydney, Australia: Ashton Scholastic.

HOSKISSON, K., & TOMPKINS, G. E. (1987). *Language arts: Content and teaching strategies.* Columbus, OH: Merrill.

KIEFER, B. (1988). Picture books as contexts for literary, aesthetic, and real world understandings. *Language Arts, 65,* 260–271.

LASS, B. (1982). Portrait of my son as an early reader. *The Reading Teacher, 36,* 20–28.

LUKENS, R. L. (1986). *A critical handbook of children's literature* (3rd ed.). Glenview, IL: Scott, Foresman.

MARTIN, B. (1983). *Brown bear, brown bear.* New York: Holt.

McCONAGHY, J. (1985). Once upon a time and me. *Language Arts, 62,* 349–354.

McGEE, L. M. & TOMPKINS, G. E. (1981). The videotape answer to independent reading comprehension activities. *The Reading Teacher, 34,* 427–433.

NEUMAN, S. B., & ROSKOS, K. (1990). Play, print, and purpose: Enriching play environments for literacy development. *The Reading Teacher, 44,* 214–221.

NEUMAN, S. & ROSKOS, K. (1993). Access to print for children of poverty: Differntial effects of adult mediation and literacy-enriched play settings on environmental and functional print tasks. *American Educational Research Journal, 30,* 95–122.

PALEY, V. G. (1981). *Wally's stories: Conversations in the kindergarten.* Cambridge: Harvard University Press.

PALEY, V. G. (1984). *Boys and girls: Superheroes in the doll corner.* Chicago: University of Chicago Press.

PALEY, V. G. (1986). *Mollie is three: Growing up in school.* Chicago: University of Chicago Press.

PALEY, V. G. (1988). *Bad guys don't have birthdays: Fantasy play at four.* Chicago: University of Chicago Press.

PALEY, V. G. (1990). *The boy who would be a helicopter: The uses of storytelling in the classroom.* Cambridge: Harvard University Press.

ROSKOS, K. (1988). Literacy at work in play. *The Reading Teacher, 41,* 562–566.

SCHICKEDANZ, J. A. (1986). *More than the ABCs.* Washington, DC: National Association for the Education of Young Children.

STAUFFER, R. (1980). *The language experience approach to teaching reading* (2nd ed.). New York: Harper and Row.

TOMPKINS, G. E., & McGEE, L. M. (1989). Teaching repetition as a story structure. In D. M. Glynn (Ed.), *Children's comprehension of text* (pp. 59–78). Newark, DE: International Reading Association.

TOMPKINS, G. E., & WEBELER, M. B. (1983). What will happen next? Using predictable books with young children. *The Reading Teacher, 36,* 498–502.

WASON-ELLAM, L. (1988). Using literary patterns: Who's in control of the authorship? *Language Arts, 65,* 291–301.

WILKES, A. (1989). *My first cookbook.* New York: Alfred A. Knopf.

CHAPTER 8

Supporting Literacy Learning in Kindergarten

In this chapter, we discuss techniques for supporting literacy learning in kindergarten. We begin by describing what happens in one kindergarten class as the teacher, Mrs. Poremba, uses a sign-in procedure and informational books to teach about dinosaurs and to facilitate children's exploration of written language. We describe the unique context of kindergarten and our design for an exemplary classroom layout.

In the remainder of the chapter we present four methods of supporting kindergartners' language and literacy development. We show how Mrs. Poremba responds to her children's reading and writing of classroom print; we discuss shared reading experiences, including effective large-group instruction; and, we describe using writing and play as important learning settings. We end the chapter with a discussion of teachers' roles in supporting kindergartners' literacy learning.

Key Concepts

extended sign-in procedure

sign-in question

kindergarten-style research

self-scheduled copying

writing the room

the wall

wall work

pocket chart

classroom print

"All Around You" print

informational print

specials schedule

weather chart

opening-of-the-day routines

Words for Today

listening to the big sounds

finding the word somewhere in the room

birthday chart

shared reading

orienting children to print

What Can You Show Us? activity

word frames

choral reading

text reconstruction

"I helped" record sheet

cooperative learning

instructional writing

journals

language experience

language experience chart

sign making

dramatizing information from nonfiction

READING AND WRITING IN MRS. POREMBA'S KINDERGARTEN

Mrs. Poremba is a kindergarten teacher whom we have visited frequently over a two-year period. She teaches in a public school serving a rural community that is fast becoming suburban. Mrs. Poremba uses routines as an opportunity for children to learn more about content units and as a place where they talk about written language. She is especially effective in challenging children to think and to discover. The following example is from February, when the children are a few weeks into a dinosaur unit. The children talk about what they know about dinosaurs, and they read and write. Mrs. Poremba uses particularly supportive talk to encourage children's reading and writing efforts.

Extended Sign-In Procedure

The children in Mrs. Poremba's kindergarten sign in on arrival each day. Because of the way she uses this procedure, not only to take attendance but also to teach about many aspects of written language, we call it the **extended sign-in procedure.** First, each child goes to an assigned table where he or she shares a sign-in sheet with the other three children at that table. At the beginning of the year, the top of the vertically arranged 8-½-by- 11-inch sign-in sheet has the message "Please sign in," and the bottom has the message "Thank you." Between these messages are four lines for four signatures. In February, the sign-in sheet is arranged horizontally, with the messages "Can a dinosaur jump?" at the top and "Today is Wednesday, February 24, 1993" at the bottom (see Figure 8.1). The four lines are numbered 1 through 4 and there is room for each student to write his or her name and answer the question yes or no.

Talking about a Sign-In Question

Mrs. Poremba has included yes-or-no questions on the sign-in sheet before, but until today the question has been followed by the words "yes or no" to provide children a model when writing their answers. Children talk among themselves as they enter the classroom and take their turns signing in and considering the **sign-in question.**

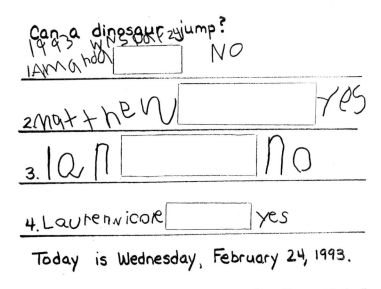

Figure 8.1 *A Sign-In Sheet with Sign-In Question (Last Names Masked)*

Mrs. Poremba walks among the tables and talks with the children as they sign in. The following is the exchange among the first children to arrive at their tables.

Bill: I know what the sentence says, Josh.

Josh: What?

Bill: "Do dinosaurs jump?"

Josh: No—It says, "*Can* a dinosaur jump?"

Several children: "Can—a—dinosaur—jump?"!

Bill: Look it—all it says is, "Can a dinosaur jump?" . . . No *yes* or *no*.

Mrs. Poremba: What are you thinking about, Bill?

Later, two other children have this exchange:

Child 1: It says, "Can a dinosaur jump?"

Child 2: No, no, no, no *nos* or *yeses*.

Child 1: No.

Child 2: See she says that we already know how to spell *yes* or *no*.

A little later:

Mrs. Poremba: Do you know what the question says, Jen?

Jenny: Yeah.

Mrs. Poremba: Are you sure? Maybe you need to work with a friend.

Several children: I know! I know! I know!

One child: "Do dinosaurs jump?"

Another child: "Does dinosaurs jump?"

Several children: No!

Another child: "Does a dinosaur jump?"

Another child: "Can a dinosaur jump?"

Another child: (for the first time, really asking) Can a dinosaur jump?

This question results in several children's saying "No!" and several more children's saying "Yes!" One child says, "I say yes!" another, "The answer is no!" and still another, "Yes they can!"

During the several more minutes of sign-in time, groups of children discuss other things besides their sign-in question. For example, they talk about a sports event two children attended and the class's plans for today—to stuff several big paper dinosaur models they decorated yesterday.

Whole-Class Writing of the Sign-In Question

The second step of the extended sign-in procedure involves writing the sign-in question. Mrs. Poremba writes a copy of the sign-in question on the board, and as she does this she discusses spacing between words and spellings of words. She begins by eliciting directions from the class about how she should write the question on the board. The children still have their sign-in sheets and can refer to them as they give directions.

> Mrs. Poremba: If you are still working on your sign-in sheet, go ahead and keep signing in. We'll write our question of the day up on the board. Can someb—what we need to figure out first . . . is how many words are in our question for today. How many words? Christina, want to work on that?
>
> Christina: Four.
>
> Mrs. Poremba: . . . Bill, want to read it for us?
>
> Mikey: How come you wrote no, Bill?
>
> Bill: 'Cause they can't jump.
>
> Mrs. Poremba: (as Bill now takes some time to begin reading the sentence) He's thinking hard. That guy is thinking!
>
> Bill: "Can a dinosaur jump?"
>
> Mrs. Poremba: Did you say, "Can—a—dinosaur—jump?" (She pauses between the words.) Those four words?
>
> Bill: Yes.

Mrs. Poremba then asks the children about the spelling of each word, as children look at their sign-in sheets to help her. She also talks about spaces between words.

> Mrs. Poremba: So we're finished with the word *can*. Now I need to scoot over and leave a space because we're all finished with the word *can* and we're going to start a new word. Dan, what's the next word?
>
> Dan: *a!*

Later, after the word *dinosaur:*

> Mrs. Poremba: Are we finished with our question?
>
> Some children: No.
>
> Others: Yeah.
>
> Mrs. Poremba: We're all done? Let's read what we've got so far.

They read "Can a dinosaur" and decide that it still needs the word *jump.*

> Mrs. Poremba: Samantha, I'm not sure where to write the word *jump*. Does it, any ideas how, where to tell me about that up here?

Samantha: Um, scoot over a little bit and then write it.

After writing *jump:*

Mrs. Poremba: And a *p* on the end. Are we finished?

One child: Yeah.

Bill: And a question mark!

Mrs. Poremba: Question mark! Bill, tell me about that.

Bill: It's asking, it's asking, it's asking you a question.

Then Melissa reads the sentence as "Does a dinosaur jump?"

Mrs. Poremba: Melissa, let me write the word *does* here and see if . . . I'll write the word *does* right over here. (She writes the word.) Does. Is that what your sign-in sheet says? You might want to take a peek and check.

And then Mrs. Poremba leaves Melissa and immediately goes on with the routine of dismissing children from their tables as she picks up their sign-in sheets and acknowledges their sign-in writing.

Mrs. Poremba: Oh, Matt, Matt's seen some jumping dinosaurs in books. Good for you. Ian says no. . . . Derek, great that you are writing your last name. Good for you. Derek says no . . .

Kindergarten-Style Research

Later, as the children gather on the floor in the large-group area, Mrs. Poremba begins a discussion about dinosaurs that will lead into what she calls **kindergarten-style research.**

Mrs. Poremba: I have a question for you. On the sign-in sheet today, it asked you a question. Bill said it was an asking question. It needed to know something. It said, "Can a dinosaur jump?" Some of you said yes and some of you said no. What could we do, what could we do to find out more information about that?

Two children: Look in a book!

Mrs. Poremba: What is it called when you're, when you're trying to get more information, you need to learn something, and you decide to do things like look in books to find answers? What did we call that?

One child: Research.

Mrs. Poremba: Research! That's right! Kindergarten-style research. And we've been researching a lot lately. One day we tried to research to see if dinosaurs could lay eggs. And many of you went to the dinosaur books. You started poring through the dinosaur books. And sure enough, we found pictures of dinosaurs doing real dinosaur things like laying eggs.

I need some kindergartners to do some kindergarten-style research. We need to know if dinosaurs can jump.

Reading for Information

Mrs. Poremba has already introduced several books about dinosaurs. Some are narratives and some are informational books. Some are from her own collection, some from the school library, and some from the children, who have been invited to bring dinosaur books from home to support the dinosaur unit. The children know these books can be found on a book cart in the reading center, and they know how to work in pairs on a learning task. All the children volunteer to do kindergarten-style research about the question "Can a dinosaur jump?" Soon they are working in pairs all about the room.

Bill:	I found one! I found one jumping!
Another child:	Some could jump.
Another child:	I found one that's jumping!
Another child:	Oh, there's one jumping!
Another child:	That one's *not* jumping.

As they work, Mrs. Poremba moves from group to group and talks with children about their discoveries.

Mrs. Poremba: What do you think helps that dinosaur to be able to jump?

She asks one group about the difference between the fictional and nonfictional dinosaur books in the classroom library.

Mrs. Poremba: If you needed to know the truth, which one helps you the most?

One child: The *real* books!

And with another group:

Mrs. Poremba: Very interesting! You might want to save this for us, Samantha. Would you just hang on to that picture—because we need to talk about that.

Discussing the Evidence

After several minutes of kindergarten-style research, Mrs. Poremba rings a bell.

Mrs. Poremba: We need to gather as a team over on the carpet.

The children share what they have found in the books and Mrs. Poremba attempts to guide them to think about a new question.

Mrs. Poremba: Samantha, any ideas of what helps that dinosaur to be able to jump?

Samantha:	His legs . . .
Derek:	I think there's a special . . . muscle . . .
Mrs. Poremba:	Possibly.
Derek:	. . . that helps him.

Some interpret Mrs. Poremba's question as "How does this picture prove dinosaurs can jump?"

Mrs. Poremba:	Bill, tell me what your thinking is about that.
Bill:	. . . his whole body is up in the air instead of on the ground.

Some children are still not convinced by the pictorial evidence of jumping.

Mikey:	. . . they can't be jumping, I don't think, because like one foot's up, the other foot's down.
Matt and Dan:	Well, Mike . . . *about* to jump.
Mrs. Poremba:	Matt and Dan think they are getting, they are just about ready to jump. Any ideas on what might help these dinosaurs here, this, this kind of dinosaur to be a jumper? Ian, what do you think—could this be a jumper?
Ian:	I think they're jumping.
Mrs. Poremba:	Any ideas about that? Derek?
Derek:	. . . could be jumping . . . possible . . . or could not be, too. Could just be walking or running.
Mrs. Poremba:	So you're not convinced yet. Is anybody convinced about this? Dan?
Dan:	I know why, I know, I know why they don't think he's jumping. 'Cause he's not in the air yet.

After a bit more discussion:

Mrs. Poremba:	You know we really need to move on. I've got something I want to show you right now. If you need to continue your research, you're welcome to go to the dinosaur book cart during your free-choice time.

But Melissa and Samantha each still want to share their evidence, and the children are willing to continue for their sakes. After more discussion:

Mrs. Poremba:	Okay. I think we've done a good amount of research. And I think we've got some good ideas on, on whether dinosaurs could jump or can't jump. Now if you saw on your sign-in sheet "Can a dinosaur jump?" now that you've done some research and you've gotten some ideas, how would you answer that question now?

Several children:	Yes.
One child:	Well, actually, I think yes.
Several other children:	No.
Bill:	Some dinosaurs can jump, some can't.
Mrs. Poremba:	. . . Bill, you made an interesting comment. . . . (to the whole class) How would you feel about that for today?

Literacy Learning from "Can a Dinosaur Jump?"

This case study contains many examples of literacy and content learning in kindergarten. Mrs. Poremba continually emphasizes the meaning-making nature of reading and writing. The sign-in procedure is not an empty exercise. It serves as an attendance-taking device, which Mrs. Poremba makes explicit when she uses it to dismiss children from their tables. It contains important content for the children; in addition to telling them the date, it asks them a question, the deciphering and answering of which are important business for the beginning of the day. In this classroom, reading from books is meaningful; informational books can provide information relevant to the group's goal of answering the question. With her alterations to the sign-in procedure, Mrs. Poremba has extended children's opportunities to read and write as well as her own opportunities to model reading and writing. She capitalizes on this opening-of-the-day routine as a place for thinking, hypothesizing, and learning.

Mrs. Poremba emphasizes the form of written language when she reinforces concept of word by asking children how many words are in the question for today and by drawing attention to spacing between words. Mrs. Poremba emphasizes meaning-form links when she expects children to be able to spell *yes* and *no* without a model; when she elicits children's spelling of the words of the question; when she direct's Melissa's attention to the difference between the appearances of the words *can* and *does;* and when she gives time for discussion of the punctuation at the end of a question. Mrs. Poremba emphasizes the functions of written language when she acknowledges children's *yes*es and *no*s on the sign-in sheets as a record of their opinions and when she provides an organic, noncontrived reason for using books in kindergarten-style research.

Mrs. Poremba is especially skillful at helping children think for themselves. Her crafting of questions such as "Can a dinosaur jump?" and using the kindergarten-style research activity illustrates her role as a facilitator of thinking. Because of these questions, children formulate hypotheses and test them through their research and thinking. Children know that it's okay to have differences of opinion and that marshalling evidence for an idea is an important part of what they do in research. Children formulate hypotheses not only about the content they are learning, but also about written language. Children read the sign-in sheet carefully and make hypotheses about what it says. They work together to explore the print and to test their hypotheses about what it says.

WHAT'S NEW HERE?

In this and the next two chapters, we will discuss the context for instruction and learning in terms of how it is different from that presented in the preceding classroom chapters. In this case, we distinguish between the preschool context discussed in Chapter 7 and the unique kindergarten context.

Academic Expectations

One word captures this difference: *academic*. In the last twenty-five years, there has been a shift toward a more academic kindergarten experience. No longer is kindergarten viewed as merely a socialization for school, a year to get used to how to behave for teachers and with other children. Many children have already been away from home and in the organized, long-time company of large numbers of their age cohort for several years before coming to kindergarten.

Knowledge Bases

Although kindergartners are not usually bound to a goal of mastery, most educators expect them to show at least some knowledge that twenty-five years ago was introduced only at the beginning of first grade. This knowledge includes being able to recognize and write alphabet letters, write first and last names, know sound-letter correspondences, distinguish between fact and fiction, respond to characterization in stories and emotions in poetry, appreciate differences among multiple versions of traditional tales, recognize and write numerals, count, and understand the number line. Often the academic agenda for kindergarten contains some actual reading, writing, and computing. That is, some kindergartners are expected to learn a few sight words for reading, some conventional spellings for writing, and how to write number sentences. The academic agenda also includes knowledge in a variety of mandated social studies and science curriculum units (e.g., the neighborhood or the life cycle).

Constraints on Teachers

The constraints inherent in this new academic kindergarten context often are not limited to content. Frequently, kindergarten teachers feel less independence than in the past, not only in terms of what they teach but also how they teach it. Teachers' manuals and children's practice booklets and work sheets accompany mandated curricula in many kindergartens.

We feel that it is possible for kindergarten teachers who are knowledgeable about the characteristics of young children as they emerge into literacy to turn this academic expectation to their advantage. Furthermore, we believe that it is possible and desirable for kindergarten teachers to maintain the child-centered approach that has always been part of their outlook, even while addressing the new academic agenda. Kindergarten teachers can still be attentive to and responsive to individual children's interests and abilities; they can still be flexible.

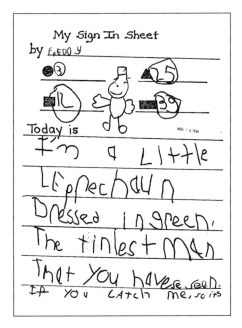

Figure 8.6 *Freddy's Sign-In Sheet (Front and Back)*
with Self-Scheduled Copying of "I'm a Little Leprechaun"

Lyrics by Betty Ruth Baker. Taken from *More Piggyback Songs*. Used with the permission of Warren Publishing House, Inc., P.O. Box 2250, Everett, WA 98203.

Freddy:	Mrs. Poremba—
Mrs. Poremba:	Freddy, you're still thinking about this, aren't you?
Freddy:	I noticed something.
Mrs. Poremba:	What did you notice? (She again places the tooth poem next to "I'm a Little Leprechaun.")

Freddy points to *you* in "I'm a Little Leprechaun." He doesn't say anything for several seconds; he doesn't know what the word says.

Mrs. Poremba:	Oh, are you looking at the word *you?*
Freddy:	And right here. (He points toward the tooth poem but can't immediately find *you* there.)
Mrs. Poremba:	It's on there. There—your finger almost touched it.
Freddy:	(Then Freddy finds it and points to *you* in both poems.) The same thing.
Mrs. Poremba:	You noticed the word *you* (pointing to *you* in the tooth poem) and the word *you* in the [leprechaun] poem. Freddy, thank you for finding that word *you*, Y-O-U.

Then Ian steps to the easel and points out that there are a lot of *you*s in "I'm a Little Leprechaun."

Freddy's self-scheduled copying had created a naturally occurring opportunity for exercising his visual discrimination. Mrs. Poremba used the opportunity to teach that the word Freddy noticed was *you*. Ian showed that he had benefited from this teaching; he could apply his learning to his reading elsewhere in the poem. Furthermore, at least one other classmate, Meagan, also a frequent self-scheduled copier, became newly interested in the tooth poem; she copied it on her sign-in sheet during wall work two days later.

THE KINDERGARTEN SETTING: SPACE AND MATERIALS

As with all teachers, an important part of being a kindergarten teacher is arranging the classroom and gathering materials. Figure 8.7 presents our design for a well-appointed and well-arranged kindergarten classroom. It has many similarities to Mrs. Poremba's classroom. One whole-group area in this classroom is the large, open, carpeted area in front of a bulletin board. Mrs. Poremba used an area like this when her class met to share the results of their kindergarten-style research and to conduct opening-of-the-day activities, such as their calendar activity. Mrs. Poremba and her students call the bulletin board **the wall** and their opening activities **wall work.**

In our exemplary classroom, the wall includes a Helpers' Tree on which the names of each day's two helpers are displayed (on apple-shaped cutouts taken from an apple basket containing every child's name); a tooth graph (on which the names of children who lose teeth are written); a calendar; a specials schedule and hook for displaying a sign that tells each day's special class (gym, music, art, or library story); and a weather chart with yes and no options for reporting whether it is sunny, cloudy, windy, rainy, or snowy.

A **pocket chart** hangs from a nearby stand. This large vinyl chart has several horizontal pockets running the width of the chart in which words on cards can be placed to make sentences or lines from poems. Also near to the carpeted whole-group area is a piano for music activities and an easel used for displaying big books, chart paper, and an erasable marker board.

This classroom has a second whole-group area where children can sit at tables near the chalkboard. Mrs. Poremba used an area like this when she wrote the question, "Can a dinosaur jump?" as a part of her extended sign-in procedure.

There are five centers in the classroom: blocks, make-believe play, home and restaurant, writing, and reading. In addition, children play in the large-group center when it is not being used for group activities. Play props are stored in bins and low cupboards in these centers and in the home center's kitchen furniture.

The writing center looks much like the one in the preschool classrooms described in Chapter 7. There is a large, round table where children are able to see others' work and to share their own work. There is also a smaller table with a typewriter and space for one or two children to write without interruption or distraction. On low shelves, there are many kinds of writing tools and paper; picture dictionaries; several letter-stamp sets and ink pads; several laminated cards, each

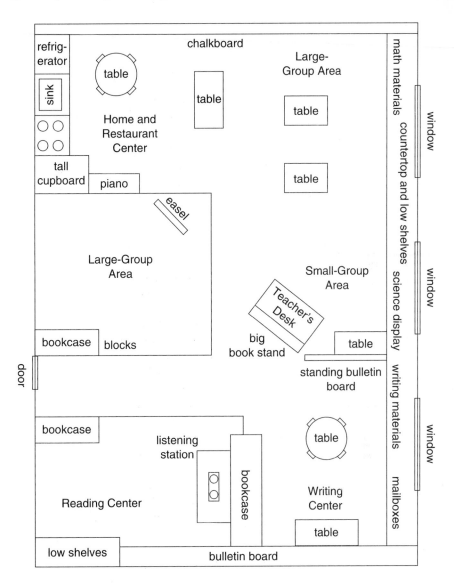

Figure 8.7 *A Kindergarten Classroom*

showing the alphabet in uppercase and lowercase letters; and a file box filled with words that children have written on cards and saved for future reference, some of which are illustrated. On the countertop above the shelves are pigeonhole mailboxes, one for each child. They hold unfinished writing and letters to kindergartners from classmates or the teacher.

In Mrs. Poremba's writing center, there is a special writing resource: two laminated, plastic-spiral-bound "My Friends" books. These are about Mrs. Poremba's students, one each for the morning and afternoon classes. Each page has a photograph of a child, the child's name, and a list of the child's favorites (foods, colors, activities). Parents sent the photographs from home and Mrs. Poremba gathered the information during individual interviews during the first few weeks of school. Children enjoy reading about themselves and their classmates, and they use these books to look up the spelling of classmates' names.

In the reading center, children's books stand on low, deep shelves and lie on low cupboard tops, where they are easily accessible. These include story and informational picture books, often chosen to complement a unit of study (such as the dinosaur books Mrs. Poremba's class used during their dinosaur unit); class made books (such as a book of bear stories written from children's dictation on bear-shaped pages during a bear unit); big books that the class has read; and multiple standard-sized copies of some of the big books. There are soft cushions on which the children can make themselves comfortable when they read. The cushions can be stacked out of the way when the reading center is used for a small group area. The listening station is set up on a small table in the reading center, with chairs for four children to use a tape player with headsets.

LEARNING AND TEACHING ABOUT LITERACY IN KINDERGARTEN: ROUTINES AND QUALITY TALK

The space and materials just described provide the setting for kindergarten teachers to support literacy development in a flexible, child-centered way. This flexibility and response to individual children is critical—a kindergarten class is likely to include some children from each of the descriptions given in Chapters 3 through 5—some novices, some experimenters, and some conventional readers and writers. In the examples from Mrs. Poremba's classroom that follow, some children are learning to recognize alphabet letters whereas others can read words and notice spelling patterns. Still others can read poems independently. Mrs. Poremba plans activities that allow all children to show what they know. We describe activities using classroom print, shared reading, writing, and play as support for children's language and literacy development in kindergarten.

Using Classroom Print

The exemplary kindergarten setting is filled with print. An important part of the teacher's role in this classroom is to invite children's responses to that print that reveal their current understandings about written language. This practice allows the teacher always to validate those understandings and at times to give children support for expanding those understandings. We will share examples of Mrs. Poremba's playing this role with two kinds of **classroom print:** "All Around You" print and informational print.

"All Around You" print in a kindergarten includes labels that the teacher introduces to the environment: object labels, such as *chair, table,* and *door;* picture labels, such as *ghost* on the picture of a ghost on the Halloween bulletin board; and other labels, such as *Helpers* or *Writing Center*. It also includes environmental print that comes with everyday things, such as packaging print—brand names and other print placed by manufacturers on everything from typewriters to T-shirts, and pencils to pennies. **Informational print** is writing that provides information in an organized format, such as a chart, a list, a picture dictionary, or an informational book.

"All Around You" Print
in Mrs. Poremba's Classroom

A guiding principle of using "All Around You" print is that it is always appropriate if presented to children in a supportive way. Teachers ask, "What can you read here?" and then accept the child's interpretation of that task. Some children will identify the object on which the print is found. When asked to read a toothpaste box, they may reply "toothpaste." Teachers celebrate their reading, saying, "Yes, it is a *toothpaste* box and it says *toothpaste* right here" (pointing to the appropriate word). Other children may identify letters (replying, "C-R-E-S-T"). Teachers celebrate this reading by saying, "Yes, you're right, and it says *Crest.*" Still other children may identify words (replying, "Crest"), and others may read connected text (replying, "Tartar control Crest"). In each case, teachers recognize children's reading as valid.

Mrs. Poremba includes "All Around You" print in a variety of ways in her units and activities. During a unit about taking care of the environment, children were examining bottles, cans, and other packaging that Mrs. Poremba had collected in a recycling bin. She had told the class about using the recycle symbol, a triangular shape formed from three interlocking arrows with a number in the center, to determine which numbered items their trash collectors would accept for recycling. Jason noticed a similar symbol on an empty cottage cheese carton. This was a symbol used by the dairy to indicate a real dairy product, an oval formed from two interlocking curves with the word *REAL* printed in the center. It was very similar in appearance to the recycle symbol. Jason asked, "Does this mean anything?" He knew that this symbol should have meaning, that it did not appear on packaging randomly—in effect, that it was readable.

It is also appropriate for children to copy "All Around You" print *if the task is self-initiated.* Even if children cannot read what they have copied, the teacher can read it and celebrate it. "All Around You" print is a continually available model and resource for children's writing. Mrs. Poremba has children "find the word you want somewhere in the room" as one possible writing strategy. They frequently find words in unexpected places.

For example, Freddy was playing in the home center. He sat at a counter where children regularly took orders at their pretend pizza parlor. He often wrote in this center, writing lines of mock cursive for each order. Now he had a pencil and clipboard—but no customers. While waiting for some pizza business, he entertained himself by carefully and very legibly copying the brand name embossed on the metal clip of his clipboard. His writing is shown in Figure 8.8. The brand name on the clipboard that he was copying was STEMPCO COLEMAN; he wrote STEMPCO COVEMAN.

Figure 8.8 *Freddy's Pizza Parlor Writing (A Pizza Order and Self-Scheduled Copying of a Brand Name, STEMPCO COLEMAN)*

Informational Print in Mrs. Poremba's Classroom

A guiding principle of using informational print in the classroom is that even young children whose literacy knowledge is not fully developed can benefit from the ways in which print is organized in informational formats if the teacher calls their attention to that organization and models its use.

When Mrs. Poremba's kindergartners engaged in kindergarten-style research about dinosaurs, they used two important understandings about informational print. First, they knew that some books are fictional and some are nonfictional. They knew to look in nonfictional books for information about what dinosaurs were really like. When Mrs. Poremba asked, "If you needed to know the truth, which one helps you the most?" a child answered, "The *real* books!" Mrs. Poremba had contrasted real and make-believe books with the class on many other occasions.

Second, Mrs. Poremba's kindergartners knew an important aspect of how information is organized in informational books—that there are text and illustrations, and both give reliable information (Pappas, 1993). When informational books contained text beyond the ability of even the experimenters and conventional readers among them, their reading strategy was to read the pictures. They even used high-level thinking when reading the pictures, that is, they read critically. When one child exclaimed, "Oh, there's one jumping!" a classmate replied, "That one's *not* jumping." Later, Mikey disputed Matt and Dan's interpretation of a picture: " . . . they can't be jumping, I don't think, because like one foot's up, the other foot's down," and Matt and Dan explained their thinking, "Well, Mike . . . *about* to jump." Still later, Dan attempted to accommodate both theories, "I know why, I know, I know why they don't think he's jumping. 'Cause he's not in the air yet."

Books are not the only informational print in Mrs. Poremba's classroom. Several charts provide information that children use frequently. Three examples are a specials schedule, a weather chart, and a birthday poster.

Using the specials schedule.   On the **specials schedule** are the words "Today we have:". Underneath are a hook and an envelope. The envelope contains four laminated signs, one each for art, music, gym, and library story, to hang on the hook. On the envelope is the word *Specials*. Each sign has a word telling the special class and a picture: a gym shoe for gym, a paintbrush for art, a musical note for music, and a book for library story. In early October, Mrs. Poremba posted a specials schedule beneath the specials envelope. Information is organized in this schedule by column, color, and picture. Across the top is the word *Specials*. Heading the left column is the word *Morning;* heading the right column is the word *Afternoon*. Each column has five cells, one for each day; in each is the name of the day of the week, the name of the special class that day, the time of the class, and the same picture symbol for that class as on the special signs. The day names are color coded, pink for Monday, yellow for Tuesday, green for Wednesday, blue for Thursday, and orange for Friday.

As part of wall work each day, one of the two helpers posts the specials sign for that day. For a time after introducing the specials schedule, Mrs. Poremba directed the helper's attention to the appropriate column, cell, and picture. By the middle of the year, children knew the schedule and helpers seldom needed to consult it, but if they forgot what day it was, Mrs. Poremba said, "You can look at the schedule. Today is Tuesday," and if necessary, "That's in a yellow rectangle." Often children wrote the name of the special class in the "Today is _____ " part of their sign-in sheets (see Figure 8.4).

The specials schedule is a resource for self-scheduled practice using informational print. In October, Jeff and Tara were reading the specials schedule together during free-choice time. Tara pointed to the appropriate columns and cells on the schedule and said, "On Tuesday we have library; on Tuesday, they have gym, the afternoon class. On Wednesday we have gym and they have library story."

Using the weather chart.   Mrs. Poremba's wall includes a **weather chart,** and reporting the weather is one of her **opening-of-the-day routines.** As a part of this activity, Mrs. Poremba writes weather words on a piece of paper posted next to the weather chart. At the beginning of the year, Mrs. Poremba wrote words the children suggested. She used this as an opportunity to model alphabet letter formation, letter identification, and spelling strategies. Usually children would repeat words from the weather chart for Mrs. Poremba to write. By midyear, they often suggested weather words not on the weather chart (e.g., *foggy*) or even nonweather words (e.g., *Easter*). As Mrs. Poremba wrote these words, she would ask children to identify letters or hear big sounds in order to spell. In February, she changed the activity by giving one of the helpers the option of writing the **"Words for Today."** As children wrote, Mrs. Poremba would ask them to **listen to the big sounds** or to **find the word somewhere in the room.**

Figure 8.5 showed Zack's Words for Today writing in March. He wrote the children's favorite weather word, *Brrrr,* with an exclamation mark. When Ian suggested writing "totally sunny," Zack copied *sunny* from the weather chart, but at first did not want to attempt *totally.* Then he agreed to write just the first sound in *totally,* fitting a *T* before *sunny.* Last, Jeff suggested writing "damp," and Zack received help spelling that word from his classmate Deborah.

On the second-to-last day of school, Freddy was the helper. After a discussion about how the grass had turned brown from a lack of rain, a classmate suggested that Freddy write "brown" as one of his Words for Today. He had already written *water* (*WtR*) using invented spelling—or, as Mrs. Poremba often suggested, "listening to the big sounds." Now Freddy remembered the color chart and another strategy Mrs. Poremba had often suggested, "Find that word somewhere in the room and copy it." With no hesitation, he located a color chart the children frequently used, brought it to the wall, and copied *brown* as *bROWn* on the Words for Today paper. Freddy's Words for Today writing is shown in Figure 8.9.

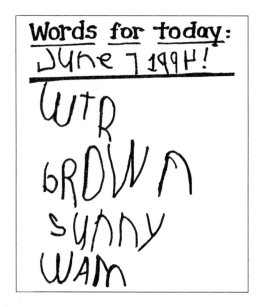

Figure 8.9 *Freddy's Words for Today*

Using the birthday chart.   Near the door in Mrs. Poremba's room is a laminated **birthday chart.** It organizes important information, the children's birthdays, using pictures for the months (e.g., a pumpkin for October). With erasable marker, so she can use it again next year, Mrs. Poremba has written each student's name and birthday on the appropriate month's picture. When lined up at the door to go home at the end of the morning, children often read the birthday chart, especially as they became better at reading one another's names.

On May 19, Deborah, as helper, was writing Words for Today. Mayra suggested writing "June," because "One more month is my birthday." Deborah, who had already used invented spelling to write "Jacob is sick" (*jAkup is sik*), immediately ran to the birthday chart. She came back and wrote *j*. When she made another trip to the birthday chart, Mrs. Poremba suggested she look at all the rest of *June*. When Deborah returned, she was able to write the rest of Mayra's word, *une*. After Deborah read all her writing to the class, Mayra said, "June 16!" Deborah said she would check the chart and again returned to the birthday chart, now not as a spelling guide, but as a source of information to verify Mayra's birthday. She added to her last entry for Words for Today so that it read *jUNe 16* as shown in Figure 8.10.

As these examples show, opportunities to use classroom print are not limited to activities planned as part of special units. They arise during routine activities as well, such as Mrs. Poremba's wall work (completing the opening-of-the-day routines, including the calendar, weather chart, and Words for Today). Making use of such opportunities is one way to vary activity within a routine. In this way, a routine can provide the structure and security that children often desire, while at the same time supporting their learning as teachers affirm existing understandings and provide scaffolding for next steps.

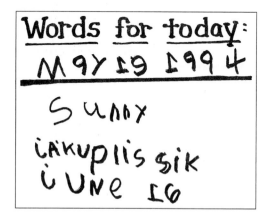

Figure 8.10 *Deborah's Words for Today*

What Is Learned about Written Language from Classroom Print?

Mrs. Poremba's students' experiences with classroom print are opportunities to learn much about written language. Her kindergartners learn that classroom print provides models of how to form letters and spell words for their own writing. Deborah demonstrated this when she copied the word *June* from the birthday chart. They know that environmental print has meaning, as Jason showed when he asked about the meaning of the *REAL* symbol on a cottage cheese container. They know that books serve many purposes, including telling stories about pretend characters and giving information about real people and things. They know that reading informational print sometimes requires knowing how content is organized. Jeff and Tara, for example, used the columns and rows to locate information on the specials schedule. They know how to record information by writing personally meaningful words on their sign-in sheets.

Mrs. Poremba's role was to capitalize on the opportunities provided in daily routines to teach about written language and strategies children could use in their reading and writing. She modeled listening for the big sounds as she demonstrated writing weather words. Then she encouraged children to listen for the big sounds

as they wrote Words for Today. As a result, children learned about sound-letter relationships. She also suggested other strategies that children could use, such as finding words from somewhere in the room. Consequently, children learned strategies
for independent writing.

Shared Reading

An important way in which kindergartners learn from each other is through planned
group-literacy experiences. Several of the routines in Mrs. Poremba's classroom included such experiences: Mrs. Poremba's and her students' rewriting and rereading
the sign-in question, "Can a dinosaur jump?" at the chalkboard; their discussion of
kindergarten-style research findings; and their wall work. In this section we will describe another technique for providing group literacy experiences for kindergartners, **shared reading.** With this technique, teachers read aloud from charts or big
books (with large-sized print so that children can look at the print as teachers read).
Then the children and the teacher read together (the shared reading portion of the
activity). Finally, children read with a partner or alone.

The purpose of shared reading is to guide children's learning about print so that
they gradually learn more conventional concepts. Many of Mrs. Poremba's children
develop concepts about print, such as the concept of a written word, directionality
(left-to-right orientation), and finger-point reading (see Chapter 4). They also learn
about sound-letter relationships and spelling patterns in word families (see Chapter
5). Some children learn to read a few or many words by sight. Shared reading also
demonstrates meaning-making strategies, such as predicting, connecting with real experiences, and making inferences. However, Mrs. Poremba does not expect that her
children will master any of these skills; rather, she expects them to acquire new understandings about written language. Before we describe shared reading in Mrs.
Poremba's classroom, we address the issue of large-group instruction in kindergarten.

Large-Group and Small-Group
Instruction in Kindergarten

Shared reading includes whole-class, small-group, and individual activities. Considering the variety of levels of written language knowledge in most kindergartens and
the active, distractible nature of many young children in their first year of formal
schooling, many educators would argue that whole-class activities are inappropriate. We feel, however, that they provide excellent opportunities for quality talk. A
sound principle of whole-class work is that it can be one of the most beneficial of
children's early school experiences so long as teachers ensure that it remains open
to a variety of children's responses.

An example of Mrs. Poremba's guaranteeing that all children participate successfully is her use of wall work and sign-in writing. We have already described
how Mrs. Poremba's sign-in procedure became writing the room, in which children
were free to write in their own way (or not to write). This approach to writing carried over to wall work when Mrs. Poremba invited children to bring their sign-in
sheets and clipboards along. She encouraged them to write down what was im-

portant to them during wall work and frequently told them that when they wrote on their sign-in sheets, she could see what they were thinking.

Mrs. Poremba monitored individual writing even while conducting the whole-class wall work and frequently commented on what a child had written. For example, she would say, while revealing the two helpers' names, "If you want to remember who was helper today—if that is important to you, you can copy their names on your sign-in sheets." During calendar, she would say, "If you think you know what day it is today, write it on your sign-in sheet and hold it up for me to see," or "I can see that you're thinking ahead, Freddy—you already wrote down the number for today," or "If you know the number for today, write it on your sign-in sheet and show it to a friend."

In similar fashion, Mrs. Poremba would invite children to copy weather words or copy or write their own Words for Today (see Figures 8.4 and 8.6). At the end of wall work time, Mrs. Poremba would direct children, "Turn and read something from your sign-in sheet to a friend." She would listen in on pairs of children doing this or ask a child to read to her. In this way, within the routine of wall work and with a whole-class group, individual children were able to use their varying reading and writing abilities, and they were able to interact often with each other and with the teacher. This interactive style of whole-class group work ensures that active kindergartners are attentive and provides them with immediate opportunities to display their written work.

Mrs. Poremba's kindergartners also participate in many small-group and paired activities. These include partner reading and cooperative learning (see Chapter 6). For example, on the day the children answered the question, "Can a dinosaur jump?" they decided, in small groups randomly assigned the previous day, what to name the large, paper dinosaurs their group had stuffed and decorated. Each group worked together to write a sign displaying their names and their dinosaur's name. The following descriptions of shared reading include examples of both large- and small-group reading and writing.

Shared Reading of Charts
in Mrs. Poremba's Classroom

Shared reading is a method for using a shared text as a reading and learning experience for a group of children (Holdaway, 1979). Typically, shared reading consists of three steps: (1) The teacher reads aloud a selection printed in large text on a chart or in a big book; (2) the teacher and students read the selection together; and (3) students do individual activities with the selection. Mrs. Poremba adds a preliminary step, which occurs before she reads aloud to the children. She orients the children to print during a What Can You Show Us? activity. Mrs. Poremba frequently uses the shared reading technique with a poem or letter to the class that she has written on chart paper and displayed on the easel. We will show how Mrs. Poremba uses shared reading as children read these charts.

Step one: Orienting children to print. Before Mrs. Poremba reads a new poem or letter to them, she **orients the children to print.** She has already emphasized the poem's line-by-line structure by printing the poem on the chart in two colors of ink, alternating colors for each new line. As children enter her room at the beginning of a day when there is a new poem or letter at the easel, she invites them to begin looking at the chart: "You might want to visit the easel during your sign-in time today. There is a new poem there for you."

Some children use this opportunity to read parts of the text that they know. Often Mrs. Poremba includes little picture clues over some words as an aid for this activity. Some children copy parts of the text onto their sign-in sheets during sign-in time, as a self-scheduled copying task. (Recall Freddy's doing this, as shown in Figure 8.6.)

During a whole-class time, Mrs. Poremba continues to orient children to the text of a poem. She points out the names of the author and illustrator. When the author is unknown, Mrs. Poremba discusses what "Author Unknown" means. She orients children to the form of a letter by pointing out the date line, the salutation line, and the signature line.

Mrs. Poremba's orientation to print continues in a **What Can You Teach Us? activity.** Before she reads the poem, she invites children to come to the chart and point out something they know. Children take turns stepping up to the easel and talking about a variety of letters or words or even trying to read the poem on their own. The other children are appreciative of whatever their fellow students can teach them about the text.

In October, Erin participates in the What Can You Show Us? activity by reading a word in a chart-paper letter from the class's imaginary Uncle Wally. This letter is presented in Figure 8.11.

Dear Kindergarteners,

   It is fall!
Fall is apple time.
We picked an apple
on a tree.
   Yum! Yum!
      Love,
      Uncle Wally

Figure 8.11 *A Letter from Uncle Wally*

Mrs. Poremba:	You're pointing to that *i-s,* Erin. Tell us about it."
Erin:	It's *is!*
Mrs. Poremba:	That's the word *is?* (Erin nods, and Mrs. Poremba points to the word and reads.) "Is."

When it is Eric's turn, he shows what he has noticed about letters.

Mrs. Poremba:	(to the class) Watch Eric.
Eric:	There's a *Y* for Freddy (pointing to the first letter in *Yum*).
Mrs. Poremba:	Oooh. There's a *Y* for Freddy. What do you mean "a *Y* for Freddy"? Does Freddy have a *Y* somewhere in his name?
Eric:	Yeah, and he has an *F* (pointing to the first letter in *Fall*).

Ten days later, the class reads another letter, this time from imaginary Aunt Edith. Now Mayra, who speaks almost no English at this point in the school year (Spanish is her first language), shares what she knows about letters.

Mrs. Poremba:	Mayra has something she would like to teach you. . . .
Mayra:	A *W* (pointing).
Mrs. Poremba:	A *W!* (pointing to the same *W* that Mayra had pointed to).
Mayra:	*W.*
Mrs. Poremba:	That's a *W.* Thank you, Mayra, for showing us the *W.* Thank you.

Mayra bows and makes the American Sign Language sign for "Thank you" that Mrs. Poremba has taught the class (Bornstein, Saulnier, & Hamilton, 1983; Children's Television Workshop, 1985; Rankin, 1991; Riekehof, 1978). Then Eric shows what he learned from Mayra.

Eric:	(pointing from his place on the floor to another *W* in Aunt Edith's letter) "And there's another *W!*"

In February, when children are invited to show what they know about a new poem, Freddy makes a connection with a familiar word. He uses one of Mrs. Poremba's **word frames** (window-shaped cutouts with handles that can be placed around a word to isolate it from the other words in a text) to show the word *Little.*

Freddy:	It starts like—(He goes to the wall and points to the word *Library* in the "Library Story" sign posted there for that day's special class.)
Jason:	*Library* has the same two letters.
Another child:	And *Lisa* (his sister's name.)
Mrs. Poremba:	Okay now, Freddy, you touch the *L* and the *i* right there and I'll get the *L* and the *i* right here. Freddy, that's very interesting. What about the rest of the word, Freddy?

Freddy: No.

Mrs. Poremba: . . . Freddy noticed the *L* and the *i* at the beginning of that word—the same thing as in *Library*. Freddy, that was important.

Later in February, Alyssa points out all the words beginning with *A* in a poem about Abraham Lincoln. Ian can read individual words: *Abraham, Lincoln, you, to, A*. Mrs. Poremba reinforces his use of beginning letters.

Mrs. Poremba: Where does it say *Abraham?* Can you show us that part? (Ian points to the word *Abraham*.) How do you know that says *Abraham?*

Ian: I saw the *A* and the *b* (pointing to those letters).

Mrs. Poremba: So the *A* and the *b* in *Abraham* helped you to read that word. Where does it say *Lincoln?* (Ian points to *Lincoln*.) How do you know that says *Lincoln?*

Ian: *L* (pointing to the *L*).

Mrs. Poremba: So the *L* in the beginning of the word helped you to read it to be *Lincoln*. . . . So you looked at the words to give you some ideas. . . . You can see words that you can read here. That's great. Alyssa could read letters.

When it is her turn, Nicole shows that she can read the pattern. She says, "Orange, green, orange, green, . . . " pointing out the alternating colors Mrs. Poremba has used to write the poem.

In March, Deborah reads the entire poem "I'm a Little Leprechaun" when it is her turn to show what she knows (remember that Mrs. Poremba has not read this poem to the class yet). Mrs. Poremba asks, "What was the poem telling you, Deborah?" but another child interrupts to say, "She read the *whole* thing!" Mrs. Poremba stops to celebrate that, "She *did* read the whole thing!"

Step two: Teacher reading.

The teacher reading portion of shared reading ensures that students attend to meaning. As teachers read, they invite children's comments and questions and model using meaning-making strategies. Mrs. Poremba maintains the interactive talk of the orienting-children-to-print portion of shared reading as she reads the selection aloud to the class and as she and the children read together. When she reads, she stops to comment about character or plot, to invite predictions, to remark about illustrations, and to accept and acknowledge students' comments and questions. Sometimes she points out a familiar or an unusual word; comments about punctuation, especially a question mark or an exclamation point; or reminds the class of a student's earlier observation during their orientation talk.

Step three: Teacher and children reading together.

In shared reading in kindergarten, poems, letters, stories, and informational books are read many times. Sometimes, when a poem has become familiar enough, Mrs. Poremba's class reads it aloud together, while she directs with a pointer on the chart-paper text. She knows that it is important for children to look at the print during this reading. Before such a **choral reading** of "I'm a Little Leprechaun," she says, "Sarah, where will you look to find the first word of the poem?" Sarah points from where she is sitting on the floor with the group.

Mrs. Poremba:	Can you tell us where it is?
Sarah:	On the top.
Mrs. Poremba:	(echoing Sarah) On the top. Right here? (Mrs. Poremba points and Sarah nods.) Are you ready (individually, calling several children by name) . . . Ready—here we go—" (and the class reads the poem aloud together).

Children in Mrs. Poremba's classroom interact with the poem many times before they are ready for a choral reading. Mrs. Poremba prepares children for choral reading by engaging them again in What Can You Show Us?, but now as a teacher-and-children-reading-together activity. In these interactions, children demonstrate more and different readings than when the text was new. They have memories of the teacher's reading to help them.

During such a reading of "I'm a Little Leprechaun," Lauren uses a word frame to show that she can read *old* in the words *gold* and *told*.

Mrs. Poremba:	Lauren, what did you want to show us?
Lauren:	There's the word *old* (putting her frame around the *old* part of *gold*).
Mrs. Poremba:	She found the word *old* inside of—(Lauren moves her frame to *old* in *told*) oh!
Lauren:	And there.
Mrs. Poremba:	Look, there's *told,* but if you cover up the *t,* you just have the *old* part left. And there's *gold;* cover up the *g* and *old* is left. Isn't that interesting?
Another child:	Old—gold!

Then Lauren shows the *an* part in *man*.

Lauren:	An!
Mrs. Poremba:	Oh and you saw the *an* word inside of *man*. Thank you, Lauren!

Mrs. Poremba had given no previous instruction in analyzing words for such similarities.

During a shared reading with another poem, Eric, who can not yet usually identify individual words, remembers how to read an important element from Mrs. Poremba's reading of the poem.

Mrs. Poremba: Eric's ready. Come on up, Eric. Guys, let's see what Teacher Eric wants
                to show us.

Eric: (pointing and reading) Author unknown.

Mrs. Poremba: You remembered the "Author Unknown" part. We don't know who
                wrote this poem. That's an important thing to remember.

Step four: Response activities.   The final step of shared reading involves response activities with the text. The purpose of these activities is for children to attend
to print on their own without the support of a teacher. In kindergarten, many of these
activities take place in pairs or small groups; some are done by individuals. Mrs.
Poremba usually assigns small groups randomly by drawing children's names from a
"magic pot." For randomly assigning pairs, Mrs. Poremba has children draw strips of
paper. She cuts the strips so that there are two at each of several lengths; a child's
partner is the classmate with the strip of matching length. The children's acceptance
of this eliminates disappointments or arguments about who gets to be with whom.

After several whole-class activities with a chart-paper poem about November,
Mrs. Poremba assigned students to small groups. Each group had all the words of
the poem on separate word cards and a large piece of lined posterboard. Their job
was **text reconstruction;** they worked together to reconstruct the poem by placing the word cards onto the lines on the posterboard.

Earlier, the whole class had used the pocket chart as preparation for this activity. Mrs. Poremba wrote the poem on long strips of posterboard, one strip for
each line of the poem. She placed these strips in the pocket chart, one strip per
pocket, and the class read the poem one line at a time. Then she invited students
to step up to the pocket chart, choose a line of the poem, read it, and remove that
strip from the chart. When all the strips were removed, Mrs. Poremba returned
them to the pocket chart and repeated the activity until every student had had a
turn choosing and reading a line of the poem.

The pocket chart with the poem displayed on strips was still available as a
model for students who wanted one during their text reconstruction. As some children worked in their small groups to reproduce the poem, they used the model
from the pocket chart to match words. Some children were able to locate words
using picture clues, such as a drawing of blades of grass on the word card for *grass*
in the line "No green grass."

After they completed the activity, children evaluated their cooperation by cir-
cling *yes* or *no* after their names on an **"I helped" record sheet.** When she visited groups as they worked on the text reconstruction activity, Mrs. Poremba was
as interested in how they worked together as in whether they constructed the poem
accurately. She wrote on the record sheet what children said they had done, such
as "Kaitlynn helped with the easel and read" and "Nathan—liked reading and helping with the No's" (several lines of the poem begin with the word *No*). An "I
helped" record sheet for this activity is presented in Figure 8.12.

One reason this **cooperative learning** and recording activity worked well on
the first try, early in the school year, was that Mrs. Poremba, her classroom aide, and
one of the authors of this book modeled the processes of reading, working together,
and deciding whether to circle *yes* before Mrs. Poremba asked the children to do it.

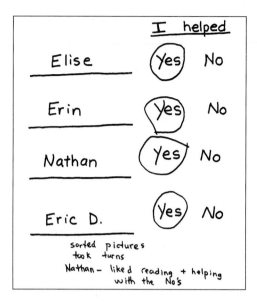

Figure 8.12 An "I Helped" Record Sheet

Mrs. Poremba provided another individual activity with the November poem. Children made their own books, each page of which contained a line from the poem and a pop-up illustration. Because they had listened to Mrs. Poremba read the poem, had read the poem together, and had done a small-group activity with the poem, all the children could read their November poem books when they took them home.

Another example of an individual activity occurred after Mrs. Poremba's class had observed the three-week long process of chicken eggs' incubating and hatching in their room. A chart-paper poem/song used during this unit began, "Cluck Cluck Red Hen" and followed the pattern of "Baa Baa Black Sheep." During free choice one morning, Zack was singing this song while visiting the brooder box that contained the class's newly hatched chicks. Mrs. Poremba noticed this and invited Zack to the easel. She pointed out that he was singing what was written on the chart paper, which the class had read together many times. She invited him to point with a pointer as he read the text (to finger-point read; see Chapter 4). She watched and listened, nodding as he read, even when his pointing did not always match his reading. Her role was audience, not instructor; she did not correct him. When he finished reading, both Mrs. Poremba and Zack were smiling broadly. She said, "You did it! Very nice, Zack!"

Zack's reading attracted Alyssa, Tara, and Elise, each of whom took a turn pointing to and reading the poem. These three varied in the accuracy of their pointing, with only Elise pointing perfectly; all three had an appreciative, fully attentive audience in Mrs. Poremba.

Even when Zack's, Alyssa's, or Tara's pointing sometimes digressed from their reciting or singing of the poem, they were able to recover, that is, to find a place in the poem where they could identify a word with confidence and proceed. Their self-correcting using sight words or beginning sound–letter correspondences demonstrated significant growth from what they were able to do in individual reading activities at the beginning of the year. Their confidence and the number of reading strategies now in their repertoires made pointing and reading a chart-paper poem a viable free choice for them in May. Mrs. Poremba was aware of this when she seized the opportunity presented by Zack's singing to the chicks and by the girls' interest in what Zack was doing at the easel.

Shared Reading with Big Books in Mrs. Poremba's Classroom

Big books (see Chapter 6) are excellent texts for shared reading. Big books can be effective in extending kindergartners' literacy knowledge, especially in helping them to appreciate written language forms, to understand the relations between what a reader says and what is written in a book, and to become increasingly influenced by a book's text in their pretend reading. Big books make text especially accessible to children who are taking these steps (Martinez & Teale, 1988; Trachtenburg & Ferruggia, 1989).

Early in the year Mrs. Poremba reads the big book *Bears, Bears Everywhere* (Connelly, undated). This is a pattern book with the title repeated on every page, followed by a three-word phrase, the last word of which rhymes with *where*.

Orienting the children to pictures and print.   Mrs. Poremba's orienting the children to *Bears, Bears Everywhere* demonstrates that a picture book's illustrations are as important as the text. She helps children to use both illustrations and text to answer questions about the book. One of these questions concerns a topic the class has been exploring. They have already made a large poster from index cards on which were written facts about bears dictated by the children. Also, Mrs. Poremba had asked parents to write bear stories their children dictated at home and send the stories to school. When Mrs. Poremba read these to the class, she always asked if they were real or pretend stories. Now, with *Bears, Bears Everywhere,* she asks the same question, and the answer can be found in the cover illustration of bears that are behaving more like humans than like bears.

Mrs. Poremba:	I want you to look at the cover of the book and get your ideas for what this book is about.
Children:	(loudly and all together) Bears!
Mrs. Poremba:	Turn and tell a friend.
Children:	(whispering to one another) Bears. Bears.
Mrs. Poremba:	I have a thinking question for you right now. . . . I want you to think about whether this book will be about pretend bears or real facts about real bears. Don't say it, just think.

After a short pause, many children answer.

> Mrs. Poremba: Can you turn and share your idea with a friend?

Children whisper their predictions to one another, but some loud *nos* and *yeses* can be heard as children disagree with one another. One child suggests that the illustration might be showing real bears who are in the circus.

> Mrs. Poremba: Now there's an idea—I hadn't thought of that. Why don't we read and then we'll get more ideas about whether these are real bears or pretend bears, bear facts, or pretend things about bears.

Now Mrs. Poremba shifts the focus to the print on the cover of the book. She helps the children to concentrate on where to begin reading, how to spell the first sound in *bears,* and how a written word looks (by counting words in the title).

> Mrs. Poremba: Where could I look to find the name of the story?
>
> Children: B! B!
>
> Mrs. Poremba: What do you mean *B?*
>
> Child: The title page.
>
> Mrs. Poremba: Well that's one place to look.
>
> Child: The cover.
>
> Mrs. Poremba: The cover? Okay . . . and I noticed that some of you said the letter *B* because that's the very first letter in the word (pointing) *Bears.* Here's another one (pointing to the *B* at the beginning of the second word *Bears*). This story is called (pointing) *Bears, Bears, Everywhere!*
>
> Child: Bears, bears everywhere?
>
> Mrs. Poremba: I'll read it again—first of all, how about if we count the words in the title, so we know how many words there are. (with some children reading and counting along) "Bears"—one. "Bears"—there's two. "Everywhere"—three words in the title.
>
> Child: No, how about that top one (referring to writing above the title)!
>
> Mrs. Poremba: Up here it says "CTP Big Book"—that's the name of the store, or the company, I should say, that printed this book.
>
> Child: There's some down there.
>
> Mrs. Poremba: Down here it says, "Author, Luella Connelly"—she wrote the words—and . . . the other words here say, "Illustrator Neena (hesitating) Chawla Koeller."
>
> Child: That's hard.
>
> Mrs. Poremba: That's a lot—she's the person who did the pictures. She's the illustrator.
>
> Child: Two people worked on it!
>
> Mrs. Poremba: (confirming) Two people worked together to make this book.

Child: Teamwork!

Mrs. Poremba: (confirming) Teamwork, teamwork—that's a very good idea!

Teacher reading.   During her first reading of the big book *Bears, Bears Everywhere,* Mrs. Poremba points out where to look when reading; contrasts the spellings of two similar words, one of which is familiar to some of the children; and demonstrates meaning-making strategies. She weaves these and other activities— many of them suggested by the children's questions and comments—into a rich interaction about a simple story. As she reads a page about bears in pairs, for example, she first establishes a focus on meaning by asking the children to look at the illustration and call to mind what the story might be about. Then she points to the text as she reads.

Mrs. Poremba: I want you to look at the pictures and get some ideas. (pause) I want you to put your eyes right down here and I'll start reading (pointing to the text at the bottom of the page).

Mrs. Poremba reads, and the children laugh. Next, Mrs. Poremba responds to a child's question, capitalizing on the opportunity to expand their understandings about the meaning of the word *pair*.

Child: Pairs?

Mrs. Poremba: I wonder what it means—bears in pairs?

Jason: Two together make a pair.

Mrs. Poremba: Oh, there are two together. So this isn't the kind of *pear* that you buy at the store and eat, like a fruit. This is a different way to use the word *pair.* Jason said that a pair is when two things are together. Look at your shoes. Like a pair of socks.

Children: Pair of earrings . . . pair of shoelaces . . . eyes . . . ears . . . arms . . . pair of legs . . . pair of elbows!

Mrs. Poremba: So things that come in twos are pairs.

Still later, for a page about bears on chairs, Mrs. Poremba shifts to form and meaning-form links. She calls attention to the picture of bears on chairs and asks what the bears are doing. Then she does some **instructional writing;** she takes a moment from the big book reading to demonstrate with her writing how written language works. Mrs. Poremba uses a small, erasable marker board that she keeps near her big book easel for her instructional writing. In this case, she reads the page about bears on chairs, but stops before the word *on*.

Mrs. Poremba: What's this word (pointing)?

Several children respond at once with their guesses, including "Sitting in chairs," "Zero," and "No."

Mrs. Poremba: Does anyone know what O-N spells? . . . Let me show you.

Child:	(still working on her own) On chairs.
Mrs. Poremba:	(writing on the erasable board) Here is how you spell *no.* How do you spell it?—with *N* first and then—
Eric:	Oh I get it! I get it. The *O* has to be on that side and the *N*'s on that side.
Mrs. Poremba:	Yes when the *O* is on this side and the *N* is second, that's the word *on.*
Tara:	It's like a pattern! (The children are used to finding patterns in the shapes on which the numbers of the calendar are written.)
Mrs. Poremba:	It *is* kind of.
Children:	(reading) On. On. On. On chairs! It's "On chairs"!

Mrs. Poremba then reads the page and comments, "Some of you have been writing *on* in your sign-in sheets."

Still later, when Mrs. Poremba points to the word *lair,* Tara says, "Just like the Blairs!" One of the class's favorite books is *Somebody and the Three Blairs* (Tolhurst, 1990), a parody of the Goldilocks and the three bears story.

Reading and responding. Over the next several days, the children frequently reread *Bears, Bears Everywhere* together. They also read their own little-book versions of this book to one another and take them home to read to their families.

Often, children who at first say that they cannot read are willing to read a big book page after a group reading and discussion. They become enthusiastic about the big books and want to return to them again and again (Combs, 1987).

A teacher who uses big books with groups of children does what anyone would do with an individual child sitting in his or her lap; that is, the teacher responds to the children's developing awareness of story form and of the role of the text in the storyreading. Such informal talking with children about what people do when they read can be very helpful to experimenters. Big books merely make that kind of talk available for more than one child at a time. Thus, they are especially effective in classroom situations in which teachers cannot do one-to-one lap reading as often as they would like.

What Is Learned about Written Language during Shared Reading?

Shared reading in the examples from Mrs. Poremba's class was the vehicle for teaching and learning about all aspects of written language. For example, children learned about meaning making when Mrs. Poremba asked them to think about what a book or a page might be about from studying a book cover or page illustration. They learned about form when she asked them where to start reading a poem or where to find the title of a big book and when they worked together to reconstruct a poem from word cards. They taught one another about meaning-form links when they pointed out sound–letter correspondences (e.g., Ian's telling how the letter *A* helped him find the word *Abraham*), word families (e.g., Lauren's *old, gold, told* discovery), and print-to-speech matches (e.g., Zack's, Alyssa's, Elise's, and Tara's finger-point reading). They learned about functions of written language, that it can provide information (e.g., "Author Unknown," "CTP Big Book") and entertain (e.g., a poem about bears in pairs, on chairs, in lairs, etc.). It can even be used to record feelings about learning together (e.g., "Nathan—liked reading and helping with the No's").

It is important to keep in mind that shared reading is only one kind of reading aloud to children that takes place in Mrs. Poremba's classroom. Mrs. Poremba frequently reads aloud quality literature, including poems, stories, and informational books. The purpose of these readings is for children's enjoyment, to find out more about a topic of study (such as dinosaurs or recycling), and to extend children's experiences with literature. During these read alouds, Mrs. Poremba focuses on meaning—responding to children's questions and comments and encouraging their predictions. Therefore, her attention to print in shared reading is balanced by her attention to meaning in a variety of other kinds of reading activities, including kindergarten-style research.

Writing

We have included descriptions of the many ways in which writing was used in Mrs. Poremba's kindergarten. Children wrote signs, orders at the pizza dramatic-play-with-print center, and Words for Today, and they wrote as they carried out the sign-in activity. Mrs. Poremba also modeled writing as a part of many activities. She modeled writing as she wrote the sign-in question, during instructional writing, and as she took dictation from the children. For example, at the start of the unit on dinosaurs, Mrs. Poremba wrote on chart paper at the easel children's dictations of things they already knew about dinosaurs. Later, she transferred this information to a huge piece of bulletin-board backing paper, with each child's comment in quotation marks (e.g., "Elise—'Dinosaurs eat leaves off trees and dinosaur teeth are stones now.' "). The children referred to this chart throughout the unit, as they learned more about dinosaurs. Here we describe two additional contexts for writing: journals and language experience charts.

Journals

Kindergartners enjoy writing in **journals** both about self-selected topics and about topics suggested by their content study. Figure 8.13 presents a journal entry written by a kindergartner after he had played in a doctor dramatic-play-with-print center. Figure 8.14 presents Nathan's journal entry on the day Mrs. Poremba's class witnessed a chick's hatching.

Another teacher included journal writing in a unit about Pilgrims. As a part of the unit, the class "gathered around a small box and talked about what they would put in it to take to the New World where there would be no stores" (Fallon & Allen, 1994, p. 547). They acted out being Pilgrims and living on a cramped ship. Each day the teacher read aloud books about the *Mayflower,* and children wrote in journals as if they were traveling on the ship.

Kindergarten journals often become places where children dictate content information of personal interest. Marina dictated about a caterpillar that she brought to

Figure 8.13 *A Kindergartner's Journal Entry*

Figure 8.14 *Nathan's Journal Entry ("A chick just hatched!")*

school on a stick. "A calipitter [*sic*] likes to climb on his stick. He's fuzzy. . . . And he gots short hair and its [*sic*] thick. I don't know how many legs he's got because he won't turn over on his back" (Fallon & Allen, 1994, p. 548). Journals are also places where teachers provide individual help with invented spellings (Freppon & Dahl,

1991). As teachers sit with children writing in journals, they help children listen for the big sounds in words and celebrate children's successes in inventing spellings.

Language Experience

We have described both preschool and kindergarten teachers' taking dictation from children. Children dictate a message, and teachers write what they say. **Language experience** capitalizes on this activity (Stauffer, 1980; Van Allen & Van Allen, 1982). Language experience usually involves three kinds of activities: experience, dictation, and language study. First, teachers provide an experience, such as baking cookies, observing eggs hatch, or interviewing a classroom visitor. Then, children record their experience by dictating what they have observed or learned. Teachers write the dictation on a chart or in a big book. Finally, teachers use the **language experience chart** to help children learn new concepts about written language. In small groups, pairs, or independently, children may reconstruct the text or illustrate a personal copy of a group language-experience chart.

The purpose of language experience is to provide opportunities for children to learn more about written language just as they do in shared reading. Children may learn to recognize alphabet letters while teachers name the letters while they write. Children may learn more about sound-letter relationships by observing their teachers slowly say words and write letters. Or teachers may invite children to help them spell words. Children learn about meaning by noticing that what is said can be written and reread.

Experience and dictation. The first step of a language experience lesson is to provide children with an experience. The experience can be concrete, such as popping corn, or it can be more abstract, such as reading a story. One kindergarten teacher, Mrs. Bellanger, brought in several kinds of animal hearts preserved in alcohol. The children looked at the hearts and listened to their own hearts through a stethoscope.

During this phase, teachers encourage children's interactions with the activity. Teachers can contribute to this phase of the language experience lesson by interjecting new vocabulary, making explanations, and providing analogies to extend children's understanding of the experience. Mrs. Bellanger provided information about each of the different hearts. She described the heart as a pump, she pointed out the veins and arteries on each heart, and she informed the children that the heart was a muscle like other muscles in their bodies. The children tried to guess which heart belonged to a deer, a chicken, and a dog; they talked about eating chicken hearts; and they tried to make their hearts beat faster by jumping up and down.

Next, children dictate. Frequently, teachers do the writing, but as children gain more experience with written language, they write parts of their language story. In this step, teachers guide children in writing a narrative or an expository text. They might want to introduce children to different names of texts, such as "story," "description," or "explanation." The words that are selected to be included in writing should be the children's own. Sometimes teachers ask children to record only a few words, perhaps in a list or as part of the longer dictation. Dictations are recorded on a language experience chart or in a big book. When individual children dictate, teachers write below the children's pictures or on letter-sized paper. Mrs. Bellanger asked the children to think of good descriptive sentences about the human heart. The children dictated the following language experience chart:

> We have a heart.
> Our heart is a muscle that pumps blood.
> It is as big as a fist.
> Animals have hearts, too.
> Hearts are usually found in the chest.

Once the chart is produced, the teacher reads it aloud and invites children to read along. The chart is reread several times without undue attention to getting it right. Mrs. Bellanger's children read and reread their chart several times; then Mrs. Bellanger placed it in the science center and invited children to read it to a friend during center time.

Pattern books are frequently used as stimuli to language experience activities (Bridge, 1986). Because pattern books are easily remembered, children can dictate them for language experience charts or for big books. Big books with their pictures covered become the materials for language study lessons.

Language study.   Language study includes rereading the language experience chart. With less experienced children, teachers usually read the chart several times and invite children to participate. Teachers generally ask more experienced children to begin reading. Several kinds of language activities can follow rereading the chart. For example, children can match sentences and then words written on sentence strips or cards to those text segments on their chart.

What Is Learned about Written Language from Writing?

Writing provides numerous opportunities to explore written language meanings, forms, meaning-form links, and functions. Children's meaning making is extended through learning new vocabulary, for example, *muscles, arteries,* and *veins,* as a part of language experiences. Children explore form as they observe their teacher writing from their dictation. They notice the teacher using left-to-right orientation and spacing between words. Children expand their understanding about meaning-form links as their teacher helps them invent spellings in journals, as they observe other children inventing spellings, and as they try spelling. Children learn more about written language functions as they keep a journal recording their experiences on a pretend journey.

Play

Play is one of the most important activities in a kindergarten classroom. We described in Chapter 7 how one of the many benefits of play in preschool is its serving as a context for literacy learning. The same is true of play in kindergarten, and many of the methods for encouraging preschool literacy-related play are equally suitable for kindergarten. In the academic context of today's kindergartens, it is important for teachers to remember the benefits for their students of having plenty of space, materials, and time for free play. In this section, we describe some of the literacy-related uses of play in Mrs. Poremba's kindergarten.

Play in Mrs. Poremba's Classroom

We have already described Mrs. Poremba's kindergartners' use of free-choice times to experiment with reading and writing from familiar texts. When previewing options for free-choice time, Mrs. Poremba always reminded the children that the reading and writing centers were open. Children frequently chose individual and partner reading with a big book that the class had already read or visiting the easel where the current chart-paper poem was posted. Reading along with a book on tape at the listening center was also a popular choice.

We described Freddy's mock cursive writing and self-scheduled copying from environmental print as part of his play at the home center (see Figure 8.8). Another example of play-related writing occurred when Deborah was taking orders at the dramatic-play-with-print pizza parlor. This was a popular play scenario for both boys and girls. Deborah chose it as a play activity for at least a small part of the free-choice time several times a week. Like Freddy and the other kindergartners, her writing during order taking was always the same—a line of mock cursive for each item in the customer's order. She took a pizza order from one of the authors of this book: seven lines of mock cursive for "extra large . . . thin and crispy . . . green olives . . . sausage . . . extra cheese . . . root beer . . . large." Later, however, when delivering the order, Deborah used a different writing strategy, one she had never before used during pizza parlor play. "Wait—you need your receipt," she said, and she used the numerals and symbols on the toy cash register to copy "¢25¢" and "$5" on the back of the paper she had used for writing the order (see Figure 8.15).

Figure 8.15 *Deborah's Pizza Parlor Writing ("Extra Large," "Thin and Crispy," "Green Olives," "Sausage," "Extra Cheese," "Root Beer," "Large" and a Receipt)*

Sign making was another use of written language during play times. In December, Mrs. Poremba turned the block center into a dramatic-play-with-print shoe store. In response to a letter asking for help stocking the store, parents sent old shoes, slippers, and boots; shoehorns; and foot sizers. The children arranged the footwear on shelves and set up a checkout counter. They also wrote signs and their own paper money.

Frequently, children in Mrs. Poremba's room wanted to work on a play project for more than one day. When they asked Mrs. Poremba what they could do to be sure that what they had done was not disturbed in the meantime (especially by the afternoon kindergartners), Mrs. Poremba always suggested that they make a sign. In January, Ian taped such a sign to his half-finished Lego creation (see Figure 8.16). Ian does not yet always make a conventional *S,* but he does know that an apostrophe shows ownership. When asked the next day to tell "what you added to *Ian,"* he replied, "Ian's."

Figure 8.17 shows another sign that several boys made in May to reserve a large dinosaur puzzle they had constructed on the floor. The sign tells others "No Stepping." As they had been doing on their sign-in sheets at this time of the year, Jeff

IAN'S

Figure 8.16 *Ian's Sign*

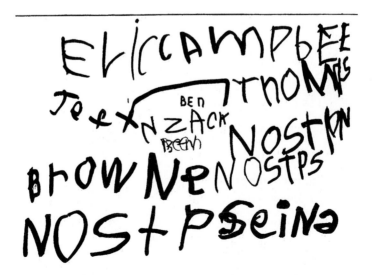

Figure 8.17 *Eric, Jeff, Zack, and Ben's "No Stepping" Sign*

Browne included his last name and Eric Thomas Campbell included his middle and last names.

Dramatizing Informational Books

Dramatizing information from nonfiction is a playful and powerful learning opportunity. After reading several informational books about bees, Mrs. Holcomb invited her kindergartners to play about being bees. "Now I would like you to pretend that you are bees looking for a flower. When I ring the bell, stop buzzing and land on a petal of a flower." After the teacher rang the bell, she said, "Suck up the nectar. All right, now brush some of the pollen to the back of your legs. . . . Now, you have the nectar in your honey stomach and the pollen on your back legs. . . . Fly home" (Putnam, 1991, p. 463).

Mrs. Poremba directed a similar play episode as part of her chick-hatching unit. Her students had read many informational books and posters about chick development and hatching. As the children anticipated their first chick's hatching, they applied what they had learned from their reading.

Mrs. Poremba:	Let's pretend that we are a chick that's been in the egg twenty-one days. You are SO crowded, your legs and your wings and your head and your back and your beak are ALL crunched together. . . . Okay, the first thing you do is you SLOOOOOWLY move your head up and you're going to poke your air sack on the top of your egg to take that breath of your first air. Poke your air sack. Okay. Take your breath. Do you like that air?
Children:	Yes. Uh huh.
Mrs. Poremba:	But you know what? That took a lot of work. So now you're tired again. . . . Ohhhh. Now a little bit of a rest. Now we're going to take our head and get your egg tooth up, part of the end of your beak. And we're going to make our very first pip in the shell—and that's very hard work. Find your place to pip.
Children:	Pip, pip, pip. Peep, peep, peep.
Mrs. Poremba:	Did you get a pip in your shell?
Children:	Yeah, Yes.
Mrs. Poremba:	Go back to sleep. You are so tired. This is HARD work hatching. Okay, now let's look at our picture to see what we need to do next.

What Is Learned about
Written Language during Play?

Play provides a rich context for extending children's understandings about written language. As children listen along with tapes in the listening center, they extend their understandings about stories. As they dramatize informational books, they show their understandings of the meanings of words such as *pollen, nectar, honey stomach, air sack, pip,* and *egg tooth.* Copying numbers, for example, copying *25* from a toy cash register, extends children's knowledge of written language forms. Using seven lines of mock cursive to write seven phrases in a pizza order allows children to test a meaning-form link hypothesis—that written language must relate to spoken language. Sign making is a functional activity—making a sign "No Stepping" means that children expect written language to be heeded.

ANOTHER LOOK: THE TEACHER'S ROLES

We have described kindergartners and their teachers as they participated in activities using reading and writing. The children had rich and numerous opportunities to learn about written language. In particular, Mrs. Poremba played at least six roles in supporting her kindergartners' language and literacy learning.

First, she *followed children's leads*. Mrs. Poremba wanted children to discuss evidence from their kindergarten-style research that revealed how a dinosaur might be able to jump (e.g., dinosaurs shown with large leg muscles). She asked, "Samantha, any ideas of what helps that dinosaur to be able to jump?" But she abandoned that idea when the children preferred to debate a simpler question—whether or not illustrations actually provided evidence of jumping ("his whole body is up in the air" versus "one foot's up, the other foot's down"). Mrs. Poremba invited children to tell what they knew as they read big books and sign-in questions. She said, "Tell us about that," demonstrating that children had something important to teach each other. Their information—what they knew about print—became part of each day's lessons. Mrs. Poremba also followed children's leads as she changed her sign-in procedures after noticing that children wanted to use the sheets for a new kind of writing—writing the room. She observed children as they talked and as they read and wrote. Each day she provided opportunities for children to show what they were learning about.

Second, Mrs. Poremba *planned routines that included functional reading and writing*. She used sign-in questions to foster reading for information and wall work to orient children to their daily schedule and the weather. She expected that children would read and write as a part of these activities.

Third, Mrs. Poremba *modeled reading and writing strategies in ways that supported children's own reading and writing*. During shared reading, she demonstrated reading from print, knowing where to begin reading, and paying attention to titles as a clue for meaning. She pointed to words as she read and provided opportunities for children to practice pointing as they read. She modeled listening for the big sounds and finding words in the room as she wrote weather words, and she expected children to use these strategies when they wrote Words for Today.

Fourth, Mrs. Poremba *drew explicit attention to print*. She used instructional writing to point out the differences between *no* and *on*, she elicited talk about print as she wrote the sign-in question, and she oriented children to print before and during shared reading by using the What Can You Show Us? activity.

Fifth, Mrs. Poremba *gradually shifted the responsibility for reading and writing to the children*. In the beginning of the year, children were expected to write only their names on their sign-in sheets. By the middle of the year, they might circle *yes* or *no* or even write those words themselves in answer to a sign-in question, or they might use their sign-ins as a personal journal-like record of the opening-of-the-day events. In the beginning of the year, Mrs. Poremba wrote the weather words, but by the middle of the year she offered children the option of writing themselves. By the end of the year, the children were writing Words for Today.

Finally, Mrs. Poremba *planned individual and group activities involving reading and writing*. She planned shared reading activities, including special small-group- and individual-related activities, such as text reconstructions and pop-up books. She planned ways to make group learning more effective, including having children evaluate their performance on "I helped" record sheets.

Chapter Summary

Kindergarten teachers, like all teachers in elementary school, have many academic expectations for their children's learning. In general, kindergartners are expected to learn to write and name the alphabet, write their names, learn sound–letter relationships, expand their understandings of words, understand stories, and learn from listening to informational books. These academic expectations are met when classrooms are filled with print, when teachers and children model reading and writing, and when children participate in reading and writing activities.

Kindergartners' literacy learning is supported through classroom routines using print. Routines such as the extended sign-in procedure, wall work, and Words for Today encourage children's reading and writing as well as provide opportunities for teachers and children to talk about written language. Shared reading is a rich context for literacy learning; teachers orient children to print, read with children, and plan response activities. Shared reading is used with poems, songs, letters, chants, stories, and informational texts presented on charts and in big books.

Writing is another context for language and literacy learning in kindergarten. Teachers model writing through instructional writing, language experience, and other dictation activities. Children write as a part of dramatic-play-with-print centers, at the writing center, and while writing the room, writing Words for Today, and keeping journals. Finally, play is a critical component of the kindergarten curriculum. As a part of play, children make signs, reread big books, and pretend to be Pilgrims and bees.

Applying the Information

We suggest two activities for applying the information. First, make a list of the nine characteristics of literacy-rich classrooms from Chapter 6. Then reread this chapter and identify classroom activities appropriate for kindergartners that are examples of each of these nine characteristics. Discuss with your classmates why these activities fit the characteristics.

Second, make a list of all the literacy learning activities described in this chapter, including the teacher activities of following children's leads, planning routines, modeling, focusing on print, transferring responsibility, and planning activities. List the group activities—writing the sign-in question, wall work, shared reading, text reconstruction and pocket-chart activities, and language experience—as well as individual activities—signing in, writing the room, Words for Today, using dramatic-play-with-print centers, bookmaking, keeping journals, finger-point reading, and sign making. For each of these activities, describe what children learn about written language meanings, forms, meaning-form links, or functions. For example, children who participate in text reconstruction activities with a pocket-chart text as a model are learning about written language forms as they match words by matching letters. Children who finger-point read a familiar poem are learning about meaning-form links as they adjust their pointing using what they know about sounds and letters.

Going Beyond the Text

Visit a kindergarten and observe several literacy activities. Take note of the interactions among the children and between the teacher and the children as they participate in literacy experiences. Make a list of the kinds of literacy materials and describe the classroom routines in which children read and write. Talk with the teacher about the school's academic expectations for kindergarten. Find out how the teacher meets those expectations. Compare these materials, interactions, and activities with those found in Mrs. Poremba's classroom.

References

BAKER, B. R. (1984). I'm a little leprechaun. In J. Warren (Compiler), *More piggyback songs: New songs to the tunes of childhood favorites* (p. 30). Everett, WA: Warren Publishing. Warren Publishing House, Inc., P.O. Box 2250, Everett, WA 98203.

BRIDGE, C. (1986). Predictable books for beginning readers and writers. In M. R. Sampson (Ed.), *The pursuit of literacy: Early reading and writing* (pp. 81–96). Dubuque, IA: Kendall/Hunt.

COMBS, M. (1987), Modeling the reading process with enlarged texts. *The Reading Teacher, 40,* 422–426.

BORNSTEIN, H., SAULNIER, K. L., & HAMILTON, L. B. (Eds.). (1983). *The comprehensive signed English dictionary.* Washington, DC: Gallaudet University Press.

CHILDREN'S TELEVISION WORKSHOP. (1985). *Sign language ABC with Linda Bowe.* New York: Random House.

CLAY, M. (1975). *What did I write? Beginning writing behavior.* Exeter, NH: Heinemann.

CONNELLY, L. (undated). *Bears, bears everywhere.* Cypress, CA: Creative Teaching Press.

FALLON, I., & ALLEN, J. (1994). Where the deer and the cantaloupe play. *The Reading Teacher, 47,* 546–551.

FREPPON, P., & DAHL, K. (1991). Learning about phonics in a whole language classroom. *Language Arts, 68,* 190–197.

HOLDAWAY, D. (1979). *The foundations of literacy.* New York: Ashton Scholastic.

MARTINEZ, M., & TEALE, W. H. (1988). Reading in a kindergarten classroom library. *The Reading Teacher, 41,* 568–572.

PAPPAS, C. C. (1993). Is narrative "primary"? Some insights from kindergartners' pretend readings of stories and information books. *Journal of Reading Behavior, 25,* 97–129.

PUTNAM, L. (1991). Dramatizing nonfiction with emerging readers. *Language Arts, 68,* 463–469.

RANKIN, L. (1991). *The handmade alphabet.* New York: Scholastic.

RIEKEHOF, L. L. (1978). *The joy of signing: The new illustrated guide for mastering sign language and the manual alphabet.* Springfield, MO: Gospel Publishing House.

STAUFFER, R. (1980). *The language experience approach to teaching reading* (2nd ed.). New York: Harper and Row.

TOLHURST, M. (1990). *Somebody and the three Blairs*. New York: Orchard.

TRACHTENBURG, P., & FERRUGGIA, A. (1989). Big books from little voices: Reaching high risk beginning readers. *The Reading Teacher, 42,* 284–289.

VAN ALLEN, R., & VAN ALLEN, C. (1982). *Language experience activities* (2nd ed.). Boston: Houghton Mifflin.

Supporting
Literacy Learning
in First Grade

Chapter 9 describes how teachers support first graders' reading and writing. First we present Mrs. Walker's first grade classroom as an example of using opening-of-the-day routines, read alouds, shared reading, and writing to support children's literacy development. We describe the classroom layout and the materials that provide the foundation for Mrs. Walker's reading and writing program.

We next introduce two approaches to beginning reading and writing instruction: the basal approach and approaches based on whole language. We describe how two teachers combine basal approaches with literature-based approaches more aligned with whole-language philosophy. We also discuss the writing process approach and provide three examples of teachers who use this approach. Mrs. Robb includes the writing process approach along with a more traditional basal reading approach. Mrs. Walker uses process writing to help children publish stories. Mrs. Zickuhr uses process writing to support children's writing of poetry. We end the chapter with a review of what children learn about written language meanings, forms, meaning-form links, and functions as a part of the classroom activities described in the chapter.

Key Concepts

graph-question atten-
    dance routine

graph question

Daily Oral Language
    (DOL)

words for the week

spelling poem

flashlight reading

word wall

shared reading

basal reading series

scope and sequence of
    skills

partner reading

pattern writing

take-home books

daily journal writing

author's chair

mail center

letter-writing models

story sentences

word identification
    problems

daily news sentences

word identification

phonics

structural analysis

contextual analysis

vocabulary

sight vocabulary

comprehension

literal comprehension

inferential comprehen-
    sion

critical comprehension

directed reading lessons

directed reading-think-
    ing activity (DRTA)

guided reading

high-frequency words

whole language

literature based

extensions

writing process
    approach

process writing

rehearsing

collecting

drafting

revising

editing

publishing

minilessons

cluster

| writers' conference groups | legibility | Things I Can Do list |
| editing checklist | topic list | composition record sheets |

READING AND WRITING
IN MRS. WALKER'S FIRST GRADE

Mrs. Walker is a first grade teacher in a suburban public school. She is especially effective at meeting the needs of her thirty students. The following example is from November, when Mrs. Walker provided multiple reading and writing experiences in routine opening-of-the-day activities and shared reading. She begins the day with a special attendance routine in which children read and answer a question. Then the children read a short text in which Mrs. Walker has intentionally inserted errors. The children talk about what they need to do in order to make the text conventional. Next, Mrs. Walker introduces six words that her children will learn to read and spell as a part of their reading and writing activities during the week. Finally, Mrs. Walker reads a story aloud, and children read a similar story in a shared reading activity.

Opening-of-the-Day Routines

The first opening-of-the-day routine in Mrs. Walker's classroom is the **graph-question attendance routine.** For this routine, each child answers a question that Mrs. Walker has written on the chalkboard as the daily attendance taking. Coleen volunteers to read today's **graph question,** and then the whole class reads it together: "Have you ever gone fishing with your dad?" Mrs. Walker records children's *yes*es and *no*s by placing their name cards in two vertical columns, making a bar graph. She also converses briefly with each child, encouraging students to tell more about their answers and responding positively to what they say. Valerie elaborated on her *yes* answer by saying, "My brother, he put the worm on." Mrs. Walker and the class use the bar graph to talk about the results of this survey and to determine how many children are present today.

Mrs. Walker uses the graph question to foster oral language. Each child gets to share daily, and Mrs. Walker uses this opportunity to talk with the children individually—an important task with so many children in her classroom. It also serves as an informal math activity.

The second routine is called **Daily Oral Language (DOL)** (Vail & Papenfuss, 1982). It involves a three-line text that Mrs. Walker writes on the chalkboard and into which she has inserted errors in spelling, punctuation, and usage. Today's DOL text is

jimmy he CAN wach
the car jast lik his dad
what can you do

Mrs. Walker first asks children to read the text; then they determine whether the information in the text is true.

| Mrs. Walker: | Let's find out if that's true first. Jimmy, can you wash the car like your dad? (Jimmy nods.) He can! |
| Jimmy: | I can wash it better! |

Then the children offer suggestions about how to correct the text.

Laura:	(about CAN) You put all capitals. . . .
Mrs. Walker:	There's no real reason to have all capitals here, although I'm still seeing a lot of capital letters in some of [your] journals. . . .
Kasey:	We don't need the *he*.
Mrs. Walker:	Okay, when we have that *he*, it's just like we said "Jimmy Jimmy," isn't it?

Robert suggests a period after *do*.

Mrs. Walker:	Think about this—"What can *you* do?" (with question intonation and emphasis on *you*)
Child:	It's a question!
Mrs. Walker:	I'm asking you something, aren't I? I'm asking you what you can do. So does it need a period? What does it need, Robert?
Robert:	A question mark. . . .
Kara:	You need a *e* in *like*.
Mrs. Walker:	Is this how I spell *like?*
Children:	No! No!
Mrs. Walker:	L-I-K, actually if I were sounding it out, that sounds pretty good—/l/, /ī/—but if I wouldn't put the *e* on it, it would be /l/, /i/. Sometimes—
Child:	Like "Lick a stick!"
Mrs. Walker:	Sometimes we put an *e* on the end, and the *e* helps the other vowel say its name—/l/, /ī/. . . . Look at the word *just*. Now look real close at what I put—/j/-/a/-/ja/—I used the wrong vowel. Take a look at the vowels (points to short vowel posters at the side of the room). Vowels are special because every word has one.
Child:	I!
Child:	E!
Mrs. Walker:	Which one of those vowels do you think would make—listen—would make the /u/ sound?
Child:	I!
Child:	U!
Child:	E!
Mrs. Walker:	Like in what, A.J.?

A.J.:   U!

Mrs. Walker: It would be the *U*—like in—

Child: /u/, /u/.

Mrs. Walker: —*fun tub* (These words are written on the short-*u* poster.)—hear the /u/ sound there?

Eventually they find all the errors, and the text is now written correctly on the chalkboard.

Mrs. Walker uses Daily Oral Language to teach a variety of skills that first graders are expected to learn. She carefully crafts the sentences to focus on sound–letter relations she wants to teach, to include words that children will need to read in other reading activities, and to highlight errors that she has noticed in children's writing.

Spelling and Reading Words

Later, Mrs. Walker introduces six **words for the week.** These are words that the children will encounter during today's shared reading activity and that they will practice reading and spelling throughout the week. For many of her literacy lessons, Mrs. Walker uses poems displayed in a pocket chart at the front of the room (McCracken & McCracken, 1986). The poem for her spelling lesson includes repetitions of the line "I can spell _____ ."

This week's new words are: *am, on, big, look, who,* and *can't.* Mrs. Walker places the first word, *am,* in one of the "I can spell _____" lines of the **spelling poem** in the pocket chart and helps children read the word. She emphasizes the known sound–letter correspondences for the short *a* sound and the *m* sound (the class has worked with short vowels since the beginning of the year). With *look,* she holds the word card over her eyes as a clue. As they read the words for the week, the children discover other strategies for reading words. For example, Mark notices *can't* elsewhere in the spelling poem. Another child comments about a classmate's reading of *big:* "He saw it on 'Big pig,'" referring to these words on the familiar short-*i* poster.

During the week the children practice reading the poem and reading and spelling the words. A favorite practice activity is **flashlight reading.** Mrs. Walker darkens the room and gives children turns shining a flashlight on words they know and reading them.

At the end of the week, the children take a spelling test on these words. Then the word cards are placed on a large wall chart, creating a **word wall** (Cunningham, 1991). Thereafter, Mrs. Walker refers the children to the word wall when she holds them accountable for knowing how to spell these words in their writing.

Mrs. Walker uses the spelling poem and activities to ensure that her children build a set of words that they know for reading and writing. Of course, these reading and spelling activities are not the only ways in which children learn sight words or develop spelling strategies. As we will see, they have many opportunities to read interesting stories that provide natural practice for developing sight words and learning about spelling patterns.

Reading Aloud

Later in the morning, Mrs. Walker reads the picture book *Just Me and My Dad* (Mayer, 1977). As she reads, she talks about both the print and strategies for meaning making. She begins by calling attention to words in the title.

> Mrs. Walker: This one has 1-2-3-4-5 words in the title. . . . Some of these words are in the morning sentences or in the morning graph question (pointing to the two texts still on the board from the opening routine). . . .
>
> Kimberly: I know some of them.

Kimberly reads *My, Dad, Me,* and *and.*

> Mrs. Walker: So the only one you don't know is the first one. "Blank me and my dad." J-U-S-T is in our morning sentence right here (pointing to the Daily Oral Language text)—remember that's the one I put the wrong vowel in?
>
> Several children: Just!

Mrs. Walker calls on Nicholas, and he reads the whole title.

> Mrs. Walker: What do you think this little boy and his dad are doing in this story?

Mrs. Walker points to the cover picture, which shows a Mercer Mayer creature and his dad fishing. She reminds the children of their responses to the morning question ("Have you ever gone fishing with your dad?") and suggests that they might have some ideas about what will happen in the story. She encourages children to use an important meaning-making strategy.

> Mrs. Walker: What's a good question we could ask ourselves? Good readers always ask themselves a question before they start reading. What do you want to know about this book? What are you wondering about?
>
> Child: I wonder where they go camping.
>
> David: I wonder what kind of fish they are going to catch.

Mrs. Walker reads the story of the boy and his dad going camping. The story contains a pattern of events: The boy starts an activity (e.g., taking the dad for a canoe ride, cooking their fish), but it goes wrong (e.g., he launches the canoe too hard and it gets a hole in it, a bear steals their dinner), and the dad fixes it (e.g.,takes them fishing, cooks eggs instead). The story is not limited to this pattern, however; other events occur (e.g., the dad takes a snapshot of the boy with the fish he caught). It is told with humor, some of which comes from its being told from the boy's perspective. For example, he says he gives his dad a big hug to make him feel better after they tell scary stories, but we know that the boy is the one who needs to feel better. The illustrations are Mercer Mayer's usual richly detailed, entertaining pictures. Mrs. Walker's students noticed and commented on the details (e.g., "There's always a spider on each page," "And a grasshopper!").

Mrs. Walker has several purposes for reading *Just Me and My Dad* aloud. Children enjoy this humorous story and naturally respond to its pattern. Mrs. Walker models comprehension (meaning-making) strategies and makes explicit that words children are learning to read and spell are found in books they want to read. The book also provides an important introduction to a story that Mrs. Walker will later expect her children to read on their own.

Shared Reading

Next, Mrs. Walker and her students do a whole-class **shared reading** (see Chapter 8) of what Mrs. Walker calls their "first grade story." Each week the class reads one story from the **basal reading series** adopted by their school. The basal reading series is a published reading program with materials for kindergarten through the eighth grade. Mrs. Walker has materials intended for the first grade, including a set of preprimers, primers, and first readers. These are anthologies of stories on increasingly difficult reading levels. Mrs. Walker also has a teacher's manual for each of the readers, and workbooks are available if she wants them. The teacher's manual specifies a list of skills that are taught along with each reader (called the **scope and sequence of skills**). We will see that Mrs. Walker teaches many skills related to reading but does not use the basal workbook in order to do so.

Today's shared reading is carefully orchestrated with the graph question, the DOL sentences, and the story *Just Me and My Dad* in preparation for the children's reading of the first grade story *Just Like Daddy* (Asch, 1984). This simple pattern story about father and son bears who go fishing with their mother has been reproduced in the basal reader that Mrs. Walker uses. The pattern in *Just Like Daddy* is that the boy tells about performing a series of acts (yawning a big yawn when he gets up, having breakfast, getting dressed, picking a flower, baiting a hook) and each time adds the phrase "Just like Daddy." The twist that ends the story is that the boy catches a big fish "Just like Mommy" (Daddy is pictured with a much smaller fish).

The sentences in this story are shorter than those in *Just Me and My Dad;* the vocabulary is more regular; the pattern is more obvious; and the structure of the story is simpler (everything leads to the one joke of Mommy's big catch, in contrast to the multiple funny mishaps that befall the boy in *Just Me and My Dad*). There is an almost one-to-one correspondence between the illustrations and what the text tells. This story is typical of texts that provide the best kind of support for beginning readers.

Mrs. Walker combines the first two steps of shared reading (the teacher's reading and then the children's reading together) in order not to give away the joke at the end of the story. All the children have their own basal readers, which include this story. Mrs. Walker reads a page from her basal reader, and then the class rereads the same page together. They talk about the story and the illustrations as they go.

Mrs. Walker:	(after the third occurrence of the pattern) Does anybody see the same thing happening a lot in this story? No one sees a pattern? Jake, do you?
Jake:	First he does something, then he says, "Just like Daddy." Then he does something else and he says, "Just like Daddy."

Next is **partner reading.** Mrs. Walker assigns each child a partner, and each pair has one book. The partners take turns: one reads while the other looks on and, as Mrs. Walker explains, "gets to be the teacher and help with any words they don't know."

Mark and Jacob are partners; they find a corner of the room, and Mark reads first. This text is easy for him; he reads fluently, with expression and no mistakes. Jacob follows Mark's reading with his eyes. When it is Jacob's turn, he works harder than Mark did, but with Mark's help he is able to finish the story with comprehension. He substitutes words that make sense in the story. He reads "jacket" for *coat,* "Mom" for *Mommy,* and "put on my worm on my hook" for *put a big worm on my hook.* As Jacob reads a page with the phrase "Just like Daddy," he moves his finger across the text quickly, saying the words without looking at them. "I can read that part easy," he comments to his partner.

The next day, the children do an individual response activity, the third step of their shared reading of *Just Like Daddy.* Each child makes his or her own "Just Like Daddy" or "Just Like Mommy" books using **pattern writing.** Mrs. Walker types the phrase "Just like Daddy" (or "Mommy") and duplicates it so that each child has four pages of the pattern. She and the children discuss the things they like to do with their own moms and dads. Then the children write, using invented spelling, on their pattern paper and illustrate their pages. Two pages of Jacob's "Just Like Daddy and Mommy" pattern book are shown in Figure 9.1.

Mrs. Walker uses shared reading as a context for children to orchestrate their knowledge of sound–letter relationships, meaning-making strategies, and sight words. She uses the stories from her basal series because they are appropriate for supporting her beginning readers, but she has other stories, poems, and informational texts not found in a basal reader that are also appropriate for this purpose and that she also uses to teach reading (Scott, 1994).

Additional Reading

Children in Mrs. Walker's class have many other reading experiences. A daily event is OTTER time, *Our Time To Enjoy Reading* (like the sustained silent reading activity described in Chapter 6). Mrs. Walker plays soft music on her tape player, and children read big books that the class has already read together, books from Mrs. Walker's extensive classroom library, or library books (children are free to go to the school library daily). Mrs. Walker monitors her students' reading during OTTER, helps them when they ask, and encourages them to read challenging and interesting books. Children are free to share their reading with one another and to ask one another for help (this time is far from silent, and, therefore, OTTER is a better name for this activity than SSR).

In October, a few weeks before their reading of *Just Like Daddy,* Jacob's selection for OTTER was a big book that the class had read together earlier. The book is based on a pattern song ("Did you ever see a _____ , doing _____ , down by the _____") and was made from handwritten pages laminated and bound by a parent volunteer. Among Jacob's classmates' selections for OTTER reading on this day were other big books, other class-made books, including a scrapbook full of envi-

Classroom Print

Mrs. Walker's classroom spaces are filled with print materials, and these materials reveal a great deal about how she teaches. We describe here just some of the classroom print that was displayed in October. To the left of the chalkboard is a seasonal bulletin board containing a Halloween word game. To the right of the chalkboard is a pocket chart containing the spelling poem that Mrs. Walker uses with each week's new vocabulary words. To the right of that is a football-game bulletin board that Mrs. Walker is using this month to keep track of students' reading of at-home books. Next to the front door is a set of posters and a poem about consonant letters. A standing pocket chart contains word cards forming a poem about a jack-o'-lantern and picture cards that provide clues to the content of each line of the poem (after the children read the poem together, they used the word cards to reconstruct the poem on the pocket chart). The bulletin boards at the back of the room display children's birth dates by month on a vertical bar graph, posters about the four seasons, and a story dictated by the class.

Next to the calendar on the standing bulletin board are five **daily news sentences,** for the current day and each of the last four school days. The daily news sentences are dictated by the "superstar" student each day. When the new sentence for the current day is added, the oldest sentence (from five days ago) is taken down and given to the student who dictated it. These sentences are reviewed and reread each day during the calendar routine.

Mrs. Walker's classroom library with its hundreds of books is housed in the low shelves at the front of the room. There are books made by the children, such as the environmental print scrapbook one child read during OTTER and hardcover storybooks that children have written and published. There are many selections of children's literature. Most are picture books, including storybooks, informational books, books related to holidays, and books related to science or social study units that the class is studying. Mrs. Walker rotates books to this area from her storage cupboards to maintain interest and relevance to ongoing classroom events. She supplements her own collection with books she borrows from the school library.

In Mrs. Walker's classroom library, there is also a set of basal readers. Her class used these books when they read *Just Like Daddy.* In first grade, materials and methods are more closely interrelated than they are in preschool and kindergarten. Methods come with their own special materials; a choice of materials implies a philosophy of instruction. In the next section, we describe the basal approach and the philosophy that provides a foundation for this approach. Then we explain the whole-language philosophy and the approaches associated with it. Both the basal approach and the whole-language philosophy have implications for how reading and writing are taught in first grade.

THE BASAL APPROACH
TO BEGINNING READING

Basal reading programs are associated with a systematic, skills-based approach to instruction. The philosophy behind this approach is that literacy is most easily learned when the skills of literacy—its component parts or behaviors—are identified and taught in a systematic way. This orientation has a long history and a strong hold on American literacy instruction.

Most reading-skills programs are organized around three major skill areas: word identification (decoding), vocabulary, and comprehension. **Word identification** skills include knowing how to sound out words by relating sounds to letters (**phonics**), recognizing and using prefixes and suffixes (**structural analysis**), and being able to use context or the surrounding words in a text to understand an unknown word in the text (**contextual analysis**). **Vocabulary** skills include being able to read a large store of words without having to sound them out (**sight vocabulary**) and learning meanings for vocabulary words. **Comprehension** is taught in terms of many skills for understanding and remembering what the author says (**literal comprehension**); inferring what the author implies but does not directly state (**inferential comprehension**); and using the author's ideas and determining whether or not they are relevant, biased, or logical (**critical comprehension**). (Table 9.1 lists examples of skills.)

Basal Reading Lessons

Basal programs are usually organized around directed reading lessons or activities. **Directed reading lessons** have three steps: preparation for reading, directed reading, and follow-up. The preparation phase involves helping children relate their background experiences and interests to the story they will be reading. Teachers introduce vocabulary words in oral discussion, followed by a presentation of a few of the words printed in sentences and in isolation. Word identification skills are often taught in this phase and applied to the new story vocabulary. In the directed reading phase, teachers ask questions to stimulate and guide children's silent reading of the story. The story is usually read in small segments, which are interspersed with questions and discussion. Silent reading is followed by reading aloud particular parts of the story, usually to provide answers to questions. The follow-up phase involves teaching skills that can be applied to further understanding or appreciating the story.

A frequently used alternative to the directed reading portion of the directed reading lesson is the **directed reading-thinking activity** (DRTA) (Stauffer, 1969). In DRTA lessons, the teacher reads the title and shows pictures to the children. The children make predictions about what will happen in the story, which the teacher may record on chart paper. Then the children read a short segment of the story to see which of their predictions are accurate and whether or not their predictions need adjusting. This three-step cycle (predict, read, prove) is repeated several times throughout the story (Davidson & Wilkerson, 1988).

Beginning Reading Instruction with Basals

Basal programs provide a comprehensive approach to reading instruction. They identify skills to be taught with each basal story, suggest methods of teaching those skills, and provide practice activities in the form of workbooks or pages for duplication. The traditional basal approach to teaching beginning reading is to teach chil-

Table 9.1 *Some Reading Skills*

Word Identification

Identifies rhyming words

Identifies sounds of initial and final consonants, blends, and diagraphs

Identifies long and short vowels

Forms new words by substituting initial and final letters

Forms new words by adding *-ing, -ed, -s*

Recognizes contractions (*I'm, shouldn't*)

Recognizes and uses prefixes and suffixes

Vocabulary

Describes pictures

Classifies objects

Identifies and understands concrete nouns (*dog, cat, man, horse*)

Identifies and understands pronouns (*it, she, he, they, us, we*)

Identifies synonyms, antonyms, and homonyms

Identifies descriptive words

Identifies and understands abstract words (*love, honesty*)

Comprehension

Recalls and sequences story details

Recognizes main idea and supporting details

Predicts outcomes

Makes inferences

Draws conclusions

Distinguishes fact and fantasy, fact and opinion

Describes character traits

dren a few sight words before reading a story (these words appear in the story as new sight words, and other words in the story are words that have been taught as sight words in previous stories). Then children read the story using **guided reading** (a part of the directed reading lesson in which the teacher asks a question, children read, and then they talk about the question after reading). Children usually read aloud in early beginning reading lessons so that teachers can assess how well they can read sight words and apply phonics skills. Then children practice sight words and phonics skills by completing workbook or other practice pages on these skills.

The sight words in most first grade basals are **high-frequency words,** words that occur frequently in text. Only one hundred words make up 50 percent of all the words found in almost any English-language text. Learning to read high-frequency words—such as *the, is, of, are, were, they, in, it,* and *has*—is a powerful tool for reading, because these words appear so often in stories, poems, and informational books.

Other words in most first grade basal texts follow phonics patterns and are easily decoded using phonics. For example, the word *cat* is easily decoded because it follows the rule that the vowel sound is short in a word with one vowel between two consonants. It is an example of a word that follows the CVC (consonant-vowel-consonant) pattern. Table 9.2 presents some phonics generalizations taught in the first and second grades.

Table 9.2 *Some Phonics Generalizations*

1. Each of the consonant letters corresponds to one sound, as in the words:

*b*ag	*h*air	*n*est	*t*oe
*d*og	*j*ar	*p*ipe	*v*iolin
*f*an	*k*ite	*q*ueen	*w*ig
	*l*amp	*r*ug	*b*ox
	*m*ilk	*s*un	*z*ebra

2. Consonant clusters are composed of two or three consonant sounds blended together (e.g., *bl, cr, dr, fl, gl, pr, sm, st, scr, str, thr, nt*)

3. The consonant digraphs correspond to the sounds in the words:

      *ch*urch   *sh*oe   *ph*one   *th*umb   *wh*istle

4. The vowel letters take several sounds, such as

long	*short*	*r-controlled*	*l-controlled*
*a*pe	*a*pple	h*er*	h*all*
*ea*gle	*e*gg	s*ir*	t*alk*
*i*ce	*i*gloo	f*or*	
*o*boe	*o*ctopus	f*ur*	
*u*nicorn	*u*mbrella		
tr*y*			

5. When a word has a VCe pattern, the V usually takes the long sound (*like*).

6. When a word has a CVC pattern, the V usually takes the short sound (*sat*).

7. When the letter *g* is followed by the letters, *e, i,* or *y,* the *g* usually takes the soft sound, as in the letter *j* (*gym*). Otherwise, it takes the hard sound, as in the word *gum*.

8. When the letter *c* is followed by the letters *e, i,* or *y,* the *c* usually takes the soft sound, as in the letter *s* (*cycle*). Otherwise, it takes the hard sound, as in the letter *k* (*cake*).

Some basal reading programs published recently draw extensively from published children's literature and have modified their approach to beginning reading to suggest using the shared reading approach (Hoffman, et al., 1994). In these basal programs, children reread predictable pattern stories with their teacher and with partners. They write in special journals and read and write in other response activities, such as retelling the story using storytelling props or writing a pattern story. These basals are more like approaches based on the whole-language philosophy (which we will discuss later in this chapter).

Criticism of the Basal Approach

Basal reading materials have been criticized on at least three important points. First, the language used in the stories is not like the language of children nor like the language in other "real" literature (Goodman, 1988). Children comprehend stories better when the stories conform to their language patterns (Wilkinson & Brown, 1983). More recently published basals have more natural sounding language that resembles other literature.

Second, there is little connection between the phonics generalizations taught along with particular basal stories and the stories themselves (Anderson, Hiebert, Scott, & Wilkinson, 1985). Most basal stories contain very few words that illustrate the generalizations that have been taught, and children have few opportunities to practice using those generalizations in the context of reading meaningful text (Beck, 1981).

Last, skills-based instruction is deprofessionalizing. If teachers must teach skills in isolation, then their job is not one of thoughtful consideration, but rather one of technique. Within the skills-based approach taken by most basal reading programs, there is an implication that teachers should not think about what literacy really is. Their job is to be technicians; they should deliver a product that comes as close to predetermined specifications as possible (Shannon, 1993).

In defense of basal materials, there are some positive features about the theory of the skills-based orientation. Many learners need a systematic approach and explicit directions for some literacy learning (Baumann & Schmitt, 1986). The notion that there are many things to learn about reading and writing that should be identified and carefully considered *by teachers* is also important (Baumann, 1992). Teachers *certainly* would not be effective if they did not know about literacy or how to respond to children's literacy efforts in ways that increase children's literacy learning. The problem with the skills-based approach is that the lists of skills we currently have focus on very small, disconnected bits of knowledge, and not on how to use knowledge while reading and writing.

Basal reading programs were never intended to be the entire reading program in a classroom. Reading professionals who author these programs believe that children should also be encouraged to read literature and to engage in developmentally appropriate activities. They do not recommend rigid adherence to a basal series as the only component to a reading program, exclusive use of workbooks as the only independent reading activity, or requiring a child to master every skill in a basal reader as a prerequisite to moving forward in a program.

WHOLE-LANGUAGE APPROACHES
TO BEGINNING READING

As often happens to widely used terms in our public discourse, **whole language** no longer serves as a label for a specific referent. It has become so burdened with political, social, and economic associations that it almost ceases to mean. We think it is helpful to reemphasize the notion that whole language instruction is simply instruction in which language remains whole. Many implications follow from this definition—implications about literacy materials and instruction. Materials should come from the real world, presenting whole, "real" texts, as opposed to texts specially composed to control exposure to written language. For this reason, the term **literature based** is sometimes used to describe a whole-language approach.

In whole-language approaches, children use reading and writing to communicate meaning (Altwerger, Edelsky, & Flores, 1987; Goodman, 1986). Whole-language advocates argue that children learn to read and write by reading and writing, and not by learning skills. Children learn because they use reading and writing to accomplish real tasks. Whole-language teachers also use the study of content, such as science or social studies, or the study of literature as the major component of their literacy programs. What gives a literacy program a whole-language orientation is the teacher's philosophy about literacy and literacy learning (Newman, 1985).

Whole-Language Philosophy

Because the whole-language approach is not embodied in a special set of materials as is the basal approach, its advocates emphasize its philosophical identity. Newman (1985, p. 1) described whole language as a philosophical stance. Whole-language advocates are united by a common set of assumptions about language, learning, teaching, and children. They believe that the literacy and language curriculum is not a set of literacy materials (basal readers), nor a set of predetermined skills (a scope and sequence chart). Rather, the literacy and language curriculum comprises the unique literacy learnings constructed by learners. Therefore, learners and not skills or materials are the heart of the whole-language orientation. Children are viewed as active learners capable of selecting information and constructing knowledge for themselves. Whole-language advocates believe that children can lead the way. Children not only can acquire knowledge on their own, but they can also inform observant teachers about what they might need to learn.

Newman (1985) describes three other tenets. First, children learn by participating in demonstrations of literacy. There are many kinds of knowledges presented in a literacy demonstration, and children select any number of these knowledges to learn. Therefore, rather than using a narrow, isolated skill or knowledge as the focus of a lesson, teachers should offer demonstrations of a reading or writing experience that is rich with many potential learning opportunities.

One literacy demonstration a teacher might provide is to help children compose a letter to a classmate who has recently moved away. As the teacher and children compose the letter, the teacher would offer comments, ask questions, and invite children to make comments, ask questions, and make suggestions. The children might learn any number of literacy lessons from this demonstration. They might learn about the conventions of letter form, the need to consider the person to whom one is writing when deciding what to say in a letter, or how to spell the words *Dear* or *love.*

The second tenet is that children should be invited to select literacy activities rather than be assigned particular literacy tasks (Newman, 1985). It follows that if children are viewed as capable learners who can take away many different potential knowledges from a literacy demonstration, then they can select literacy experiences that are personally interesting and offer their own unique potential for literacy learning. Offering children choices and invitations to literacy activities is an important way in which teachers empower children as learners.

The third tenet is that reading and writing are social activities; they are interactive processes involving authors and readers sharing ideas. Children's knowing about and communicating with authors of published books is seen as vital to literacy learning. Whole-language teachers encourage children to write to authors and invite authors to their classrooms to share their work with children. Publishing children's writing and sharing their writing with real audiences is another important part of whole-language programs. These activities stress the communication of meaningful ideas as the goal of reading and writing.

Learning is viewed as a social activity as well. Whole-language advocates believe that children and teachers collaborate and share information, and that learning occurs in situations where children talk together and with their teacher about literacy experiences (Hansen, 1987). Cooperative learning groups, small groups of children who complete projects together, are often a critical component of whole-language programs.

Whole-language advocates believe that children can learn much literacy information and that no single set of materials or practices is synonymous with the whole-language orientation. Gunderson and Shapiro (1988) describe teaching phonics as a part of a writing program. Bridge and her colleagues (Bridge, 1986; Bridge, Winograd, & Haley, 1983) use predictable books in a patterned language approach to teach sight words. Holdaway's (1979) shared book approach using big books includes teaching children sight vocabulary, use of context clues, and phonics. What makes these programs compatible with whole-language philosophy is their foundation on a belief in children as learners and their use of information gathered from observing children to guide instruction.

Whole Language and Beginning Reading and Writing

Many approaches are based on whole-language beliefs and are intended to support beginning reading and writing. No one approach identifies whole-language instruction; teachers applying whole language use a variety of approaches throughout the day that they consider instruction in reading and writing. In addition, teachers applying whole language do not believe that beginning reading and writing instruction begins in first grade. It begins earlier, certainly in kindergarten (Mrs. Poremba's kindergarten, described in Chapter 8, is an excellent example of whole-language beginning reading and writing instruction in kindergarten). It is extended in first grade (Mrs. Walker's classroom from this chapter provides an example of whole-language beginning reading and writing instruction in first grade) and extends beyond first grade into the primary grades.

Mrs. Walker uses Daily Oral Language, shared reading, take-home books, OTTER, journals, and the mail and listening center activities as her beginning reading and writing program. In each of these areas, children read whole texts and learn skills embedded within a variety of activities. Children are expected to acquire sight words, strategies for making meaning, and strategies for decoding words as a part of their reading and writing activities. Mrs. Walker stresses appropriate use of punctuation and knowing rules for decoding and spelling vowels. She expects her children to learn an ever increasing set of sight words. However, children are not expected to master skills in a predetermined order (Jacob is learning different skills during reading, for example, than his partner Mark).

Criticisms of Whole Language

The whole-language approach is not a comprehensive, systematic program for literacy instruction. It lacks the teachers' manuals, skills lists, students' workbooks, and tests that come with a basal reading series. Parents and administrators may be uneasy about whether teachers are providing the reading instruction expected at each grade level. Thus whole-language teachers must make very deliberate efforts to demonstrate to parents and administrators that they are aware of individual students' strengths and weaknesses, that they are meeting each student's needs, that they are facilitating each student's progress—in short, that no student is falling through the cracks. A whole-language approach requires more teacher initiative in planning, obtaining reading materials, assessing (see Chapter 12 on assessment), and record keeping than does the basal approach.

A whole-language approach provides no scope and sequence of skills; hence teachers must make themselves aware of the range of skills and strategies that conventional readers use (see Chapter 5). They may consult a scope and sequence of skills provided in a basal reading series or in a school system's reading curriculum guide. They must then monitor children's self-selected reading and model reading and writing skills that foster children's learning.

Also, because the whole-language approach is not systematic in the way the basal approach is, it lacks the continuity of the basal approach. There is no predictability about what children will have read and what skills they will have mastered at specific points in their schooling. It is therefore difficult to place students moving from a whole-language classroom to a basal classroom as a result of a transfer from one school to another or a promotion from one grade to the next. As with the other limitations of the whole-language approach, the solution to this problem lies in teachers' attending as professionals to students' individual development and communicating as professionals with their fellow teachers.

BASALS AND LITERATURE TOGETHER

Because so many school districts require that teachers use basal readers, many teachers combine basal reading instruction with instruction using literature. In this section we discuss how two first grade teachers use a literature-based, whole-language approach to teaching reading *and* a basal series provided by their school systems. Both are among the best teachers we know. They meet the needs of all their students in stimulating, child-centered, literature-rich classrooms. One is Mrs. Walker, whose classroom we described at the beginning of this chapter; the other is Mrs. Zickuhr.

Mrs. Walker's Approach to Combining Basals and Literature

Mrs. Walker uses a basal reader as a source of first grade stories. She embeds the reading of the basal story, for example, *Just Like Daddy,* in a rich context of other literacy events, including the personally relevant morning graph question, the DOL text, and an interactive reading of literature (*Just Me and My Dad*). She uses the basal texts because they provide her students with a common, expanding core of reading vocabulary words and common texts for weekly shared reading.

This practice places Mrs. Walker in the middle of a continuum of possible ways to use (or not use) a basal reading series. Some teachers accomplish the same purposes without using a basal series at all. They use high-frequency word lists to determine which words children should be learning and to make decisions about spelling development. They use multiple copies of trade books for shared reading. Other teachers depend on a basal reading series to a much greater degree than Mrs. Walker does. For them, a basal series is the primary source of reading material and of reading instructional activities. They place their students according to ability in one of three or more reading instructional groups, each reading in a different basal reader; they teach the reading skills suggested in the teachers' manuals for those different levels of the basal reading series; and their students complete skills exercises in workbooks matched to each basal reader. (Later we will describe Mrs. Robb's reading and writing instruction, which relies on the basal reader more heavily than does Mrs. Walker's instruction.)

A significant factor in Mrs. Walker's use of the basal is that the students all read at the same level of the series, that is, they are all in the same book, reading the same stories together. For some children, this at-grade-level basal reader would be too difficult if it were their primary or only reading text; for others, it would be too easy and nonmotivating. During partner reading, Mark's modeling and prompting guided Jacob's fluent, comprehending reading of *Just Like Daddy,* which is a more difficult text than Jacob can read on his own. At other times, both Mark and Jacob read other texts (e.g., OTTER selections and take-home books) at their own ability levels. If the basal reader were Mark's only reading material, he would be unavailable to help Jacob; he would need to be placed at a more difficult level in a different group from Jacobs'. Then, rather than considering themselves partners in reading, Jacob and Mark might identify themselves as good or poor readers based on their reading-group memberships. With the whole-group and partner reading activities in Mrs. Walker's class, all can proceed quite comfortably together.

Mrs. Zickuhr's Approach
to Combining Basals and Literature

Mrs. Zickuhr, a first grade teacher in an urban district, also uses an at-grade-level basal reader a few times per week along with her literature-based approach. At the end of her second year of using a literature-based approach, Mrs. Zickuhr described the decisions she makes as a teacher. She described what she calls **extensions.** Extensions are response activities based on shared reading, similar to writing the pattern books "Just Like Daddy" and "Just Like Mommy" that Mrs. Walker's students wrote after reading *Just Like Daddy* together. Mrs. Zickuhr rarely uses the workbook or other duplicated papers as follow-up activities for reading. Instead, she creates her own extension activities, such as one based on David Small's *Imogene's Antlers* (Small, 1988).

> When we did *Imogene's Antlers* about the little girl who grew antlers, I just made up a folder, and here inside the folder is . . . my master pattern [for a class-made book using pattern writing]: "On Saturday, when Imogene woke up, she found she had grown *blank.*"

The children use the blank spaces to insert their own ideas just as Mrs. Walker's students wrote their own activities with their moms or dads. Mrs. Zickuhr commented about pattern writing.

> It's a way to step out of the book and then a way to step back into the book. Because I realized that once we had done the story extension from *Brown Bear, Brown Bear [, What Do You See?]* (Martin, 1983), where we had done our own book, *Brown Bear* still continues to be a very popular book too—they feel very comfortable with it. . . . It's not like "I've read that book, I'm finished with it."

Students in Mrs. Zickuhr's class do not always use patterns for writing. They might write their own story about *Imogene's Antlers* without using a pattern. However, she recognizes that many of her beginning writers need the support of a pattern.

> My friend who [teaches] second grade loves *Imogene's Antlers* . . . But she feels second graders don't need this format done for them—they can do it on their own. And so she puts the book together and gives them free rein to follow the pattern, but independently without the teacher. I feel that when I introduce it, this gives kids a certain frame to work with, and first graders can take off with that. She feels that second graders are more than able to take off on their own.

Mrs. Zickuhr talked about accountability for the materials and skills in the basal series provided by her school system.

> I usually use the basal twice a week, and on the other three days I'm doing other activities. . . . I feel a lot of their skills are being acquired through their writing. . . . Like when we first started journals . . . the digraphs came up right away. "Mrs. Zickuhr, what [letter] makes /th/?" or "What's the beginning of /th/?" And so right away I knew that it was time to do digraphs. So we did do some digraphs on the overhead; I did give [the students] a copy of [basal] worksheets to do. . . . Once they had a handle on it, and I can see day to day—everyday when they are working in their journals and I am walking around—I know who has a handle on [digraphs] and

who doesn't. And it's much more diagnostic to look at a journal entry than a worksheet.

THE PROCESS APPROACH
TO WRITING INSTRUCTION

We saw that both Mrs. Walker's and Mrs. Zickuhr's students wrote in journals. In both classrooms, the teacher observes and confers with students as they write, and students regularly read their journal entries to their classmates and answer their classmates' questions about those entries. We saw that Mrs. Zickuhr considered journal writing the true test of her students' skills learning. This journal writing is the beginning of an approach to writing instruction known as the **writing process approach,** or **process writing** (Calkins, 1986; Graves, 1983). It involves many opportunities for students to interact with each other and with their teacher about self-assigned writing projects. We will first describe process writing in general; then we will give examples of process writing in three teachers' classrooms.

Writing Processes

The process approach to writing has become a strong force in children's literacy instruction (Calkins, 1986; Graves, 1983). Within this approach, the focus of instruction is on supporting children's use of writing processes rather than on making sure that children write conventionally correct compositions—hence the "process approach" label. Spelling, handwriting, grammar, and usage are taught within the writing program.

There are many descriptions of writing processes (e.g., Murray, 1987). In general, writing processes fall into five categories: rehearsing, drafting, revising, editing, and publishing. However, it is misleading to think of these processes as occurring linearly or sequentially; rather, they are interactive, and they often occur simultaneously.

One writing process is called **rehearsing** (Calkins, 1986) or **collecting** (Murray, 1987). This process includes a writer's search for a topic, identification of audience and purpose, and collection of ideas about which to write. Many young children draw pictures as rehearsal for writing. Other children rehearse by talking to a friend or to their teacher, by writing a list of ideas, by role-playing an experience, by listening to or reading literature, or by simply thinking. The purpose of rehearsing is to generate ideas and formulate plans for writing.

Another writing process is called **drafting** (Calkins, 1986). In this process children commit their ideas to paper. Drafting for young children may consist of as much talking and drawing as it does writing. First drafts of conventional readers and writers can be short, sometimes consisting of only a few words. More accomplished readers and writers write longer first drafts and more consciously consider the necessity of writing details.

A third writing process is **revising;** it consists of children's rethinking what they have written. In revising, children reread their drafts; add or delete words, phrases, or sentences; and move sentences. The focus of these activities is the content of the writing. In another writing process, **editing,** children focus on misspellings and errors in capitalization, punctuation, and usage. Children gradually learn to edit their own writing. The last writing process, **publishing,** consists of making writing available for a wider audience. Table 9.3 presents several ideas for publishing children's writing.

Table 9.3 *Suggestions for Publishing Children's Writing*

Draw pictures for children's magazines (*Humpty Dumpty, Turtle*).

Write poems, essays, reports, or stories for children's magazines (*Stone Soup*).

Write class, grade-level, or school newspapers or literary magazines.

Read writing in the author's chair.

Post writing on an "Author of the Week" bulletin board.

Read writing at a "Parents Share Fair" once a month.

Write letters to children's authors, public figures, government agencies, or members of the community.

Write greeting cards.

Write poems, essays, reports, or stories to be bound into books. (The books can be composed by a class or an individual and can be kept in the class or school library.)

Bind books for Mother's and Father's Day gifts.

Bind books for a nursing home or the children's ward of a hospital.

Bind books to present to obstetricians or pediatricians for use in their waiting rooms (Temple, Nathan, Burris, & Temple, 1988).

Make a class yearbook (Temple et al., 1988).

Enter local and state library contests.

The Teacher's Role

Teachers play several roles in the writing process approach. First, they interact with and respond to individual children and their writing. Second, they help children learn strategies for rehearsing, drafting, revising, editing, and publishing their writing. Third, they provide knowledge about written language and literary conventions. Teachers help children learn effective strategies or procedures for writing (Bereiter & Scardamalia, 1982). Teachers usually provide this kind of help in short minilessons conducted in writers' workshops.

Minilessons in Writers' Workshops

Minilessons on writing strategies are often conducted in writers' workshops as part of whole-group activities (Calkins, 1986). During minilessons, teachers might talk about the importance of drawing as rehearsal. For more accomplished writers, teachers might demonstrate writing a list of possible topics about which to write. (See Graves, 1983, for a discussion of helping children choose writing topics.) Teachers might also demonstrate writing a **cluster,** ideas related to a topic written in a weblike diagram. Figure 9.7 presents Sarah's cluster of ideas for a story about the mysterious disappearances of her friends on a camp-out.

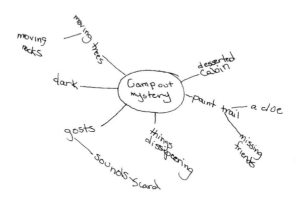

Figure 9.7 *Sarah's Cluster for the Camp-Out Mystery*

Writers' Conferences

Some teachers form **writers' conference groups** to serve as collaborative learning groups. Writers' conference groups can be used to provide additional time and support for small groups of children to try out various strategies introduced in mini-lessons. They can also be used to teach children knowledge related to literary and written language conventions, such as letter writing, using similes or metaphors, and sequencing of events, as well as proper use of capital letters, periods, commas, quotation marks, and even colons. Many teachers use editing conferences to deal with two additional writing tools—spelling and handwriting. Table 9.4 presents an **editing checklist.**

Table 9.4 *An Editing Checklist*

☐ I have reread my writing to a writing partner.

☐ I have listened for sentences.

☐ I have a capital letter at the beginning of each sentence.

☐ I have a period, question mark, or exclamation mark at the end of each sentence.

☐ I have a capital letter for every time I used the word *I.*

☐ I have a capital letter for every person's name.

☐ I have checked spellings of the word wall words.

Spelling in the Process Approach

Writing process advocates recommend that spelling come from children's writing and that it be taught as a tool to help writers and as a convention to help readers. This approach suggests that teachers should not use the predetermined, arbitrary word lists presented in spelling books. The spelling words that conventional writers should study and learn should be words they have misspelled in their writing, words they need to learn as a part of their content study, and words for which they ask the spellings (Johnson, Langford, & Quorn, 1981).

Teachers can use high-frequency word lists and notes they have made about spelling problems in children's writing to help them select the words common to all children's spelling lists. Table 9.5 presents a list of high frequency words that children learn to spell as part of process writing.

Handwriting

Handwriting is an important part of composing. When children labor over remembering how letters are formed, not to mention over listening to the sounds they hear in each word, their compositions suffer. The best ideas disappear when children focus on pencil and paper instead of on the content of what they are writing.

Instruction in handwriting should focus on **legibility** rather than on imitation of examples; it should provide children with language with which to talk about their handwriting and letters, and it should be connected with publishing children's writing.

There are four aspects of legibility that young writers need to learn. First, letters should conform to expected formations as defined by the writing program. Expected formations, especially of capital letters, differ from one handwriting program to another. Zaner-Bloser, a publisher of writing programs, is famous for its "ball and stick" manuscript letter formations (Barbe, Wasylyk, Hackney, & Braun, 1984). The D'Nealian handwriting program is known for slanted manuscript letters that are formed with a continuous stroke producing more curved lines (Thurber, 1981). Making expected letter formations does not always mean using the strokes suggested in a handwriting program. Children who begin making the letter *e* by writing it from bottom to top will probably not develop an unbreakable bad habit.

The second aspect of legibility is that letters should be of uniform size, proportion, and alignment. Third, letters and words should be evenly spaced. Fourth, letters should have a consistent slant.

The time to be concerned about legible handwriting is when writing is for an audience. Just prior to binding children's writing into a hardbound book is an opportune time for handwriting instruction.

Process Writing and Reading
Instruction in Mrs. Robb's First Grade

Mrs. Robb is a first grade teacher in a university laboratory school. Figure 9.8 shows her daily schedule. It includes independent reading time (sustained silent reading), independent writing time (concentrated writing time), instruction in reading (during small-group reading), instruction in writing (during writers' workshop and writ-

Table 9.5 *High-Frequency Words for Writing*

I	there	do	see
and	with	about	think
the	one	some	down
a	be	her	over
to	so	him	by
was	all	could	did
in	said	as	mother
it	were	get	our
of	then	got	don't
my	like	came	school
he	went	time	little
is	them	back	into
you	she	will	who
that	out	can	after
we	at	people	no
when	are	from	am
they	just	saw	well
on	because	now	two
would	what	or	put
me	if	know	man
for	day	your	didn't
but	his	home	us
have	this	house	things
up	not	an	too
had	very	around	

From R. L. Hillerich, *A Writing Vocabulary for Elementary Children* (p. xiii), 1978. Courtesy of Charles C Thomas, Publisher, Springfield, Illinois.

ers' conference groups), and read aloud (during literature sharing). Mrs. Robb's process writing approach accompanies a more traditional approach to reading instruction.

Every morning Mrs. Robb participates in SSR (sustained silent reading) with the children. The children take one or two books each from the library center to their desks as they enter the classroom. During this time the children and Mrs. Robb read books or other materials of their choice.

At 8:45 Mrs. Robb conducts a minilesson. Some of her minilessons focus on showing children how to find topics to write about, how to brainstorm ideas, and how to conduct peer conferences. During some minilessons, Mrs. Robb provides a

Figure 9.8 *Mrs. Robb's Daily Schedule*

8:15	Children arrive, sign in, sign the lunch list
8:30	Sustained silent reading (Mrs. Robb and whole class)
8:45	Writers' workshop (whole class)
9:00	Concentrated writing time (Mrs. Robb and whole class)
9:15	Transition time (Mrs. Robb circulates for five mintues) Reading group (small group)
9:45	Transition time Reading group (small group)
10:15	Recess
10:30	Transition time Reading group (small group)
11:00	Individual conferences, writers' conference groups, author's chair:

	Monday	**Tuesdsay**	**Wednesday**	**Thursday**	**Friday**
11:00	Group A	Author's Chair	Group C	Group B	Author's Chair
11:20	Group B		Group A	Group C	

11:45	Lunch
12:30	Literature sharing (Mrs. Robb shares with whole class)
12.45	Mathematics (whole class)
1:00	Mathematics (small groups)
1:30	PE (Tuesday and Thursday) Music (Monday)
2:00	Social studies and science block (Wednesday and Friday begins at 1:30) Art (Thursday every other week)
2:50	Clean up
3:00	Dismissal

brief experience that stimulates a class collaborated composition. The children brainstorm and dictate ideas. They read and reread their compositions and make revisions together (Karnowski, 1989). Some minilessons focus on editing compositions for periods and capital letters. Mrs. Robb often uses the writers' workshop to read to the children a special book that can be used as a model for their writing. In one writers' workshop, she shared *Would You Rather* . . . (Burningham, 1978). She discussed the pattern found in this book and suggested that it might be a pattern the children could use in their writing.

At 9:00 Mrs. Robb and the children begin writing. They may talk to a friend about what they might write, reread previous drafts they have written, or revise. After she writes for several minutes, Mrs. Robb circulates among the children and stops to make a comment or two to several children about their writing.

At 9:15 Mrs. Robb calls a group of children to the small-group instruction area for reading instruction. During reading, the children read stories from their basal readers or from children's literature. For example, Mrs. Robb and the children read *Shoes* (Winthrop, 1986) during reading group time. Sometimes she shares children's literature by having the children read a big book. She and the children frequently write together as part of reading group time. They sometimes write retellings of the stories or poems they have read, make their own big books of a story or poem, or compose original stories or poems (Trachtenburg & Ferruggia, 1989; Wicklund, 1989).

Mrs. Robb often demonstrates how to use a reading strategy as she reads or writes, or she has the children describe strategies that they use in their reading. The children discuss alternative strategies for what to do when they are reading and something does not make sense. The group talks about using the sound–letter correspondence knowledge that they use to spell words to figure out unknown words in their reading. They discuss children's different interpretations of a story. They talk about the different meanings that words have in different sentences and different stories.

Mrs. Robb uses her previous observations of the children as they read and write to determine what knowledge or strategy might be most useful to them (Johnson, 1987). She also consults the teachers' manual of her basal readers to check that the children are learning information related to the skills identified in the basal reading program. (The children must take an end-of-the-year competency-based test in reading that reflects many of the skills in the basal reading series.)

At 11:00 and 11:20 Mrs. Robb has writing conferences or author's chair (Graves & Hansen, 1982). Sometimes Mrs. Robb plans to use the entire time to have conferences with individual children about their writing. Sometimes she forms special writers' conference groups consisting of children who have similar writing needs or who want to explore a common writing theme together. These children meet with her during writers' conference time. Mrs. Robb uses writing conference groups to present language, handwriting, and spelling lessons as they apply to the children's writing. She teaches these lessons as part of children's editing of their writing.

When Mrs. Robb has writers' conference groups, she calls one of her three writing groups at 11:00. Each group meets two or three times a week; the schedule is posted each week, and children know to check the conference schedule for their group's meeting times. On Tuesdays and Fridays Mrs. Robb has author's chair; children who have indicated they are ready to share their writing sit in a special chair, read their compositions, and receive feedback from classmates.

Story Writing in Mrs. Walker's First Grade

Mrs. Walker also uses the writing process approach. In February she introduced story writing. She began by conducting a minilesson on collecting ideas for writing. She read *Earrings!* (Viorst, 1990), the story of a young girl's pleading with her parents to have her ears pierced. Then Mrs. Walker asked, "Where do you suppose Judith Viorst got the idea for this story?" The class speculated that the idea came from Judith Viorst's own life. Mrs. Walker then shared a picture book that she wrote,

Poppa's Coal Oil Story. This story is her father's telling about an event in his child-hood. Mrs. Walker tells her class how she got the idea for her book (from a favorite family story), planned her story, wrote several drafts, edited and typed her final draft, had a friend illustrate it, and bound it.

Mrs. Walker asks parents to help with topic selection. She sends home a letter to the parents explaining that children will be writing stories and that the best sto-ries are based on personal experience. She invites the parents to help their children collect ideas for writing by looking through family photo albums and finding three ideas. Parents write the list of possible topics and send it to school.

Each child has a writing folder containing a **topic list** of ideas sent to school by the parents and other ideas the children brainstorm as a part of minilessons. Fig-ure 9.9 presents Karissa's topic list, which includes five ideas for possible stories. The writing folders also contain a **Things I Can Do list,** on which Mrs. Walker writes the skills that she expects the writer to apply in his or her writing. And the folders include **composition record sheets** on which children write the titles of pieces that they have finished writing or are working on.

Mrs. Walker has several objectives for her students' story writing: "writ[ing] one idea per page—or maybe add some more about that idea"; being more careful about illustrations than in journal writing; and structuring stories with beginnings, middles, and ends. An example of her teaching with these objectives is a minilesson that began with her reading *My Cousin Katie* (Garland, 1989). This richly illustrated pic-ture book tells about Katie's life on a farm. Each page contains one idea, sometimes with a sentence or two of elaboration. Its beginning-middle-end structure coincides with one day on the farm, beginning at dawn ("Katie wakes up early.") and ending at sunset ("the cows come home to sleep in the barn."). Mrs. Walker reads the story, and then she and the children talk about the beginning, middle, and end structure that she expects them to use in their writing.

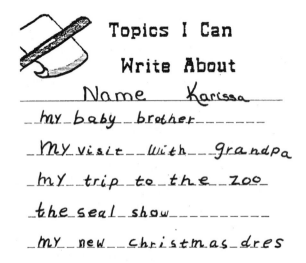

Figure 9.9 *Karissa's Writing Topics List*

During process writing time, the children plan and write stories in six-page sta-pled booklets; Mrs. Walker staples more pages in these books if needed. One day when we were visiting, Corey asked us to staple an additional page at the begin-ning of a book he was drafting. He explained that his story needed a beginning. Children share final versions by reading from the author's chair. They choose one story to be published in a special way. The text is typed and pasted into a hard-bound, blank book. The student adds illustrations, Mrs. Walker adds a photograph and a note about the author, and the children share their published books at an au-thors' tea at the end of the school year. Figures 9.10 and 9.11 show two pages of a draft of Jacob's story "I'm going to col sitee" and several pages of his published book *When I Go to Coal City.*

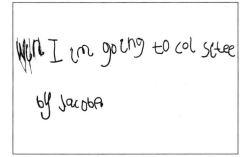 

Figure 9.10 *Two Pages from Jacob's Draft for Story Writing ("I'm going to Coal City by Jacob P." and "We are going to fish at Coal City.")*

Poetry Writing in Mrs. Zickuhr's First Grade

Poetry reading and writing is an important part of literature enjoyment and literacy instruction in Mrs. Zickuhr's room. Children respond to poems through choral read-ing, collecting poems, drama, art, music, talking, and writing. Mrs. Zickuhr teaches several minilessons about poetry as a part of process writing. With one, she stresses the importance of feelings in writing and responding to poetry. She reads a poem about which she feels strongly, shares her feelings about it, and invites the students to respond in small groups. Another minilesson is about topic selection ("Poetry has to hit a person right in the heart or it won't work"). Another is about form. Mrs. Zickuhr suggests that after writing a draft, her young poets should think about struc-ture: "Just like buildings have architecture—some are tall and thin, some are short and wide—poems also have to be built according to a design which works." She finds that first drafts often look proselike, so she has students read their poems aloud and add slashes for line breaks where they naturally pause. Another miniles-son is about endings, that they can hold the rest of the poem together, can surprise the reader, make the reader think.

As inspiration, Mrs. Zickuhr reads poems that make use of sounds, such as the sound "vroom" found in the poem "The Go-Go Goons" from *Street Poems* (Fro-man, 1971). Children use these ideas in their own poetry compositions. Figure 9.12

Figure 9.11 *Three Pages from Jacob's Published Book (last name masked)*

shows a poem that Mike wrote, revised, edited, and published about motorcycles. Michael's poem shows attention to the sound words introduced in Mrs. Zickuhr's minilesson (see his use of the word *vrooming*). All published works in Mrs. Zickuhr's class bear the embossed seal of UKP, Unicorn Kids Press, a name they chose for their publishing company.

WHAT IS LEARNED ABOUT WRITTEN LANGUAGE?

Throughout this chapter, Mrs. Walker and Mrs. Zickuhr described the skills they teach. Our discussion of the basal and whole-language approaches also included a

<u>Motorcycle</u>

Motorcycle,

Fast, too loud,

Racing, driving, vrooooooming,

I like motorcycles!

Bike.

by Mike Kotowski

Figure 9.12 *A First Grader's Poem*

discussion of skills in terms of traditional categories of skills and strategies (e.g., phonics, word identification, comprehension). Here we emphasize that first graders—whether learning from a basal reading lesson, a shared reading activity, an individual reading or writing conference, a question from a classmate during an author's chair reading, or a process writing minilesson—are still engaged in expanding their literacy knowledge and competence in the four areas of meaning making, form, meaning-form links, and written language functions.

The process approach to writing, in particular, focuses on children's meaning-making knowledge. A major thrust of this approach is supporting children's learning of both information about writing processes and strategies for meaning making. Children in the writing process approach learn to read for information, to generate a list of ideas by brainstorming or clustering, and to use talking with a friend as a way of finding ideas. They also learn to use these idea-generating strategies before they write and when they get stuck writing. Thus, children know that writing is communicating ideas, they know how to generate some ideas about which to write, and they know when to use their idea-generating strategies.

One of the most important ways in which teachers can support children's use of meaning-making strategies is to encourage children to monitor their own meaning as they read and write. Effective readers seem to ask themselves, "Does this make sense? What does this mean to me?" When readers realize that what they are reading does not make sense, they reread and self-correct reading errors to make sense. Effective teachers foster self-monitoring by frequently asking children, "What does that mean to you?" They encourage children to skip words that they do not know, to keep reading portions of text that they do not understand, and then to return to reread. Some teachers encourage children to say "blank" when they come to an unknown word as they read aloud.

First graders extend their knowledge of forms and meaning-form links. They learn about structure in poetry and about the relations of sounds and letters, orthography, and the morphology (prefixes, suffixes, and base words) of written language. More important, they learn how to use this information more consciously in their reading and writing. We saw this learning taking place in the many impromptu phonics lessons in Mrs. Walker's daily routine, such as when she used the short-vowel posters to teach about the short *u* sound in *just* during DOL.

Teachers help children expand their knowledge of written language functions in environments that call for children to use language in meaningful ways (Loughin & Martin, 1987). Mrs. Walker understands this process when she combines attendance taking with reading and talking about a daily graph question that will be relevant to that day's activities. Mrs. Zickuhr understands this process when she says, about a report activity that children completed and took home following a parent's presentation to the class, "And so it's a language arts activity and it's sharing with parents. It's meaningful writing."

Chapter Summary

First grade marks an important time in children's schooling. They are expected to begin "really" reading and writing; at the end of first grade, society expects children to have made great strides toward conventional reading and writing. We have shown that there are many ways in which this journey is taken. In Mrs. Walker's first grade, children read and write as a part of the graph-question attendance routine, Daily Oral Language, shared reading, partner reading, journal writing, writing letters, and listening to and writing about stories. Mrs. Walker's literacy program is an example of using basal readers in a way that is consistent with the whole-language philosophy.

The basal reading approach to beginning reading is systematic. It provides a scope and sequence of all the skills that children are expected to master, materials for children to read, suggestions for instruction, and practice activities. As a part of this program, children develop word identification skills (including phonics, structural analysis, and contextual analysis), vocabulary abilities (including sight and meaning vocabularies), and comprehension skills (including literal, inferential, and critical comprehension). Lessons follow the directed reading lesson format, with vocabulary and skills taught before reading, then guided reading of the text, and finally, follow-up activities. The basal approach can be criticized for its deskilling of teachers, for its inauthentic texts, and for its lack of match between skills and text.

In contrast, whole language is a philosophy in favor of children's reading and writing authentic texts and learning skills as a part of reading and writing activities. Shared reading and other literature-based reading approaches are consistent with the whole-language philosophy. The whole-language approach can be criticized for not being systematic and for re-lying on teacher-developed lessons and activities.

Most teachers use a blend of the basal approach and other approaches consistent with the whole-language philosophy. Mrs. Walker uses the basal reader stories in a shared reading approach. Mrs. Zickuhr teaches the skills listed in the scope and sequence of skills in her basal reader series as a part of journal and process writing. She assesses how well her children know skills by observing their use in writing activities.

The writing process approach is an important part of a first grade literacy program. As a part of this approach, teachers use minilessons to model the processes of writing, rehearsing, drafting, revising, editing, and publishing. Children learn to use strategies such as writing a cluster, getting feedback when reading in the author's chair, and conferring with the teacher in order to bring compositions to publication. Mrs. Walker helps her children collect topics for personal stories, and Mrs. Zickuhr helps children use ideas from poems in their own poetry compositions.

As a part of these activities, children continue developing their understandings of written language meanings, forms, meaning-form links, and functions.

Applying the Information

We suggest two applying-the-information activities. First, make a list of the nine characteristics of a literacy-rich classroom presented in Chapter 6. Then reread this chapter to locate an activity that is consistent with each of these characteristics. Discuss your examples with a classmate.

Make a list of all the literacy learning activities described in this chapter, including the graph-question attendance routine, Daily Oral Language, spelling poem, flashlight reading, word wall, shared reading, partner reading, pattern writing, take-home books, journals, mail center, listening center, word identification problems, daily news sentences, directed reading lessons, directed reading-thinking activity, writing minilessons, topic lists, and composition record sheets. For each of these activities, describe what children learn about written language meanings, forms, meaning-form links, or functions. For example, during Mrs. Walker's Daily Oral Language activity, children were learning about long and short vowels, increasing their understandings of meaning-form links. In Mrs. Zickuhr's poetry minilessons, children were learning interesting new words and the special lining associated with poetry—they were attending to meaning and poetry form.

Going Beyond the Text

Visit a first grade classroom and observe several literacy activities. Make a list of all the print and literacy materials in the classroom. Take note of the interactions among the children and between the children and the teacher during literacy activities. Talk with the teacher about his or her philosophy of beginning reading and writing. Compare these materials, activities, and philosophies with those of Mrs. Walker, Mrs. Zickuhr, and Mrs. Robb.

References

AHLBERG, J., & AHLBERG, A. (1989). *The jolly postman*. Boston: Little, Brown.

ALTWERGER, B., EDELSKY, C., & FLORES, B. M. (1987). Whole language: What's new? *The Reading Teacher, 41,* 144–154.

ASCH, F. (1984). *Just like Daddy*. New York: Simon & Schuster.

ANDERSON, R. C., HIEBERT, E. H., SCOTT, J. A., & WILKINSON, I. A. (1985). *Becoming a nation of readers: The report of the commission on reading*. Washington, DC: The National Institute of Education.

BARBE, W. B., WASYLYK, T. M., HACKNEY, C. S., & BRAUN, L. A. (1984). *Zaner-Bloser creative growth in handwriting (Grades K–8)*. Columbus, OH: Zaner-Bloser.

BAUMANN, J. F., (1992). Basal reading programs and the deskilling of teachers: A critical examination of the argument. *Reading Research Quarterly, 27,* 390–398.

BAUMANN, J. F., & SCHMITT, M. C, (1986). The what, why, and when of comprehension instruction. *The Reading Teacher, 39,* 640–646.

BECK, I. L. (1981). Reading problems and instructional practices. In G. E. MacKinnon & T. G. Waller (Eds.), *Reading research: Advances in theory and practice* (Vol. 2, pp. 53–95). New York: Academic Press.

BEREITER, C., & SCARDAMALIA, M. (1982). From conversation to composition: The role of instruction in a developmental process. In R. Glaser (Ed.), *Advances in instructional psychology* (Vol. 2, pp. 1–64). Hillsdale, NJ: Erlbaum.

BRIDGE, C. A. (1986). Predictable books for beginning readers and writers. In M. R. Sampson (Ed.), *The pursuit of literacy: Early reading and writing*. (pp. 81–96). Dubuque, IA: Kendall/Hunt.

BRIDGE, C. A., WINOGRAD, P. N., & HALEY, D. (1983). Using predictable materials vs. preprimers to teach beginning sight words. *The Reading Teacher, 36,* 884–891.

BURNINGHAM, J. (1978). *Would you rather . . .* New York: Harper.

CALKINS, L. M. (1986). *The art of teaching writing*. Portsmouth, NH: Heinemann.

CUNNINGHAM, P. (1991). *Phonics they use: Words for reading and writing*. New York: HarperCollins.

CUTTING, J. (1988). *Just look at you!* San Diego: The Wright Group.

DAVIDSON, J. L., & WILKERSON, B. C. (1988). *Directed reading-thinking activities*. Monroe, NY: Trillium.

FROMAN, R. (1971). *Street poems*. New York: McCall.

GARLAND, M. (1989). *My cousin Kate*. New York: HarperCollins.

GOODMAN, K. (1986). *What's whole in whole language?* Exeter, NH: Heinemann.

GOODMAN, K. (1988). Look what they've done to Judy Blume: The basalization of children's literature. *The New Advocate, 1,* 29–41.

GRAVES, D. H. (1983). *Writing: Teachers and children at work*. Exeter, NH: Heinemann.

GRAVES, D., & HANSEN, J. (1982). The author's chair. *Language Arts, 60,* 176–183.

GUNDERSON, L., & SHAPIRO, J. (1988). Whole language instruction: Writing in the first grade. *The Reading Teacher, 41,* 430–437.

HANSEN, J. (1987). *When writers read*. Portsmouth, NH: Heinemann.

HOFFMAN, J. V., McCARTHEY, S. J., ABBOTT, J., CHRISTIAN, C., CORMAN, L., CURRY, C., DRESSMAN, M., ELLIOTT, B., MATHERNE, D. & STAHLE, D. (1994). So what's new in the new basals? A focus on first grade. *Journal of Reading Behavior, 26,* 47–73.

HOLDAWAY, D. (1979). *Foundations of literacy*. Sydney, Australia: Ashton Scholastic.

JOHNSON, P. (1987). Teachers as evaluation experts. *The Reading Teacher, 40,* 744–748.

JOHNSON, T. D., LANGFORD, K. G., & QUORN, K. C. (1981). Characteristics of an effective spelling program. *Language Arts, 58,* 581–588.

KARNOWSKI, L. (1989). Using LEA with process writing. *The Reading Teacher, 42,* 462–465.

KREMENTZ, J. (1987). *A visit to Washington, D.C.* New York: Scholastic.

LOUGHLIN, C. E., & MARTIN, M. D. (1987). *Supporting literacy: Developing effective learning environments*. New York: Teachers College Press.

MARTIN, B., Jr. (1983). *Brown bear, brown bear, what do you see?* New York: Holt, Rinehart and Winston.

MAYER, M. (1977). *Just me and my dad*. Racine, WI: Golden Books.

McCRACKEN, R. A., & McCRACKEN, M. J. (1986). *Stories, songs, and poetry to teach reading and writing: Literacy through language.* Chicago: American Library Association.

MURRAY, D. M. (1987). *Write to learn* (2nd ed.). New York: Holt Rinehart and Winston.

NEWMAN, J. M. (1985). Introduction. In J. Newman (Ed.), *Whole language.* Portsmouth, NH: Heinemann.

OMMANNEY, F. D. (1979). *The fishes.* Alexandria, VA: Life's Young Readers Nature Library.

SCOTT, J. E. (1994). Teaching nonfiction with the shared book experience. *The Reading Teacher, 47,* 676–678.

SHANNON, P. (1993). Commentary: A critique of false generosity: A response to Baumann. *Reading Research Quarterly, 28,* 8–14.

SMALL, D. (1988). *Imogene's antlers.* New York: Crown.

STAUFFER, R. G. (1969). *Directing reading maturity as a cognitive process.* New York: Harper and Row.

TEMPLE, C., NATHAN, R., BURRIS, N., & TEMPLE, F. (1988). *The beginnings of writing* (2nd ed.). Boston: Allyn and Bacon.

THURBER, D. N. (1981). *D'Nealian handwriting. (Grades K–8).* Glenview, IL: Scott, Foresman.

TIME-LIFE TELEVISION (1976). *Wild, wild world of animals: Reptiles and amphibians.* Alexandria, VA: Time-Life.

TRACHTENBURG, P., & FERRUGGIA, A. (1989). Big books from little voices: Reaching high risk beginning readers. *The Reading Teacher, 42,* 284–289.

VAIL, N. J., & PAPENFUSS, J. F. (1982). *Daily oral language.* Racine, WI: D.O.L. Publications.

VIORST, J. (1990). *Earrings!* New York: Atheneum.

WARD, C. (1988). *Cookie's week.* New York: Putnam.

WICKLUND, L. K. (1989). Shared poetry: A whole language experience adapted for remedial readers. *The Reading Teacher, 42,* 478–481.

WILKINSON, I. A., & BROWN, C. A. (1983). Oral reading strategies of year one children as a function of the level of ability and method of instruction. *Reading Psychology, 4,* 1–9.

WINTHROP, E. (1986). *Shoes.* New York: Harper and Row.

hanging. I don't feel like I understand what you are talking about. Who did that?" So that they will [follow my] model when they are doing their own [sharing] activities together.

Ms. Vaughn uses writing workshop as a time to assess children's learning and identify skills that she needs to teach. She consults the school's language arts textbook for a list of skills that she is expected to teach and uses it, in part, to guide her decisions about skills teaching.

I try to assess [children's learning] through writing workshop. Are they applying quotation marks? . . . Are they trying to put conversation into their writing? . . . With permission from one of the kids, if I see a sheet, where if we've just worked on contractions, maybe, and I notice in a few papers that they are just not [getting it]— or capitals and periods or we started learning how to do paragraphs and we indent—I'll ask them if I can [photocopy] their page and I'll take their name off . . . And I'll do it on the overhead, and then we'll do a group kind of [lesson on] that. . . . [I do] lots of individualized instruction [in grammar] through their conferencing in writing workshop. . . . There are language books [in the school]—the only thing I've done with them is I've copied the scope and sequence [of grammar skills].

Reading Time

During **reading time** students read in their basal readers. They are not grouped for instruction, but may select to read alone, with a partner, or with Ms. Vaughn or a student teacher or to listen to a selection in the listening center.

A lot of times I tell the kids, "You can choose somebody to read with." Or I have ten headsets [at a listening station], and I usually have four or five kids who really could not get anything out of [reading an anthology selection] on their own. And I try to either make myself available to them, or a student teacher or an aide, or I let them be at the headsets. But I always make sure that it's a big mix [of ways to read the selection], because I always want everyone to feel good about what they are doing and not feel that they are the ones who can't do it.

Ms. Vaughn goes beyond the selections in the basal anthology.

I do a lot of prereading activities. . . . If we're going to do *Strega Nona* [by Tomie de Paola, 1979], for example, maybe I'll have lots of books [by] Tomie de Paola. . . . We'll talk a lot about spaghetti [because Strega Nona's spaghetti cooking is a big part of the story]. I take a lot of fiction stories—for some reason this is just the way I've enjoyed doing it—I bring a lot of nonfiction into it first. . . . I try to enrich their background on whatever we're doing. With *Strega Nona,* we would maybe make spaghetti before . . . or get an encyclopedia . . . and I would come up with some questions and they would in their cooperative learning groups, for example, find Italy . . . and then report that back or have a way to present that to the class.

Ms. Vaughn provides choices about selections. At the beginning of the year everyone is in the same place in the basal anthology, reading the same selection. But this changes.

It's usually by choice. Once we establish ourselves at the beginning of the year and they know my expectations and what kind of person I am and what I want from

> them, I'll give them—let's say there are three stories in "Best Friends" [a unit in the
> anthology]—three stories about friendship, they can rank 1, 2, and 3 which one they
> want to read the most, and then I'll group the kids in those.

And Ms. Vaughn does not even always use the basals for such reading time experiences.

> You know I just don't spend tons of time in the [basal] anthology. They're good sto-
> ries, but I have so many other [sources to read from]. . . . Whatever I have multiple
> copies of, I'll pull them out and I'll say, "Okay, if you want *The Ugly Duckling* (An-
> dersen, 1986), sign up for this one; if you want *The Paper Bag Princess* (Munsch,
> 1980), choose this one." And then they get in those groups. . . . I would do this at
> reading time, as just kind of a break from the anthology. . . . There are other good
> stories out there too, and I would never want to be locked in [to the basal]. . . .
> There are skills [in the basal series] that we have to teach, and so long as a I focus
> on those, I don't see what difference it makes what they are reading. I want them
> to read things that are age appropriate, but not be bored with it. I always read some-
> thing on slavery and something on Chinese New Year. . . . [I ask children to do a
> lot of] responding—their thoughts . . . if there's an issue there. I try to make them
> aware of things out there [in the real world].

Reading Beyond the Basal and Novel Reading

After lunch, Ms. Vaughn has yet another reading time, **reading beyond the basal,**
when children read books of their choice. Ms. Vaughn uses this time for a modification of **readers' workshop** (Atwell, 1987; Reutzel & Cooter, 1991). In readers'
workshop, teachers begin by teaching a minilesson about a reading skill or demonstrating writing in a **response log.** Response logs are special journals in which children write responses to what they have read. After the minilesson, children read
books of their choice and then respond to the books either by writing in their response logs or by participating in another response activity.

Ms. Vaughn forms four **reading workshop groups** with children of mixed
ability levels. She prepares a group of reading materials for each group and places
the materials in a basket. These materials might consist of small copies of big books;
easy-to-read series books; picture books, including informational books; and chapter books. These materials are on a variety of different difficulty levels. During beyond-the-basal reading, children read books in reading workshop groups. Twice a
week they are expected to write in their response logs. Children also work on response-to-literature projects as extensions of their reading.

> I call it reading beyond the basal, but with some structure to it, it's not like silent
> reading, it's not reading instruction per se. I've taken all these books that I've got-
> ten through grants and that you get through *Weekly Reader* with your bonus points
> (and you can get tons!). And I've tried to code them with a sticker on the reading
> level—easy, medium, or hard—and I've got that posted in my room, so the kids
> know. I've got four baskets around the room. . . . Now they are in their reading
> workshop groups, and they go to their basket with a variety of books (high,
> medium, or low). . . . They bring their spiral notebook that I've written "Response
> Log" on. . . . At least twice a week, if we meet every day, they have to respond to
> me at least two ways in their response books on what they have read. . . . [For ex-

ample,] they could write me a letter about what they have read; they could write about the favorite part of what they've read; they could write something they don't understand; they might even make—for that one day—a list of words that they didn't know; or they can draw a picture, but that's something I don't let them do a lot. . . . So they're all reading something different. . . . They'll read for a certain amount of time . . . and I'll say, "Okay, your fifteen minutes is up. If today's the day you're going to respond, respond; if it's not, continue reading." I set a timer a lot so that they can walk by and look at it. They can get up and down a lot. . . . You will have your lower readers who will [just write, for example,] "The teeny, tiny woman was scared in the end." And that's okay, but before they even write that, they have to write the title and the author and underline the title . . . which is another way of throwing a type of a skill in. . . . [As extensions to reading workshop,] they could make a big book about their little book or share it with another classroom. . . . If when we go on, they haven't finished [a book], I say, "Take it with you, and put it back when you're done."

Figure 10.4 shows a book that Carrie wrote as an extension of her reading *The Mud Pony* (Cohen, 1989) during reading workshop.

Another reading time in Ms. Vaughn's class is **novel reading,** when she reads a novel aloud to the children. She knows that students beyond first grade are not too old to enjoy being read to.

I'm always reading a novel. And we keep track of all the books we read out loud. That's our favorite time; I read daily; and I read for at least twenty minutes. . . . I hype up the stories; I get so excited. . . . And I hope my enthusiasm rubs off on them. And if a day were to go by [when something precludes novel reading], they don't like it! . . . I might hold up three books and say, "Let's take a vote—which one do you want to hear?" I try to vary what I read, from fiction to nonfiction.

During her reading, students may listen at their desks or on the floor by Ms. Vaughn's rocking chair; they may draw as they listen; or they may even read something else, but . . .

. . . my rule is you can't get up and you can't talk when I'm reading. . . . Everybody loves it, and they don't want their [novel reading] time interrupted.

Occasionally, Ms. Vaughn combines listening, writing, and drawing in a special way.

A couple times a year with my novel reading, I do something called story painter. . . . The person that's the story painter gets to illustrate that [day's] chapter. And then [the students] retell it to me [for me to write as a caption to the picture]. And I staple [these pages] together and then we make a big book out of it—daily, I keep adding chapter[s]. . . . And they love the [big] book.

Center Time and Small-Group Reading Instruction

During center time, children work at classroom centers that are related to a topic the class is studying (center time occurs during science and social studies time). For example, several centers provide learning activities about spiders, including a hands-on center with magnifying glasses, observation recording sheets, and spiders that children have brought to school; a reading center stocked with books that Ms. Vaughn and the students have collected about spiders; a listening center with National Geographic books on audiotape about spiders; and an art station.

Figure 10.4 *Carrie's Writing Extension Based on* The Mud Pony
(Cohen, 1989)

Children work in centers in **center groups.** These groups are randomly assigned or self-selected (e.g., "when we get to where we study states, they get to pick which state they study").

During center time, Ms. Vaughn is able to meet with **reading instruction groups.** Each group includes five or six children with similar reading abilities. Ms. Vaughn uses reading instruction groups to teach skills and to provide opportunities

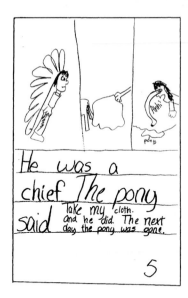

Figure 10.4   *(Continued)*

to read and to respond to literature. When Ms. Vaughn calls for one of these groups, its members leave whatever center groups they are in to receive reading instruction matched to their needs.

> When we were doing centers, . . . I would pull, out of the whole, five kids. They weren't all clumped in one [center] group. But now [they form] an ability-based group. Meanwhile, the others are doing their centers, and I'm at the back of the room at a table [with these reading instruction groups] doing various things with stories, writing new endings to stories, using big books, taking words out, doing different consonant sounds. And then with the higher kids, it was a lot of predicting . . . different levels of thinking skills.

With the children, Ms. Vaughn refers to these as "continent groups" because each group chooses to call itself by the name of a continent.

> A kid's not going to walk out and say, "Boy am I the dumbest one in my class!" Nobody really knows. . . . There's not a high group, there's not a low group that they are ever aware of. They all think that what they do is great.

One reason that these groups avoid being identified as high or low is that they are not associated with a set of materials. Ms. Vaughn does not use a basal reading series for this part of her reading instruction. She uses a variety of literature and other reading materials.

> I had some big books, . . . I ordered a bunch of the lower materials—that was my goal for one year. I really needed to meet the lower kids, because I [already] have a lot of stuff for the kids that can really read—I've got lots of multiple copies of chapter books and things like that. . . . And then we would do language experience activities. [For example,] from *The Sounds of Laughter* [by Bill Martin, Jr.], I showed a picture. It was a really funny picture of funny stuff going on with these animals

in a rainstorm. And then as a small group, everybody wrote a page, dictated it to me, and then I went home, typed it on my computer, we made it into a book, they illustrated it, they had to share it with the class. There's lots of sharing. I try to do the follow-through.... [For example] this year I want to get my kids ... involved ... with kindergartners and first graders, ... doing things for their classes. I am going to have them make different kinds of nonfiction books and give them to those classes, like an A-B-C book.

Ms. Vaughn makes decisions about the skills she teaches to reading instruction groups by carefully examining the materials that she uses in instruction and by observing the needs of the children in the group.

Themes and Cooperative Learning

There are extensive opportunities for students to cooperate and communicate about content-area learning in Ms. Vaughn's classroom. She includes eight thematic units for content study each year, and the children determine the topics of four of these.

I've got eight slots, and I'm going to fill in probably three or four of them [e.g., occupations, holidays, agriculture].... These are my content-area things. And then the kids are going to choose three or four things that they as a class [will study]. So they're going to get in their **cooperative learning groups** ... and then they're going to make the decisions on things that they want to learn about.

The first of these content units, which takes place beginning around Labor Day, is one for which Ms. Vaughn determines the topic. It is a unit about occupations. Although cooperative learning groups do not determine the topic of this unit, they are an important part of children's learning *about* the topic.

The kids as a [whole class] group are going to brainstorm important people and their jobs in a school. And then they are going to choose jobs to interview and they're going to meet in cooperative learning groups. Let's say three people have decided that they want to interview the nurse. So they will meet in their group and they'll decide their ten questions that they are going to ask the nurse.

As we have seen, groups like these—formed from members' sharing a common purpose and charged with a specific task—play a large part in the way in which Ms. Vaughn's students learn. On some occasions, they may be called cooperative learning groups; on others, they are called response groups or center groups. Ms. Vaughn's role is to facilitate. Part of that role is to teach children their roles in these groups.

I try to help them, but I don't solve it for them. I'm their facilitator, and they're in charge of their outcome.... [For example, in response to the story "A Maker of Boxes," (Wittram, 1972)], they're going to make a box. But they're going to have to write an outline on how they're going to make a box, and have a materials list on how they're going to do it.... [In articles] about cooperative learning groups, there are a million different job titles, and that gets confusing for the kids—I think—in second grade. I do have a group leader. [He or she] wears the tag, and that's the person in charge of the group for that day, and it rotates. There's going to be only one person who can come and ask me a question if they are confused, so they really have to think it through.... I make it a point to meet with each group, and once they've done their activity—and especially if there are problems—I always like to say, "How did it go for everyone?" And if there is a problem, I especially call everyone together to focus on [that]. . . . And then as a class we discuss it and then work [on it], and then the next day [they have another chance]. They're in cooperative learning groups I would say a big part of the day, and next time it usually works better.

Teaching this way involves giving children choices.

They have a lot of choice. [For example,] if they need to present some type of information to me—or to the class—they in their cooperative learning groups would devise a way. It might be a poster; it might be an overhead; it might be a chart on the board; it might be a skit.

WHAT'S NEW HERE?

In grades beyond first grade there are explicit outcomes for all subject areas. A second or third grade teacher is helped in planning for those outcomes by a new level of student competence. As a part of children's new competence, they are given greater responsibility. The teacher's role remains one of flexibility and careful attention to individual students' needs.

Increasing Expectations for Traditional Skills and Child-Centered Classrooms

In the primary grades and beyond, children are held accountable for mastering an ever-increasing number of academic skills in all subject areas. They are expected to apply sophisticated word identification strategies, including using spelling patterns and knowledge of familiar word parts such as prefixes and suffixes. They are expected to attend to the meanings of words and to learn thousands of words by sight. They are expected to comprehend a variety of literary genres at increasingly more interpretive levels. They are expected to know literary elements found in stories and to use these elements in their own compositions. Children are expected to learn several spelling strategies, including using a dictionary, and to learn the conventional spellings of hundreds of words. Finally, they are expected to write many kinds of compositions of increasing complexity.

Still, it is possible to master these skills within the child-centered classrooms that we have described in this and the preceding three chapters. Ms. Vaughn provided instruction tailored to the children's reading abilities in small-group reading instruction, yet, her children had multiple other opportunities to learn with classmates at a variety of reading levels. Children worked in cooperative learning groups, response groups, center groups, and reading workshop groups. As a part of these groups, children were expected to read and write together. Ms. Vaughn continually observed children as they read and wrote in order to make decisions about instruction. The curriculum came from children's needs, but Ms. Vaughn was also cognizant of her school's expectations about second grade skills.

One of Ms. Vaughn's resources for reading time was the basal reading series provided by her school. She made sure that her students learned the skills associ-

ated with the basal series. She did not, however, use other textbooks, including social studies or language arts textbooks. Ms. Vaughn relied on her extensive classroom library and the school library to supply the materials needed for her content
units (Tunnell & Ammon, 1993).

Ms. Vaughn is proof that child-centeredness does not have to end in the primary
grades. Her students' responsibility and excitement are the foundations of her child-
centered teaching. We saw many examples of Ms. Vaughn's giving her students
choices and respecting those choices. As a part of allowing student choice, Ms.
Vaughn teaches her students to take responsibility and to respect self and others.

> [At the beginning of the year] I do a thing where we talk about ways to treat each
> other in a classroom . . . the way you treat other people, and I weave it into [the
> way] we do this cooperative learning. . . . I want them to respect other people; first
> I want them to have self esteem; I want them to know that they can do anything
> they put their mind to do. That is more important than what five times five is any
> day, to me—what they think of themselves and how they treat their fellow man or
> woman. If you have those things down, everything else just happens. . . . And re-
> spect—I see that word *respect* as like an umbrella and everything just falls under
> it. . . . You look at our world; our world is so scary. . . . But if I can get them to treat
> their fellow students and people in their lives with respect, I just think everything
> else just happens.

New Competence

An important aspect of the context beyond first grade is that a class as a whole usually has achieved a critical mass of literacy competence. Teachers can rely on this
competence to allow a degree of subject-matter integration and student independen-
dence that is impossible in the earlier grades. Even in second or third grade, not all
students are conventional readers and writers, but a large enough proportion of
them are so that all students can work together with increasing independence on
tasks that require literacy competence. All can function in the sort of heterogeneous
cooperative-learning groups, whose strategies for problem solving and content
learning include reading and writing, that we saw in Ms. Vaughn's classroom.

This critical mass of literacy competence results in learning and communicating
in a variety of ways, as evidenced by Ms. Vaughn's description of her class's unit
about occupations.

> I'm going to go to the public library, and I'm going to bring in all kinds of books
> on jobs, and we're going to brainstorm jobs—things that are their real life. . . .
> They're going to interview people in our building, and then they are going to have
> to rewrite it, and they're going to have to have some kind of factual information
> about [, for example,] a nurse that they're going to have to have gotten from a book.
> And then they are going to come up within their group—we're going to set my
> classroom up like the [principal's] office, like the nurse's office, like the gym—how
> to use your lunch ticket, how to use the library. And they're going to have learned
> that information by interviewing the person mostly, and then by reading and study-
> ing that. And then we're going to do an [assembly] to teach the rest of the kids in
> the building. And they are going to have posters and ways to demonstrate. So all it
> is is reading and writing . . . and that's what second grade *is* mostly.

Activities like these have a characteristic that we can call **social construction of meaning** (Wells & Chang-Wells, 1992). They involve both a social component and a process of revision. In social construction of meaning, children work together to create an understanding, by which we mean that they interact with others in order to construct compositions and understand literature. This creative process, whether for composing or comprehending, always involves more than one pass at a text; it usually involves several rounds of remaking a message.

A piece of writing is sometimes only part of what results from social construction of meaning. Continued growth in oral-language competence is another important part of this broader concept of literacy. Ms. Vaughn's students often gave oral reports. Similarly, Joao reported the progress his group of third and fourth graders were making in their study of chick hatching and growth. In his classroom in a school in Toronto where the majority of students come from homes in which English is not the dominant language, the author's chair is also a speaker's chair.

> Joao is one of the first to be chosen. He picks up his papers and goes to sit in the speaker's chair, facing the rest of the class. He waits for silence. Then, holding up a piece of paper, he explains. . . . Immediately after he finishes, a number of children ask questions . . . (Wells & Chang-Wells, 1992, pp. 3–4)

THE SETTING: SPACE AND MATERIALS

Figure 10.5 shows our design for a well-appointed and well-arranged classroom for second or third graders. As in Ms. Vaughn's room, the teacher's desk is at the back of the room and students' desks are in clusters.

The whole-class instruction area is the largest area of the classroom. It is defined by the twenty-six desks arranged in clusters and the front-wall chalkboard. A rolling cart is kept in the front of the whole-class instruction area. It holds a variety of writing materials and supplies available to children when they work at their desks. The materials are similar to those that might be found in a writing center in a first grade classroom: lined and unlined paper; pots full of markers, colored pencils, pens, and pencils; boxes of scissors; several tape dispensers; a stapler; and erasers.

There is no writing center in this classroom. Students write throughout the day and in many locations. For example, during writing workshop or in cooperative learning groups for a science unit activity, they may write at their desks, in the small-group area, at the project center, at the typing and computer center, or on the floor.

The centers are arranged around the perimeter of the room. The library center is defined by tall bookcases that set off a corner of the room. It includes floor pillows, a couch, and a bulletin board containing child-made displays. Some are book reports, written by hand or by word processor and mounted on colorful tagboard; some are reports of surveys that children have conducted about their classmates' preferences (favorite fairy tale, favorite book about kids their age, favorite science fiction book, and favorite character in a book they have all read or heard read to them); and some are child-made posters about books. The counter holds other student-made displays about books, such as dioramas. The shelves on the bookcases are labeled and contain as many as 250 books.

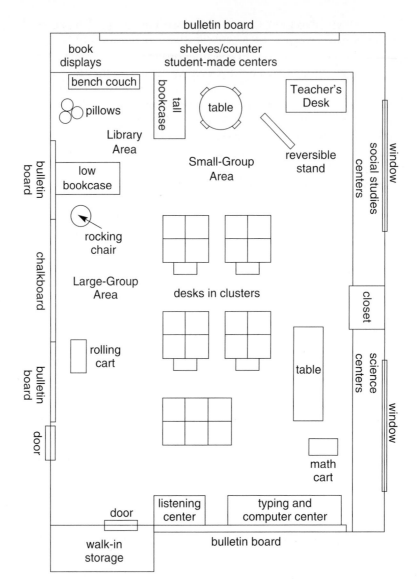

Figure 10.5 *A Second or Third Grade Classroom*

The shelves under the counter in the library center contain child-authored books in different forms: hardbound books, plastic-binder books, and photo album books. These books were written both by the room's current class of students and by children from previous years' classes. For example, in Ms. Vaughn's classroom children produce published books as a part of the writing workshop, and they make books from language experience stories and story painter pages.

The library center also features authors of children's books. The center includes a display of letters written by children's authors in response to student queries (children receive photocopies of the letters to take home). A scrapbook holds all the letters that the class has received over the years. The library center also has a special display of books autographed by authors. Children especially enjoy borrowing these, reading the authors' inscriptions, and reading the books. These books are gathered in part through field trips for an author's appearance at a nearby bookstore or at academic conferences.

There are displays of books all around the classroom including displays of new books, books with a common theme, books by the same author, fiction and nonfiction books to accompany a unit of study in social studies or science, books that a single student has read in the last month and recommends to his or her classmates, books that the teacher has read and is planning to read to the class, and books that the teacher has read and is reading for his or her personal reading.

The small-group instruction area, located at the side of the classroom, includes a round table and a reversible stand holding a pocket chart on one side and a large newsprint tablet on the other. A small chalkboard hangs on the back of the library center's tall bookcases. Open shelves below the counter hold reference books and basal readers. The counter holds student-made centers and displays, such as a student's bug collection.

The small-group instruction area is also a talk area. The bulletin board in this area contains the messages "Let's talk about books" and "Let's talk about writing." Children gather at this area for booktalks and for responding to writing as children in response groups did in Ms. Vaughn's classroom. At the end of a silent reading time, for example, the teacher may invite interested students to discuss with one another what they have been reading. At the beginning of the year, the teacher may need to be present to model talking about books and to ask discussion-starting questions. Later, students can discuss on their own what they have been reading.

The project center is located on a large table and on nearby shelves, counters, and a rolling cart. It is used for art, math, social studies, and science projects. It is also available when the teacher wants to create a larger listening center than will fit at the usual listening center location. Math manipulatives are stored on the rolling cart. Science and art materials are stored on open shelves. Science projects and centers are displayed on the counter to one side of the small closet, social studies projects and centers on the other. The teacher uses the shelves beside the teacher's desk for his or her professional library, and the walk-in storage room for instructional materials not in use at a given time.

The listening center and typing and computer center are located on tables pushed against a side wall. The listening center includes seats for five children and a box filled with books and tapes in plastic bags. A typewriter and computer are on an adjacent table.

INSTRUCTION BEYOND FIRST GRADE: SOCIAL CONSTRUCTION OF MEANING

In many ways, literacy instruction found in the late primary grades is similar to that found in the preschool, kindergarten, and first grade classrooms we have described. Story retelling, drama, and reading aloud are still important literacy activities. Ms.

Vaughn's instruction builds from the strong foundation provided in kindergarten and first grade. Her writing workshop is based on the process approach to writing described in Chapter 9, and her newsletter activity resembles Mrs. Walker's Daily Oral Language. Here we describe additional oral-language, reading, writing, spelling, and thematic activities that support children's social construction of meaning beyond first grade.

Oral-Language Activities

In this section we describe using readers' theater, choral reading, and storytelling.

Readers' Theater

Readers' theater is a simply staged form of dramatization in which players read their lines rather than memorize them (Shanklin & Rhodes, 1989; Sloyer, 1982; Trousdale & Harris, 1993; Wolf, 1993). Players usually sit on stools but may stand in groups. There are few props and only the simplest of costumes. To begin readers' theater, teachers can write their own script from a simple story or informational text. They demonstrate how dialogue from stories is translated into dialogue in script form and how narrative in text is translated into a narrator's words in a script. Eventually, students compose their own readers' theater scripts from a picture or informational book they have selected. Composing a script gives readers' theater its social, revisionary potential. As children work together to write a script, they are revising in the most literal sense: re-seeing, creating their personal version of a text. With a variety of on- and offstage roles and a built-in need for collaboration, this use of drama in the classroom is ideal for heterogeneous groups.

Because children need not memorize lines, they are free to work on interpretation as they read the script aloud, they feel less anxiety, and, overall, there is less emphasis on the performance than in traditional drama. Instead, as in writing workshop, process takes precedence over product. Many processes lead to the actual performance: choosing a favorite story from a basal reader or children's literature, identifying characters who will have dialogue and one or more narrators' parts, determining which parts of the story are to be copied directly from the story or informational text and which parts can be summarized in narration, writing dialogue, planning simple staging (e.g., characters' miming actions or facing the audience only at times when they are "on stage"), and rehearsing, which may, in turn, necessitate further revision. All these processes are social—they are done in groups, such as Ms. Vaughn's cooperative learning groups.

The Judge: An Untrue Tale (Zemach, 1969) was a second grade class's choice for its first readers' theater (Trousdale & Harris, 1993). Next the class worked from a teacher-scripted version of *Leo the Late Bloomer* (Kraus, 1971) and a published readers' theater adaptation of *Where the Wild Things Are* (Sendak, 1963). Each child had a speaking part in one of the plays, and the class presented all three plays at their annual young authors' tea for parents.

In the readers' theater, rehearsals begin with the teacher's gathering the whole class so that all groups report progress. The children ask questions and make suggestions for solutions to problems in play making and playacting. Then the groups disperse to different parts of the room for rehearsals as the teacher circulates among them.

Once children (or the teacher) have composed a readers' theater script, teachers read it aloud during rehearsal. Then players experiment with reading the script by varying their voices and rate of speaking. The teacher assists students who are having difficulty (Hoyt, 1992). Even the least able readers can participate in readers' theater, however. They are helped by the repeated reading of the scripts that occurs as a natural part of rehearsal. These students' success is one of the greatest benefits of readers' theater. "[O]ne child whom the teacher described as 'basically a nonreader' stood up and read her part with as much aplomb as the most advanced readers" (Trousdale & Harris, 1993, p. 204).

Nonverbal contributions are as important as spoken parts. For example, "[t]he child who played 'the horrible thing' in *The Judge* had no lines but simply suddenly appeared at the end of the story affecting a misshapen form under his white sheet; he crossed to the unbelieving judge and enveloped him in the folds of the sheet" (Trousdale & Harris, 1993, p. 203).

Readers' theater works just as well using nonfiction books as an alternative to content-area textbooks. It "gives the words on the page a voice, and the students in the classroom an active role in internalizing and interpreting new knowledge" (Young & Vardell, 1993, p. 405).

Choral Reading

Choral reading involves children in reading poetry or other short narratives together. An important difference between readers' theater and choral reading is that in choral reading the text itself is not altered. Instead, groups of children make decisions about interpretation and manner of performance. Choral reading is especially appropriate with shorter texts than those used in readers' theater and with texts in which the author's exact wording is important. Poems meet both these criteria. Table 10.1 presents guidelines for choral reading, and Table 10.2 presents methods for arranging poems for choral reading.

Storytelling

Storytelling is another way to revise and perform a printed text (Mallan, 1991). It differs from readers' theater in that it is an oral performance rather than a reading performance. In storytelling, the performer chooses a favorite story, revises the text to suit his or her performing style and the characteristics of the audience, decides what props to use, and rehearses.

Although a storytelling is usually by only one person, revision can be a social process. Whether from a rehearsal before a group chosen to give critical feedback or from interaction with a performance audience, good storytellers are always modifying their tellings. The storyteller does not memorize the text; no two tellings are the same.

Teachers provide important models for storytelling. They not only read to their classes, they also tell stories. When storytelling is a regular part of their weekly

Table 10.1   *Guidelines for Choral Reading*

1. *Silent reading of the poem.* The entire group reads the poem silently.

2. *Oral reading of the poem.* One or two students read the poem aloud.

3. *Discussion of the poem.* After the poem has been read aloud, discussion follows. Here any unfamiliar words may be cleared up.

4. *Deciding on the method.* Various methods of reading the poem chorally should be tried and discussed. Multiple interpretations are to be expected and encouraged—and tried out. Experimentation with tempo, volume, and the treatment of particular lines contributes to the students' understanding of the poem.

5. *Performance.* The group decides upon a method of choral reading, rehearses, and is ready to perform. A leader reads the title and gives the downbeat to get the group started off together.

From Ann Trousdale and Violet Harris in "Missing Links in Literary Response: Group Interpretation of Literature," *Children's Literature in Education,* Vol. 24, p. 199. Copyright © 1993. Reprinted with permission from Human Sciences Press, Inc.

Table 10.2   *Methods for Arranging Poems for Choral Reading*

1. *Antiphonal or two-part arrangement.* One group of voices is balanced with another, each group speaking alternately.

2. *Soloist and chorus.* One voice reads particular stanzas or lines, and the rest of the group joins in on other lines or the refrain.

3. *Line-a-child.* One child or a pair speak a line or couplet. Then the next child or pair speak the next line or lines, and so it continues. The poem may end with all speaking the last line or couplet.

4. *Increasing or decreasing volume.* Voices are added or subtracted, building up to and moving away from the climax of the poem.

5. *Increasing or decreasing tempo.* The rate of speaking is increased or decreased as the poem is read.

6. *Unison.* The whole group speaks as one. The most obvious but the most difficult to do well because of the tendency to become singsongy.

7. *Accompaniment by music, movement, or sound effects.* The speaking of the poem   is accompanied by musical instruments, movement, or sound effects such as snapping fingers or clicking tongues.

8. *A combination.* Some poems may be interpreted using a combination of two or more of the other methods.

From Ann Trousdale and Violet Harris in "Missing Links in Literary Response: Group Interpretation of Literature," *Children's Literature in Education,* Vol. 24, p. 198. Copyright © 1993. Reprinted with permission from Human Sciences Press, Inc.

schedule, teachers share the enjoyment of interpreting a favorite story and they model methods of storytelling. If they begin with stories that are familiar and contain repeated dialogue and repeated action, their students will take the step of becoming storytellers themselves. Folktales are often well suited for this.

To help children become storytellers, teachers may use interactive storytelling. **Interactive storytelling** involves the teacher's beginning a story, but inviting children to add dialogue or make up new episodes. Stories with repetitive episodes and dialogue are especially appropriate for this kind of storytelling. "By making storytelling an interactive event we can help children feel comfortable enough in storytelling to be confident of their own emergent narrative ability, to take risks, to elaborate, to invent, to explore, and thereby to grow" (Trousdale, 1990, p. 173). This is a prescription for children's growth not only as storytellers, but as story writers and comprehenders of their world.

Storytellings do not always have to derive from a printed text. Other sources include personal experiences or oral traditions, such as favorite family anecdotes. Everyone has a fund of personal narratives. "Storytelling is so basic to human existence that we often cannot see that we all engage in telling some form of story every day of our lives" (Mallan, 1991, p. 5). Storytelling viewed in this way can have the same power for second and third graders and adults that Paley's (1990) story telling and playing has for preschoolers (see Chapter 7).

Reading

A variety of reading activities invite children to construct meaning as a social process through revisiting literature again and again. We describe booktalks and book productions. We also elaborate on using readers' workshop, the core-literature approach, and the basal reading program with students who are beyond the first grade.

Booktalks

Booktalks are variations on the traditional book report. During booktalks teachers or children tell about a favorite story, giving the title, author, and illustrator. Teachers identify the genre of the book. For stories, the teller describes the setting, characters, and major events. For informational books, tellers discuss the topic and present its main points. Tellers may talk about their reasons for selecting the book, an interesting event or fact from the book, information about the author, and why others might like to read the book.

Booktalks can be informal conversations (e.g., when teachers invite any children interested in talking about the books they are reading to spend five to ten minutes talking together about their books in small-group areas). For more formal booktalks, children sign up to give a booktalk on a particular day. They use a booktalk checklist (shown in Table 10.3) to prepare for their talk and rehearse the talk with the teacher or an aide. Then they present their booktalk to a small group of their classmates.

Teachers give many booktalks as a way of introducing children to the variety of books in their classroom libraries. Giving booktalks is an important part of a self-

Table 10.3 *A Booktalk Checklist*

Book Talk Checklist

Be sure to include:

_____ Title of the Book

_____ Author's name

_____ Illustrator's name (if there is one)

_____ Is your book a storybook or information book?

(For storybooks)

_____ Setting   _____ Characters   _____ Problems

(For information books)

_____ Topic   _____ Way topic is presented   _____ Charts, maps?

You may include:

_____ Sample to share

_____ Reason for chosing the sample

_____ Something your audience might like—or wonder about

_____ Information about the author

_____ A question for the author

_____ This question for your audience: "What questions do you have about my book?"

selected reading program (such as Ms. Vaughn's readers' workshop). Children are more eager to read books that their classmates or teachers have described. Teachers' booktalks also provide models for children's booktalks.

Book Productions

Book productions are major responses to literature and require considerable time and effort. Two or three times each year, the teacher announces a book production time. During this time, which may last from a few weeks to a month, children team up to make some production based on books. One group may choose to dramatize a favorite book. Another may choose to make a video based on a book. A video may take the form of a dramatization of a book's story or a "You Are There" interview of the characters at crucial points in a story. Other children may choose to write their own book using a similar theme or setting or the same characters as a book they like. They work together on composition (writing several drafts before producing a well-edited final copy), on illustrations, and on production (typing on a word processor, photocopying several copies, and binding). Another group may produce a literary review, a newspaper-like publication containing children's reviews of books that they have read recently. Multiple copies are made for the whole class.

Parents can be enlisted to help with these productions, if the teacher announces a book production time several weeks before work begins and lists the kinds of help that he or she would like. Help may include videotaping and editing assistance, costuming, typing, bookbinding, helping with rehearsals, taking dictation, and assisting with revisions and editing. Parents are always invited to attend productions.

Readers' Workshop

Readers' workshop is a form of reading instruction based on wide, self-selected reading. Ms. Vaughn uses a modified form of the readers' workshop as a part of her program. The six components of a readers' workshop (Reutzel & Cooter, 1991) are:

- Reading aloud to students
- Teaching minilessons on reading skills and other matters related to the readers' workshop
- Reading independently
- Responding to literature
- Holding conferences with students
- Sharing books and response activities

Teachers begin readers' workshop by reading aloud to students. Through read alouds, teachers demonstrate reading strategies by talking aloud sometimes as they read (for example, stopping to imagine a scene in a story or to comment on connections among ideas in an informational book). In **minilessons** teachers may demonstrate reading strategies; provide information about authors, illustrators, styles of illustration, genres, or literary conventions; model response activities, including ways of writing in a response log; and provide information about record keeping, such as how to record in a response log the titles and authors of books read during readers' workshop. Students read independently for extended periods of time as a major part of the readers' workshop. The purpose of this reading is to develop reading fluency, to create interest in reading, and to enhance children's reading ability.

Students respond to the literature they are reading in a variety of ways. One way in which Ms. Vaughn's students responded was to write twice a week in response logs. They also wrote stories that were extensions of their reading. Suggestions for response-to-literature activities include

- Compose readers' theater scripts
- Perform informal dramatizations
- Retell stories with homemade props
- Construct dioramas
- Give booktalks
- Make bookmarks or book jackets

- Experiment with art media used in illustrations

- Write and publish a retelling or an extension of a book

Teachers have **reading conferences** with students about the books they are reading. During these conferences, teachers talk with students about their books, listen to students read, and discuss response-log entries and other response projects. Teachers use conferences to teach skills and make assessments of students' progress and needs. As a last part of readers' workshop, students share their response projects and talk about books they are reading. Small groups of students act as audiences for response activities such as dramatizations and readers' theater productions.

Core-Literature Approach

The **core-literature approach** involves a class or a small group of students reading a common literature selection (Zarrillo, 1989). Ms. Vaughn used a modification of this approach when she provided multiple copies of such books as *Strega Nona* for students to read together.

The core-literature approach includes four components.

1. Reading the core selection

2. Responding to the selection

3. Teaching about reading and literature

4. Reading independently

This approach can be used with one literature selection in which the whole class reads the same book or with several selections. Teachers select a group of five to seven books related to the same theme or topic, written by the same author, or in the same genre. The books represent a variety of difficulty levels. Teachers give booktalks about each of the books, and children then select which book they want to read.

The core-literature approach can be based on **book clubs,** or **literature-response groups.** To start a book club, the teacher provides multiple copies of a book, she previews it for the class, and then signs up a club of children who are interested in that book. They read (or are read) assigned parts between sessions, and then they discuss and share favorite parts when the club gets together. Usually the teacher or an aide or volunteer meets with the club to participate in and guide the discussion. Often clubs (or some of the members) want to stay together when they finish a book. Sometimes they read another book with a similar theme or topic, or another book by the same author. Other times they become a theme or topic club, and each child reads whatever books he or she wants that come under the theme or topic (for example, fantasy, hobbies, sports, animals, folktales, mysteries, and biographies).

Children respond to the core selection either independently or as a group. Teachers provide instruction by modeling a variety of reading strategies, including using word identification strategies, predicting, summarizing, questioning, and forming images. They provide a daily time for children to read books of their own interest. Teachers may provide a selection of additional books written by the same author, on the same theme, or about the same topic as the core selection.

The Basal Approach beyond First Grade

Basal reading programs extend beyond the first grade. These programs include anthologies of stories written on increasingly difficult levels and teachers' manuals that specify skills and suggest activities for teaching these skills. Workbooks are available for skills practice. Stories and other texts in some more recently published basal reading programs are reproductions of children's literature. They also suggest additional literature that complements the basal texts and response activities. Basal reading programs continue to focus on developing word identification, sight-word learning, and comprehension skills. As we have seen, Ms. Vaughn combines basal instruction with other approaches to reading.

Writing

Writing is an important part of the literacy program in the grades beyond first. We have seen how Ms. Vaughn includes a writers' workshop and journal writing as a part of her program. She also encourages writing as a way to extend reading (for example, see Carrie's story in Figure 10.4). Next we describe other writing activities that encourage children's social construction of meaning; these activities use graphic organizers, word clusters, character clusters, comparison charts, and computers.

Graphic Organizers

Much of children's writing in grades after first reflects their increasing control over expository text (see Chapter 5). Children write reports using the many printed resources in their classroom and school libraries. They are invited to write reports for many purposes. The writing workshop overlaps the rest of the day when students write current events reports, descriptions of family vacations for which they were excused from school attendance, historical essays for social studies, or descriptions of individual- or team-conducted experiments in science class.

Much of the formal instruction about writing (in minilessons and in small-group and whole-class activities) in these grades is about how to write expository passages. Teachers can use a modified language-experience approach to model expository writing (Kinney, 1985). Another method uses special outlines called graphic organizers to teach about different text structures that authors use to write about causes and effects, about problems and solutions, or about contrasts and comparisons (McGee & Richgels, 1985).

Graphic organizers are special visual displays that present information from a text in an organized fashion. Figure 10.6 presents a graphic organizer for the text "Forest Fires" that was presented in Figure 5.8 in Chapter 5. Major points from the text are written in boxes, main points are written inside ovals, and important details are written under the ovals and marked with dots. Relationships among ideas are signaled with connecting lines. In Figure 10.6 the relationship between the ideas "fires destroy forests" and "staff lookout stations and have helicopters ready," "have experts and bulldozers ready", and "build fire lanes" is that "fires destroy forests" is a problem and the other ideas are three solutions to that problem.

Young readers can use graphic organizers to guide their reading and writing (McGee & Richgels, 1985). Teachers present the organizer before reading as a stimulus for group discussion. They point out not only the information included in the organizer, but also the relationships among ideas as shown on the organizer.

Teachers can use graphic organizers to call attention to compare–contrast, main idea–detail, sequence, and cause–effect structures as well as to problem–solution. To construct a graphic organizer, teachers read short passages noting main ideas and details. They pay attention to the relationships among ideas. Then they write a graphic organizer that presents the passage ideas and relationships in visual form. After making the organizer, teachers can make a skeleton organizer by taking the text out and leaving behind the boxes, ovals, dots, and lines.

Children can use skeleton organizers as a prompt for writing as well as for reading. For example, after reading several books about alligators and crocodiles, children could use a skeleton compare–contrast graphic organizer to organize information about the two animals in preparation for writing a report. The value of graphic organizers during reading and writing lies more in the discussion surrounding their use than in the actual organizer that children produce. As children talk together in cooperative learning groups to fill in a graphic organizer after reading, they share and revise their ideas. This kind of talk is another example of social construction of meaning.

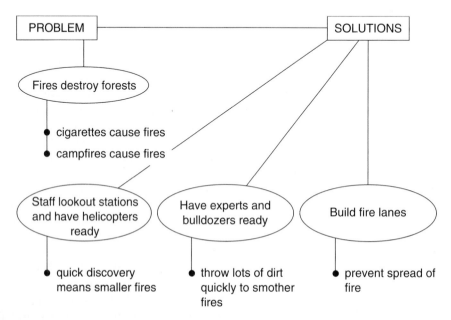

Figure 10.6 *A Graphic Organizer for "Forest Fires"*

Word Clusters

Word clusters are visual displays of knowledge related to a concept (Pearson & Johnson, 1978). A word is placed in the center of a circle, and around the circle, information related to the word is written. Figure 10.7 presents a word cluster for the word *polar* written by a third grader before and after reading *The Polar Express* (Van Allsburg, 1985). First, Fran wrote about *polar* that "it's a train" and "it's big and black," reflecting her knowledge of the story but little awareness of the meaning of the word *polar.* After reading the story and discussing how *polar* was used in the story (to describe the polar ice cap and the polar sky), Fran became more aware of the word's meaning. However, when she spontaneously said, "Hey, polar bear! It's like a *polar* bear. They must live at the North Pole," she finally made the connection between the word *polar* and its referent *North Pole.*

Group construction of word clusters is more useful than having individual students write their own clusters. Groups of students can pool their knowledge to come to a richer understanding of words.

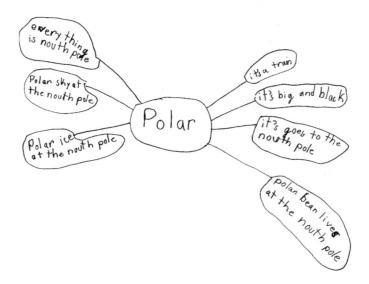

Figure 10.7 *A Word Cluster for the Word* Polar

Character Clusters

Character clusters are visual webs that present character traits. For example, Figure 10.8 presents a character cluster written by third graders for the main character, the boy, in *The Polar Express* (Van Allsburg, 1985). These children noticed the boy's altruism (although they did not have the sophisticated vocabulary to label this concept) when they said, "[I]t was more important to have the bell instead of a toy." They also clearly identified the boy as a believer and as brave, two character traits strongly implied in the text. They were able to find two details from the text as support for one character trait (the boy was brave "because he went on the train" and "he sat on Santa's lap").

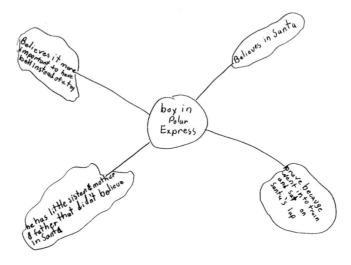

Figure 10.8 *A Character Cluster for* The Polar Express
(Van Allsburg, 1985)

Again, the value of character clusters lies in their generating quality talk about stories, their supporting social construction of meaning. As children work together to make hypotheses about characters' traits, they challenge one another to find supporting details. This kind of talk allows children to move back and forth between the literal information provided in the text and inferential ideas that they construct.

Computers

Classrooms beyond the first grade usually include at least one microcomputer. We suggest using computer time for word processing and creating data bases, *not* for the many computer games (or "skill-and-drill software") that are available. These games are fun and attractive to students (at least when they are new), but they are too expensive and too narrowly focused.

Students can do some of their writing on microcomputers, using a word processing program, but it is not practical for them to do all their writing that way. Most students can do much of their planning and drafting with paper and pencil, rather than with a word processor. They are adept at making revisions with cross-outs, arrows, and brackets and cut-and-paste (see Figure 10.9). Then students can sign up for word processor time to do third-, second-to-last, and final drafts, to run spelling checks, and to print final copies of their pieces for publication in the classroom. They appreciate the ease of making changes with the word processor and the clean look of their computer-printed final copies.

Some students never use the word processor because they do not like waiting for a sign-up time or because they lack keyboard skills. Either they are quite satisfied with their handwritten products—many of which are very neatly produced— or they can get a classmate or teammate to type their pieces for them.

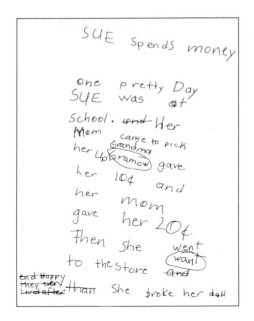 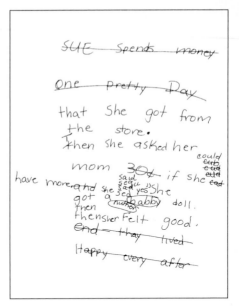

Figure 10.9 *Brittney's Draft with Revisions*

Data bases are cross-referenced computer files that students create as they are doing research for a subject-area project or report (Strickland, Feeley, & Wepner, 1987). Instead of leaving their notes in notebooks, on three-by-five-inch cards, or on scraps of paper, they enter them into the computer (see Figure 10.10). It is easier for the children to use these files in their final products, and the files remain available for anyone else in the class.

Spelling

Spelling is an important part of the literacy program beyond first grade. Children need to learn to spell many words to use in their writing, to become aware of alternative spelling patterns, and to develop strategies for spelling unknown words (Wilde, 1992). We describe here an approach to teaching spelling in second and third grades that we feel is consistent with the emphasis in this chapter on functional, social uses of language and on child-centered instruction. Such a spelling program has five necessary features:

1. A large number of words that children are expected to learn to spell must come from the children's needs, for example, from their own writing and reading, from current and upcoming content-area units, and from current events.

2. There should be a balance between individualization and whole-class work. Students work with spelling lists that include personal words, which only they are expected to learn, and words that the whole-class is expected to learn.

Figure 10.10 *A Microcomputer Data File*

Data File

Explorer: Ferdinand Magellan

Nationality: Portuguese

Dates: 1480?–1521

Accomplishments: Organized the first expedition to sail around the world. (Note: People sometimes say he was the first to sail around the word, but he didn't make it all the way himself—he was killed on the way. His sailors did go all the way around.)

Other information: The Strait of Magellan at the south end of S. America (between it and Antarctica) is named for him. So is the Magellanic Cloud—a galaxy you can only see from the southern part of the world (Southern Hemisphere)—and one of the closest galaxies to our galaxy.

Source of information: *World Book Encyclopedia* and the dictionary

Books about this explorer: don't know

File name: Magellan

Cross reference words: Magellan/explorers/Southern Hemisphere/South America/Antarctica/galaxies

This file was created by:
date:

This file was amended by:
date:

This file was used by:
dates:

---

3. There should be a balance between words that follow generalizations (e.g., *ight* words) and high-frequency words that do not follow generalizations (e.g., *said*). The teacher may have a master list of high-frequency words and generalizations that children will encounter at some point in the year.

4. There should be a routine in the teaching and learning of spelling, including some routine way to begin a spelling unit and a routine way to bring closure to that unit.

5. Children should be involved in identifying words to learn and in discovering spelling generalizations or rules.

With these features in mind, we suggest a three- or four-week **spelling cycle** approach. For each spelling cycle unit, children generate a large pool of words with which they will work for three or four weeks. During this time children are expected to be able to read these words and to know their meanings. Each week small groups of children select a short list of words from the word pool for spelling. Each student learns to spell these words and two or three other words of personal interest or need. Each week for the three or four weeks of the spelling unit, children continue to generate a new spelling list from the word pool. At the end of the unit, the teacher and students work together to generate a final list of words from the word pool that all children will be expected to be able to spell. These words go on a master spelling-editing checklist posted in the classroom for use during children's editing of their writing pieces.

Creating a Word Pool

At the start of each spelling unit, the teacher and the children generate a **word pool** of seventy to eighty words from content units, high-frequency words, words that follow spelling patterns, words whose spellings children have requested during writing workshop, words collected from personal reading, or words that children find interesting. Children keep their own lists of words (Ms. Vaughn's children keep a spelling log in which they write words for which they asked about spelling during writing workshop; we describe spelling logs later). They know that every three or four weeks they will have the opportunity to give input in the creation of a word pool for spelling.

Whole-Class Vocabulary and Spelling Activities

In some activities, the whole class works with words from the word pool for understanding, not for spelling. For example, children may categorize the words or make word clusters, resulting in adding related words to the word pool. In other activities, the class works together to discover spelling rules or devices to help remember spellings (such as mnemonics). Children may divide the pool into easy and difficult words, words that follow spelling generalizations, words that do not follow spelling generalizations (most high-frequency words do not), proper nouns, long words, and short words. Word groupings should highlight features of the words that will aid in learning to spell them.

Small-Group Activities

Small groups of children choose twelve to fifteen words from the word pool to create a list of words to study and learn to spell for the first week. Each child is expected to add one or two personal challenge words to the group list that are unique to that child. The teacher works with the class and with groups to help them to see what makes a good list, for example, words of similar difficulty, words that follow a generalization and some exceptions to that generalization, and topic-related words.

Sequence of Lessons

The children learn the words from their group's list. They test each other on Friday. Then groups generate new lists for the next week, still using the pool of seventy to eighty words that began the unit. Each group may share what it learned the first week, telling the whole class how the list came to be, what was easy or difficult, and how the words were used in writing or seen in print.

The cycle continues through several weeks. Three or four weeks seem long enough to make good use of the original pool of words, but not so long that it gets boring. At the end of the unit, the teacher makes a smaller list from the original word pool that reflects some words from each group's weekly lists. This smaller word list is added to the **spelling editing checklist,** a list of words that the children are expected to spell correctly in final drafts of writing projects. The next three-to-four-week unit begins with a new pool of words, and children form new spelling study groups.

Spelling Challenge

To review and expand on words that children have already learned to spell, and as a break from the spelling cycle, the teacher may want to provide a **spelling challenge** from time to time before starting a new spelling cycle unit. Figure 10.11 shows an example of a spelling challenge activity.

Spelling Logs

The best spelling approaches connect children's daily reading and writing. One way to do this is to use spelling logs. **Spelling logs** are records of words that students have difficulty spelling and the strategies they used for correctly spelling those words. Ms. Vaughn tells about her class's spelling logs:

> [On our spelling logs] we have this sheet that's got two columns [one for the student to write his or her way and the second for trying to fix it]. . . . And then we

Figure 10.11 *A Spelling Challenge Test Activity*

Spelling Challenge

This week's spelling challenge words are:

fight	eight	caught
night	height	though
light	straight	cough
slight	thought	rough
tight	through	ghost

Most of these words have a silent *gh,* but in the last three words, the *gh* sounds like a hard *g* or an *f.*

I challenge you to find more words with a silent *gh* and a *gh* that sounds like an *f* or a hard *g.* Think about it. Pay attention to words while you read. Start keeping a list. Compare lists with your classmates. Can you know anything for sure about where a *gh* will be silent or where it will sound like an *f*—or at least where it *won't* sound like an *f*?!

There will be a special challenge test on Friday with words not from this list.

> make sure that [the word written on] the other side is right. . . . Then they have to record their words with the date in their spelling logs, and they have to be spelled correctly. They can not [ask] . . . if they need to know how to spell a word, unless they've tried it in their spelling log. . . . And it's wonderful how many times they get it, or they are so close and I show them, "See, you got that *th*. Now so what if you didn't know it was an *e* or it was an *i*?"

Ms. Vaughn teaches spelling of high-frequency, often-irregular words using a high-frequency list such as the one presented in Table 9.5 in Chapter 9. She photocopies it and staples it in each child's spelling log.

> At least it's there. At least it's one more way to have a word. It's alphabetized. I tell them, "If you always get stuck on the word *with*, put a star by that one."

Self-Evaluation of Spelling

Teachers and children need to evaluate spelling growth. Ms. Vaughn:

> I try to keep a lot of self-evaluation in [the students'] portfolios. And I really do get to know the kids when I do that. [Their self-evaluation includes their writing:] . . . "What I know about spelling" . . . "What I learned in today's minilesson" . . . "What do I do when I don't know how to spell a word?"

Chapter Summary

Second grade and third grade are an exciting time for children and their teachers. The great strides that students make toward becoming fully competent readers and writers present teachers with great challenges, opportunities, and satisfactions. In this chapter Ms. Vaughn describes how she teaches her engagingly literate second graders. The day begins with children writing a daily newsletter, searching for the answer to a geography question, and writing in dialogue journals. Ms. Vaughn conducts an extensive writing workshop in which she teaches lessons and confers with children about their writing. Children compose, revise, and edit. As a help for these processes, they belong to response groups, which meet regularly to talk about compositions. Ms. Vaughn teaches children how to give compliments about compositions as well as how to ask questions and give honest reactions. Children read at least three times each day,

during reading time, beyond-the-basal reading time, and center time. During reading time they read stories from the basal or other multiple-copy reading materials that Ms. Vaughn has collected. During beyond-the-basal reading time, children participate in a readers' workshop in which they read from a variety of books selected by Ms. Vaughn. They write about their reading in a response log and participate in response activities. During center time, children work at social studies or science centers and Ms. Vaughn calls on small groups of children who have been grouped by ability. She teaches reading skills and guides children in response activities. Ms. Vaughn reads aloud from a novel daily, and children read and write as a part of content units. They learn much about their content units through work in small cooperative-learning groups.

We have emphasized the social and revisionary nature of literacy and content-area learning in a classroom that functions like Ms. Vaughn's, as a true community of literate thinkers. This social construction of meaning takes place in additional oral-language activities, including readers' theater, choral reading, and storytelling. It occurs in additional reading activities, such as booktalks, book productions, and core-literature activities. It takes place in writing activities that support reading, such as using graphic organizers, word clusters, character clusters, and data files. Finally, it occurs in spelling approaches, such as the spelling cycle.

Applying the Information

We suggest two activities for applying the information. Make a list of the nine characteristics of a literacy-rich classroom presented in Chapter 6. Then reread this chapter to locate one activity from Ms. Vaughn's classroom that is consistent with each of these characteristics. Discuss your examples with a classmate.

Next, make a list of all the literacy learning activities described in this chapter (see the list of key concepts). For each of these activities, describe what children learn about written language meanings, forms, meaning-form links, or functions.

Going Beyond the Text

Visit a second or third grade classroom and observe several literacy activities. Write a list of all the print and literacy materials in the classroom. Take note of the classroom layout and the interactions among the children and between the children and the teacher during literacy activities. Talk with the teacher about his or her philosophy of literacy instruction. Compare these materials, activities, and philosophies with those of Ms. Vaughn.

References

ANDERSEN, H. (1986). *The ugly duckling*. New York: Knopf.

ATWELL, N. (1987). *In the middle*. Portsmouth, NH: Heinemann.

COHEN, C. (1989). *The mud pony*. New York: Scholastic.

de PAOLA, T. (1979). *Strega Nona*. New York: Simon and Schuster.

GAMBRELL, L. (1985). Dialogue journals: Reading–writing interaction. *The Reading Teacher, 38,* 512–515.

HOYT, L. (1992). Many ways of knowing: Using drama, oral interactions, and the visual arts to enhance reading comprehension. *The Reading Teacher, 45,* 580–584.

KINNEY, M. A. (1985). A language experience approach to teaching expository text structure. *The Reading Teacher, 38,* 854–856.

KRAUS, R. (1971). *Leo the late bloomer*. New York: Crowell.

MALLAN, K. (1991). *Children as storytellers*. Portsmouth, NH: Heinemann.

MARTIN, B. Jr. (1972). *Sounds of laughter*. New York: Holt, Rinehart and Winston.

McGEE, L. M., & RICHGELS, D. J. (1985). Teaching expository text structure to elementary students. *The Reading Teacher, 38,* 739–748.

MUNSCH, R. (1980). *The paper bag princess*. Toronto: Annick Press.

PALEY, V. G. (1990). *The boy who would be a helicopter: The uses of storytelling in the*

of expected knowledge within a reasonable time frame when they are given adequate opportunities and instruction. For young children, this time frame and range of expected knowledge is wide and allows for much individual variation. However, teachers also recognize that some children seem to struggle to acquire literacy even within literacy-rich classrooms and with a wide variety of instructional experiences. We call these children **at-risk learners**. At-risk learners need teachers who are especially observant and adept at modifying instructional techniques. Effective teachers are aware of the variety of special literacy-intervention programs that have been successfully used to accelerate the literacy learning of at-risk learners.

Using Observations to Modify Instruction

At-risk learners are more likely to experience school failure if their teachers do not use observations to modify instruction to better fit their needs. For example, a kindergarten teacher noticed that two children in her class had a great deal of difficulty listening to stories read aloud. Most children in her class were interested in the stories and informational books that she read aloud in whole-class gatherings. The children eagerly responded to questions and made thoughtful comments during short grand conversations. They sat still and watched the illustrations intently as she read the text. However, these two children were obvious exceptions to this general pattern of behavior. John and Pedro seemed to be behavior problems at storytime. They often brought small toys to play with, rolled around on the rug, and disrupted the group by attempting to talk with other children while the teacher was reading.

The teacher realized that both boys needed experiences with books. John had had few experiences with storybook reading prior to coming to school, and Pedro could benefit from more interaction with books to support his learning English as a second language. She hypothesized that the boys' behavior during storytime reflected John's lack of experience interacting with books and Pedro's problems understanding English. She decided to read with just Pedro and John for a few minutes every day. Both boys listened more intently in this small group, and the teacher was able to select books that were more engaging for them. However, she could not coax either boy to contribute much in discussions about the books she read; they used one or two words to answer her questions. The teacher decided to include other children in the group, who could model talking about books. She carefully selected two children who were sensitive to Pedro's attempts to communicate in English. Now the small-group discussions were more lively, and gradually both John's and Pedro's responses became longer and more complex.

As this teacher discovered, most at-risk children learn better in small-group settings than in whole-class gatherings (Kameenui, 1993). This setting provides more opportunities for children's active participation and allows teachers to provide explicit instruction targeted to children's needs. At-risk learners need immediate interventions, instruction that moves them quickly toward successful reading and writing behaviors and understandings, and more frequent opportunities to engage in reading and writing activities.

Teachers who support at-risk learners are sensitive to children's responses to instructional settings and techniques. They make hypotheses about the difficulties that children experience and plan modifications in their instruction to overcome these difficulties. They are patient and understanding of children's unwillingness to take risks and fear of failure (Allen & Carr, 1989). They are watchful for small signs of success, and help children celebrate their new accomplishments.

Literacy-Intervention Programs for At Risk Learners

Researchers have developed several intervention programs designed to ensure the success of young at-risk learners (Hiebert & Taylor, 1994). Teachers who are aware of these programs may be able to adapt some of their procedures to support at-risk learners in the regular classroom. The best-known literacy-intervention program for at-risk learners is Reading Recovery, a literacy program designed by Marie Clay in New Zealand (Clay, 1985) and implemented widely in the United States.

Reading Recovery

Reading Recovery is targeted at first graders who are experiencing difficulty learning to read, who are identified early, and who receive daily one-on-one instruction fine-tuned to match their instructional needs. Instruction is intended to accelerate their learning so that on leaving the program (generally after twelve to fifteen weeks), children achieve at the average reading level of the other children in first grade and continue adequate reading improvement without special instruction.

Reading Recovery teachers provide daily thirty-minute lessons in which children read, write, and analyze language. The materials used in the lesson and the way in which teachers respond to children during the lesson are highly dependent on daily observation of children's reading and writing strategies. The materials are organized from easier to more difficult according to repetition and language patterns. Easier texts have fewer words, more repetition, and spoken language patterns. More difficult texts have more words, less repetition, and literary language (Peterson, 1991). Children are taught to use several reading strategies, including using the meaning (does that make sense?), language patterns (does that sound right?), and orthographics (do you expect to see that letter?). Each lesson has five components: reading familiar stories, taking a running record, working with letters, writing a message or story, and reading a new book (Pinnell, Fried, & Estice, 1990).

Reading Recovery Lessons

Reading Recovery lessons begin with reading a familiar book. Familiar books are books read in previous lessons. Sometimes teachers select a particular book for instructional purposes, and sometimes children select familiar books for rereading. Familiar books provide children with opportunities to read fluently and practice using a variety of reading strategies.

Each day the teacher takes a running record of the child's independent reading of a book that was read for the first time during the previous lesson. Running records are used to gauge reading level and to reveal children's reading strategies (see Chapter 12 for a discussion of running records). The results of running records are used, in part, to make decisions about the next lesson.

Working with letters is an optional component of the Reading Recovery lesson. In this portion of the lesson, children work with magnetic letters on a magnetic board. They may use the letters to write words or to engage in word analysis.

Children write a message or story every day. The message may be related to a book the child has read or to a school event. The message is relatively short (only one or two sentences), but the writing may extend over several days. The child composes the message and then writes it word for word with the teacher's assistance as needed. All words are spelled conventionally, but the teacher uses every opportunity to call attention to sound–letter information or spelling patterns. The child predicts letters, analyzes sounds, and practices writing correctly spelled words. Immediately after the message is composed, the teacher writes it on a sentence strip and cuts it apart. The child reassembles the message and reads it. The sentence is taken back to the classroom to share with the teacher and other children.

An important part of each Reading Recovery lesson is reading a new book. The teacher thoughtfully selects a book that will push the child's abilities forward, yet still be accessible. The teacher introduces the book by having the child look at and talk about the illustrations. The teacher may interject several vocabulary words during the discussion and may have the child locate the words in the text before reading (Clay, 1991). After the teacher has helped the child become familiar with the plot, the important ideas, and some of the language of the text, the child reads the book with the teacher's assistance when needed. As the child reads, the teacher draws attention to the child's successful use of strategies and gently nudges the child to use different strategies and strategies in combination. Children are taught to use more than one reading strategy to cross-check their reading.

Whereas Reading Recovery is intended for use in one-on-one settings, it also incorporates many features that we recommend for all children. For example, children read and write every day, and instruction is embedded within reading and writing activities. Teachers can implement a variety of other Reading Recovery principles and procedures for use in the regular classroom. They can regularly assess children's learning. Taking stock of each child's reading and writing abilities several times during the school year highlights successes, identifies potential problems, and signals the need for instructional modifications. Teachers can provide many opportunities for children to reread favorite books. Finally, teachers can encourage children to discuss their use of reading strategies and teach children to use several strategies to cross-check their reading.

At-Risk Revisited

Our definition of at-risk learners focuses on children who have difficulties learning in a literacy-rich classroom with many opportunities to read and write. Other definitions of at-risk learners include children from backgrounds with historically high drop-out rates and low achievement levels: children with special needs, children from low socioeconomic or minority backgrounds, and English-as-a-second-language learners.

Many children who have special needs, have diverse cultural backgrounds, and speak English as a second language are at-risk learners. Of course, not all of these children are at-risk learners, but there are many reasons to give special attention to these diverse learners. The remainder of this chapter describes issues related to supporting the literacy learning of children with special needs, from diverse cultural backgrounds, and from diverse language backgrounds.

SPECIAL-NEEDS LEARNERS

Children with special needs include children with challenging social and emotional behaviors, pronounced differences in learning styles or rates, or deficits in hearing, vision, or mobility (Truax & Kretschmer, 1993). Despite being singled out as having special learning difficulties, most special-needs children develop literacy knowledge in patterns that are similar to those found in all children's literacy understandings. For example, one researcher examined the literacy development of young children who were prenatally exposed to the drugs crack or cocaine (Barone, 1993). The children were asked to reread a favorite storybook, write a story, and spell words once a month over a year. During this time, the children's emergent readings became more advanced and their writing evidenced more sophisticated concepts about written language. In a similar study, profoundly deaf preschoolers with delayed receptive language were found to have understandings of written language that were developmentally appropriate (Williams, 1994).

Therefore, we could conclude that the most effective way to support special-needs children's literacy learning is similar to the way in which we support all children's learning. Many special education professionals recommend the use of holistic, integrated approaches to reading and writing instruction similar to the activities and approaches proposed in the preceding chapters (Cousin, Weekley, & Gerard, 1993; Truax & Kretschmer, 1993).

Supporting Special-Needs Children's Literacy

Many educators argue that *all children* acquire literacy when they pursue topics of personal interest, interact with others who share similar interests, and make connections between known and new information. Of course, children with special needs "may vary from their age peers, making connections in their own time and in their own ways; but the steps in the learning process" are similar (Truax & Kretschmer, 1993, pp. 593–594). Effective teachers carefully observe children, including special-needs children, and make adjustments in activities and instruction to meet their needs. Adapting instruction to serve special-needs learners often means careful observation of children as they participate in reading and writing activities in order to make modifications that will allow all learners to take small risks and reap large rewards (Salvage & Brazee, 1991).

The early childhood classroom is an especially supportive environment for young children with developmental or learning differences. Here, children select activities that promote growth in all areas and levels of development. Because teachers spend less time in whole-group instruction and more time with small groups and individual children, accommodating instruction for the special-needs child is usually not difficult.

Children with developmental or learning differences in elementary school are placed in regular classrooms when special education teachers feel they can benefit from instruction and activities planned for non-special-needs children. With some adjustments, children with special needs can benefit from instruction along with other children in the regular classroom.

All special-needs children from the age of three who have identified developmental or learning differences have an **individualized educational plan (IEP)** developed by a team of specialists and the child's parents. Teachers should ask for a copy of the plan and quickly become familiar with it so that they can prepare activities to help the child achieve the goals outlined in the IEP.

Modifying Instruction for Children with Developmental Delays

One of the most effective techniques for supporting the literacy learning of children with developmental delays is to provide instruction that is compatible with the child's developmental level, rather than with the child's age. A second effective technique is to provide social experiences that involve interacting with other children on similar social developmental levels, rather than with children of similar ages. Many of the techniques that we have described for younger novice readers and writers or experimenters with reading and writing are appropriate for older children with developmental delays.

Dramatic-play-with-print centers are effective learning tools for children with developmental delays through the elementary-school years. Environmental print reading is also especially effective in helping children with developmental delays learn about written language and reading. Teaching children how to write the names of their friends and family members is another meaningful literacy activity. Both environmental print reading and name writing activities provide opportunities for teachers to help children with these special needs transfer knowledge from one situation to another. As children learn to write the names of many of their special friends and family members, the teacher can point out the names of letters that are found in more than one name. Teachers need to explain how learning to write the letter *B* in *Brandi* is like writing the letter *B* in *Brad*. When children read a Raisin Bran cereal box, the teacher should explain again the connections between the letters found in *Brandi, Brad,* and *Bran*.

More formal techniques for teaching children with developmental delays to read and write are similar to techniques that support all children's learning to read and write (Dixon, 1987; Sindelar, 1987). Special educators suggest that if children are to become effective readers, they need to read whole texts (not isolated words); however, children with developmental delays may need more practice and may take a longer time than other children. There are several ways for teachers to help children read whole texts and give them the extra practice they need to become good readers. Teachers can read stories first as children follow the text. The method of **repeated reading** provides practice with whole texts (Dowhower, 1989; O'Shea & O'Shea, 1987). In this method, children repeatedly read stories (or parts of stories) that are about fifty or one hundred words in length until they can read the selection with only three to six errors. Children begin the repeated readings only when they understand the story.

Modifying Instruction for Children with Emotional, Learning, and Language Disabilities

The writing process is an effective approach in helping emotionally and learning-disabled children successfully communicate their feelings (D'Alessandro, 1987). Daily writing encourages children by implying that they have something meaningful to communicate. A process approach to writing deemphasizes spelling and mechanics, which can be significant stumbling blocks for special-needs children. By focusing on ideas, the writing process supports these children's self-esteem.

As the children brainstorm ideas, teachers can record their ideas on a chart. Then teachers can help the children cluster their ideas into groups. Teachers can demonstrate how to use the cluster by writing a group-collaborated composition that in turn may also be used in reading instruction. During revision, teachers need to be especially careful, because too much revision can frustrate the child into discarding a good composition. The most effective motivation for revision occurs when children discover that they have difficulty reading their own compositions as they present their work in the author's chair (D'Alessandro, 1987).

There are many ways in which teachers can help special-needs children become more actively involved in reading and writing. One way in which children are active during reading is by making predictions about what they are going to read and by drawing conclusions about what they have already read (Norris, 1988). Pattern books are effective for supporting active reading and writing of learning-disabled children. These books have predictable sequences that make it easier for children to draw inferences as they predict what will happen next.

Avoiding Reductionist Teaching

Opponents of integrated, holistic approaches to literacy learning argue that children learn better when instruction is systematic and explicit (Dolman, 1992; Shapiro, 1992). Because of the tendency of many special-needs children to be easily distracted from completing tasks, teachers have been encouraged to break tasks into smaller or easier-to-complete components and to use tasks that are highly structured. One activity that might seem to make learning to write letters easier is to have children copy only three letters several times. Although learning-disabled children might learn to form the three letters from this activity, they will not learn how letters operate within the written language system, which is much more important than merely learning to form a few letters. We recommend that teachers rarely use drills on isolated written language tasks with any child, and especially with children who may have trouble figuring out the complexities of reading and writing.

LEARNERS FROM DIVERSE CULTURAL BACKGROUNDS

Children from **diverse cultural backgrounds** may be distinguished by their ethnicity, social class, or language (Au, 1993). **Ethnicity** is determined by one's national heritage, and most children from diverse cultural backgrounds are included in groups we call African American, Hispanic American, Asian American, or Native American, although people usually identify their ethnicity more precisely with a country of family origin, for example, Puerto Rican, Haitian, or Vietnamese. **Social class** is related to socioeconomic level as reflected in parents' occupations and family income. Children from diverse cultural backgrounds may speak a nonmainstream dialect of English or a language other than English (we discuss the influence of diverse language backgrounds in the next section of this chapter).

Cultural Influences on Learning

Some cultural groups have different ways of helping children learn. In some Native American communities, children are expected to learn by observing adults as they perform tasks; this implies that little verbal interaction takes place. Children who expect to learn from watching adults may not learn well in writing centers, where teachers expect children to learn by talking with each other as they write. In other communities, children learn cooperatively with other children; the emphasis is on developing a group understanding and performance rather than on individual achievement. Children from these communities may have difficulty in reading groups, where teachers expect only one child at a time to answer a question.

Culture also influences how children are socialized into being readers and writers. That is, all cultural groups share attitudes and beliefs about the uses and values of literacy and have preferred literacy practices. In general, children from mainstream backgrounds are socialized to use language and literacy within a tradition that places a large responsibility on the primary caregiver, usually the mother (Faltis, 1993). Mainstream mothers often talk with babies from birth and share books with their young children, asking questions that call for labels and clarifications. They include their children in dinner-table talk that supports their recounting of their daily activities or telling stories (see Chapter 2).

In contrast, Mexican American families recently immigrated to the United States often distribute caregiving among family members and close friends (Heath, 1986). In general, children are expected to observe adults' actions and conversation. In a working-class African American community, children observe parents and other adults as they read aloud and talk together about the meaning of texts (Heath, 1983).

There is considerable variation among families in the ways in which they socialize their young children into language and literacy use. However, we do have evidence of distinctive methods used by particular cultural groups to socialize children to become readers and writers. In mainstream cultural groups, children are expected to share in the construction of meaning with a parent during storybook reading and to construct stories on their own. Children from Mexican and African American backgrounds are less likely to be included in storybook reading experiences and are more likely to learn by observing rather than by participating in language activities.

Differences between mainstream and other cultural groups in how they socialize their children into language and literacy use provide an example of **cultural discontinuity** (Au, 1993). Cultural discontinuity means that there may be a mismatch between the literacy culture of the home and that of the school (which usually represents mainstream practices and values). Children who experience a cultural discontinuity are more likely to have learning difficulties in school. This is one possible explanation for the difference in achievement between children from mainstream and from other cultural backgrounds.

If teachers are to support the literacy learning of children from diverse cultural backgrounds, they need to be sensitive to the possibilities of cultural discontinuities as well as knowledgeable of how to change the classroom to better fit the learning of all children (Gee, 1990). Instruction that supports all children's learning and capitalizes on their cultural ways of learning is called culturally responsive instruction (Au, 1993).

Culturally Responsive Instruction

Culturally responsive instruction is instruction that is "consistent with the values of students' own cultures and aimed at improving academic learning" (Au, 1993, p. 13). We describe four examples of culturally responsive instruction. In these examples, teachers develop instructional strategies that are compatible with the learning styles of their children and at the same time help their children learn to operate more successfully with the learning styles usually associated with schools. This kind of instruction is called *culturally responsive.* The first example of instruction is from Au and Kawakami's (1985) description of the Kamehameha Early Education Project (KEEP); the second is from Heath's (1982) description of a project examining children's questions and talk conducted in schools in a southeastern city. The third example describes a teacher adjusting to a cultural style of sharing (Michaels, 1986), and the last example presents learning in school and in the community at the Warm Springs Indian Reservation (Philips, 1972).

KEEP: The Talk Story Lesson

Teachers in a special school in Honolulu for children of Polynesian-Hawaiian ancestry studied carefully the kinds of interactions or talk used by Hawaiian children. They researched talk in the community and talk in the classroom. These teachers discovered that their Hawaiian children engaged in interactions resembling "talk stories." In talk stories many speakers participate together, jointly speaking—often at the same time—to create a narrative. There are few times in a talk story when only one child is speaking. Leaders in talk stories are skillful in involving other children, rather than in carrying the conversation alone. This way of interaction is not compatible with interaction that teachers traditionally expect during reading instruction.

Once teachers recognized that children who "spoke out" during reading group time were not being disruptive, they began to consider ways of using this type of interaction to foster reading growth. They decided that they would plan the questions they asked, but allow children freedom in the way they answered questions. They allowed more than one child to respond at a time. The teachers tape-recorded reading lessons to examine whether allowing children to talk in what seemed to be a disruptive manner helped children to learn better. They found that 80 percent of the children's responses in "talk story" reading lessons focused on the story. In contrast, only 43 percent of the children's responses in a traditional lesson focused on the story (Au & Kawakami, 1985).

Questioning at School

An important way that children learn and demonstrate their learning is by answering questions. As teachers, we assume that the kinds of questions we ask make sense to children. Heath (1982) discovered that children from different communities in nearby towns and cities in the southeast were exposed to different kinds of questions from their earliest language experiences. In one community, the kinds of questions toddlers and preschoolers were familiar with were not the kinds of questions that were later used by their teachers. In another community, toddlers and preschoolers were exposed to questions much like those their teachers would use later in elementary school. When children from these two different communities began attending elementary school together, differences in their achievement were noted. When faced with unfamiliar school-like questions, some children seemed unable to learn and were considered less able than other children.

Teachers in these schools were concerned with helping their children achieve success. They worked closely with Heath to identify ways to help their students, especially the less successful ones, to learn more effectively (Heath, 1982). First, the teachers tape-recorded the kinds of questions they asked in their classrooms and compared them to the kinds of questions children were exposed to in their communities. They discovered that the questions they used in the classroom were requests for labels (for example, "What is that?" about an object in an illustration), were veiled attempts to control or direct behavior ("Is someone not following the rules?" which really means, "Someone had better sit down and be quiet"), or were requests for displays of book-related knowledge or skill ("Where should I begin reading?"). Many of their children seldom heard such questions in their communities. At home children were asked questions that were like analogies ("What is that like?"), questions that started stories ("What happened to Maggie's dog yesterday?"), and questions that accused them of wrongdoing ("What's that all over your face?") (Heath, 1982, p. 116).

Once teachers realized that their questions were not the kind their students were accustomed to answering, they began planning ways to use different kinds of questions in their instruction. They prepared social studies units based on pictures taken in the children's communities. Teachers asked questions that did not require children to label or name objects in the pictures; rather, they asked questions such as "What is going on here?" and "What is this like?" that were similar to the questions children were familiar with. Only later did teachers ask naming and labeling questions. When the teachers tape-recorded the lessons, the children enjoyed listening to the questions and their answers. The tape also provided children with valuable practice in listening to new kinds of questions and their answers.

Adjusting to Topic-Associating Style

A frequent activity in many early childhood classrooms is sharing, or show-and-tell. When children share, generally in a whole-class gathering, they tell something about themselves. Most teachers use this as an opportunity to develop children's oral-language abilities and expect children to select a topic and discuss the topic in some detail. This style of talking—sticking to a topic and describing it in detail—is called

topic-centered discourse style (Michaels, 1986). Teachers and children from the mainstream culture are familiar with this style of sharing because it is a familiar discourse style used in the mainstream culture.

However, not all children use topic-centered discourse during sharing. Many African American children are more likely to use a **topic-associated discourse style** during sharing because this language pattern is frequently used in the African American culture (Michaels, 1986). In this style of discourse, events are linked to some person or theme, but the links are not made explicit as they are in the topic-centered style. Children who use this language style during sharing are often interrupted by mainstream teachers because they fail to see the connections among children's ideas. Teachers often urge children to talk about just one thing or to stick to the topic (Michaels, 1986) even though the topic-associated style is closer to the desired style used in high school creative writing and studied in literature courses (Gee, 1990).

Teachers who understand that some children are likely to use a topic-associated style both in their sharing and in their compositions are more likely to support children's learning. For example, as one teacher read a child's composition, she noticed the topic-associating style.

> I have a cat and my cat
> never go to the bathroom
> when my cousin eating over
> my house and we went to
> the circus my cousins
> names are LaShaun Trinity
> Sherry Cynthia Doral
> (Michaels, 1986, p. 114)

After reading the composition, the teacher acknowledged the child's writing by responding, "Boy, you've got a lot of cousins!" Then the teacher chatted with the child about her cousins and asked, "Just one more thing . . . what do your cousins . . . have to do with the circus . . . and your cat?" The child responded, "Oh, my cousins always eat over my house, and they sleep over my house, too. And one day last week, we all went to the circus" (Michaels, 1986, p. 114). Finally, the teacher signaled to the child that she should make the connections among the ideas in her composition explicit to other readers.

Learning on the Warm Springs Reservation

The final example of culturally sensitive instruction comes from a study of Native American children's learning in school and in their community (Philips, 1972). On the Warm Springs Indian Reservation, Native American adults work together to solve problems. Leadership is assumed by many adults who have special skills or knowledge, rather than by an appointed leader, and adults choose whom they follow. Adults participate in group activities only when they feel they will be successful, and they participate at the level at which they feel comfortable. Children are observers in community meetings, but are often included in conversation.

These cultural ways of interacting are very different from the behaviors usually expected in school. In school, teachers expect children to follow their directions, to speak when asked a question, and to participate willingly in classroom activities. In contrast, Native American children expect to choose their own leader and make decisions about whether to participate in an activity. It is not surprising that Native American children do not volunteer to answer questions and often refuse to speak when called on in whole-class discussions.

One reason for the lack of participation by Native American children in whole-class recitation activities in school is that the **participation structures** in classrooms and in the community differ. Participation structures include the different rules for speaking, listening, and turn taking. Native American children are uncomfortable in the participation structures of whole-class recitations and discussions used frequently in school. They are more comfortable in the participation structures of small groups in which children initiate and direct their own activities. These participation structures have patterns of interaction more like those that the children have observed in their community.

Culturally Sensitive Instruction: A Summary

These four projects demonstrate how teachers can alter their ways of instruction and help children develop new ways of interacting in the classroom. Two characteristics distinguished these projects. First, teachers researched not only their children's community, but also their own way of teaching. They were willing to make changes in how they conducted lessons in order to support their students' learning. Second, teachers sought methods of helping their children make the transition from community ways of learning to school ways of learning. Teachers not only helped children learn, but they also helped children learn how to learn in school. These projects were fortunate in having the support of anthropologists who supplied much insight into the communities in which the teachers worked. Not all teachers will have the support of such professionals. Yet, tape-recording lessons, visiting community activities, and talking to parents can provide all teachers with valuable information about developing culturally sensitive learning activities for their children.

Culturally Sensitive Instruction in Multicultural Settings

Many classes, especially in urban settings, comprise children from several different cultural backgrounds. For example, a classroom might include Hispanic American children from different Spanish-speaking countries, African American children, and Vietnamese children. In these situations, developing culturally sensitive instruction cannot be a matter of merely matching instruction with cultural features. Instead, teachers employ instructional approaches that are successful with most of the children, and at the same time provide extra support for those children who are struggling. They are willing to depart from familiar approaches to instruction and to experiment with different ways of learning and teaching (Au, 1993). Teachers craft culturally sensitive instruction when they invite collaboration from families and the community, use interactional styles of instruction, strive for a balance of rights, and seek culturally relevant content (Au, 1993; Cummins, 1986).

Community Collaboration

Involving parents from diverse cultural backgrounds in educational activities is an important part of teachers' responsibilities. In mainstream cultures, most parents acknowledge the importance of their involvement in school activities. Mainstream parents are likely to participate in school activities by helping their children with homework, participating in fund-raising activities, attending school functions, such as open houses or music performances, attending parent–teacher conferences, and accompanying children on field trips.

Parents from nonmainstream cultures are also concerned about their children's education (Flores, Cousin, & Díaz, 1991). However, their perceptions about their involvement in schools may differ from the school's expectations. For example, many recently immigrated Mexican American families teach their children to be respectful of elders and to be accountable for their actions. However, they rarely work with their children on homework or other school activities. This may be because they assume that the school is responsible for educational matters.

Teachers using culturally sensitive instruction assume that all parents are interested in their children's success in school. They initiate contact with parents early in the school year through telephone calls, notes, and a weekly newsletter to parents. Inviting parents or other family members to school to share a family story is another way of initiating contacts with parents. Teachers communicate with parents often about the progress of their children's learning and provide concrete suggestions about how parents can help their children. Research has shown that nonmainstream parents are effective in supporting their children's learning at home (Goldenberg, 1989).

Instruction through Interaction

Children from diverse cultural backgrounds learn best when instruction involves children in constructing their own meaning, when higher-level thinking strategies are stressed, and when students set their own goals for learning (Cummins, 1986). This style of instruction is consistent with the instruction that we have recommended throughout this book and is called **constructivist models of instruction.** The essential ingredient of constructivist approaches is that children actively construct understandings. At first, children construct understandings with the support of others. The support that teachers provide for children's learning is sometimes called **scaffolding** (Cazden, 1988). The child accomplishes as much of the task as possible, and the adult scaffolds, or assists (see Chapter 1 for a discussion of the zone of proximal development). The constructivist model recognizes that learning begins with what children already know. Children's understandings about concepts are the beginning point of all learning experiences. In this way, children's experiences become a central part of the classroom.

Examples of interactive or constructivist models of instruction in literacy learning include using grand conversations to build understandings about literature, using writing workshop and the author's chair to support children's writing development, and using small, cooperative groups to learn new concepts, vocabulary, and spellings. In each of these teaching approaches, the children and teacher jointly

identify topics of interest about which to talk and write, children's talk is acknowledged as an important avenue for encouraging critical thinking, and children learn
to value the insights of their classmates.

Balance of Rights

The concept of balance of rights is similar to an interactive style of teaching in which
both the children and the teacher have input into what is learned. **Balance of rights**
recognizes that in a classroom there are three dimensions of control over who gets
to speak, what topic is discussed, and with whom children speak (Au & Mason,
1981). In mainstream classrooms with conventional recitation lessons or discussion-
participant structures, teachers control

- Who will speak—children speak one at a time when called upon to speak
  by the teacher

- The topic—teachers ask questions that frame the topic of discussion

- To whom children will speak—children speak to the teacher when answering questions, and the teacher provides feedback about the appropriateness
  of answers

These conventional recitation lessons reflect the IRE (initiate, respond, evaluate)
question-asking routine (see Chapter 6) in which the teacher controls all dimensions
of the interaction. Achieving a balance of rights means allowing children choices
about one or more of the three dimensions of interactions (Au & Mason, 1981).

For example, in grand conversations, teachers and children together choose
topics of discussion. Children talk about events or characters of interest to them, but
the teacher also poses one or two interpretive questions. Children may speak without raising their hands, but the teacher helps quiet children hold the floor or facil-
itates turn taking when many children want to speak at once. The children listen
carefully to one another and react to each other's comments, and teachers encourage such interactions by asking such questions as, "Jane, did you want to comment
on what Jeff just said?"

The teachers in our classroom case studies provide other examples of teaching
styles that give children a share in control of classroom talk. Recall, for example,
Mrs. Poremba's (see Chapter 8) use of the What Can You Show Us? activity as a part
of shared reading. Similarly, Ms. Vaughn (see Chapter 10) repeatedly spoke of children's selecting topics and activities and their learning in cooperative groups.

An example of a lesson in which teachers and children share a balance of control is the **experience-text-relationship approach** to guiding reading lessons (Au,
1979). In this approach to reading stories, poems, or informational books, teachers
first select a major theme that will help the children understand the text as a whole.
They decide how the theme might be related to their children's background experiences (the *experience* phase of the lesson). For example, a second grade teacher
guided some of her students in reading *Annie and the Old One* (Miles, 1971). In this
story, a young Navajo girl does not wish her grandmother to die. Her grandmother
helps Annie see that she must return to Mother Earth and complete the cycle of life.

The teacher decided that the children needed to understand the natural cycle of life and death in order to understand the story. She began the lesson by inviting children to talk about their own grandparents and what it was like to lose a grandparent (Au, 1993).

In the second part of the experience-text-relationship approach, teachers guide children as they read the text (the *text* phase of the lesson). Teachers may divide the text into segments and have grand conversations about each segment. In this part of the lesson it is crucial for teachers to help children grasp the main theme identified in the experience phase of the lesson. For example, the second grade teacher used considerable prompting and questioning to ensure that the children understood that Annie was trying to keep her grandmother from dying and that the grandmother was trying to help Annie see why she must go to Mother Earth (Au, 1993).

In the last phase of the experience-text-relationship approach, children relate their experiences to what they learned from reading (the *relationship* phase of the lesson). In this part of the approach, children discuss the theme of the text and relate it to their own experiences discussed prior to reading. The second graders recalled their own feelings when they lost a grandparent and compared them with Annie's feelings in the story.

Achieving a balance of rights does not mean that the teacher turns control over the classroom to the children or that the teacher does not establish expected behaviors or routines. It does mean that children are given many more choices than in an IRE-dominated classroom.

Culturally Relevant Content

Children who perceive that what they are learning affirms their cultural heritage are more likely to become engaged in learning (Ferdman, 1990). Teachers can draw on three sources to provide culturally relevant content in the classroom: multicultural literature that is culturally authentic, children's experiences, and community resources.

Multicultural literature.   Multicultural literature is literature that incorporates people of diverse cultural backgrounds, including African Americans, Hispanic Americans, Asian Americans, Native Americans, and people from other cultures (see Chapter 6). Culturally authentic multicultural literature is usually written by members of a particular culture and accurately reflects the values and beliefs of that culture.

Children from diverse backgrounds need access to literature that includes characters from those backgrounds. Seeing children like themselves in literature increases children's self-esteem and enlightens others about the worth of different cultural backgrounds. All children need experiences with culturally authentic literature about a variety of different cultural backgrounds.

Teachers must carefully choose the literature they share with children so that the literature does not distort children's concepts about others. Aoki, an Asian American, reported a childhood incident that illustrates this point (Aoki, 1981). She remembered when her teacher read the story *The Five Chinese Brothers* (Bishop & Wiese, 1938) to her class. (While this book is often considered a classic, it portrays

Asians as stereotyped characters.) As her teacher showed the illustrations, a few children darted quick glances at her. Aoki began to sink down in her chair. She recalled that other children taunted her by pulling their eyes so that they slanted. This incident makes a point about helping diverse learners, and all children, to develop more positive attitudes and self-esteem—diverse learners need to feel welcome and safe in their classrooms, and they need to believe in their own worth and abilities.

Children's literature offers many opportunities to explore both language differences and cultural heritages with children. There are many literature selections about different cultural groups and heritages that present nonstereotyped characters. As teachers read these selections to children, they can help children explore common heritages, customs, and human qualities. If Aoki's teacher had been sensitive to stereotypical portrayals in children's books, she might have instead shared *Umbrella* (Yashima, 1958). Then the children would have learned to identify with the little girl in the story. Their teacher could have asked them to describe their common experiences.

Using multicultural literature in the classroom should entail more than merely highlighting the heroes or holidays of a culture or reading works of culturally authentic literature (Rasinski & Padak, 1990). Rather, teachers go beyond mere tokenism by using multicultural literature to help children see issues from multiple cultural perspectives. For example, when studying a local community, children can examine the contributions of Native Americans, European Americans, African Americans, Hispanic Americans, and Asian Americans. As children study literature, they should have opportunities to read folktales from different cultures, to examine historical fiction about a variety of American people, and to read poetry composed by members of several different cultural groups. Table 11.1 presents a list of multicultural literature including folk literature, poetry, fantasy, and realistic fiction that reflect the culture of African Americans, Asian Americans, Hispanic Americans, and Native Americans.

Children's experiences.   Children's experiences provide an important starting point for many kinds of literacy activities. Having children write about their experiences is a critical component of process writing and the writing workshop approach (see Chapters 9 and 10). Children identify topics of interest about which they wish to write, and teachers help them shape their writing by teaching mini-lessons, guiding writers' groups in which children revise and edit their compositions, and offering opportunities for sharing through the author's chair or other kinds of publishing.

Having children talk about events and people in their experiences is a base for guided reading lessons, especially using the experience-text-relationship approach. Teachers identify broad themes related to what children will read and then invite children to talk about their experiences related to these themes.

The **KWL (know, want to learn, and learn)** approach (Ogle, 1989) is another instructional activity that draws on children's experiences. In this approach, children first tell what they know about a topic as they or the teacher write the information on a KWL chart (the *know* phase of the lesson). Then children brainstorm what they

Table 11.1 *Multicultural Literature*

African Americans

Bryan, A. (1977). *The dancing granny.* New York: Atheneum.

Bryan, A. (1986). *Lion and the ostrich chick and other African folk tales.* New York: Atheneum.

Caines, J. (1982). *Just us women.* New York: Harper and Row.

Clifton, L. (1970). *Some of the days of Everett Anderson.* New York: Holt, Rinehart and Winston.

Greenfield, E. (1978). *Honey, I love.* New York: Harper and Row.

Greenfield, E. (1988). *Grandpa's face.* New York: Philomel.

Greenfield, E. (1988). *Nathaniel talking.* New York: Black Butterfly Children's Books.

Hamilton, V. (1985). *The people could fly.* New York: Knopf.

Hamilton, V. (1992). *Drylongso.* New York: Harcourt Brace Jovanovich.

Havill, J. (1989). *Jamaica tag-along.* Boston: Houghton Mifflin.

McKissack, P. (1986). *Flossie and the fox.* New York: Dial.

McKissack, P. (1989). *Nettie Jo's friends.* New York: Knopf.

Price, L. (1990). *Aida.* New York: Harcourt Brace Jovanovich.

Steptoe, J. (1987). *Mufaro's beautiful daughters.* New York: Lothrop, Lee and Shepard.

Asian Americans

Coutant, H., & Vo-Dinh. (1974). *First snow.* New York: Knopf.

Say, A. (1988). *The lost lake.* Boston: Houghton Mifflin.

Say, A. (1990). *El Chino.* Boston: Houghton Mifflin.

Say, A. (1991). *Tree of cranes.* Boston: Houghton Mifflin.

Takeshita, F. (1988). *The park bench.* New York: Kane/Miller.

Yashima, R. (1958). *Umbrella.* New York: Viking.

Young, E. (1989). *Lon po po.* New York: Putnam.

Zhensun, A., & Low, A. (1991). *A young painter.* New York: Scholastic.

Hispanic Americans

Cruz Martinez, A. (1991). *The woman who out-shone the sun/La mujer que brillaba aun mas que el sol.* San Francisco: Children's Book Press.

Delacre, L. (1989). *Arroz con leche: Popular songs and rhymes from Latin America.* New York: Scholastic.

Delacre, L. (1990). *Las Navidades: Popular Christmas songs from Latin America.* New York: Scholastic.

Garcia, R. (1987). *My Aunt Otilia's spirits.* San Francisco: Children's Book Press.

Pena, S. (1987). *Kikiriki: Stories and poems in English and Spanish for children.* Houston: Arte Publico Press.

Rohmer, H. & Anchondo, M. (1988). *How we came to the fifth world: Como vinimos al quinto mundo.* San Fransisco: Children's Book Press.

Tafolla, C. (1987). *Patchwork colcha: A children's collection.* Flagstaff, AZ: Creative Educational Enterprises.

Native Americans

Baylor, B. (1986). *Hawk, I'm your brother.* New York: Scribner's.

Bruchac, J. (1985). *Iroquois stories: Heroes and heroines, monsters and magic.* Freedom, CA: The Crossing Press.

Bruchac, J., & Longdon, J. (1992). *Thirteen moons on turtle's back: A Native American year of moons.* New York: Philomel.

Connolly, J. (1985). *Why the possum's tail is bare and other North American Indian nature tales.* Owings Mills, MD: Stemmer House.

Erdoes, R. (1976). *The sound of flutes and other Indian legends.* New York: Pantheon.

Goble, P. (1989). *Iktomi and the berries.* New York: Orchard Books.

Goble, P. (1992). *Crow chief: A Plains Indian story.* New York: Orchard Books.

Ortiz, S. (1988). *The people shall continue.* San Francisco: Children's Book Press.

Sneeve, V. (1989). *Dancing teepees: Poems of American Indian youth.* New York: Holiday House.

Strete, C. (1990). *Big thunder magic.* New York: Greenwillow.

would like to learn about the topic and write this information on the KWL chart (the *want to learn* phase). Children read about the topic (usually in informational books) and then tell what they learned from their reading and record it on their chart (the *learn* phase of the lesson). Finally, children compare what they knew before reading, what they wanted to learn, and what they learned.

Community resources.   The community can provide many rich resources for the classroom. Inviting local storytellers into the classroom is especially useful when teachers have difficulty locating children's literature representative of a child's cultural heritage. For example, a first grade teacher had a few children in her classroom from Cape Verde, an island off the African coast. When she failed to locate literature that included children from this cultural background, she turned to the community liaison in her school for help and learned that the neighborhood included many families from Cape Verde. The community liaison helped the teacher locate a storyteller from the neighborhood, who came to class and shared several stories from Cape Verde. After the storyteller's visit, the children retold two stories, which the teacher recorded in big book format. The children illustrated the big books, and these books became class favorites.

Culturally sensitive instruction is inclusive—it invites participation from children, parents, and the community. It recognizes the value of cultural heritage and children's experiences. It uses children's knowledge as a beginning point for instruction, and it is evolving. Teachers constantly fine-tune the ways in which they invite children to participate in activities and seek new and more relevant content for instruction.

CHILDREN FROM DIVERSE LANGUAGE BACKGROUNDS

An increasing number of children in school are from **diverse language backgrounds.** They speak a nonmainstream dialect of English or a language other than English in their homes.

Learners Who Speak Nonmainstream Dialects of English

The way we speak English varies according to our social class, gender, occupation, locale, and ethnic background. Variations of a language are called *dialects*. All dialects of a language are understandable by all speakers of a language, but they are sufficiently different from one another to be distinctive (Bryen, 1982). Many speakers from New York City, for example, have what speakers from other parts of the country consider a dialect, but New Yorkers are easily understood by English speakers from San Francisco, Atlanta, or any other location in the United States.

Dialects are distinguished by differences in pronunciation, word choice, grammatical structure, and communicative style or usage. For example, the words *park* and *car* are pronounced *pahk* and *cah* in Boston or New York and *pawk* and *caw* in New Orleans (Barnitz, 1980). A sandwich on a long roll is called a *hoagie* in

Philadelphia and a *Po Boy* in parts of Louisiana. Some people say they must be home by *quarter til 5*, while others say they must be there by *quarter of 5*.

Nonmainstream and Mainstream Dialects

There is no one variety or dialect of English that is the standard or **mainstream dialect.** This is a difficult concept to accept. As speakers, we are capable of, and unconsciously make, judgments regarding other people's use of language. When we consider their language use to be standard or nonstandard, we are not applying any consistent criteria. Many speakers would label, "I ain't parkin' no car," as **nonmainstream** (or nonstandard) **dialect**. When asked why, they usually say that it violates rules of grammar. Yet they may consider the sentence "None of the cars were parked" to be standard even though it violates a rule of grammar: the use of a singular subject (*none*) with a plural verb (*were*). In other words, although the word *standard* implies otherwise, there are no objective criteria for determining whether a dialect is standard. All speakers have a range of language patterns that they use depending on situation and audience. This is called *code switching* or *register switching*. Again, the point is that nonstandard English and standard English are not absolute language patterns; rather, they represent a range of language patterns.

> ***Dialects considered nonmainstream.*** There are many dialects frequently considered nonstandard or nonmainstream by large segments of the population, especially by teachers and other educated groups. Some of these dialects are tied to locale, and others are tied to social class (Labov, 1966). Many researchers have described a dialect referred to as Black English (for example, Smitherman, 1977). Black English as a dialect has perhaps received the most attention and has engendered the largest controversy of any American English dialect (see, for example, Turner, 1985). Many African Americans do not use Black English, and many of the features of Black English are found not only in so-called standard English, but also in many other dialects. However, an important court case, *King Elementary School Students* vs. *The Ann Arbor, Michigan, School District Board* highlighted the need to recognize children's dialects, and in particular the dialect known as Black English, as an important consideration in children's education (Smitherman, 1985). The court ruled that teachers need to be familiar with the home language, in this case Black English, and to become more sensitive to children's special needs.

We will not be able to explore different dialects in detail here. Nevertheless, there are two facts related to dialects that early childhood educators need to know. First, all language systems, including dialects considered nonstandard or nonmainstream, are rule-bound, and the rules describing both nonstandard and standard dialects are often similar. Rule-bound means that the features of the language can be described. Linguists' rules are *descriptive* rather than *prescriptive*. They do not tell speakers what to do and they do not explain why speakers do what they do; they do allow us to predict what speakers of a given dialect will say under certain conditions. For example, many speakers of dialects considered nonstandard pronounce the word *left* as *lef;* that is, they simplify the word by deleting the final consonant sound of the letter *t* (Bryen, 1982). However, when the word *left* precedes a word beginning with a consonant, as in "She left *To*m all her money," even speakers of dialects considered standard do not pronounce the final consonant sound of the letter *t*.

Second, some features of dialects are more stigmatizing than others (Wolfram, 1970). Listeners use just some features of language to label a speaker's dialect. One such feature of a dialect considered by many to be nonstandard is the absence of the copula (a form of the verb *to be*), as in "He good to me." This feature of the dialect is more likely to be used as a labeling criterion than another feature of the same dialect, such as embedding of direct questions, as in "I wonder, did the package come?"

Nonmainstream dialects and attitudes. We not only make subjective judgments about whether speakers have standard or nonstandard speech patterns, but we also make other kinds of judgments based on our assessment of their language. Sometimes people unconsciously think that speakers of a different dialect might not be very intelligent or may have a low social status. Such judgments are especially harmful when teachers make them about children (Gee, 1990). Children who speak dialects that their teachers consider nonstandard are more likely to be identified as having cognitive lags, needing language therapy, and needing special remedial reading and writing instruction (Bartoli, 1986). They are more likely to be placed in lower ability groups for instruction and to receive lower achievement scores than their peers. This is an injustice. We must understand why it occurs so that we will not perpetuate it.

There are three reasons that children who speak dialects considered nonstandard are more likely to be included in remedial or lower ability groups. The first reason is related to the unconscious practice of using language patterns to judge the worth of a whole person. Teachers are not exempt from the phenomenon of unconsciously deciding on a person's intellectual capacity by virtue of his or her speech. In one study, teachers rated students' potential for academic success after listening to them answer questions on an audiotape. Half the students spoke in dialects considered by many teachers to be nonstandard, and half spoke in dialects considered to be standard. In spite of the fact that all the children's answers were correct, teachers rated the answers of students with nonstandard dialects lower than the answers of students with standard dialects (Crowl & MacGinitie, 1974).

The second reason that students who speak dialects considered nonstandard are at risk is that tests that assess reading and writing do not use their dialect. While we know that written English is different from anyone's spoken English dialect, there are degrees of difference. When test questions are phrased in syntax that is greatly different from a speaker's dialect, the speaker is penalized. Dialect difference, and not content knowledge or intelligence, is measured.

The third reason that students who speak dialects considered nonstandard are at risk is that teachers may spend more time helping them acquire standard or mainstream English than they do helping them learn to read and write. Some preschool teachers insist that children speak in complete sentences and use what they consider standard language when the children talk about stories or answer questions. Some elementary teachers spend considerable time correcting children's reading "errors," insisting that children read, "He is coming home" instead of "He comin' home." Time spent achieving dialect conformity takes away from time spent learning reading and writing. We are not saying that children ought never to be taught a dialect that employers and other powerful people in our society will accept as standard. We are saying that teachers of young children ought not to postpone children's literacy learning by first requiring them to learn a new dialect.

Literacy Instruction for Children with Nonmainstream Dialects

One of the most hotly debated topics in language education is whether, how, and when children should be taught to speak what is considered standard English. Because language is so closely interwoven with a person's sense of identity and self-worth, using language in a different way can be threatening. However, it is hard to counter the argument that people who speak so-called standard English have more access to educational and economic opportunities.

Teaching children to speak English that is considered standard in their region.   Most experts agree that preschoolers should be encouraged to communicate, whether their language is perceived as standard or as nonstandard (Genishi & Dyson, 1984). Teachers need to be more concerned with what children have to say than with how they say it. The practice of requiring children to speak in complete sentences or to "say it right" is not recommended. As all children get older and as they hear a greater variety of language models, they naturally begin to include in their speech more forms considered standard by most people in their region (Padak, 1981). Reading aloud to young children provides a model of written English, which is actually different from any spoken dialect, yet is often the standard against which people compare their so-called standard dialects (Feitelson, Goldstein, Iraqi, & Share, 1993).

Children in elementary school should have opportunities to use language in many different situations. Role-playing activities can provide children with opportunities to use a variety of language patterns. For example, they may practice interviewing a community leader, a minister, and a senior citizen as preparation for data gathering in a social studies unit. Children in elementary school are capable of discussing how different kinds of language are appropriate in different situations.

Children's literature provides rich models for language growth. Children enjoy hearing and saying many kinds of language found in literature. There are many fine examples of literature in which a dialect considered nonstandard contributes to the authenticity and enjoyment of the story. These selections can be used to demonstrate the variety and richness of language. As children explore language variety through literature, they can also explore language that most consider standard (Cullinan, Jaggar, & Strickland, 1974). Children naturally use the language of literature as they retell stories, role-play story actions, and write stories of their own.

Teaching reading and writing.   No special techniques are necessary to introduce written language to preschoolers who speak with a dialect considered nonstandard. All children, whether in preschool or in elementary school, learn about reading and writing when written language is presented in meaningful activities.

In more formal reading and writing programs in the elementary school, teachers need to be knowledgeable of how children's dialects are reflected in their reading and writing. We will give two examples of how dialect is reflected in reading and writing. First, because reading and writing are language activities, children's language influences how they read aloud and write. Children who speak with a dialect considered nonstandard will use that language as they read aloud—they may translate the text into their own speech patterns. Similarly, they may use their language as a basis for writing—what children write may reflect their oral-language patterns. Teachers of children who speak with a dialect considered nonstandard should recognize that children translate text into their own oral-language patterns. As children read the *text*, they may translate it into their spoken language. These translations from text language to spoken language are expected based on what we know about dialects considered nonstandard (Bryen, 1982). Teachers who are sensitive to children's language recognize dialect translations as positive indications that children comprehend as they read.

Our second example of how dialect is reflected in reading and writing involves homonyms, words that sound alike. Because dialects involve differences in pronunciation of sounds, many word pairs are homonyms in one dialect, but not in another (Barnitz, 1980). Teachers should be aware of these differences. For example, in many dialects considered standard, the words *pear* and *pair* are pronounced the same (homonyms), although they have different meanings. On the other hand, in many dialects considered nonstandard, the words *toll* and *told* are homonyms because they are pronounced the same (Barnitz, 1980). Not surprisingly, the use of the homonyms *toll* and *told* in phonics lessons and in spelling lessons is confusing when teachers and students do not have the same perceptions of which words are homonyms. Teachers need to be careful, however, not to assume that all nonstandard dialects are alike. Not all children's dialects are the same, even when they live in the same neighborhood.

Children's dialects are reflected in what and how they write. Figure 11.1 presents a story written by a boy whose dialect is considered nonstandard by many (Meier & Cazden, 1982, p. 507). Even when we are sensitive to Darryl's dialect, we know that he has several problems with writing. His story lacks the details that make writing vivid, although it is certainly startling. He has many misspelled words (over a fourth of the text), and most of the sentences are ineffective. Although teachers do not need to know a great deal about dialects to see Darryl's weaknesses, they may need this knowledge to see his strengths (Meier & Cazden, 1982). For example, Darryl's use of *in* for both the words *in* and *and* may reflect that he says the word *and* like the word *in*. Similarly, the deletion of the letters *ed* on some of his past tense verbs reflects that the pronunciation rules of his dialect include simplification of past tense verbs (that is, dropping the pronunciation of the final sounds /t/, /əd/, or /d/).

There are many more important strengths to this story that reflect both what all children learn, and specifically, what Darryl is learning, about good stories. His story has a beginning, complications, and an ending all centered on a single character, Eddie Mcdevitt. Darryl's story also contains features of a "trickster tale" (Smither-

Figure 11.1 *Darryl's Story: "The Spooky Halloween Night"*

The Spooky Halloween Night

One there was a mummy named Eddie Mcdevitt he was so dume at he dump his head in the can in then he chod his head off and then he went and to his house and then he went outside and chod his arm off then the cops came and chase him away and then he tuck some lade and kidl here in then she came alive and chod his bode off and then his spirt comed in kill everybody.

From "Research Update: A Focus on Oral Language and Writing from a Multicultural Perspective," by T. R. Meier and C. B. Cazden, 1982, *Language Arts, 59,* p. 507. Copyright © 1982 by the National Council of Teachers of English. Reprinted with permission.

---

man, 1977). This is a special kind of story told by African Americans that usually involves an African American male who triumphs over adversaries through cunning and unusual feats (Meier & Cazden, 1982). Although he lacks a head or a body, Eddie lives on at the end of the tale. Teachers who are sensitive to children's language recognize what children bring to writing and are in a better position to build on children's strengths. Writing may be the most effective way to help children gain control over language considered standard.

   Dialects and dictation.   Although many teachers are sensitive to their children's language and they view *oral* language diversity as valid, they wonder what to do when writing down children's dictations. Should teachers translate children's speech into standard text or should they write what children say? Figures 11.2 and 11.3 present a kindergartner's dictated story and a first grader's dictated retelling of *There's Something in My Attic* (Mayer, 1988). These child-authored texts include some language that many consider nonstandard. Many teachers are concerned that parents will object to such a text, since it is not regarded as standard English. They wonder if children's reading of such texts will somehow be harmful.

Figure 11.2 *Natasha's Story*

They was hiding eggs in the grass.
When they went to bed the Easter Bunny come.

Figure 11.3 *Latosha's Retelling*

There was a little girl.
She had a dream about a ghost.
She got off the bed and her dad put her back in the bed.
He say, "Go to sleep."
She got off her bed and went upstairs to her attic.
The little girl tooks a rope and catch the ghost.

There are at least three arguments for writing what children dictate, although words should be spelled conventionally and not as children pronounce them (Jaggar, 1974). First, the main reason for writing down children's dictations, such as stories about their art work, is so that children can realize that what they say is what is written. Children whose dictations are not written as they are dictated may not discover this concept. Second, one of children's most valuable reading strategies is their understanding of what language is like. Therefore, teachers will want to write what children say in dictations so that children can use this strategy as a method of reading. Finally, writing what a child says demonstrates acceptance of the child; it suggests that teachers find children's ideas important and that they recognize the validity of children's expressions.

One method of helping children build bridges from the oral-language patterns they use in dictations to patterns found in written texts is to use more than one language story for some dictation experiences (Gillet & Gentry, 1983). In some dictation exercises, the teacher might prepare an experience story that is similar to the children's dictated story, but in language considered standard. Figure 11.4 presents a language story dictated by six-year-olds that includes some language considered nonstandard. Figure 11.4 also presents a story written by their teacher.

Figure 11.4 *"The Holiday Memory Book"*

Children's Dictated Story

The Christmas Tree and Hanukkah Candles

We put seven ball on the Christmas tree.
We puts some lights on the Christmas tree.
We put a lot of candy cane on the Christmas tree.
We lighted candles for Hanukkah.

Teacher's Story

Holiday Celebrations

We celebrated Christmas and Hanukkah. We decorated a Christmas tree. First, we put lights on the tree. Then we put balls and candy canes on the tree. Last, we lit Hanukkah candles. We enjoyed our celebration of Christmas and Hanukkah.

This story includes many of the same words used in the children's dictation. The teacher and children read and reread both stories many times. Teachers need to use this technique with care so that the children's stories are as valued as their teacher's stories.

Another technique all young children enjoy is signing. This involves combining the teaching of American Sign Language with the teaching of English. Many books show American Sign Language signing for words, phrases, and letters of the alphabet. The teacher demonstrates signing of routine phrases (e.g., "good morning," "thank you"), content-related words (e.g., "dog," "cat," "bird" for a unit about pets), behavioral directions (e.g., "sit down," "hands to yourself"), poems, and songs. This practice emphasizes English vocabulary while teaching something novel and interesting to the whole class. Mrs. Poremba (see Chapter 8) used this technique with her kindergartners (see the example of English-as-a-second-language student Mayra's signing "Thank you" on p. 273). All the children in her classroom learned signing. They learned to sign the names of their special classes (music, art, gym, and library story) and often did so along with saying the names when it was their turn to announce the day's special class as part of the opening-of-the-day routine. Many enjoyed researching signs and writing with an alphabet sign stamp set in the writing center.

Learners Who Speak English as a Second Language

Children whose home language is not English are **English-as-a-second-language-learners** and may speak English fluently, a little, or not at all. When they come to preschool or elementary school, it may be the first time they are expected to speak English, or they may have had many opportunities to speak English prior to their school experiences. One of the first concerns that teachers voice is how to teach children, especially children who speak little English, to speak and to understand English.

Teaching Spoken English

The easiest way to learn to speak English is to participate in meaningful activities (Genishi & Dyson, 1984). The structure provided by familiar objects and activities supports children's language learning. To be effective, the objects must be real and the children must use them in real activities. Just as many toddlers first learn familiar phrases or words associated with repeated activities (called "routines"), so do English-as-a-second-language learners first learn familiar phrases and words in English (Urzua, 1980). Many children learn to say "Night night," "go to sleep," and "read books" because these routine phrases are repeated daily as they participate in the activity of getting ready for bed. Preschool English-as-a-second-language learners can learn the same phrases as they interact with their teacher and other children in their play with dolls, blankets, beds, and books in the housekeeping center. Many dramatic-play activities, such as grocery shopping, visiting the dentist, and taking a trip to McDonald's, provide rich language-learning experiences. Teachers can join in play and provide models of language. At first, many English-as-a-second-language learners will be silent in their play as they internalize the sounds of English and discover the actions of routines. They may switch between using English and using their home language (this practice should not be forbidden; Lara, 1989).

Even in elementary school, props and dramatic play can be used as a bridge to English. All children enjoy a pretend trip to McDonald's that includes such props as bags, hamburger containers, drink cups, and hats for the employees. As part of the McDonald's play, children will learn the English words *hamburgers, French fries, Coke, milk, ketchup, salt,* and *money.* They might learn routine phrases such as "Welcome to McDonald's," "May I take your order, please?" "I'd like a hamburger," or "Give me a Coke." Pictures of familiar activities can also be used to increase English as second language learners' oral-language proficiency (Moustafa & Penrose, 1985).

Teaching Reading and Writing

Children need not be proficient speakers of English in order to begin reading and writing in English (Abramson, Seda, & Johnson, 1990). In fact, reading and writing instruction supports learning spoken English. Effective strategies for literacy instruction in English include using additive approaches, developing comprehensive input, using shared language, and providing opportunities for extended discourse.

Additive approaches.   **Additive approaches** build on children's home language and culture (Cummins, 1986) and are in contrast with **subtractive approaches,** which replace children's home language and culture with English and mainstream values. The best approaches to supporting the literacy learning of English-as-a-second-language learners are those in the children's home language. But in many classrooms this approach is not possible. Sometimes children speak many different languages, and at other times, parents request that children receive instruction in English.

All teachers can take an additive approach to their literacy instruction when they allow students to use their home language in some reading and writing activities. For example, a third grade teacher who had several Spanish-speaking children in her class introduced the characters and events in *Mirandy and Brother Wind* (McKissack, 1988) by using simple props to act out important parts of the story. As part of her introduction, the teacher used descriptive phrases from the story and illustrated the meaning of these phrases through her dramatic portrayal of the characters in action. Then the children divided into pairs to read the story. Next the children gathered together to have a grand conversation about the story. As part of the conversation, the teacher shared many responses in which she used several of the vocabulary words from the story. These portions of the lesson were all conducted in English. Finally, the class broke into small groups to act out portions of the story, and several children planned their dramatic reenactments in Spanish. Although most groups presented their dramas to the class using English, one group used Spanish in its enactment.

Using a class or school postal system provides another example of how teachers can support children's use of home language in literacy activities. Children can help make mailboxes and establish a routine for delivering and receiving mail. Teachers can encourage children to write to them, to each other, to school personnel, and to famous people (including favorite children's authors). Writing letters and notes can become part of free-time activities, or it can become part of more formal reading and writing lessons. Teachers who have used this system have found that English-as-a-second-language learners begin writing in their home language. This practice should be encouraged as a way for children to continue their literacy growth in their home language. Teachers in areas where a majority of children come from families whose first language is not English will welcome this opportunity to demonstrate the value of being literate not only in English, but also in other languages. This cross-cultural literacy can be reinforced by including materials written in languages other than English in the classroom, sending notes home to parents in both the language of the home and English, and posting signs and labels in both the predominant language and English (Ortiz & Engelbrecht, 1986).

Gradually, English-as-a-second-language learners begin to write their notes and letters in English to communicate with children who write in English (Greene, 1985). English-as-a-second-language learners may find letter and note writing especially motivating because the emphasis is placed on communicating meaning to friends, rather than on correct conventions. Writing may be a particularly meaningful bridge to literacy in English (Urzua, 1987).

Instruction can also be additive when written language and spoken language are used as mutually supportive systems (Fitzgerald, 1993). For example, teachers can reinforce their spoken questions by writing the questions as well. Before having children read to find answers, teachers write two or three questions on the chalkboard. As children read, they can refer to the written questions as a guide for their reading (Gersten & Jiménez, 1994).

Another way in which spoken and written language support reading is through the use of the language experience approach. Dialogues that emerge from activities such as a pretend trip to McDonald's provide material for reading and writing (Feeley, 1983). After participating in dramatic play about a visit to McDonald's, children can learn to read and write many words found on the environmental print at McDonald's and associated with going to a McDonald's restaurant, such as *McDonald's, restrooms, men, women,* and *push* (Hudelson & Barrera, 1985). The teacher can prepare a story about the children's activities incorporating English words and phrases used as part of the McDonald's play experience. Children can also dictate or write about their experiences (Moustafa & Penrose, 1985). Photos of the children taken during the activity provide useful supports for reading these stories or writing about the experience (Sinatra, 1981). These language stories can be used to help children

Figure 11.5 *English-as-Second-Language Learner's Dictation*

Lim Makes Play Doh

I can use two cup flour.
I put one cup salt.
I am mix with spoon.
I am measure with water and flour.
I put spice in bucket.
I put two tablespoon oil in bucket.
We put color in bucket.

---

develop sight words or practice decoding skills. Figure 11.5 presents a story dictated by an English-as-a-second-language learner in second grade after he made Play Doh.

In addition to language experience materials, English-as-a-second-language learners need frequent and early experiences with children's literature both to read and as a support for their writing (Hough, Nurss, & Enright, 1986). Pattern books are particularly effective as first reading materials for all children, including English-as-a-second-language learners. Pattern books are especially useful in developing English-as-a-second-language learners' sense of syntax as well as giving them experience with new vocabulary. Chapter 9 describes how pattern books can be used to encourage children's reading and writing. Wordless picture books are also useful to stimulate dictation and writing.

Finally, additive approaches invite participation from parents and the community. Teachers make every effort to communicate with parents despite language differences. School systems provide community liaisons—people who know the different school communities and are native speakers of the languages spoken in the various communities. English-as-a-second-language and bilingual teachers are also useful resources and may be able to locate bilingual parent volunteers to help communicate with parents or to work in classrooms. Teachers make sure that all notes and newsletters sent to parents are written in the home language. They check with community liaisons or school volunteers to find ways of showing respect to parents during parent–teacher conferences or telephone conversations. They invite parents or other community members to school to share family stories or traditions, to read books related to their culture, or to demonstrate special skills.

Comprehensible input.   **Comprehensible input** is language that has been adjusted to accommodate the learner's needs (Krashen, 1985). It can be understood by the learner but still presents structures that are beyond what the learner currently uses or understands. Comprehensible input is characterized by a slower speaking rate, repetitions of important words, simple sentence structure, and high-frequency words. The following is an example of comprehensible input using simplified speech patterns (Scarcella, 1990, p. 68).

> Native-English speaker: Do you want the book?
>
> Non-native-English speaker: What?
>
> Native-English speaker: Book. Book. Big red book. Do you want this book? (picks up book and hands it to non-native speaker)

This example demonstrates comprehensible input that includes repetition of important content words, simplified sentence structure, gestures, and the use of concrete objects (picking up the book to identify the meaning of the word *book* and handing it to the speaker to demonstrate the meaning of the phrase *do you want*).

Comprehensible input also depends on the amount of contextual support available during language use (Cummins, 1981). That is, language is easier or more difficult depending on the setting in which it is used. Language is easier to understand and produce when children are involved in or observe an activity or event. For example, it is easier for children to describe going to a McDonald's restaurant when they are visiting the restaurant. Being at McDonald's when describing it provides contextual clues and concrete referents for description. In contrast, telling about a trip to McDonald's using only a picture of the outside of a McDonald's restaurant is more difficult. Some contextual clues are available from the picture, but not as many as are available when in the restaurant. Finally, telling about a trip to McDonald's relying only on memory is most difficult of all. No contextual clues are available to support the activity. The most comprehensible input is that which includes more of the contextual support provided by hands-on activities, drama, objects, films, and pictures.

Comprehensible input also depends on the cognitive demands of an activity (Cummins, 1981). Some language is easier to understand because it involves lower levels of thinking. Cognitive activities that require different levels of thinking include

- Describing (telling who, what, and where)

- Sequencing (describing events in order, cycles, processes, procedures)

- Classifying (grouping according to properties)

- Generalizing (making interpretations, inferring principles, and drawing conclusions)

- Evaluating (judging or critiquing based on criteria) (Mohan, 1986; Faltis, 1993)

In general, it is easier to describe and sequence than to generalize or evaluate. Therefore, a description of people, events, objects, or sequences of events is more comprehensible input than presenting an argument or drawing conclusions.

The two dimensions of context and level of thinking interact. That is, the most comprehensible input requires learners to use lower levels of thinking and provides contextual support, such as when a teacher describes the changes that occur in autumn while taking children on a walk in the woods and collecting leaves and nuts. The least comprehensible input requires learners to use higher levels of thinking without contextual support, such as when a teacher tells children why leaves change colors in the fall without the support of diagrams or pictures.

Shared language.   Effective teachers of English-as-a-second-language learners realize that students can be easily overwhelmed by too many changing instructional techniques. These children need repeated use of familiar instructional routines and activities using shared language. **Shared language** refers to vocabulary that is used repetitively when talking about a reading or writing task (Gersten & Jiménez, 1994). For instance, one teacher who taught many children with limited knowledge of English repeatedly used a few familiar words when talking about literature. She taught her children the components of a *story grammar* (see Chapter 2 for a description of a story grammar and its components), and her students understood the English words *character, goal, obstacle, outcome,* and *theme.* The students knew how to look for *character clues* because the teacher frequently asked questions such as, "What kind of character is he? What are the clues?" (Gersten & Jiménez, 1994) and modeled answer-finding techniques.

Another teacher taught students the vocabulary needed to conduct writers' conferences with partners. Using whole-class minilessons the teacher taught children to talk about " 'favorite part,' 'part you didn't understand,' 'part you'd like to know more about,' and 'part you might like to work on' " (Blake, 1992, p. 606). Through modeling, the teacher showed children the kinds of language that he expected them to use and the kinds of information that he expected them to talk about in a writer's conference.

These teachers focused on teaching their children how to participate in highly successful activities. They did not use many different strategies, but instead used only a few strategies routinely. As children gained confidence using these strategies, these teachers gradually added other instructional strategies.

Extended discourse. Mastering English and becoming competent readers and writers of English is possible only when students use English for a variety of purposes in situations that are not anxiety producing (Faltis, 1993). That is, children need opportunities for **extended discourse,** or talking and writing extensively in a variety of settings (with a variety of partners, including the teacher, in small groups, and in whole-class gatherings). Teachers can encourage extended discourse by acknowledging children's input to lessons and by providing models of more complete English-language structure, as in the following example (Gersten & Jiménez, 1994, p. 445).

Teacher: What does he hope will happen when he shoots the arrow?

Child: The rain (gestures like rain falling).

Teacher: Right, the rain will fall down.

Another way to engage students in extended discourse is to elaborate on vocabulary meanings. It is crucial for English-as-a-second-language learners to grasp the meanings of core vocabulary in stories. Engaging children in talk about vocabulary words and their meanings helps teachers confirm that the children understand vocabulary meanings and provides opportunities for extended discourse. For example, in one story that a teacher was reading aloud a character was eavesdropping. The teacher stopped reading, told the children the meaning of the word *eavesdropping,* and then invited children to demonstrate what the word meant. Several children acted out eavesdropping and talked about their experiences with eavesdropping. Another teacher stopped reading to talk about the meaning of the word *pierced* by relating the word to the pierced ears of many of the girls in the classroom and by piercing a piece of paper with scissors. These teachers often wrote key words on the chalkboard as they talked about their meanings and encouraged children to use the words as they talked and wrote about stories (Gersten & Jiménez, 1994).

A kindergarten teacher provided opportunities for extended discourse using repeated reading of a favorite book, storytelling with flannel-board props, and emergent reading of the favorite book (Carger, 1993). First, the teacher read aloud an engaging picture book that appealed to young Hispanic children. After each reading, the teacher invited individual children to reread the story using the pictures in the picture storybook as prompts (for emergent readings). The teacher accepted the children's attempts at reading using their limited English. Then the teacher reread the story and retold the story in Spanish, using flannel-board props. She invited the children to retell the story once again in English, this time using the flannel-board props.

Issues Related to Teaching Children from Diverse Backgrounds

The models of instruction that we and others (Au, 1993) have proposed for supporting children from diverse backgrounds are called by many names, including constructivist, interactional, socio-psycholinguistic, process oriented, and holistic. They share the underlying principles that learning is more effective when learners actively construct understandings for themselves rather than passively repeat what teachers tell them, when teachers stress processes rather than adultlike products, and when learners engage in meaningful activities that involve reading and writing rather than practice skills in isolation.

However, it is important to keep in mind that children from diverse backgrounds also need instruction that ensures their academic success. "If students from diverse backgrounds are to have access to opportunities in the mainstream culture, schools must acquaint them with the rules and codes of the culture of power, such as the grammar of standard English" (Au, 1993, p. 51). Many children from diverse backgrounds will benefit from explicit teaching of the conventions of writing. One educator put it this way: "Unless one has the leisure of a lifetime of 'immersion' to learn them, explicit presentation [of the rules of the culture of power] makes learning immeasurably easier" (Delpit, 1988, p. 283).

Explicit teaching, however, does not mean that teachers necessarily need to resort to traditional drills and recitation. Instead, teachers can provide explicit teaching within the context of reading and writing activities, as is done during the writing phase of Reading Recovery lessons, during minilessons in the writing workshop approach, or through guided reading lessons. All teachers must strike a balance between allowing children to construct their own understandings and providing direct, explicit instruction (Spiegel, 1992). All good instruction includes both opportunities to explore and explicit teaching.

Careful observation and assessment of learners is the key to making thoughtful decisions about when to step back and allow children time and space to develop their own understandings and when to step in and direct children's learning. This may be particularly true for children for whom English is a second language. For these children, for example, merely inviting them to read books of their choice or to write about topics of personal interest may not be enough to support their literacy growth (Peréz, 1994; Reyes, 1991). Teachers may find that they need to model how to find an appropriate book and teach strategies for decoding unfamiliar print. Teach-

Chapter Summary

At-risk learners are children who are especially at risk for school failure. At-risk learners include children who struggle to

acquire literacy concepts despite quality classroom support. Teachers use observations to modify their instruction for at-risk learners and may adapt techniques from Reading Recovery. Reading Recovery, a special intervention program for first graders, engages children in daily reading, writing, and language analysis. It focuses on teaching independent reading strategies.

Children who may be at-risk learners may also include those with special needs, from diverse cultural backgrounds, and from diverse language backgrounds. As with other at-risk learners, observant teachers adapt instructional activities to meet the needs of special learners without resorting to reductionist methods of instruction.

Teachers recognize that culture influences the way in which children learn and how they interact with each other and with adults. For example, children of Hawaiian ancestry are familiar with interaction styles in which more than one speaker talks at a time; children from some African American communities are not exposed to known-answer questions often used by teachers; when sharing, some children from African American cultures are more likely to use a topic-associated discourse style than the topic-centered discourse style that many mainstream teachers expect; and children from one Native American culture are more familiar with talking in small informal groups than in whole-class recitation. Once teachers recognize the ways in

which culture affects how children learn and interact, they are on the way to crafting culturally sensitive instruction. Culturally sensitive instruction is characterized by interactive instruction, a balance of rights, and culturally relevant content. Culturally relevant content includes multicultural literature, resources from the community, and children's own experiences.

Children who speak a nonmainstream or nonstandard dialect of English may be the victims of teachers' unconscious judgments about their academic potential. To counter this possibility, teachers understand that all dialects, including nonmainstream dialects, reflect an underlying logic and structure. They help children feel comfortable and accepted when using their dialect to communicate while they help children to expand their language use to include the dialect that is considered standard in their region.

Children who speak English as a second language learn spoken English at the same time that they learn to read and write in English. Teachers support this process when they use additive approaches, comprehensible input, shared language, and extended discourse. All teachers of diverse learners must strive for a balance between supporting children as they construct their own understandings and providing explicit instruction.

Applying the Information _____

Julia Felix is a first-year teacher in a large urban school that serves children from a variety of cultural and language backgrounds. This year she will be teaching third grade (or, you may assume that she will be teaching kindergarten). She opens her class list and reads the following names (X = ESL Student) (Faltis, 1993, p. 5).

1. Brown, Leon

2. Cavenaugh, Kimberly

3. Cui, Xiancoung   X

4. Cohen, Daniel

5. Evans, Lisa

6. Fernandez, Maria Eugenia   X

7. Freeman, Jeffrey	
8. Garcia, Aucencio	X
9. Gomez, Concepcion	X
10. Hamilton, Jessica	
11. Mason, Tyrone	
12. O'Leary, Sean	
13. Pak, Kyung	X
14. Petruzzella, Gina	
15. Quinn, Frank	
16. Rosen, Chatty	
18. Rojas, Guadalupe	X
19. Sandoval, Kathy	
20. Tran, Do Thi	X

21. Vasquez, Jimmy	X
22. Williamson, Amy	
23. York, Leonard	
24. Zbikowski, Antonin	

Julie thinks to herself, "I especially want the ESL students to fully join in my class" (Faltis, 1993, p. 6). How will Julie accomplish this task? What suggestions can you make about her room arrangement, the materials she will need, and the modifications she can be expected to make in instruction? Suppose that Julie decides to teach a unit about animals. Make suggestions for materials that she can include in the unit, and plan at least one lesson that will meet the needs of the English-as-a-second-language learners in her class.

Going Beyond the Text

Visit a preschool or elementary school that has special-needs children. Observe the children in their classroom as they interact with the other children and during literacy activities. Take note of ways in which the special-needs children are similar to and different from the other children. If possible, talk to a teacher about supporting the literacy learning of special-needs children. Take at least one reading and one writing activity that you can share with a special-needs child. For example, take a children's book and literature props for the child to retell the story, plan a hands-on experience, such as popping corn, that will stimulate writing, or prepare a special book that you can give to the child for his or her own journal. Carefully observe the child's language and behaviors during these literacy activities. Be ready to discuss what this child knows about literacy.

References

ABRAMSON, S., SEDA, I., & JOHNSON, C. (1990). Literacy development in a multilingual kindergarten classroom. *Childhood Education, 67,* 68–72.

ALLEN, J., & CARR, E. (1989). Collaborative learning among kindergarten writers: James learns how to learn at school. In J. Allen & J. Mason (Eds.), *Risk Makers, risk takers, risk breakers: Reducing the risks for young literacy learners* (pp. 30–47). Portsmouth, NH: Heinemann.

AOKI, E. (1981). "Are you Chinese? Or are you just a mixed-up kid?" Using Asian American children's literature. *The Reading Teacher, 34,* 382–385.

AU, K. (1979). Using the experience-text-relationship method with minority children. *The Reading Teacher, 32,* 677–679.

AU, K. (1993). *Literacy instruction in multicultural settings.* New York: Harcourt Brace Jovanovich.

AU, K. H., & KAWAKAMI, A. J. (1985). Research currents: Talk story and learning to read. *Language Arts, 62,* 406–411.

AU, K., & MASON, J. (1981). Social organizational factors in learning to read: The balance of rights hypothesis. *Reading Research Quarterly, 17,* 115–152.

BARNITZ, J, G. (1980). Black English and other dialects: Sociolinguistic implications for reading instruction. *The Reading Teacher, 33,* 779–786.

BARONE, D. (1993). Wednesday's child: Literacy development of children prenatally exposed to crack or cocaine. *Research in the Teaching of English, 27,* 7–45.

BARTOLI, J. S. (1986). Is it really English for everyone? *Language Arts, 63,* 12–22.

BISHOP, C. H., & WIESE, K. (1938). *The five Chinese brothers.* New York: Coward, McCann and Geoghegan.

BLAKE, B. (1992). Talk in non-native and native English speakers' peer writing conferences: What's the difference? *Language Arts, 69,* 604–610.

BRYEN, D. (1982). *Inquiries into child language.* Boston: Allyn and Bacon.

CARGER, C. (1993). Louie comes to life: Pretend reading with second language emergent readers. *Language Arts, 70,* 542–547.

CAZDEN, C. (1988). *Classroom discourse.* Portsmouth, NH: Heinemann.

CLAY, M. (1985). *The early detection of reading difficulties* (3rd ed.). Portsmouth, NH: Heinemann.

CLAY, M. (1991). Introducing a new storybook to young readers. *The Reading Teacher, 45,* 264–273.

COUSIN, P., WEEKLEY, T., & GERARD, J. (1993). The functional uses of language and literacy by students with severe language and learning problems. *Language Arts, 70,* 548–556.

CROWL, T. K., & MacGINITIE, W. H. (1974).The influence of students' speech characteristics on teachers' evaluation of oral answers. *Journal of Educational Psychology, 66,* 304–308.

CULLINAN, B. E., JAGGAR, A. M., & STRICKLAND, D. S. (1974). Oral language expansion in the primary grades. In B. E. Cullinan (Ed.), *Black dialects and reading* (pp. 43–54). Urbana, IL: National Council of Teachers of English.

CUMMINS, J. (1981). The role of primary language development in promoting educational success for language minority students. California State Department of Education (Ed.), *Schooling and language minority students: A theoretical framework* (pp. 3–49). Los Angeles: Evaluation, Dissemination and Assessment Center, California State University, Los Angeles.

CUMMINS, J. (1986). Empowering minority students: A framework for intervention. *Harvard Educational Review, 56,* 18–36.

D'ALESSANDRO, M. E. (1987). "The ones who always get the blame": Emotionally handicapped children writing. *Language Arts, 64,* 516–522.

DELPIT, L. (1988). The silenced dialogue: Power and pedagogy in educating other people's children. *Harvard Educational Review, 58,* 280–298.

DIXON, R. (1987). Strategies for vocabulary instruction. *Teaching Exceptional Children, 19,* 61–63.

DOLMAN, D. (1992). Some concerns about using whole language approaches with deaf children. *American Annals of the Deaf, 137,* 278–282.

DOWHOWER, S. L. (1989). Repeated reading: Research into practice. *The Reading Teacher, 42,* 502–507.

FALTIS, C. (1993). *Joinfostering: Adapting teaching strategies for the multilingual classroom.* New York: Merrill/Macmillan.

FEELEY, J. T. (1983). Help for the reading teacher: Dealing with the Limited English Proficient (LEP) child in the elementary classroom. *The Reading Teacher, 36,* 650–655.

FEITELSON, D., GOLDSTEIN, Z., IRAQI, J., & SHARE, D. (1993). Effects of listening to story reading on aspects of literacy acquisition in a diglossic situation. *Reading Research Quarterly, 28,* 70–79.

FERDMAN, B. (1990). Literacy and cultural identity. *Harvard Educational Review, 60,* 181–204.

FITZGERALD, J. (1993). Literacy and students who are learning English as a second language. *The Reading Teacher, 46,* 638–647.

FLORES, B., COUSIN, P., & DÍAZ, E. (1991). Transforming deficit myths about learning, language,and culture. *Language Arts, 68,* 369–379.

GEE, J. (1990). *Social linguistics and literacies: Ideology in discourses.* London: The Falmer Press.

GENISHI, C., & DYSON, A. H. (1984). *Language assessment in the early years.* Norwood, NJ: Ablex.

GERSTEN, R., & JIMÉNEZ, R. (1994). A delicate balance: Enhancing literature instruction for students of English as a second language. *The Reading Teacher, 47,* 438–449.

GILLET, J. W., & GENTRY, J. R. (1983). Bridges between nonstandard and standard English with extensions of dictated stories. *The Reading Teacher, 36,* 360–364.

GOLDENBERG, C. (1989). Making success a more common occurrence for children at risk for failure: Lessons from Hispanic first graders learning to read. In J. Allen & J. Mason (Eds.), *Risk makers, risk takers, risk breakers: Reducing the risks for young literacy learners* (pp. 48–79). Portsmouth, NH: Heinemann.

GREENE, J. E. (1985). Children's writing in an elementary school postal system. In M. Farr (Ed.), *Advances in writing research, volume one* (pp. 201–296). Norwood, NJ: Ablex.

HEATH, S. B. (1982). Questioning at home and at school: A comparative study. In G. Spindler (Ed.), *Doing the ethnography of schooling: Educational anthropology in action* (pp. 102–131). New York: Holt, Rinehart and Winston.

HEATH, S. (1983). *Ways with words: Language, life, and work in communities and classrooms.* New York: Cambridge University Press.

HEATH, S. (1986). Sociocultural context of language development. In California State Department of Education (Ed.), *Beyond language: Social and cultural factors in school language minority students* (pp. 143–186). Los Angeles: California State University.

HIEBERT, E., & TAYLOR, B. (Eds.). (1994). *Getting reading right from the start: Effective early literacy interventions.* Boston: Allyn and Bacon.

HOUGH, R. A., NURSS, J. R., & ENRIGHT, D. S. (1986). Story reading with limited English speaking children in the regular classroom. *The Reading Teacher, 39,* 510–514.

HUDELSON, S., & BARRERA, R. (1985). Bilingual/second-language learners and reading. In L. W. Searfoss & J. E. Readence, *Helping children learn to read* (pp. 370–392). Englewood Cliffs, NJ: Prentice-Hall.

JAGGAR, A. M. (1974). Beginning reading: Let's make it a language experience for Black English speakers. In B. E. Cullinan (Ed.), *Black dialects and reading* (pp. 87–98). Urbana, IL: National Council of Teachers of English.

KAMEENUI, E. (1993). Diverse learners and the tyranny of time: Don't fix flame; fix the leaky roof. *The Reading Teacher, 46,* 375–383.

KRASHEN, S. (1985). *The input hypothesis: Issues and implications.* New York: Longman.

LABOV, W. A. (1966). *The social stratification of English in New York City.* Washington, DC: Center for Applied Linguistics.

LARA, S. G. M. (1989). Reading placement for code switchers. *The Reading Teacher, 42,* 278–282.

MAYER, M. (1988). *There's something in my attic.* New York: Dial.

McKISSACK, P. (1988). *Mirandy and Brother Wind.* New York: Knopf.

MEHAN, B. (1986). *Language and content.* Reading, MA: Addison-Wesley.

MEIER, T. R., & CAZDEN, C. B. (1982). Research update: A focus on oral language and writing from a multicultural perspective. *Language Arts, 59,* 504–512.

MICHAELS, S. (1986). Narrative presentations: An oral preparation for literacy. In J. Cook-Gumperz (Ed.), *The social construction of literacy* (pp. 94–116). New York: Cambridge University Press.

MILES, M. (1971). *Annie and the old one.* Boston: Little, Brown.

MOUSTAFA, M. & PENROSE, J. (1985). Comprehensible input PLUS, the language experience approach: Reading instruction for limited English speaking students. *The Reading Teacher, 38,* 640–647.

NORRIS, J. A. (1988). Using communication strategies to enhance reading acquisition. *The Reading Teacher, 41,* 668–673.

OGLE, D. (1989). The know, want to know, learn strategy. In K. Muth (Ed.), *Children's comprehension of text: Research into practice* (pp. 205–223). Newark, DE: International Reading Association.

ORTIZ, L., & ENGELBRECHT, G. (1986). Partners in biliteracy: The school and the community. *Language Arts, 63,* 458–465.

O'SHEA, L. & O'SHEA, D. (1987). Using repeated reading. *Teaching Exceptional Children, 20,* 26–29.

PADAK, N. D. (1981). The language and educational needs of children who speak Black English. *The Reading Teacher, 35,* 144–151.

PÉREZ, B. (1994). Spanish literacy development: A descriptive study of four bilingual whole-language classrooms. *Journal of Reading Behavior, 26,* 75–94.

PETERSON, B. (1991). Selecting books for beginning readers. In D. DeFord, C. Lyons, & G. Pinnell (Eds.), *Bridges to literacy: Learning from Reading Recovery* (pp. 119–147). Portsmouth, NH: Heinemann.

PHILIPS, S. (1972). Participant structures and communicative competence: Warm Springs children in community and classroom. In C. Cazden, V. John, & D. Hyumes (Eds.), *Functions of language in the classroom.* New York: Teachers College Press.

PINNELL, G., FRIED, M., & ESTICE, R. (1990). Reading recovery: Learning how to make a differenece. *The Reading Teacher, 43,* 282–295.

RASINSKI, T., & PADAK, N. (1990). Multicultural learning through children's literature. *Language Arts, 67,* 576–580.

REYES, M. (1991). A process approach to literacy instruction for Spanish-speaking students: In search of a best fit. In E. Hiebert (Ed.), *Literacy for a diverse society: Perspectives, practices, and policies* (pp. 157–171). New York: Teachers College Press.

SALVAGE, G., & BRAZEE, P. (1991). Risk taking, bit by bit. *Language Arts, 68,* 356–366.

SCARCELLA, R. (1990). *Teaching language minority students in the multicultural classroom.* Englewood Cliffs, NJ: Prentice-Hall.

SHAPIRO, H. (1992). Debatable issues underlying whole-language philosophy: A speech-language pathologist's perception. *Language, Speech, and Hearing Services in Schools, 23,* 308–311.

SINATRA, R. (1981). Using visuals to help the second language learner. *The Reading Teacher, 34,* 539–546.

SINDELAR, P. T. (1987). Increasing reading fluency. *Teaching Exceptional Children, 19,* 59–60

SMITHERMAN, G. (1977). *Talkin and testifying: The language of black America.* Boston: Houghton Mifflin.

SPIEGEL, D. (1992). Blending whole language and systematic direct instruction. *The Reading Teacher, 46,* 38–44.

TRUAX, R., & KRETSCHMER, R. (1993). Focus on research: Finding new voices in the process of meeting the needs of all children. *Language Arts, 70,* 592–601.

TURNER, D. T. (1985). Black students, language, and classroom teachers. In C. K. Brooks (Ed.), *Tapping potential: English and language arts for the black learner* (pp. 30–40). Urbana, IL: National Council of Teachers of English.

URZUA, C. (1987). "You stopped too soon": Second language children composing and revising. *TESOL Quarterly, 21,* 279–304.

WILLIAMS, C. (1994). The language and literacy worlds of three profoundly deaf preschool children. *Reading Research Quarterly, 29,* 124–155.

WOLFRAM, W. A. (1970). Nature of nonstandard dialect divergence. *Elementary English, 41,* 739–748.

YASHIMA, T. (1958). *Umbrella.* New York: Viking.

CHAPTER 12

Assessment

In Chapter 12 we describe the purposes and processes of assessing children's literacy learning. We begin by telling about of a kindergarten classroom in which the teacher, Ms. Orlando, uses portfolio assessment. She collects information about her children's learning in a variety of ways, including writing notes as she observes children and collecting examples of children's reading and writing products. In the remainder of the chapter we describe effective classroom assessment and, in particular, portfolio assessment. We examine theories that support the use of portfolios and how portfolios are developed and used. We present several methods of assessing children's understandings about written language meanings, forms, meaning-form links, and functions. Finally, we explain how to use portfolios to make instructional decisions, help children evaluate their own learning, and inform parents of their children's progress as literacy learners.

Key Concepts

observation notebook	assessment planning guide	word recognition analysis
caption		
classroom assessment	alphabet recognition task	retellings
portfolio		retelling checklist
portfolio assessment	concepts-about-print task	story retelling analysis
authentic activities	emergent reading checklist	informational text analysis
anecdotal notes		response-to-literature checklist
checklists	running record	
activity checklists	accuracy rate	portfolio conferences
work samples	miscue analysis	portfolio summaries

A DAY IN KINDERGARTEN

The following is a story of a day in a kindergarten classroom that is similar to several classrooms that we have observed. Ms. Orlando and her children are studying travel in a combined literature and discipline-focused unit. As a part of this unit, Ms. Orlando has read many stories about characters who travel away from their homes (including books with a circle structure, in which the story begins at home, the character leaves home and has adventures, and then the character returns home at the end of the story) and poems about traveling (including imaginary travel of the mind). The children have learned different methods of transportation and are examining ways in which seeds travel.

A Day in Ms. Orlando's Classroom

Ms. Orlando's kindergarten day is divided into four large blocks of time. The children begin the day with a whole-class gathering, have center time, eat their snack and have recess or a special class, such as music or physical education, and then end the day with storytime.

Whole-Group Gathering

The children are gathered on the rug as the teacher reads Kovalski's (1987) version of *The Wheels on the Bus.* Two other versions of this story are displayed in the classroom library center. Ms. Orlando holds up the book and says, "I'm going to read a new version of *The Wheels on the Bus.* This one is written and illustrated by Maryanne Kovalski. It begins differently from the other 'Wheels on the Bus' stories that we have read before. Listen carefully to find out how this version is different. When I come to the part of the story that you know, join right in and read with me." Then she begins reading, and after several pages all the children are reciting the familiar story along with her.

After reading the story, Ms. Orlando asks, "Well, how was this story different from the other two versions we read?"

Datoya:	The kids were shopping with their grandma.
Maryanne:	The grandma bought them coats with um, um buttons.
Ms. Orlando:	It looks like it was cold to me. Good thing Grandma bought those girls some coats.
Josephine:	They missed the bus.
Ishmail:	They were singing the song with their grandmother.
Ms. Orlando:	When were they singing?
Several children:	(overlapping) waiting for the bus.
Jasmine:	And they missed the bus.
John:	I wouldn't miss the bus singing. I would jump right on.
Rayshawn:	I wouldn't be singing at all, no way.
Husalina:	My grandma sing.
Ms. Orlando:	Your grandmother sings! Do you sing with your grandma? Well, these kids liked singing with their grandmother so much they forgot all about the bus and missed it. Now let's see if we can remember all the verses that were in this version of the story.

The children recall several verses of the story, and Ms. Orlando confirms their guesses by locating the verse in the book and showing the children the illustration. Then Ms. Orlando asks children to compare verses in this story with verses in the other two versions of the story.

Finally, Ms. Orlando says, "Let's sing our version of the song." She flips over some charts on the chart stand until she finds the chart for "The Wheels on the Bus" song. The children dictated the words to this song earlier in the week. Ms. Orlando says, "Husalina, you can be pointer first." Husalina comes to the front of the group and takes a long pointer. The children sing the song as Husalina points across the lines of the text (she matches most of the words the children sing to the printed words). Then another child is selected to be pointer, and the class sings the song again.

Next Ms. Orlando introduces a new story. She says, "Our new story today is about another character who leaves home and travels to many different places. But instead of reading the story to you, I am going to tell it. The title of the story is *The Runaway Bunny,* and it was written by Margaret Wise Brown (1942)." Ms. Orlando hangs a copy of the front cover of the book on the classroom story clothesline as she reads the title (see clothesline props in Chapter 6). Then she says, "Who would like to guess where this little bunny might run away to?" Many of the children make guesses. Then Ms. Orlando tells the story using the clothesline props.

After telling the story, Ms. Orlando begins a grand conversation by saying, "What did you think about the story?" The children spend several minutes sharing their personal responses. Then Ms. Orlando says, "Little Bunny sure did become a lot of things in this. You might want to draw a picture in the art center about Little Bunny and his mother and all the different things they became. Let's write a list of all the things Little Bunny turned into, and I'll put the list in the art center to remind you what you might want to draw."

As the children recall what the little bunny turned into, Ms. Orlando writes the words on a chart. As she writes, she asks children to tell her which letters she will need. She says, "Flower. FFFFFlower. Everyone say out loud what letter I need to begin spelling the word *flower.*" Many of the children say "F," some children offer other letters, and a few children are silent. Ms. Orlando confirms, "Yes. *F.* FFF-Flower," as she writes the letter *F* and then continues to spell the word except for the final letter *r.* She says, "Flower. Flowerrrr. Everyone say out loud what letter I need to spell the ending of flower." Again, many children volunteer "R," and Ms. Orlando writes it. The children continue remembering what Little Bunny turned into and helping Ms. Orlando spell words until the list is complete.

Then Ms. Orlando reminds the children to think of their plan for center time (children complete an activity checklist at the end of the day and use the checklist to plan which activities they will work on—we will explain more about this check-list later in this chapter). Several children volunteer which activities they plan to work on during center time. (Figure 12.1 presents a description of the activities available in the centers in Ms. Orlando's classroom.)

Center Time: Ms. Orlando Teaches a Minilesson and Observes Children

The children select centers, and Ms. Orlando circulates among the children helping them find materials and making sure that everyone has settled into an activity. Then she calls five children over to the worktable (a table where she frequently conducts small-group lessons) for a minilesson on spelling. She has a collection of environmental print objects and small toys that the children have brought to school in the past two weeks. The objects include toys or print objects that begin with the letters *T, R, V* or *L,* including a box of rice, a toy rabbit, a scrap of rug, a bottle of Tums, a box of Tide, a toy train, a box of Vicks cough drops, a bunch of violets, a plush lion, and a box of lima beans. Each of the children has a metal pizza pan and several magnetic letters.

Figure 12.1 *Ms. Orlando's Centers*

Blocks:	sets of large and small blocks, several toy trucks, several toy cars, road maps, toy road signs, clipboards with paper and pencils (on which children pretend to keep track of mileage)
Art:	assorted art materials (including a variety of papers, crayons, markers, collage materials, scissors, and glue) and materials for making a visor, including paper plates and a pattern (for cutting the plate into a visor shape), elastic, and hole punchers (to punch a hole for the elastic)
Travel–Dramatic Play:	dress-up clothes, including purses and wallets; checkbook, play credit cards, play airline and bus tickets; materials for going to the beach, such as empty bottles of suntan lotion, towels, sunglasses, sand bucket and shovel; travel brochures and other materials, such as maps, blank postcards, paper, markers; materials for an ice-cream stand, including play money, cups, spoons, order pads, and a cash register
Library:	quality collection of literature; retelling props for "Henny Penny" and "The Gingerbread Man"; display of "Wheels on the Bus" books; display of books featuring ways to travel and toy boats, airplanes, trucks, motorcycles, and cars that the children collected; special tub of books labeled "Traveling Characters," which includes four books each in a plastic bag with an audiotape for the listening center
Letter and Word Center:	two pieces of chart paper on which Ms. Orlando has printed the letters *T* and *R* in upper- and lowercase letters and markers (children write on the charts practicing letter formations); magazines, scissors, glue, and paper (children cut letters and pictures out of magazines and glue them on the paper); a collection of environmental print items and toys with beginning sounds of /t/, /r/, /v/, and /l/, which the children have gathered, and four grocery-store sacks labeled with those letters; picture dictionaries; names of all the children in the class, and other words, such as the days of the week, months of the year, colors, and numbers
Math	assorted manipulatives and math materials for sorting and counting; toy coins; directions for playing a game with the coins (money madness)
Discovery:	a display of different kinds of seeds the children have collected; several books about seeds and how seeds travel; magnifying glass; directions for an experiment exploring how far a piece of paper can travel when it is shaped like an acorn and when it is shaped like a maple seed, string for measuring, paper for drawing and writing the results
Writing:	assorted writing materials and tools, blank postcards, paper, and envelopes, variety of stamps (which children use as postage stamps), picture dictionaries, photo album of children in the class with their pictures, first and last names, directory of children's addresses, telephone book, maps

To begin a familiar game, Ms. Orlando holds up an object and emphasizes its beginning sound. She says, "Rrrrice. Now let's spell the beginning of rrrice." The children locate the letter *r* and put it on their pizza pans. After spelling several more words, Ms. Orlando says, "Today we are going to change this game a little bit. We are going to spell the beginning and ending of words. Like this (she holds up the toy rabbit). First I listen to the beginning of the word. Rrrrabbit. I hear an *r*." (She puts the letter *r* on her pizza pan.) "Now I have to listen for the ending. Rabbit /t/ /t/. I hear a *t*." (She puts the letter *t* after the letter *r* on her pizza pan.) "Now I've spelled *rabbit* with two letters, one for the beginning and one for the ending. Now let's try one together."

Ms. Orlando holds up the piece of rug and says, "First listen for the beginning letter. Rrrrrug. Everyone put the beginning letter." The children put the letter *r* on their pizza pans and show it to the teacher. Ms. Orlando says, "Great. Now listen for the ending letter. Rug /g/ /g/. Everyone put the ending letter. If you need help, ask your neighbor or look around the room for help." Some children hesitate, until Ms. Orlando says, "Rug /g/ /g/. Rayshawn has got it. *G*." Then the rest of the children put *g*'s on their pans.

Ms. Orlando and the children spell several more words. Then Ms. Orlando says, "I want everyone to visit the writing center today or tomorrow. When you are writing, think about using beginning and ending letters." Then the five children choose centers for the remainder of center time; three of the children begin writing at the writing center.

Ms. Orlando picks up a clipboard on which she has placed six pieces of sticky notepaper with five children's names written at the top of each paper (one extra, blank notepaper is included). Ms. Orlando observes five or six children nearly every day. At the beginning of the year, she divided her twenty-two children into two groups of five and two groups of six children. Then she assigned each group of children to a day of the week. The first group of children are observed on Monday, the second group on Tuesday, and so on. One day a week she does not observe children, but uses the day for more small-group instruction, guests, films, cooking, or other special activities.

Ms. Orlando circulates among the children in the centers. She decides to watch Ishmail as he works in the letter and word center. She observes as he dumps out the bag of *R* and *T* objects that the class has gathered and separates them into two piles. He says "ro-bot," and places the toy in the *R* bag. He says "rrr-ice," and places it in the *R* bag. He says "t-t-tums," and places it in the *T* bag. He says "tr-ain," and places it in the *T* bag. Ms. Orlando writes her observations on one of the sticky notes as shown in Figure 12.2.

Then Ms. Orlando observes Jasmine as she reads the "Wheels on the Bus" chart. Jasmine says the words to the song aloud as she points with the pointer. She does not correctly match the words she says to the printed words, but at the end of each line she adjusts her pointing so that she begins a new line saying the correct word for that line.

Ms. Orlando observes Rayshawn looking at books in the block center. He has gathered several of the toy trucks in the center and is trying to match the trucks in the center to the trucks in the books' illustrations. In the library center, Ms. Orlando observes Husalina retell "Henny Penny" using the story clothesline. Husalina includes every event in the story, recalls the characters' names correctly, and repeats the dialogue, "Wanna come? Yes. Tell king sky's falled." Ms. Orlando then observes Cecelia playing in the travel dramatic-play center with Josephine and Barbara. All three girls pretend to write a letter home to their mothers. Ms. Orlando observes

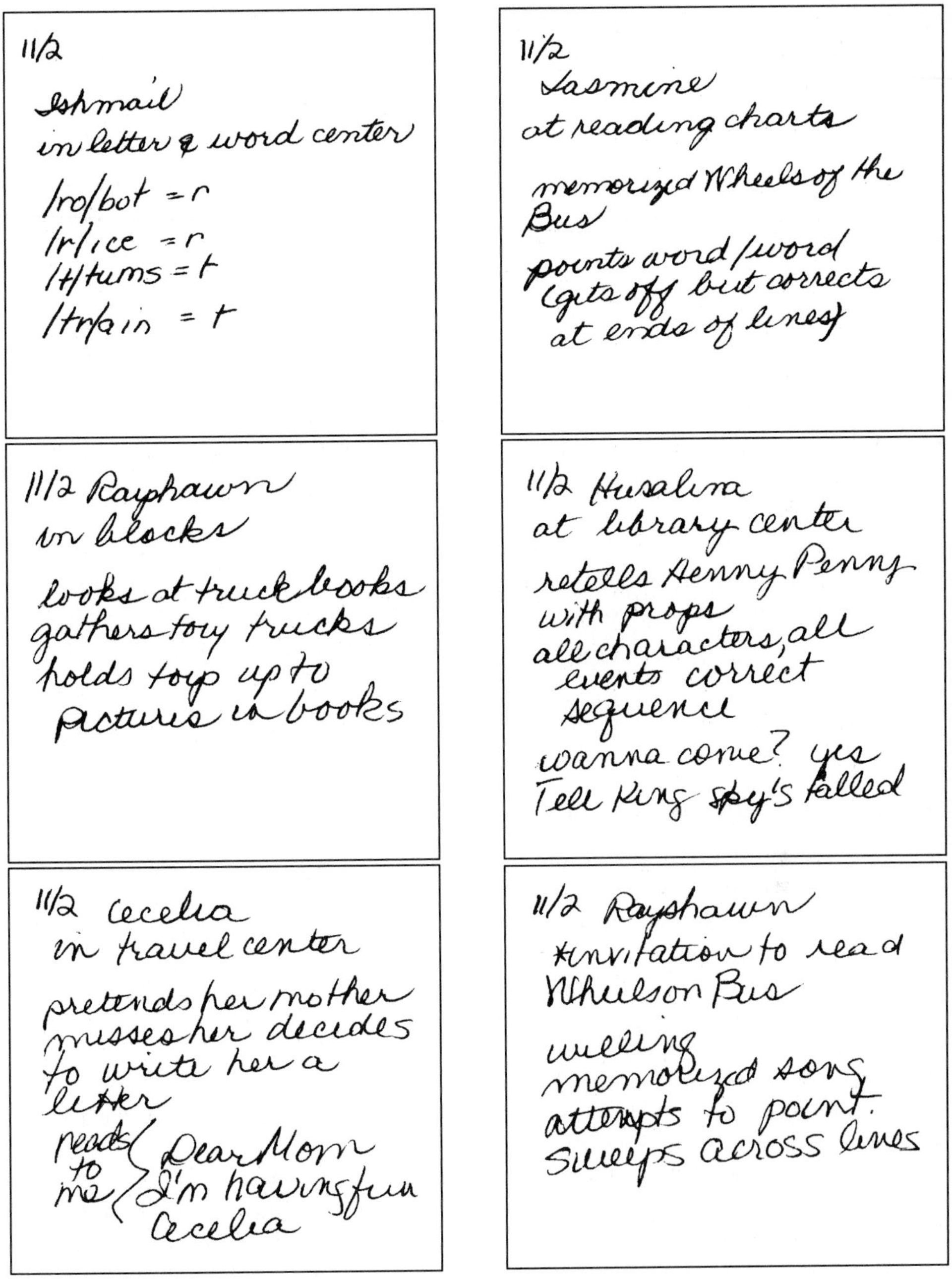

11/2
Ishmail
in letter & word center
/ro/bot = r
/r/ice = r
/t/tums = t
/tr/ain = t

11/2
Jasmine
at reading charts
memorized Wheels of the Bus
points word/word (gets off but corrects at ends of lines)

11/2 Rayshawn
in blocks
looks at truck books
gathers toy trucks
holds toys up to pictures in books

11/2 Husalina
at library center
retells Henny Penny with props
all characters, all events correct sequence
wanna come? yes
Tell King sky's falled

11/2 Cecelia
in travel center
pretends her mother misses her decides to write her a letter
reads to me: Dear Mom
I'm having fun
Cecelia

11/2 Rayshawn
invitation to read Wheels on Bus
willing
memorized song
attempts to point.
sweeps across lines

Figure 12.2 *Mrs. Orlando's Anecdotal Notes*

their writing and then asks Cecelia to read her letter. Cecelia reads, "Dear Mom, I'm having fun. Cecelia."

Last, Ms. Orlando invites Rayshawn to read the "Wheels on the Bus" chart with her; she is aware that he rarely chooses to reread the classroom charts or retell stories in the library center. Rayshawn points to the text from left to right and across the lines as he recites the words to the song. Ms. Orlando notes that he has memorized the words to the song, but is not matching the words he says with the words in the text. He sweeps the pointer from left to right across the chart without matching words or lines. The notes that Ms. Orlando wrote about her observations of these children are also included in Figure 12.2.

Storytime

As center time comes to an end, Ms. Orlando helps the children put away their center activities and get ready for snack and outdoor recess. After recess, she reads a big book version of *Rosie's Walk* (Hutchins, 1968). As she reads, she pauses to invite children to make predictions about what will happen next. She notes that Jasmine, Tuong, and Ishmail catch on to the repetitive pattern and make accurate predictions of the story.

As the last activity of the day, the children complete activity checklists, a special ditto that Ms. Orlando has prepared (see Figure 12.3). It lists all the center activities for the current travel unit. (Ms. Orlando changes some of the activities weekly and makes a new activity checklist for each week.) She reminds children to color in all the activities they have completed today and think about which activities they need to complete by Friday. She has several children share one activity that they need to work on the next day. Then the children prepare for dismissal.

Ms. Orlando Reflects and Plans

After the children are dismissed, Ms. Orlando takes time to organize her observations and make plans for instruction. First she takes the sticky notes off the clipboard and puts each note in her **observation notebook**. This notebook is divided into sections, one for each child in the classroom. As she places the sticky notes in the notebook she reflects on what the observations show about each child's understanding about reading or writing. She writes her analysis beside the sticky note in the observation notebook. Figure 12.4 presents Ms. Orlando's analyses of her observations of the children. Finally, Ms. Orlando takes a few minutes to write notes in the observation notebook about the accurate predictions that Jasmine, Tuong, and Ishmail made during reading.

Ms. Orlando decides to put Cecelia's letter, which she collected from the travel dramatic-play center, in Cecelia's portfolio. Each child has a large folder in which Ms. Orlando keeps examples of that child's work. Sometimes children select activities to include in their portfolios. Ms. Orlando also keeps information about children's performance on special assessment tasks in their portfolios. She talks with the children about the contents of their portfolios at the end of each unit and shares the portfolios with parents every twelve weeks. Ms. Orlando quickly writes a caption for Cecelia's letter and clips it to the letter. The **caption** includes the date and Ms. Orlando's analysis of what the letter reveal's about Cecelia's understanding about writing. Figure 12.5 shows Cecelia's letter and Ms. Orlando's caption.

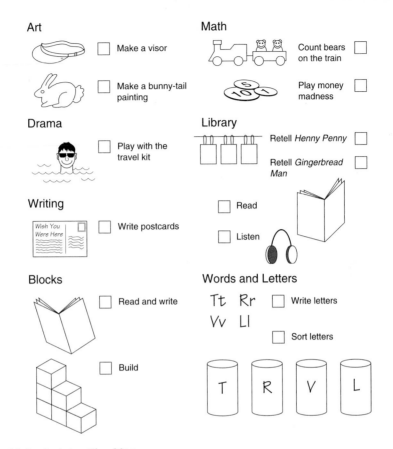

Figure 12.3 *Activity Checklist*

Figure 12.4 *Analysis of Anecdotal Notes*

Ishmail: Ishmail segments words between syllables and onset and rimes. He knows the sounds associated with *T* and *R*.

Jasmine: Jasmine knows that print is read left to right. She is developing print-to-speech match at the level of lines of text.

Rayshawn: (at block center) Rayshawn uses reading to find information. He willingly looks at books of personal interest.

Rayshawn: (reading chart) Rayshawn memorizes familiar text and knows print is read from left to right.

Cecelia: Cecelia writes to communicate with the others.

Husalina: Chooses to retell stories. Accurate recall of characters and events. English is developing in repeated dialogue.

Figure 12.5 Cecelia's Letter and Caption

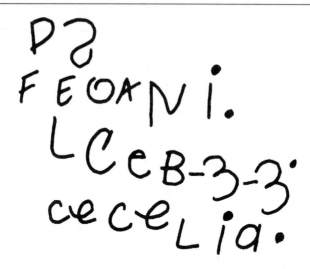

Caption: 11/2   Cecelia is using emerging letter form. Her signature is in the appropriate location for letters. She shows awareness of linearity, hyphens, and periods. Her meaning is appropriate for the situation (pretending her mother misses her) and includes language used in a letter. She uses conventional alphabet letter forms (with one reversal). She relies on contextual dependency.

Text: Dear Mom,
              I'm having fun.
              Cecelia

Then Ms. Orlando thinks back on the day's activities and her observations. She decides that she needs to teach a small-group lesson with Jasmine, Rayshawn, and a few other children on finger-point reading of memorized stories. She plans to teach a minilesson on monitoring finger-point reading and plans to include a pocket-chart activity for the "Wheels on the Bus" song.

CLASSROOM ASSESSMENT

Classroom assessment is a critical component of effective teaching; teachers use information from their assessments of children's learning to guide instructional decisions and inform parents about their children's progress in literacy acquisition. Many teachers, like Ms. Orlando, gather information from their classroom assessments of children into portfolios. A **portfolio** is a collection of samples of a child's writing and reading. It also includes teachers' observational notes or checklists documenting the child's behaviors during reading or writing. A type of classroom assessment, **Portfolio assessment** is a collection and analysis of information from several different sources, including anecdotal notes, checklists, interviews, samples of children's work, and performance on special literacy tasks. Portfolio assessment is (1) theory based, (2) multidimensional, (3) reflective, (4) systematic, (5) collaborative, and (6) concerned with process as well as product (Harp, 1991; Tierney, Carter, & Desai, 1991).

Portfolio Assessment Is Theory Based

Portfolio assessment aligns assessment, instruction, and learning with currently held theories about how children learn (Winograd, Paris, & Bridge, 1991). We believe that psycho-sociolinguistic theories provide the best explanation of how children acquire literacy concepts (see Chapter 1). According to psycho-sociolinguistic theories, children construct concepts about reading and writing as members of family and cultural groups who use reading and writing for a variety of purposes. They form hypotheses about written language and modify those hypotheses as they participate in reading and writing activities. Many of their hypotheses are not conventional; yet, children make progress toward more conventional understandings of reading and writing as they test and extend their hypotheses about how written language works.

Psycho-sociolinguistic theories also suggest that children learn through interacting with others as they read and write for authentic purposes. **Authentic activities** are those in which children read and write for a useful purpose. For example, Ms. Orlando's children engaged in many authentic reading and writing activities. They looked at books about trucks in the block center to learn more about the kinds of toy trucks available in the center. They wrote letters as a part of their play in the travel dramatic-play center, and they retold stories in the library center as an enjoyable activity.

We know that effective readers and writers are motivated and reflective (see Chapter 6) and use reading and writing to find out more about themselves and the world. Ms. Orlando noted that some children were particularly reflective; they made insightful predictions as she read a new story. Ms. Orlando planned activities that encouraged children to make choices. She developed activity checklists that children used to keep track of their own learning and to make plans for future activities. Finally, she kept records through her observational notes of the kinds of reading and writing activities in which children willingly engaged.

Portfolio Assessment Is Multidimensional

Portfolios are collections from a variety of sources of information, such as anecdotal notes, checklists, work samples, and special literacy tasks (Valencia, 1990). **Anecdotal notes** are objective recordings of what teachers observe children doing and are free from interpretation or inference (Rhodes & Nathenson-Mejia, 1992). They may focus on what children are reading and writing, children's comments about their reading and writing, aspects of text to which children attend, or strategies that children use. For example, Ms. Orlando noted Jasmine's strategy of self-correcting her pointing to words in the text at the end of each line, Ishmail's attention to smaller-than-word parts, and Husalina's use of language (see Figure 12.2).

Checklists are another source of information included in portfolios. They are prepared lists of behaviors or concepts that are used to guide observation. Some checklists are designed to document children's use of reading or writing processes. For example, teachers might use a checklist to observe children's use of writing processes during writing workshop. Other checklists are designed help children document their reading and writing. Ms. Orlando helped children complete **activity checklists** as a record of their activities and as a tool to help them plan.

Work samples are samples of children's reading and writing activities collected from ongoing classroom experiences. Work samples might include compositions, grocery lists written in a grocery store dramatic-play center, pages from journals, stories or reports, copies of improvised structure stories that children compose collaboratively, or copies of children's signatures from sign-in sheets. These samples reflect the diversity of children's classroom literacy experiences. Ms. Orlando collected a work sample when she kept a copy of Cecelia's letter.

Portfolio Assessment Is Reflective

Teachers' and children's analysis of children's current understandings about written language and progress in literacy acquisition are an important part of portfolio assessment. Ms. Orlando took time after she wrote anecdotal notes to reflect on the behaviors she observed and what those behaviors revealed about children's knowledge. For example, she recognized that Ishmail's talk at the letter and word center reflected his level of phonemic awareness (he could segment some words at syllable boundaries and segment the onset in others). She wrote her analysis for each observation in her observation notebook.

Children's reflections are also a part of portfolios. Part of children's reflections include choosing which work samples to add to a portfolio. Ms. Orlando's children selected work samples to add to their portfolios at the end of every theme unit. Children may decide to select works that are

- Best works

- Most interesting works

- Works that show learning

- Works that demonstrate variety

- Easy and difficult work

Portfolio Assessment Is Systematic

Information in portfolios is collected systematically and regularly. At the beginning of the year, teachers consider their instructional goals and make decisions about the kinds of assessments that they will use to provide evidence of children's progress toward each of the instructional goals. Instructional goals reflect the expectations of the particular grade level as dictated by district or state curriculum guides as well as teachers' understandings about children's literacy acquisition. Once teachers have identified their instructional goals, they prepare an **assessment planning guide** (Tierney, Carter, & Desai, 1991). This guide lists the instructional goals and outlines some instructional activities designed to meet the goals as well as assessments to capture information about children's learning related to the goals.

Table 12.1 presents Ms. Orlando's kindergarten assessment planning guide. This table shows that Ms. Orlando's instructional plan includes goals for children's growing knowledge about written language meanings, forms, functions, and meaning-form links. Her plan shows that each goal is extended through a variety of instructional activities. Similarly, Ms. Orlando intends to use several assessments to capture information about children's progress in each goal.

Table 12.1 *Assessment Planning Guide*

Goals	Activities	Assessment
Meanings:		
1. children demonstrate increased understanding of books read aloud	grand conversations retellings KWL	response checklist retelling checklist
2. children demonstrate increased use of meaning strategies (predicting, recalling, sequencing)	grand conversations retellings	anecdotal notes response checklist
Forms:		
3. children increase in complexity of written language forms	writing center theme activities	work samples anecdotal notes alphabet task
4. children increase in complexity of story forms used in compositions	writing center improvised structure stories sharing	work samples
Meaning-Form Links:		
5. children demonstrate increased emergent reading	independent reading chart and big books pocket charts	anecdotal notes emergent reading checklist

6. children demonstrate increased understanding of alphabetic principles	writing center
	chart and big books
	word and letter center
		anecdotal notes
		emergent reading
		   checklist
		work samples
		invented spelling
		   task

Functions:		
7. children use reading and writing for a variety of purposes	drama centers theme activities (invitations, etc.)	anecdotal notes work samples
8. children choose to read and write	center activities independent reading	anecdotal notes work samples

Ms. Orlando took considerable time stating her instructional goals so that her goals would be challenging to all the children in her classroom, regardless of the level of their entering knowledge. Therefore, she did not state her goals in terms of levels of achievement, but rather in terms of growth.

Teachers and children gather information for portfolios continuously throughout the school year. Teachers may plan to make a particular assessment each week; Ms. Orlando set up a plan whereby she observed each child in her classroom at least once a week. Other assessments might be planned at the end of each grading period or theme unit.

Portfolio Assessment Is Collaborative

Self-evaluation is a critical component of portfolio assessment (Farr & Tone, 1994). Children play an important role in assessing their own learning and setting their own goals for learning. They help select information to be included in their portfolios, and they reflect on what the information in the portfolio reveals about them as learners. Some teachers include children in parent-teacher conferences in which portfolios are shared with parents. Children show the contents of their portfolios to their parents and discuss with them what the contents show about their learning progress.

Portfolio Assessment Examines Process and Product

Portfolios contain samples of children's products (work samples) as well as documentation of their use of strategies or processes. Children can be included in analyzing their use of strategies. For example, children may be asked to select early drafts of a composition and compare it with their final, published draft. Children analyze why and how they revised their drafts and describe why the final draft is better than the early draft. Teachers can observe children as they read and write for evidence of their use of strategies. For example, children's comments and questions during read alouds and grand conversations provide a window to their meaning-making strategies. Children's mistakes or miscues as they read also reflect their use of strategies. In addition, teachers can observe children's use of writing processes during writing workshop.

ASSESSMENT TOOLS

There are a variety of assessment tools that teachers may use to assess children's literacy knowledge. These include observations, alphabet recognition tasks, concepts-about-print tasks, emergent reading checklists, running records, retellings, analyses of grand conversations and journals, and analyses of compositions.

Observations

Observation is one of the most important classroom assessment tools. As teachers observe children interacting with other children and using reading and writing in functional ways, children's concepts about written language meanings, forms, meaning-form links, and functions are revealed. Teachers capture this information for portfolios by writing anecdotal notes about their observations. Teachers usually choose to write an anecdotal note when they observe an event that reflects a child's current level of understanding about written language or a new level of understanding. For example, Ms. Orlando recognized that her observation of Rayshawn's reading books in the block center was a reflection of his current level of interaction with books. She knew that Rayshawn rarely visited the library center or willingly retold books using the many props available in the classroom. Therefore, Ms. Orlando decided to write an anecdotal note of this behavior.

An important part of observation is reflection. That is, teachers not only note behaviors, but also consider what those behaviors mean. Teachers capture the behavior in their anecdotal notes, that are objective recordings of behaviors. Then they write an analysis that identifies children's concepts. Ms. Orlando's anecdotal notes are good examples of objective reportings of behavior (see Figure 12.2), and her analyses identify children's literacy knowledge (see Figure 12.4).

Analysis of anecdotal notes depends on the teacher's awareness of children's knowledge. For example, suppose that a first grade teacher is concerned about a child's inability to select and sustain interest in a book for independent reading. The teacher observes that the child selects three different books in five minutes and does no more than look quickly through the books at the illustrations. Figure 12.6 presents the teacher's anecdotal note and analysis of this behavior. Several months later, the teacher may observe the same child spending more than fifteen minutes reading *Hop on Pop* (Seuss, 1963) with a friend in the library center. The teacher writes an anecdotal note about this event because the teacher knows that it documents significant growth in the child's ability and willingness to sustain interest in reading. Figure 12.6 also shows the teacher's anecdotal note about this new behavior and analysis of the child's progress.

Figure 12.6 *Anecdotal Notes Showing Development*

Note 10/15	Analysis 10/15
10/15 Barbara	Barbara willingly participates in independent reading. She browses through books looking at pictures. (needs support in selecting books and strategies for sustaining interest)
sits near bookcase, pulls books out at random, flips through looking at pictures, spends 4 minutes then leaves center	
Note 2/7	Analysis 2/7
2/7 Barbara searches for and retells Hop on Pop, sustains retelling for over 10 minutes	Barbara enjoys reading books to others. She is comfortable reading books she has memorized and spends long periods of time rereading these books. She selects these books for independent reading. Note progress from unable to sustain interest in books to sustains interest for prolonged periods of time from 10/15.

Teachers frequently read over their anecdotal notes about children to assess any patterns of growth. Ms. Orlando reads through her anecdotal notes every two to three weeks. Whenever her anecdotal notes indicate a change in a child's learning, she notes this change in the child's observation record.

Alphabet Recognition Task

To assess children's knowledge of alphabet letter names, teachers can prepare an **alphabet recognition task.** They write (or type) all the uppercase and lowercase alphabet letters in random order on a sheet of paper or on index cards. Children are asked to name the letters, and teachers record the letters that children fail to identify. Preschool and kindergarten teachers are particularly interested in recognizing children's progress in identifying letters correctly.

Concepts-about-Print Task

The **concepts-about-print task** is designed to assess children's understanding of familiar words used to talk about books, awareness of directionality in how print is read, and understanding of the conventions of written language (Clay, 1985). Teachers can construct their own concepts-about-print test. They select an unfamiliar picture book and ask children to point to the front and back of the book, to the beginning and ending of the story, and to the top and bottom of a page. They have children point to where to start reading (upper left), where to go next (across to the right), and then where to read next (return sweep to the next line of text). Using a big book, teachers can have child locate one word, the first and last letter in a word, a period, and a capital letter.

Children's concepts about print continue to expand through their preschool, kindergarten, and first grade years. Children's progress with this task reflects that they have shared books with their parents and teachers; using the concepts-about-print task is one way to assess children's familiarity with books.

Emergent Reading Checklist

An **emergent reading checklist** is a list of behaviors that signal children's movement toward more conventional reading. Table 12.2 shows an emergent reading checklist that can be used to document young children's growth from emergent to conventional reading (adapted from Tompkins & McGee, 1993, p. 358). Teachers use the checklist as they observe children reading independently, with partners, and in small groups. They observe children several times throughout the school year, using the checklist to document changes in children's reading abilities. Teachers may use the information from emergent reading checklists to plan instruction.

Running Record

A **running record** is used to analyze children's reading; it provides information about reading level and children's use of cueing systems during reading. A running

Table 12.2 *Emergent Reading Checklist*

Child's Name _____ Date _____

Emergent Reading

_____ reading related to pictures but not text

_____ reading closely matched to text but not coordinated with pages of text

_____ reading closely matched to text and coordinated with pages of text

_____ reading exact match to text and pages of text

Directionality (pointing while reading)

_____ sweeps across text (uncoordinated)

_____ sweeps from left to right across lines of text (continuous and coordinated sweep across lines of text)

_____ sweeps from left to right across text pointing to words

Speech-to-Print Match

_____ points to words and assigns segment of speech

_____ points to a word in text and assigns a spoken word

_____ tracks print correctly (points to a word in text and assigns correct spoken word)

Word Identification

_____ matches words

_____ tracks print to identify words

_____ identifies words in text without tracking

_____ identifies words out of text

_____ learns new words from reading

Cue Systems

_____ uses memory to read text

_____ uses pictures and memory to read text

_____ uses tracking, memory, and pictures to monitor reading

_____ uses sound–letter relationships to monitor reading

_____ uses tracking, memory, pictures, and sound–letter relationships to monitor reading

record includes several steps. First, teachers listen to children read and record children's miscues or errors. Then, they analyze the running record using a miscue analysis. Teachers may also analyze the miscues to determine children's knowledge of word recognition strategies. As an optional part of a running record, children may retell the story or informational book after reading, and then teachers analyze the retelling.

Taking a Running Record

The first step of a running record is to obtain a record of the child's reading—the running record. To begin, teachers select texts of at least one hundred words at a variety of difficulty levels. These texts can be selected from basal readers or from commercial materials have an indication of difficulty level (see, for example, materials published by The Wright Group). Reading Recovery also has a list of books at several levels of difficulty (Peterson, 1991, pp. 139–147).

Next, children read several of the texts, and the teacher records the kinds of miscues they make as they read. Figure 12.7 presents a running record of Charlie's reading "The Three Little Pigs." This figure indicates words that Charlie omitted—crossed out in text; words that he inserted—added above the text; words that he substituted—written over the text; and words that he self-corrected—marked with "SC." The figure also shows the teacher's running record, which captures Charlie's omissions, insertions, substitutions, and self-corrections (see the directions included in the figure).

Teachers then determine the **accuracy rate** of the child's reading by counting all miscues except miscues that children self-correct. This number is subtracted from the total number of words in the passage and the result divided by the total number of words. The accuracy rate provides an indication of whether the text is easy, appropriate for instruction, or difficult. According to Clay (1985, p. 17), the accuracy rates for easy, instructional, and difficult texts are easy text, 95 to 100 percent; instructional text, 90 to 94 percent; and difficult text, less than 90 percent.

"The Three Little Pigs" text that Charlie read has 181 words; he made 14 miscues and 3 self-corrections for an accuracy rate of 93 percent. "The Three Little Pigs" is an instructional text for Charlie. His teacher has Charlie read increasingly difficult texts until his reading falls below 90 percent accuracy. The highest level of text that he reads with 90 percent or better accuracy is his current reading level.

Miscue Analysis

A **miscue analysis** provides information about children's use of semantic (meaning), syntactic (language), and graphophonic cueing systems (Goodman & Burke, 1972). To assist in a miscue analysis, teachers construct a miscue analysis chart. Table 12.3 displays the miscue analysis for Charlie's reading of "The Three Little Pigs." First, the teacher analyzes all substitutions to determine whether they are semantically acceptable (miscue has a similar meaning as the text word), syntactically acceptable (miscue is syntactically acceptable in the sentence), or graphophonically acceptable (miscue matches the text word at the beginning, middle, or end). The teacher also records whether the miscue was self-corrected.

According to the miscue analysis presented in Table 12.3, none of Charlie's miscues were semantically acceptable, but Charlie self-corrected three miscues. In addition, all his miscues up to the point of the error made sense. Over half his miscues were syntactically acceptable. All the miscues except two had the same beginning letters as the text word. According to this analysis, Charlie attends especially to beginning letters, but also to meaning. His miscues make sense and are often syntactically acceptable.

Figure 12.7 *Running Record for "The Three Little Pigs"*

TEXT: The Three Little Pigs

$\overset{three \, ^{sc}}{}$
Once upon a time there were three pigs. Mother pig $\underset{\rfloor}{\overset{said \, ^{sc}}{sent}}$ the

$\overset{the}{}$ $\overset{T}{}$
three little pigs ~~out~~ to make their way in the world. The first

$\overset{sticks}{}$
pig made a house of straw. The second pig made a house of

sticks. The third pig made a house of bricks. A wolf came to

the first pig's house and said, "I'll huff and puff and blow your

house down." The wolf blew the house down and the little pig ran

$\overset{little}{}$
away fast. The wolf came to the second $_\wedge$pig's house and said,

$\overset{fast}{}$
"I'll huff and puff and blow your house down." The wolf blew the

house down but the little pig ran away faster. The wolf came to

the third pig's house and said, "I'll huff and puff and blow your

$\overset{did}{}$ $\overset{down}{}$
house down." He blew and blew but could not blow ~~down~~ the house$_\wedge$

$\overset{s \ T}{}$
He tried to sneak down the chimney but the pig put a big pot of

water on the fire. The wolf came down the chimney and burned his

$\overset{fast}{}\overset{sc}{}$
tail. He ran away the fastest of all.

EXAMPLES:

child matches text   ✓

child substitutes $\dfrac{child}{text}$

child omits $\overset{\bullet}{text}$

child inserts $\underset{\bullet}{child}$

child repeats $\lfloor text$

child self-corrects   sc

teacher prompts   T

RUNNING RECORD

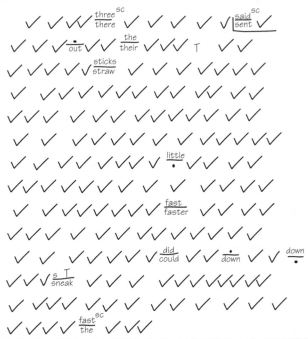

Table 12.3 *Miscue Analysis Chart for "The Three Little Pigs"*

CHILD/TEXT	SEMANTICALLY ACCEPTABLE	SYNTACTICALLY ACCEPTABLE	GRAPHOPHONICALLY SAME AS			SELF-CORRECTS	COMMENTS
			B	M	E		
three/there			✓			✓	*
said/sent			✓			✓	*
the/their	✓		✓				
sticks/straw	✓		✓				
fast/faster	✓		✓	✓			
did/could	✓				✓		
fast/the						✓	*
s/sneak			✓				
	0/8	4/8	6/8	1/8	1/8	3/8	

* sentence makes sense up to point of miscue

Word Recognition Analysis

Children's miscues in running records provide excellent resources for determining their knowledge of word recognition cues, including phonics (knowledge of sound-letter relationships) and structural analysis (knowledge of prefixes, suffixes, and familiar word parts). Teachers examine children's miscues for knowledge of

- Consonants
- Consonant clusters (*br, gl, st,* etc.)
- Consonant digraphs (*sh, ch, th, ph, wh,* and *ng)*
- Short vowels (m*a*d, etc.)
- Silent *e* long vowels (m*a*de, etc.)
- Long vowel combinations (m*ai*l, p*a*y, m*ea*t, etc.)
- Prefixes
- Suffixes
- Familiar word parts (*le* in *bottle,* etc.)

A third grade teacher recorded the following miscues in Raymond's running record.

Text	**Child**
street	stairs
strutting	starting
mournful	m

deserted	distant
abruptly	ab
mysterious	mysteries

In a **word recognition analysis** of Rayond's miscues, his teacher noted that Raymond consistently used beginning consonants but frequently omitted the *r* in the *str* consonant cluster and had difficulty decoding multisyllabic words (all the miscues were words of more than one syllable, except for *ceased*). However, Raymond is aware of some prefixes and familiar word parts (for example, he correctly read the *ab* prefix).

Retellings

Retellings are tasks in which children read and then retell a text. To retell, children recall everything they can remember from the story or informational text either orally or in writing. Retellings reflect children's understand of text; but of course, retellings also reflect children's memory and their level of spoken or written language competence. Retellings usually assess children's recall of the literal facts of a story.

To assess retellings, teachers prepare a retelling checklist that includes all the important information from a story or informational text. Table 12.4 is a **retelling checklist** for assessing children's retelling of *Fly Away Home* (Bunting, 1991). As a child retells the story, the teacher checks off each event included in the child's retelling. After the child finishes retelling, the teacher may use several prompts to see whether the child has understood more about the story than he or she recalled at first. Depending on the parts of the story that were not recalled, teachers ask, "Do you remember any other characters?" "Where (when) did the story take place?" "What was (the main character's) problem?" "How did (the main character) solve the problem?" "Can you remember anything else that happened in the story?" "How did the story end?" Children's original retelling is called *unprompted recall,* and their

Table 12.4 *Retelling Checklist for* Fly Away Home *(Bunting, 1991)*

Unprompted	Prompted	
_____	_____	1. Boy and dad live in airport.
_____	_____	2. They have no home.
_____	_____	3. They are careful they don't get caught.
_____	_____	4. The important thing is not to get noticed.
_____	_____	5. Boy and Dad don't get noticed.
_____	_____	6. The boy and his dad sleep in different parts of the airport.
_____	_____	7. One day a bird got caught inside the terminal.
_____	_____	8. After a few days the bird flew out the door.
_____	_____	9. The dad works on weekends as a janitor.
_____	_____	10. The boy stays with the Medinas.
_____	_____	11. He returns luggage carts for tips.
_____	_____	12. Dad looks for an apartment but can't find one.
_____	_____	13. The boy is sad he lives in the airport.
_____	_____	14. The boy knows he will be free of the airport like the bird.

responses to these questions is called *prompted recall*. The *retelling score* is the percentage of total ideas (prompted and unprompted) recalled.

To make retelling checklists, teachers select short stories of 100 to 300 words, read the stories carefully, and make a list of the important events. Retelling checklists can be constructed for informational texts as well. In this case, teachers make a list of all main ideas and supporting details or examples.

In addition to measuring the quantity of ideas recalled (retelling score), teachers can examine the quality of retelling. To do so usually requires that teachers tape-record retellings or gather written retellings. Teachers examine whether children include the major literary elements of stories in expected order or whether children remember the main ideas and supporting details in the organizational pattern used by the author. Table 12.5 presents a **story retelling analysis sheet,** which teachers can use to analyze the quality of retellings of stories (Morrow, 1989). Table 12.6 presents an **informational text analysis** sheet (Cooper, 1993).

Teachers may analyze retellings along with running records. First, children read a text aloud and teachers take a running record. Then children retell the text so that teachers can assess their understanding of the text. The running record provides evidence of the level of text that children can read fluently and of the kinds of reading strategies they employ. Retellings provide evidence of children's comprehension.

Table 12.5 *Story Retelling Analysis Sheet*

Setting
_____ States introduction (1 point)
_____ States place or time (1 point)
_____ Names main character (1 point)
_____ Names other characters (1 point)

Problem
_____ Names or implies problem (1 point)

Plot
_____ Recalls most major events (2 points)
_____ Recalls some major events (1 point)

Resolution
_____ Recalls climax (1 point)
_____ Recalls ending (1 point)

Sequence
_____ Recalls story in sequence (2 points)
_____ Recalls story with some sequence (1 point)

Theme (1 point)
_____

Total score (possible 12 points)
_____

Adapted from L. M. Morrow, "Using Story Retelling to Develop Comprehension," in K. Muth (Ed.), *Children's Comprehension of Text: Research into Practice*, p. 187. Copyright © 1993 by the International Reading Association.

Table 12.6 *Informational Text Retelling Analysis*

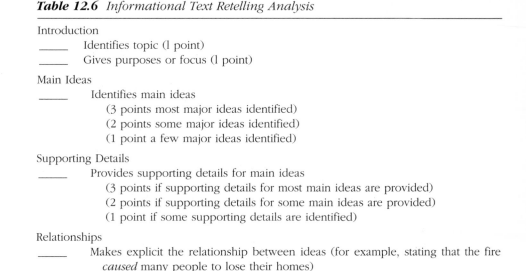

Introduction
_____ Identifies topic (1 point)
_____ Gives purposes or focus (1 point)

Main Ideas
_____ Identifies main ideas
          (3 points most major ideas identified)
          (2 points some major ideas identified)
          (1 point a few major ideas identified)

Supporting Details
_____ Provides supporting details for main ideas
          (3 points if supporting details for most main ideas are provided)
          (2 points if supporting details for some main ideas are provided)
          (1 point if some supporting details are identified)

Relationships
_____ Makes explicit the relationship between ideas (for example, stating that the fire
          caused many people to lose their homes)
          (2 points if many relationships are stated)
          (1 point if some relationships are stated)

Organization
_____ Recalls information in a sequence similar to text
          (2 points for well-organized recall)
          (1 point for somewhat organized recall)

Total score (12 points possible)

_____

From J. David Cooper, *Literacy: Helping Children Construct Meaning*, Second Edition, p. 581. Copyright © 1993 by Houghton Mifflin Company. Adapted with permission.

Grand Conversations and Response Journals

Children construct meaning beyond the literal level. One way of assessing their comprehension beyond the literal level is to examine their responses to literature in grand conversations and response journals. As children participate in grand conversations or write in response journals, they recall events, evaluate the text globally, make inferences or evaluations of characters and events, identify with a character, state themes, relate personal experiences, make connections to other literature, and comment on or evaluate literary structures or languages (McGee, 1992). Children also make predictions, hypothesize about outcomes or reasons for actions, and ask questions or identify confusing parts of the text. These responses indicate children's personal involvement with the story or informational text and their ability to construct inferential, evaluative, and interpretive understandings. Figure 12.8 presents five first graders' grand conversation about *Hey, Al* (Yorinks, 1986), which illustrates the variety of different responses that teachers can expect in grand conversations (see also Figure 5.3 in Chapter 5).

Figure 12.8 *Grand Conversation about* Hey, Al *(Yorinks, 1986)*

Teacher (T): What did you think of the story?

Chris: I like the part when he turns into a bird. The dog and Eddie.

Ryan: Hey! Eddie's the dog. I like the part when he's laying down in the water, and the birds bring him food and stuff and he's wearing the old hat that he used to have and I like the dog, too.

Annie: I like the part when they were going back to their own house and Eddie fell into the ocean.

T: Why did you like that part?

Annie: Because it was gonna be okay.

T: Did you know that for sure?

John: No, no.

Chris: Yeah, because if they were on earth they wouldn't be birds.

Annie: I like the part when they got home and they painted everything yellow so everything would be okay. Al's dog came back so Al wouldn't be afraid that he didn't have a dog anymore.

Alice: I liked the part when he was a janitor but then he said, there's no—like when he was gonna go up there, and he was gonna change his mind, but he didn't.

Ryan: I like the part when the bird comes to say, "Hey, Al," and he jumps when he's shaving his face and the bird came and says, "Al, Al," and he jumped and said, "Who's that?" and the razor came out of his hand.

John: Yeah, it was funny.

Alice: I liked those birds with all those big, big legs.

Annie: I like the part when they were going up there and Al lost his luggage. Hey! Look at that! Look at that hand! (Annie points to illustration in which a bird has a human hand)

T: Oh, where?

Annie: He's turning back.

T: Look what Annie's found.

John: He was a person.

Annie: All of them were persons.

Ryan: They were all persons?

Annie: People! All of these were people! Look at his hands.

John: I know. That's what I said.

Chris: If they all stay there, they'll all be birds.

Annie: Oh, look. How can he be changed back?

Alice: I could tell he was an old man because look at his skin.

Annie: I think all the animals were humans before they came out there because one of these animals was the real one and they turn real people into

John: animals.

Figure 12.8 *(Continued)*

Ryan: Yeah, birds and they have to go back but they don't know how to get back because some of them don't have wings.

Eric: I like the bird there with the hand in the cage with the funny mouth.

John: I liked the part when he fell in that place up in the air.

Annie: In the water.

John: No. When he fell in the place in the sky. When the bird was dropping him down into the place.

T: Well, what do you think Al found out at the island?

Annie: I think he would be better as a janitor instead of up there. He learned never talk to strangers.

Ryan: If he stayed up there, he would really be a bird and we don't know if he could change back again and his whole body would be a bird.

John: He loves his home.

T: How do you know?

John: Because he was happy to be back and the dog came back and they painted it.

Annie: They painted it yellow like the place. He was happy at the end.

Chris: Yeah, and he got a new shirt like it wasn't the shirt from, like he was a janitor again, but he's got a nicer shirt and he looks happy.

Alice: Eddie is smiling. Yeah. The story has a happy ending.

Reprinted with the permission of Simon & Schuster from the Macmillan College text *Teaching Reading with Literature: Case Studies to Action Plans* by Gail Tompkins and Lea McGee, pp. 366–367. Copyright © 1993 by Macmillan Publishing Company, Inc.

To analyze grand conversations or response journals, teachers examine children's responses. Responses in which children note details in the illustrations, recall story events, and make global evaluations (such as "it was funny," "I liked it," "it was awesome") are at the first level. Responses that indicate connections to the story are at the next higher level. For example, children may remember experiences in their own lives associated with the story or recall a similar event in another story. They may identify with a character by acting out what the character does or says or relating to the character on an emotional level ("I would like to do that, too!").

Responses that indicate that children have made inferences or evaluations of characters or events are at the third level. They may note elements of an author's craft (noticing, for example, that *The Pain and the Great One* [Blume, 1974], is written from two points of view), or they may make hypotheses about events, outcomes, or motivations. At the fourth level, children make interpretations about the story that include making theme statements tied to the story. For example, in response to *Hey, Al* (Yorinks, 1986) one child interpreted the story as meaning "Al learned to be happy" and another child stated the theme as "Al was better off as a janitor than on that island." Both of these are abstract interpretations or generalizations, but they are still tied to the content of the story.

At the fifth and most abstract level, children's responses indicate that they interpreted the story abstractly. However, they apply the theme to universal truths about humans or the world in which we live, or they apply the theme to their own lives. For example, an abstract interpretation of *Hey, Al* is that "the story is about taking charge of life," and an abstract theme is that "people have to make their own happiness." Readers might apply the abstract theme in *Hey, Al* to their own lives with such observations as "I'm always like Al—just letting other people decide what I should do."

Figure 12.9 presents a **response-to-literature checklist,** which can be used to analyze children's responses in grand conversations and response journals. To use the response checklist, teachers audiotape or videotape grand conversations or collect entries from children's response journals. They review their recordings and focus on the contributions of one child at a time. They complete a checklist for each child participating in the grand conversation and note the levels of understanding reflected in children's responses.

The response-to-literature checklist in Figure 12.9 includes the teacher's analysis of Annie's participation in the grand conversation presented in Figure 12.8. The checklist shows that Annie recalled story events, responded to a symbol, made inferences, and used illustrations to support her responses. Her responses ranged from the first level to the fourth level.

Compositions

Teachers and children select compositions to include in portfolios. These compositions may be written during writing workshop and may be highly polished stories that have gone through several drafts, or they may be informal compositions written at a writing center. Compositions can be written, dictated, or presented orally. Teachers analyze compositions for children's understanding of written forms, meanings, and spellings.

Analysis of Form

Young children's compositions can be examined for the following forms.

- Mock cursive (indicates awareness of linearity)
- Mock alphabet letters (indicates awareness of letter features)
- Conventional alphabet letters (indicates knowledge of alphabet formations)
- Copied words (indicates awareness of words in environment)
- Words such as the child's name or other learned words such as *mom, dad,* and *love* (indicates learned spellings)

In addition, teachers note whether children's writing shows awareness of linearity (for example, writing mock letters from left to right in lines) or spacing (for

Figure 12.9 Response-to-Literature Checklist

Name ___Annie_____ Date ___4/16_____

Title __Hey, Al_____

Other Children in Group ____Chris, Ryan, John,_____

___Alice, Eric_____

Product (What child said or wrote)	**Comments**
Level 1: Recall and global evaluation	
✓ recalls story events and characters	Eddie fell ocean
makes global evaluations	
recalls text language	
✓ notes details in illustrations	notes hand
Level 2: Connections	
identifies with character	
relates personal stories	
relates personal feelings	
connects to other literature	
Level 3: Inferences and evaluations	birds are people
✓✓makes inferences about characters' motivations,	Al doesn't have to be afraid
feelings, traits	doesn't have dog
makes evaluations of characters' actions, traits,	
motivations, feelings	
✓ makes inferences about events	gonna be ok
makes evaluations of events	
makes inferences about language meaning	
Level 4: Intrepretation at the Story Level	
✓ states theme related to the story	better off janitor
✓ interprets literary elements (symbol, etc.)	yellow/happy
interprets author's use of literary structures	(symbol?)
Level 5: Intrepretation at the Abstract and Personal Level	
✓ states theme at abstract level	don't talk to strangers
states theme at personal level	
interprets story as relection of society	
Processess: Child's participation in group interactions	
✓ asks questions	how can be turned back?
✓ makes hypotheses	one person "real one"
acknowledges comments of others	
✓ contributes ideas to argument	
asks for clarifying or supporting evidence	
✓ uses appropriate turn-taking procedures	
	high level participation

example, leaving spaces between strings of conventional letters as if writing words). Young children frequently circle words, place periods between words, or separate words with dashes. These unconventional strategies indicate that children are experimenting with word boundaries.

Older children's compositions can be analyzed for their knowledge of conventions, such as capital letters and punctuation. Teachers note all examples of children's use of these conventions and keep a list of all conventions the children use correctly. For example, a teacher may note that a child capitalizes the beginnings of sentences, the word *I*, the name of the local town, and the name of the school; consistently uses a period or question mark at the end of a sentence; uses apostrophes in the contractions *don't* and *I've;* and uses a comma after *Dear* in a letter.

Story form. Teachers take special note of children's control over story form. Chapter 5 described the literary elements found in the story form (see Table 5.1), which include

- Setting, which identifies time, place, and weather

- Characters, who are revealed through their thoughts, actions, appearance, and dialogue

- Plot, which includes a problem, episodes, climax, and resolution—episodes consist of actions toward solving the problem and outcomes

- Point of view, which reveals who tells the story

- Style, including use of imagery, figurative language, and word choice

- Mood

- Theme

Teachers may use their knowledge of literary elements to analyze children's compositions (written, dictated, or told).

Figure 12.10 presents a story composition dictated by five-year-old Kristen to her kindergarten teacher. The composition contains sixteen pages and a title page. As Kristen's kindergarten teacher analyzed the form of Kristen's story, she noted that Kristen had included three characters: a little girl, a cat, and baby cats. These characters were developed through the illustrations (which showed what the characters looked like), a few revelations of the cat's thoughts (she wanted to go home and she was happy), the girl's and cat's actions, and dialogue.

Kristen's story incorporates three plot episodes (rescuing the cat, the cat's birthday, and taking the baby cats to live in the woods). The first episode, about rescuing the cat, has a fully developed plot. It includes a problem (the cat was caught in a trap), actions toward solving the problem (the girl pulled and pulled, and pushed and pushed on the trap), a climax (the cat was almost out), and an outcome (the cat was out). The other episodes are descriptions of actions, and all the episodes are loosely connected through common characters.

Kristen relied on having the cats go to sleep to resolve the story. The story is told in the third person with the cat's thoughts revealed. She used repetition, and the

Figure 12.10   *"The Girl with the Cat and the Babies"*

Title:	The Girl with the Cat and the Babies
page 1	The little girl took her cat for a walk.
page 2	She got caught in a trap.
page 3	The little girl came.
page 4	And she pulled, and she pulled, and she pushed, and she pushed on the trap.
page 5	She opened the cage and the cat was almost out.
page 6	The little cat was out. She was happy.
page 7	The cat was purring because the little girl was rubbing her.
page 8	The little girl was taking her home.
page 9	The sun was coming down.
page 10	Tomorrow was the cat's birthday. She was happy because she was going to have a party.
page 11	It was the cat's birthday and the people were fixing it up because they were awake.
page 12	One day the cat was knocking on the little girl's door because she had four babies on her birthday.
page 13	The cat asked, "Can I go out in the woods with my babies to live?"
page 14	Far, far away they went. She waved good-bye and so did the babies.
page 15	The cat built five houses.
page 16	They were all ready to go to sleep.

mood of the story is pleasant except for when the cat is caught in the trap. Kristen's story shows her ability to manipulate all the literary elements of a story form except for theme.

Expository text form.   Teachers also analyze the form of children's informational writing. At the simplest level, children's expositions consist of labels (see Chapter 5). They may be one word, phrase, or sentence labels identifying objects, people, or events. At the next level, children's expository texts are organized into attribute lists, in which the ideas included in the text are related to a single topic. At the third level, children's expositions consist of initial ordered paragraphs, which include at least three ideas on a single topic related to one another through cause–effect, compare–contrast, problem–solution, or sequence. At the highest level, children's expositions are ordered paragraphs that include ideas divided into two or more related topics, with ideas within each topic related to each other.

As teachers analyze children's compositions, they use their knowledge of these four levels of text forms to describe children's expository text forms. First, they determine whether the composition consists of labeling or whether children have included a main topic. Then, teachers determine whether the ideas are consistently related to the main topic and whether they are related to one another.

Meaning

In analyzing the meanings in children's compositions, teachers consider the characters, events, settings, or information in relation to children's own experiences and to literature. They analyze the ideas included in compositions for consistency, believability, and unity. They examine children's use of dialogue, literary word order, or literary language such as alliteration, rhyme, repetition, simile, or imagery.

In the story presented in Figure 12.10, Kristen included a familiar character (she has a cat). Many of the actions of the story are from Kristen's own life—her cat often follows her on walks, she likes to rub her cat until he purrs, her birthday was less than a month away, she often explores the woods around her house, and she wishes that her cat could have babies.

Kristen also incorporated three examples of literary language in her composition. She used repetition of words and actions, including actions similar to those in the familiar folktale *The Enormous Turnip* (Parkinson, 1986) (And she pulled, and she pulled, and she pushed, and she pushed on the trap). She also used literary word order (Far, far away they went) and dialogue (Then the cat asked, "Can I go out in the woods with my babies to live?").

Spelling

Teachers assess children's spelling development by analyzing the spellings in their compositions. To do this, teachers can make a chart with five columns: non-spelling, early invented spelling, purely phonetic spelling, transitional spelling, and conventional spelling. They analyze all the spellings in a composition by writing each word in its appropriate column. For example, suppose that a child wrote the following sentence using invented and conventional spellings: *The kat ran doun the steet but the man cawt him.*

The teacher would include the words *the, ran, but,* and *him* under conventional spellings, the words *doun, cawt,* and *steet* under transitional spellings, and the word *kat* under purely phonetic spellings. Over time, teachers expect more of children's spellings to fall into higher levels of invented spelling.

USING PORTFOLIOS

Portfolios serve several functions in the classroom. They are used to make instructional decisions, help children reflect on what they have been learning, and share with parents information about their children's literacy growth. For portfolios to be useful, they must be manageable and up-to-date.

Using Portfolios to Make Instructional Decisions

We have stressed that teachers' observations and analyses focus on what children *can* do (Neuman & Roskos, 1993). Ms. Orlando's notes and analyses were positive statements about what children had learned or currently knew. Making instructional decisions means that teachers look beyond what children can do and consider the next steps in learning. For example, Ms. Orlando noticed that Jasmine could correct her finger-point reading at the end of each line of text and that Rayshawn attempted to point to text while he recited a familiar song. These are positive statements that identify what children can do. But Ms. Orlando is also sensitive to the next step in the children's learning. She knows that eventually the children need to be able to match the text word-for-word. With this objective in mind, she made plans to provide instruction to nudge children in this direction.

Kristen's kindergarten teacher was careful to include positive comments about Kristen's story "The Girl with the Cat and the Babies." However, she was also aware of problems with Kristen's composition. The three episodes were only loosely connected, the reasons for the character's actions were not obvious, and the story did not have a real ending. Because Kristen is a kindergartner, the teacher may not plan any instruction. After all, this is a fairly sophisticated story for a five-year-old. But suppose that this composition had been written by a third grader. In this case, the teacher might plan minilessons on tightly focusing the ideas in stories or writing effective story endings. Teachers always keep in mind the next step in learning and consider whether (or not) they need to plan instruction to help children take that next step.

Using Portfolios to Support Children's Reflections

One way to encourage children to reflect on their learning is to hold portfolio conferences. **Portfolio conferences** provide opportunities for children to select pieces to include in their portfolios and to reflect on their learning. Ms. Orlando holds short portfolio conferences at the end of each of her theme units (which usually last from four to six weeks). She gathers small groups of children and helps them select work samples to include in their portfolios. Children talk about reasons for selecting samples to add to a portfolio (most interesting story, best writing, favorite poem, and so on). Then Ms. Orlando helps the children prepare a caption for each piece they select. The caption includes the reasons for selecting the sample and reflections on what the child can do as a reader and writer. Ms. Orlando also shares any anecdotal notes, checklists, or samples that she has collected during the unit.

At the end of each grading period (every nine weeks) Ms. Orlando has the children review their entire portfolio and prepare a statement about what the portfolio shows about their literacy growth. After the conferences, Ms. Orlando prepares **portfolio summaries,** which summarize the children's literacy growth and achievement toward the literacy goals. To prepare the summaries, she reviews all her anecdotal notes and checklists, children's work samples, and children's performances on any literacy tasks that she has administered. She carefully reads through the children's captions and summaries and her analyses, looking for patterns of growth. The portfolio summary is an important step in preparing to share the portfolio with parents.

Using Portfolios to Inform Parents

Portfolios provide teachers with an excellent resource for sharing information about children's learning with parents. To prepare to share with parents, teachers consider information that parents will find useful and make a list of a few of each child's key new understandings. Then they select eight to ten work samples, anecdotal notes, or checklists to illustrate each child's learning. Finally, teachers think about one or two areas in which the child needs further practice or instruction.

Teachers can begin parent conferences by inviting parents to share what they have observed their child doing at home and to discuss any concerns they may have. Then, teachers describe the child's learning and share the selected examples, highlighting what the child says about his or her learning. Teachers are careful to share with parents positive experiences that show what the child is learning. Teachers may then want to highlight one or two areas in which they plan to work with the child in the future, and they may have suggestions for possible home activities.

Children may be involved in the parent conferences. If so, teachers help children prepare for the conferences by having them identify two or three things that they have learned and find evidence of this learning in their work samples. During the conferences, children share what they have learned. Teachers extend the conferences by sharing their analyses with both parents and children. The conferences might end with having the children formulate one or two goals for future learning.

Keeping Portfolios Manageable

Teachers' time is limited, and collecting and analyzing assessment information is time-consuming. Teachers need to make manageable plans and then stick to those plans. For example, Ms. Orlando takes fifteen minutes four days a week to observe her children. She writes anecdotal notes as she observes in the classroom and analyzes those notes the same day. She realizes that collecting notes on children over time is extremely valuable in helping her to know individual children. She is careful to plan her observations so that she observes behaviors related to each of her instructional goals (see Table 12.1). She uses an emergent reading checklist with each child three times a year—at the beginning of the year, after the second grading period, and at the end of the year. She collects compositions from each child about once a month and analyzes the samples on the day she collects them. She is especially careful to analyze children's invented spellings in the compositions. Finally, she administers a retelling task twice a year—at the end of the first and third grading periods.

Ms. Orlando has found this plan to be workable. During the first month of school she concentrates on getting the children used to centers, administering the emergent reading checklist, and collecting samples of children's compositions. In the second month of school she begins her weekly observations of each child and begins collecting a variety of work samples. She continues to observe children and gather work samples, and she selects one composition for each child per month of the school year. In the middle of the third month (the end of the first grading period), Ms. Orlando collects a retelling from each child and prepares portfolio summaries. At the end of the second grading period, Ms. Orlando completes another emergent reading checklist for each child and again prepares portfolio summaries. At the end of the third grading period, she collects a second retelling. Near the end of the year, she completes the last emergent reading checklist and writes portfolio summaries.

Ms. Orlando finds that her assessments are time-consuming—especially completing the retelling and emergent reading checklists and writing the portfolio summaries. However, she believes that the information provided by these activities is worth the time. All teachers must make decisions about how much time they have to devote to assessment and which assessments will provide them with the information they need. Teachers cannot use all the assessments described in this chapter—they would do nothing but assess! Nevertheless, teachers are responsible for documenting children's growth as readers and writers. Their assessments reflect their commitment to a quality, child-centered program that supports the literacy learning of all children.

Chapter Summary

Teachers are responsible for supporting children's literacy learning, and assessing children's learning is an important part of that process. Classroom assessment relies on teachers' observations and analyses of children's work. Portfolio assessment is a systematic form of classroom assessment based on an assessment planning guide. Portfolios are theory based, multidimensional, systematic, reflective, collaborative, and concerned with process and product. Portfolios may include anecdotal notes, checklists, work samples, and performances from special literacy tasks, such as running records. Portfolios also include children's and teachers' reflections in the form of analyses, captions, and summaries.

Teachers assess children's knowledge of written language meanings, forms, meaning-form links, and functions. Teachers analyze retellings, grand conversations, response journals, and compositions to reveal information about children's meaning making. They administer alphabet recognition tasks and concept-about-print tasks and analyze children's compositions for understandings of written language forms. Emergent reading checklists, miscue analyses, word recognition analyses, and analysis of spellings in compositions provide evidence of meaning-form link knowledge. Finally, observations of children's reading and writing document their understandings of the functions of written language.

Portfolios are used to make instructional decisions, encourage children's reflections on their own learning, and share information about children's learning with parents. Assessments must be kept manageable by planning a reasonable time frame for collecting assessment information, selecting only a few most informative assessments, and collecting information on a systematic basis.

Applying the Information

Two case studies follow. The first case study is a collection of work samples from Katie's third grade reading and writing portfolio. Katie selected a letter that she wrote to her grandmother and included the first two drafts as well as a copy of the final draft of the letter in her portfolio.

Her teacher took a running record from her reading of *Addy's Surprise: A Christmas Story* (Porter, 1993). Figure 12.11 presents Katie's drafts of her letter, and Figure 12.12 presents her teacher's running record. Write a caption for the letter analyzing Katie's knowledge of written

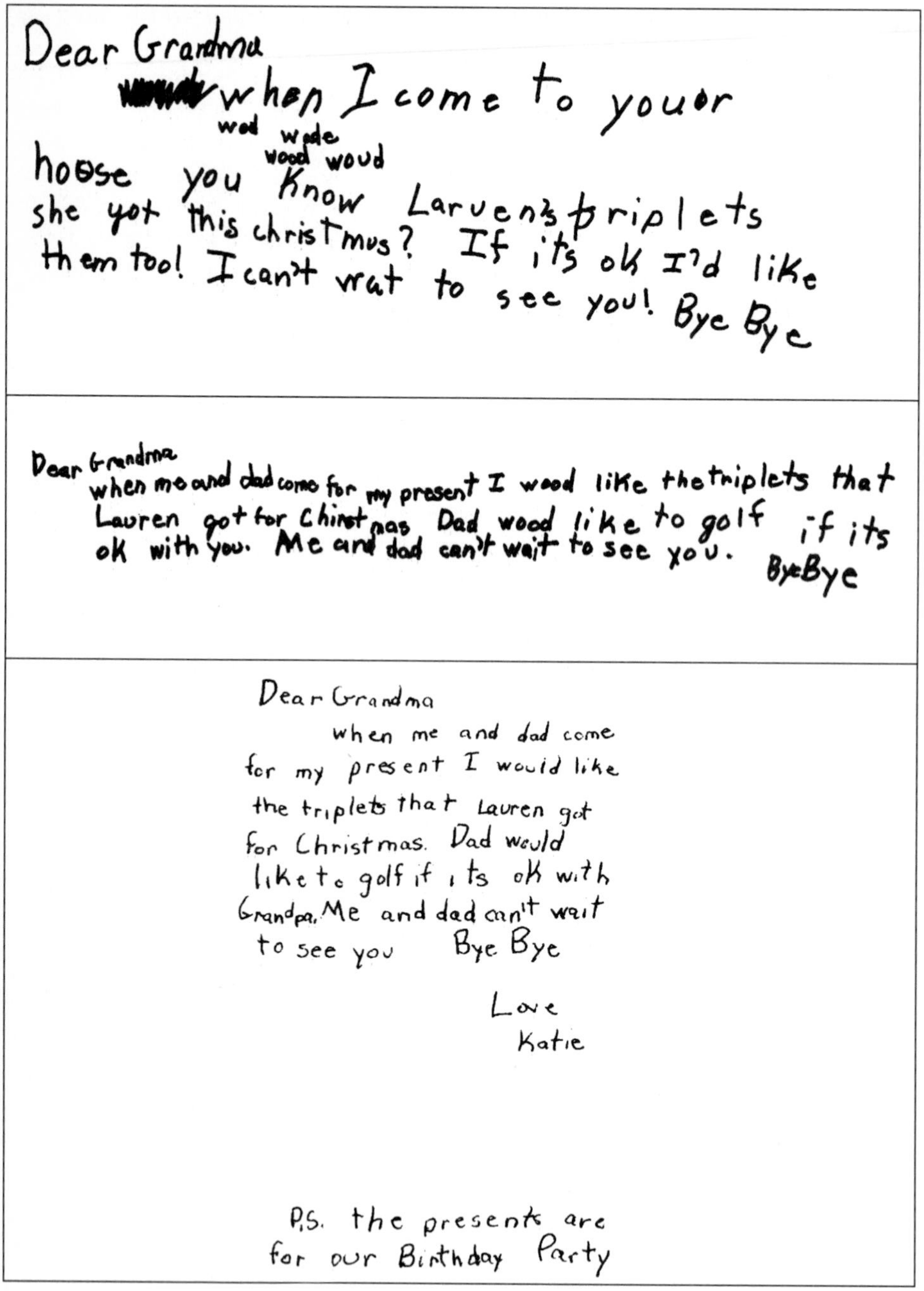

Dear Grandma
~~word~~ when I come to youer
hoose   you   ~~wod~~ ~~wode~~ ~~wood~~ ~~woud~~ know Larvens triplets
she yot this christmus? If its ok I'd like
them too! I can't vrat to see you! Bye Bye

first draft

Dear Grandma
when me and dad come for my present I wood like the triplets that
Lauren got for chirstmas Dad wood like to golf if its
ok with you. Me and dad can't wait to see you. Bye Bye

second draft

Dear Grandma
        when me and dad come
for my present I would like
the triplets that Lauren got
for Christmas. Dad would
like to golf if its ok with
Grandpa. Me and dad can't wait
to see you   Bye Bye

                Love
                Katie

        P.S. the presents are
        for our Birthday Party

final draft

Figure 12.11 *Katie's Letter*

language meanings, forms, meaning-form links, and functions. Construct a miscue analysis chart for Katie's running record. Finally, write a portfolio summary.

Figure 12.12 *Katie's Running Record of* Addy's Surprise:
A Christmas Story

Addy Walker knew that winter had come to Philadelphia even

before she opened her eyes. An icy wind whistled through the

gur-ent
crack in the ~~garret~~ window. Momma had just gotten up, letting a

puff of cold air in the bed when she lifted the heavy quilt. But

the ⊙   *snugged*
the ⊙ her place was still warm, so Addy snuggled into it.

Momma's gentle voice called to her. "Addy, honey, I need

you to
your help over here. Snow's coming right in through the window."

pants
Its panes were white with frost. A little pile of snow had built

up on the window sill, and more snow had blown across the floor.

"I'm coming, Momma," she said.

Addy crawled out of bed and shivered over to the window to

put   *stranding*
help Momma. Together, they pulled down ~~on~~ the window, struggling

to close it. But the window wouldn't budge.

"Go get them rags next to the stove," Momma said.

Addy got the rags and returned to Momma.

"Help me stuff these in the crack, Addy," said Momma, as she

poked the rags between the window and the sill. "Stuff them

they're
good. They all we got to keep the wind from coming in."

From C. Porter, *Addy's Surprise: A Christmas Story,* pp. 1–2. Copyright © 1993 by Pleasant Company Publications.

Jonathan is a five-year-old beginning kindergarten. His teacher has observed him four times over the first two months of school. For three of the observations she also collected work samples of his writing. Figure 12.13 presents Jonathan's work samples and his teacher's anecdotal notes about her observations. Write an analysis for the anecdotal note and captions for the compositions. Then write a portfolio summary that describes what Jonathan knows about written language meanings, forms, meaning-form links, and functions.

a. Notes

9/20 Johnathan at the computer center

Johnathan complains his words are run together. He is copying words from around the room. I show him space bar. He types discovery center writing center pet mouse with spaces

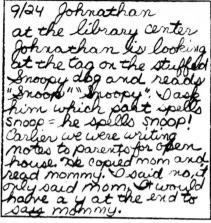

b. Notes

9/24 Johnathan at the library center Johnathan is looking at the tag on the stuffed Snoopy dog and reads "Snoop" "Snoopy". I ask him which part spells Snoop = he spells Snoop! Earlier we were writing notes to parents for open house. He copied mom and read mommy. I said no, it only said mom. It would have a y at the end to say mommy.

c. Notes

10/7 Johnathan at writing center Johnathan copies words from letterhead of scrap paper in the center. He asks me to read what he'd written. After he reads he underlines each word. He says I can spell pub-pub. He says I can spell comp-com! I spell words and he writes. I stress sounds but he wants me to tell him letters. See sample

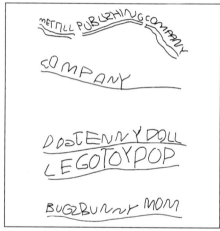

d. Sample

e. Notes

10/30 Johnathan at writing center Johnathan wants to write about Joker and Batman. He says Joker and I repeat segmenting /j/. He writes 6 he says kills I segment /k/=K people /p/=P Batman /b/=B bat= /t/=t help /h/=H people /p/=P I do all segmenting * first invented spelling I've observed see sample

f. Sample

Figure 12.13 *Jonathan's Writings and His Teacher's Observations*

Going Beyond the Text

Interview a teacher who uses portfolio assessment about his or her classroom assessments. Find out what the teacher expects to collect in the portfolios, how he or she analyzes the information, and how he or she shares the information with parents. Examine the contents of several of the children's portfolios. Talk with children about the contents of their portfolios. Compare the results of your interview with Ms. Orlando's portfolio assessment plans and procedures.

References

BLUME, J. (1974). *The pain and the great one.* New York: Bradbury.

BROWN, M. (1942). *The runaway bunny.* New York: Harper and Row.

BUNTING, E. (1991). *Fly away home.* New York: Clarion.

CLAY, M. (1985). *The early detection of reading difficulties* (3rd ed.). Portsmouth, NH: Heinemann.

COOPER, J. (1993). *Literacy: Helping children construct meaning* (2nd ed.). Boston: Houghton Mifflin.

FARR, R., & TONE, B. (1994). *Portfolio and performance assessment: Helping students evaluate their progress as readers and writers.* New York: Harcourt Brace.

GOODMAN, Y. & BURKE, C. (1972). *The reading miscue inventory.* New York: Macmillan.

HARP, B. (Ed.). (1991). Assessment and evaluation in whole language programs. Norwood, MA: Christopher–Gordon.

HUTCHINS, P. (1968). *Rosie's walk.* New York: Scholastic.

KOVALSKI, M. (1987). *The wheels on the bus.* Boston: Little, Brown.

MCGEE, L. (1992). An exploration of meaning construction in first graders' grand conversations. In C. Kinzer & D. Leu, (Eds.), *Literacy research, theory, and practice: Views from many perspectives.* Chicago, IL: National Reading Conference.

MORROW, L. (1989). Using story retelling to develop comprehension. In D. Muth (Ed.), *Children's comprehension of text: Research into practice* (pp. 37–58). Newark, DE: International Reading Association.

NEUMAN, S., & ROSKOS, K. (1993). *Language and literacy learning in the early years: An integrated approach.* New York: Harcourt Brace Jovanovich.

PARKINSON, K. (1986). *The enormous turnip.* Niles, IL: Albert Whitman.

PETERSON, B. (1991). Selecting books for beginning readers. In D. DeFord, C. Lyons, & G. Pinnell (Eds.), *Bridges to literacy: Learning from Reading Recovery* (pp. 119–147). Portsmouth, NH: Heinemann.

PORTER, C. (1993): *Addy's surprise: A christmas story.* Middleton, WI: Pleasant Company Publications.

RHODES, L., & NATHENSON-MEJIA, S. (1992). Anecdotal records: A powerful tool for ongoing literacy assessment. *The Reading Teacher, 45,* 502–509.

SEUSS, DR. (1963). *Hop on pop.* New York: Random House.

TIERNEY, R., CARTER, M., & DESAI, L. (1991). *Portfolio assessment in the reading-writing classroom.* Norwood, MA: Christopher-Gordon.

TOMPKINS, G., & MCGEE, L. (1993). *Teaching reading with literature: Case studies to action plans.* New York: Merrill/Macmillan.

VALENCIA, S. (1990). A portfolio approach to classroom reading assessment: The whys, whats and hows. *The Reading Teacher, 43,* 338–440.

WINOGRAD, P., PARIS, S., & BRIDGE, C. (1991). Improving the assessment of literacy. *The Reading Teacher, 45,* 108–116.

YORINKS, A. (1986). *Hey, Al.* New York: Farrar, Straus and Giroux.

Author Index

Subject Index